MOVIES GO FOURTH
4th Films in Fantastic Franchises

By

Mark Edlitz

Movies Go Fourth by Mark Edlitz

Copyright © 2023 by Mark Edlitz

All rights reserved. No part of this book may be reproduced in any form or by any electronic or mechanical means, including information storage and retrieval systems, without written permission from the publisher, except by a reviewer who may quote passages in a review.

Cover design by Robert Ball. Illustrations by Pat Carbajal.

This book is not authorized or endorsed by any copyright holder.

DEDICATION

<u>For Suzie, Ben, and Doug</u>

TABLE OF CONTENTS

Table of Contents
Author's Note 1
Introduction 4

Section 1: Superhero Movies
Superman 4: *Superman IV: The Quest for Peace*................................... 20
Batman 4: *Batman & Robin* 35

Section 2: Horror Movies
Jaws 4: *Jaws: The Revenge* 50
Psycho 4: *Psycho IV: The Beginning* 63
Hatchet 4: *Victor Crowley* 75
Halloween 4: *Halloween 4: The Return Of Michael Myers* 83
Friday the 13th 4: *Friday the 13th IV: The Final Chapter* 96
Nightmare on Elm Street 4: *A Nightmare on Elm Street 4: The Dream Master* 100

Section 3: Action Movies
James Bond 4: *Thunderball* 111
Dirty Harry 4: *Sudden Impact* 122
Rambo 4: *Rambo* 139
Die Hard 4: *Live Free or Die Hard* 145

Section 4: Science Fiction Movies
Star Wars 4: *The Ewok Adventure* 157
Star Trek 4: *Star Trek IV: The Voyage Home* 173
Planet of the Apes 4: *Conquest of the Planet of the Apes* 184
Highlander 4: *Highlander: Endgame* 194
Terminator 4: *Terminator Salvation* 202

Section 5: Comedies
Police Academy 4: *Police Academy 4: Citizens on Patrol* 209
Ernest 4: *Ernest Goes to Jail* 216
Home Alone 4: *Home Alone 4: Take Back the House* 226

Section 6: The Sex Comedy
Eating Out 4: *Eating Out: Drama Camp* 232

Section 7: Re-Edited Fourths
Rocky 4: *Rocky IV* 238

Section 8: Lost Fourths
Porky's 4: *Pimpin' Pee Wee* 250

Section 9: Unintended Fours
Meatballs 4: *Meatballs 4: To the Rescue* 255

Section 10: Unmade Sequels
Godfather 4: *The Godfather: Party IV* 265
Spider-Man 4: *Spider-Man 4* 271

Appendix A: And So Fourth 288
Appendix B: List of Fourth Films 300

Acknowledgments 307
Footnotes 308
About the Author 313
About the Illustrator 314

Also by Mark Edlitz

How to Be a Superhero

The Many Lives of James Bond

The Lost Adventures of James Bond

AUTHOR'S NOTE

Why write a book about fourth movies in popular film series? It is a natural question that friends and interview subjects have asked as I have worked on this book. After all, fourth movies are not famously beloved by even the most enthusiastic moviegoers and are seldom embraced by critics. Moreover, the fourth film is sometimes perceived as an opportunistic attempt to separate audiences from their hard-earned cash. The answer is simple—all of the movies discussed in the volume are heart-breaking works of staggering genius.

Well, not quite.

There are instances when moviegoers consider the fourth movie to be the nadir of the series, as is the case with *Jaws: The Revenge, Superman IV,* and *Batman & Robin.* Sometimes even the stars agree. Michael Caine has joked that while he's never seen the fourth *Jaws* movie, he has seen "the house it bought for my mum. It's fantastic."[1] Christopher Reeve, who played the Man of Steel four times, believed, "The less said about *Superman IV* the better.[2] And George Clooney often jokes that his turn as the Caped Crusader nearly destroyed the superhero franchise.

Still, there are instances when the fourth film is both critically and commercially successful. *Mad Max: Fury Road*, the belated fourth film in the post-apocalypse series, was nominated for ten Academy Awards, including Best Picture and Best Director. *Avengers: Endgame*, the fourth film about the team of superheroes, earned just north of $2.8 billion and, for a time, it became the biggest box office success of all time.

Occasionally, the fourth film is when a series finds its truest identity, as in the case of *Mission: Impossible: Ghost Protocol*. Before *Ghost Protocol*, an eclectic group of directors, such as Brian De Palma, John Woo, and J. J. Abrams, imprinted their distinctive styles on each of their three films. De Palma's elaborate set-pieces, Woo's slow motion, and Abrams' penchant for starting the story with the hero in jeopardy and then cutting back in time to show how they got there were on display in their respective films. But after the success of the fourth film, subsequent *Mission: Impossible* films adopted the style and aesthetics that *Ghost Protocol* established.

A fourth installment can be an attempt to introduce new characters and launch a new franchise: such was the case with *Highlander: Endgame*, about immortal swordfighters, *The Bourne Legacy, Men in Black: International* (2019), about a secret organization that keeps the world safe from world-ending alien attacks, and *Scream IV*, a deconstruction of horror movies.

There are also instances when the fourth chapter is a tonal departure from the rest of the series: examples of this include Dirty Harry in *Sudden Impact,* about an unorthodox cop who will stop at nothing to catch a killer, *Bride of Chucky,* featuring an animated killer doll who will stop at nothing to get his bride, and *Star Trek IV: The Voyage Home*, in which Kirk and Spock time-travel to Earth to save the whales, all of which upped the comedy quotient.

Sometimes the fourth outings are not the best film in the series, but they are commercially the most successful. *Thunderball* doesn't necessarily rank as high among James Bond fans as the first three films in the spy series: *Dr. No, From Russia with Love*, and *Goldfinger*. Yet, *Thunderball* remains one of the most popular of all the Bond films. The film represents the zenith of Bondmania, and, until the Daniel Craig era, it sold more tickets than any subsequent Bond film.

But of course "four" has not always been a common benchmark; it is in fact a relative newcomer—but it has become the magic number. Trilogies used to signify a franchise's success. For many years, *Star Wars* and the Indiana Jones films stood as landmark trilogies. Other significant three-part films include Francis Coppola's *The Godfather* series, Peter Jackson's *The Lord of The Rings*, Christopher Nolan's Dark Knight movies, Sam Raimi's Spider-Man superhero films, and Sergio Leone's "Man with No Name" westerns. On the lighter side, there were *The Naked Gun* and *Austin Powers* parody-series and Robert Zemeckis's *Back to the Future* time travel comedies.

Trilogies were also a sign that a franchise had reached blockbuster status and had become part of the zeitgeist. *Star Wars* taught audiences that a trilogy, with a beginning, middle, and end, could be a powerful way to tell a story. In *Star Wars*, as *Episode IV* was originally called, Luke leaves the comfort and relative safety of his home world to join the rebellion, travel to new galaxies, and bring down the evil Empire. In *The Empire Strikes Back*, Luke learns the terrible truth that the galaxy's mortal enemy is actually his father. In *Return of the Jedi*, Luke defeats his father and brings down the Empire. Ewoks sing, story over. (Or so, audiences at the time thought.)

In the right hands, a single story told over the course of three movies could be a perfect form of storytelling and can mimic a three-act structure. As Aaron Sorkin explains it, "Act one, you chase your hero up a tree. Act two, you throw rocks at him. Act 3, you get him down."[3] After the third film, there is no more story to tell. The End. Fade to Black.

But what happens when the trilogy is ostensibly over and the filmmakers or the studios want to make a fourth movie? Do they start all over with a new story or do they expand on the original one? Do they focus on new characters, or do they continue the story of the original ones? Do those considerations change if they want to continue what is essentially a single long story told in separate parts (*Star Wars*), or if they are creating several largely self-contained stories with a recurring character (Batman, Spider-Man, Mad Max). Do their choices depend on whether they are the works of a singular artist (the Wachowskis, George Lucas) or if they are commercially driven endeavors (*Halloween, Friday the 13th*)? And what happens when the artist and the studio come into conflict? After the fourth films are made, how do they affect the legacy of the series? Do they strengthen it or diminish it? This book seeks to answer those questions and many others.

Even when a film is not universally loved, I may still have a soft spot for it. I try not to dwell exclusively on the (sometimes obvious) flaws of a film or the filmmaker's missteps; I attempt instead to consider the filmmaker's ambitions and plans for their idealized version of the film.

I begin this book with an overview of fourth movies; and in the chapters that follow, I present my interviews with the creators of some of the world's most popular franchises about the creative and practical challenges they experienced making the fourth film in an eclectic group of franchises such as *Star Wars, Star Trek, James Bond, Batman, Superman, Spider-Man, Psycho, Die Hard* to Dirty Harry to *Police Academy* to *Planet of the Apes* and *Halloween*. I have written in-depth only about projects for which I've been able to secure a primary interview. If your favorite franchise is absent from this volume, I offer my apologies; I probably tried to include them but was not able to do so.

    Certain films are meant to be "case studies" that are designed to illustrate the kinds of considerations that artists take into account when working on films in different genres. For instance, *Superman IV* can stand for a fourth *superhero* film, *Psycho IV* can be emblematic of a fourth *horror* film, *Eating Out: Drama Camp* can be illustrative of a fourth *sex-comedy*, and so on. Other chapters take different tacks. The chapter on *Star Wars* asks, which film in the series is actually the fourth film, is it the fourth episode (*A New Hope*), or is it the fourth theatrical film (*The Phantom Menace*); or could there be yet another answer? My chapter on *Meatballs 4* looks at a film that was not written to be the fourth film but became one in the middle of production; and the chapters about *Jaws: The Revenge* and *Batman & Robin* are interesting examples of what happens when talented artists try to tell the next chapter in a series but by their own standards come up short. The section on *Rocky IV* takes a look at *Rocky IV: Rocky vs Drago*, the re-edited version of Sylvester Stallone's rousing sports-drama, which is now missing the robot butler.

    I believe you will discover that good, bad, or just plain strange, fourth movies can hold a crucial place in a franchise.

INTRODUCTION

What's a fourth movie?
Let's dispense with the seemingly obvious. A fourth movie is the fourth installment of the series. For instance, *Toy Story 4* (2019) is the fourth film in Pixar's series about the secret life toys. It follows *Toy Story* (1995), *Toy Story 2* (1999), and *Toy Story 3* (2010).

The Numbers Game
Fourth movies are sometimes easily identifiable by their title, such as *Scream 4* (2011), a horror film series, *Scary Movie 4* (2006), a parody of horror movies, *Lethal Weapon 4* (1998), Richard Donner's action-comedy series, and *Critters 4* (1992), a horror-comedy about tiny but ferocious aliens from space. These examples opted for the Arabic number "4," however, the more widespread practice is to use the Roman numeral "IV." To wit, *Rocky IV* (1985), the sports-drama series and the horror films *Phantasm IV* (1998), *Prom Night IV* (1992), *Pumpkinhead IV* (2007), *Paranormal Activity IV* (2012), and *Saw IV* (2007).

In addition to including a number, filmmakers sometimes add "chapter" to the title, as is the case with *John Wick: Chapter 4* (2023), the fourth film in the Keanu Reeves series about a reluctant assassin who is lured back into his former ultra-violent world to avenge the death of his beloved dog. Others opt for "Part." The first nine of the *Friday the 13th* films use the latter naming convention: to wit, *Friday the 13th Part 2* (1981). Other series that have dropped the "part" from the title but have relied on it in sequels include such diverse franchises as *The Toxic Avenger*, *Class of Nuke 'Em High*, *Return of the Living Dead*, and *Smokey and the Bandit*.

Subtitles
Including "Part Four" in a title can unintentionally signal moviegoers that the series might be tired and lacking fresh ideas. In these instances, filmmakers opt for subtitles. For instance, the fourth *Mission: Impossible* film is subtitled *Ghost Protocol* (2011). Before *Ghost Protocol*, the Tom Cruise spy films were numbered: *Mission: Impossible II* (2000) and *Mission: Impossible III* (2006). Similarly, the second *Friday the 13th* movie used the number 2 for the second film and the Roman numeral III for the third but dropped both methods for *Friday the 13th: The Final Chapter*. The fourth film in the sci-fi series about space-marines who combat alien bugs also lost the number and chose to use a subtitle, *Starship Troopers: Invasion* (2012). *Terminator Salvation* (2009), the fourth *Terminator* film is the first one not to include a number. Choosing not to include a number in the title can also be a way to signal to audiences that they will not be lost if they missed the previous three movies. *Highlander: Endgame* (2000) and *Mad Max: Fury Road* (2015) took a similar approach, all fourth films in a franchise that for the first time didn't include a number in the title.

Some franchises use both a number and a subtitle as is the case with *Police Academy IV: Citizens on Patrol* (1987), *Superman IV: The Quest for Peace* (1987), *Star Trek IV: The Voyage Home* (1986), *Nightmare on Elm Street 4: The Dream Master* (1988), *Halloween IV: The Return of Michael Myers* (1988), *Death Wish IV: The Crackdown* (1987), *Children of the Corn 4: The Gathering* (1996), and *Psycho*

IV: The Beginning (1990).

Don't Believe Everything You Read
There are instances where even the title is misleading. For instance, you could be forgiven for thinking that *I Spit on Your Grave 4: Deja Vu* (2019) is the fourth film in the *I Spit on Your Grave* series. But it is not. *I Spit on Your Grave 4* is actually the fifth film, but it is the third sequel to 2010's *I Spit on Your* Grave and not 1978's film of the same name. The *Fist of Fury* martial arts series has similarly deceptive titles. *Fist of Fury* (1972) is the film that helped turn Bruce Lee into an international star. Three sequels followed. But moviegoers could be forgiven for assuming that *Fist of Fury III* (1980) is the third film in the series. After all, the Roman numeral III strongly indicates the film's sequel status. However, *Fist of Fury III* is, in fact, the fourth film, but it is the second sequel to *New Fist of Fury* (1976). In the *New First of Fury*, Bruce Lee is replaced by Jackie Chan, another martial artist legend in the making.

Sometimes, titles are meant to signal to moviegoers that the fourth film will be the last in the series. The fourth *Friday the 13th* and *Lake Placid* horror films were both subtitled *The Final Chapter*. In both instances, the subtitles were misleading, as each series continued. The not-so-final chapters were followed by *Friday the 13th: A New Beginning* and *Lake Placid vs. Anaconda* (2015). *Shrek Forever After* (2010) was sometimes marketed as *Shrek: The Final Chapter*. To this date, it remains the fourth and final film in the Shrek series. However, the *Shrek* spin-off film, *Puss in Boots* was released the following year.

Conversely, some subtitles are designed to indicate a fresh start of a series or a comeback, of sorts. The subtitles for the fourth *Omen, Jeepers Creepers, Anne of Green Gables,* and *Matrix* films were *The Awakening, Reborn, A New Beginning,* and *Resurrections*. In the case of *The Omen* and *Anne of Green Gables*, it did not.

Word Play
Alternatively, the film's title can tell a little story like *The Magnificent Seven Ride!* (1972), *Midnight Run for Your Life* (1994), *Billy Jack Goes to Boston* (1977), *Killer Tomatoes Eat France!* (1991), *Shrek Forever After* (2010) and *Dracula Has Risen from the Grave* (1968). The fourth film in the horror compilation *Faces of Death* series declared that the fourth movie would be *The Worst of Faces of Death* (1987). The seven movies in Bob Hope and Bing Crosby's comedy movies fashioned their names with a kind of fill-in-the-blank approach. Each movie was named "Road to…" somewhere. Their fourth trip, *Road to Utopia* (1946), took them to Alaska and earned an Academy Award for best original screenplay nomination for its script by Melvin Frank and Norman Panama. The Muppet movies employ a similar tack by inserting "Muppets" into the title. Their fourth movie is *The Muppet Christmas Carol* (1992). There were seven films in the Beach Party series, the teen comedies about bikini-clad teens that usually starred Frankie Avalon and Annette Funicello. The titles of the first three films declared the films' common settings: *Beach Party* (1963), *Muscle Beach Party* (1964) *Bikini Beach* (1964). But the name of the fourth entry signaled a change in the nature of the teens' party: *Pajama Party* (1964). Later entries took a more absurd approach: *How to Stuff a Wild Bikini* (1965) and *The Ghost in the Invisible Bikini* (1966).

The Planet of the Apes films also used variations of the film's title. The second film went *Beneath the Planet of the Apes* (1970), the third film required the chimps to *Escape from the Planet of the Apes* (1971), the fourth film had the apes and humans square off in a *Conquest of the Planet of the Apes* (1972), and the fifth film saw all the warring factions *Battle for the Planet of the Apes* (1973). Beneath, Escape, Conquest, and Battle.

While talking about the series with superfan Eddie Murphy, who calls himself an "ape maniac," comic Jerry Seinfeld quipped that a studio executive must have thought, "Just keep putting different verbs in there and we got another movie."[4] Incidentally, Eddie Murphy, who is also a *Star Trek* fan, came very close to appearing in *Star Trek IV: A Voyage Home*.

The Living Dead franchise keeps the word "dead" in each film to preserve continuity, *Night of the Living Dead*, *Dawn of the Dead*, *Day of the Dead*, the fourth film, *Land of the Dead*, *Diary of the Dead*, and *Survival of the Dead*.

Another popular method is using "and" after the main character's name, as is the case with *Indiana Jones and The Kingdom of the Crystal Skull* and *Harry Potter and the Goblet of Fire*. For the fourth film in the *Predator* series, writer-director Shane Black simply added an article and changed *Predator* (1987) to *The Predator* (2018).

All in the Family
The family lineage of the main characters can sometimes help shape the title of the fourth film. For instance, the Universal Horror series, Universal Classic Monsters, gave us *Son of Dracula* (1943), and after meeting the bride and son of Frankenstein in the second and third sequels to *Frankenstein* (1931), moviegoers were introduced to *The Ghost of Frankenstein* (1942). In *Ghost of Frankenstein*, Ludwig Frankenstein, the son of Henry Frankenstein, sees a vision of his father's ghost.

The fourth movie in the silent black-and-white Tarzan serial introduced audiences to *The Son of Tarzan* (1920). In the film, Tarzan and Jane's son goes by the name Korak. Later MGM would gain the rights to the character and make their own Tarzan series. Coincidentally, the fourth MGM Tarzan series is also about The Lord of the Jungle's son. In *Tarzan Finds a Son!* (1939), as the title promises, Johnny Weissmuller finds and raises a boy. *The Son of Rusty* (1947) is the fourth film of eight in the series about Rusty, a German shepherd. However, the title is misleading: the other dog in the movie is named Barb, and she is introduced as a friend of Rusty's, not an offspring.

Family ancestry is also the focus of the titles in the *Spy Kids* and *Four Daughters* films. *Spy Kids 4: All the Time in the World* (2011), focuses on the stepchildren of a retired spy who is recalled from retirement to help stop a mastermind hell-bent on controlling time. By the time the *Four Daughters* series about a family of musicians (begun in 1938) reached the fourth movie, the four titular daughters were about to enter motherhood. As such, the title *Four Mothers* (1941) reflects the daughters' life change.

Direct Sequels to Fourth Films
We ordinarily expect that the sequel to the fourth film in a series is the fifth. For instance, the sequel to *Halloween IV* is *Halloween V*. But there are a few instances

where the fifth movie is not the only direct sequel to a fourth film. There are two direct sequels to *Rocky IV*; *Rocky V* (1990) is, of course, the first sequel to the film. But there is another. *Creed II*, while also serving as a sequel to 2015's *Creed*, functions as a direct, albeit belated sequel to 1985's *Rocky IV*. In *Rocky IV*, Ivan Drago is famously fought and defeated by Rocky Balboa in the Soviet Union, after Drago fought and killed Apollo Creed. In *Creed II*, Drago's son Victor fights Apollo's son Adonis. Reprising their roles from *Rocky IV* are Sly Stallone as the Italian Stallion, Dolph Lundgren as Ivan Drago, and Brigitte Nielsen who briefly reappears as Ludmilla Drago, Ivan's ex-wife.

In *Creed II*, Creed watches the match where his father was killed. The footage is theoretically footage from the fight, but it is footage from *Rocky IV*. [Note: *Rocky IV* also inspired the fan-fiction book *Drago: On Mountains We Stand*, which follows Drago's exploits after being disgraced and defeated by Balboa. The novel was ascribed to Todd Noy who was identified as a Pulitzer Prize-winning sports journalist from Australia. It was later revealed that the book was written by David Allatt as a lark for his friends.]

Job Security

Various professions—superheroes, spies, private detectives, to name a few—seem especially suited to serialized storytelling. It seems natural that these protagonists would repeatedly be put in dangerous and, even potentially, life-changing situations. Cops, private investigators, and secret agents routinely operate from case to case or mission to mission.

The adolescent amateur detective Nancy Drew stumbled across four cases and reappeared in a movie for the fourth time in a mere two years in *Nancy Drew and the Hidden Staircase* (1939). *Shadow of the Thin Man* (1941) is the fourth adventure in *The Thin Man* series, about Nick and Nora Charles, a crime-solving couple who affectionately bicker, banter, and drink copiously as they go about identifying the culprit. Private dick Philip Marlowe's fourth cinematic case, *The Brasher Doubloon* (1947), was also his second that year. Perry Mason took on *The Case of the Velvet Claws* (1936) and Charlie Chan had to solve the mystery of *The Black Camel* (1931). The Basil Rathbone/Nigel Bruce Sherlock Holmes films of the late 1930s and early 1940s spawned fourteen films in just eight years, with *Sherlock Holmes and the Secret Weapon* (1942) as the detective's fourth case. Medical and doctor shows are the staple of television, but they tend not to lend themselves to movie sequels. There is no *The Verdict 2*, or *A Few More Good Men*, or *12 Angrier Men*.

Genres: Disaster Movies

Action movies, detective stories, and police procedurals are well-suited to continuing stories, but disaster movies not so much. Audiences who go to disaster movies relish the cinematic destruction of large structures and cities. In the 1970s there was a spate of disaster movies—among them, *The Towering Inferno* (1974), *Earthquake* (1974), and *Meteor* (1979)—but few spawned sequels. There was only one *Towering Inferno*, one *Titanic*, and one *Pompei* (2014). After all, the impossibly tall building can burn down just once, and after the giant meteor has been destroyed by missiles, it is no longer a threat to Earth. It is therefore somewhat surprising to me that *Airport* was turned into a four-film series. The series is united by a star-studded cast—that included such acclaimed actors as James Stewart, Burt Lancaster, Olivia de Havilland, Charlton Heston, Joseph Cotton, and Jack Lemon—with several personal dramas being enacted as the flight crew struggle with the looming plane disaster as it unfolds. The series feels like *The Love Boat* (1977–1986), in the air, as if every time the Pacific Princess went to sea it rammed into an iceberg.

The cast and the nature of the aerial crisis changed from film to film. In *Airport*, there is a man with a bomb on the plane, in *Airport 75* (1975), there is an aerial collision, in *Airport 77* (1977), the plane crashes into the ocean and is submerged underwater in the Bermuda Triangle, and in *Airport 79* (1979), an arms dealer fires a missile at the plane to protect a secret that one of the passengers, a reporter, can expose.

Airport 79 was written by Eric Roth, who would later be nominated for an Academy Award for Best Screenplay for his work on *Forrest Gump* (1994), *The Insider* (1999), *Munich* (2005), *The Curious Case of Benjamin Button* (2008), and *A Star Is Born* (2018). In *Airport 79,* Roth and the filmmakers made a surprising structural choice. We have been conditioned to expect these movies, and action movies generally, to conclude shortly after the climactic resolution of the threat, for instance with the plane's safe landing at Dulles Airport in Washington, D.C. However, in *Airport 79* the Concord survives the arms dealer's attempt to bring it down with a missile about halfway into the movie, leaving 52 minutes for the film to continue. This set up the adventure of the plane's survival of a second attack on its return flight to Paris.

Another unlikely disaster series was the made-for-tv *Sharknado* films. The primary appeal of the series is the ridiculous title, a hybrid word that combines sharks and tornados. The fourth film in the disaster-horror-comedy series is *Sharknado 4: The 4th Awakens* (2016), which included cameos by David Hasselhoff and Gary Busey, and starred *Beverly Hills, 90210's* Ian Ziering and Tara Reid who both appeared in all six films. They concluded the saga in 2018's *The Last Sharknado: It's About Time* (2018); the title referred to the film's time-travel elements and it also acknowledges that the joke had worn thin: that it was "about time" to end the series.

Comedies

The large majority of comedies, including blockbusters, peter out at the second or third film. *Airplane!*, *The Blues Brothers*, and *Caddyshack* stopped after two films. *The Naked Gun, Austin Powers,* and *Back to the Future* were all trilogies. But some notable comedies have made it to a fourth film: these include *Ghostbusters* (four and counting), the National Lampoon series (six), *House Party* (six), *Barbershop* (four, including the spin-off film *Beautyshop*), *Police Academy* (seven), and the *Pink Panther* series (twelve).

The *Pink Panther* series had a sustaining power of decades. The first was released in 1963, with Peter Sellers as Inspector Jacques Clouseau and the last was 2009's The *Pink Panther 2* with Steve Martin as the bumbling detective. Along the way, other notable actors played Clouseau, including Roger Moore in *Curse of the Pink Panther* (1983) and Roberto Benigni in *Son of the Pink Panther* (1993), as

Clouseau's heir, who proves that the apple does not bumble far from the tree.

It is not unusual for long-standing series to replace a lead actor with a new fresh face as a means to prolong the series. But the *Pink Panther* series experimented with replacing a lead actor early on in the series. In *Inspector Clouseau* (1968), the third film, Alan Arkin plays the befuddled detective. Arkin, a gifted comic actor, seemed uncomfortable in the part, so Sellers reclaimed the role for the fourth film in the series, *The Return of the Pink Panther* (1975); it was just his third performance as the chief inspector.

The first and fourth *Panther* films are quite different. 1963's *The Pink Panther*, is a stylish heist film that focuses on the mysterious Sir Charles Lytton (David Niven), who lives a double life as The Phantom, a jewel thief; Clouseau is merely a supporting character in the movie. *Return of the Pink Panther* is an over-the-top comedy that centers around Seller's performance. The first Panther film did not have two of the elements most associated with Panther: there is no Commissioner Dreyfus (Herbert Lom), or Cato (Burt Kwouk), Clouseau's valet. Both characters were introduced in the second film (*A Shot in the Dark*, 1963), were absent from the third film, and return for the fourth film.

Other comedies including *Ghostbusters* and the *National Lampoon's Vacation* films, have made it to the fourth film. But in the case of *Ghostbusters: Afterlife* (2021), the fourth film in the series would focus on the granddaughter of one of the original protagonists. The fourth vacation film *Vegas Vacation* (1989) was released about eight years after the third. However, the first six *Police Academy* films were released annually. It was not until the seventh film that there was there a break of five years between sequels. Except for Guttenberg, there was a core central cast that continued through all seven *Police Academy* films.

Budd Abbott and Lou Costello created a run of four movies in which the bickering comedy duo encountered Universal's classic monsters. *Abbott and Costello Meet Frankenstein* (1948) started the series. *Abbott and Costello Meet the Invisible Man* (1951), *Abbott and Costello Meet Dr. Jekyll and Mr. Hyde* (1953), and *Abbott and Costello Meet the Mummy* (1955) followed.

Sex Sells, Sometimes

I have not been able to identify many erotic thrillers that have reached four installments. As a rule, after a sequel or two, no more sequels have been made for even the most popular or well-reviewed erotic thrillers. John Dahl's well-received *The Last Seduction* (1994), a film about a femme fatale played by Linda Fiorentino, was unexpectedly followed up by *The Last Seduction II* (1999), which featured none of the original cast or filmmakers. Even the most notorious erotic thrillers *Basic Instinct* (1992) and *Showgirls* (1995) finished after one sequel. Both *Basic Instinct* and *Showgirls* were directed by Paul Verhoeven and written by Joe Eszterhas. Unlike *Last Seduction II*, in which Fiorentino declined to reprise her part, Sharon Stone returned to play the stylish serial killer Catherine Tramell in *Basic Instinct 2* (2006). There was also a late sequel to *Showgirls*, the camp classic about Las Vegas showgirls and topless dancers, called *Showgirls 2: Pennies from Heaven* (2011). However, *Showgirls 2* was not created by the rights-holder. Instead, it was written and directed by, and starred Rena Riffel, who played a minor character in the original film. Riffel used the crowd-funding platform Kickstarter to raise the funds to shoot the film.

Still, there are instances where erotic thrillers make it to four films. *Wild Things* (1998) is a well-reviewed neo-noir movie that is best remembered for depicting a lurid threesome between Matt Dillon, Neve Campbell, and Denise Richards. Three direct-to-video sequels followed, including *Wild Things: Foursome* (2010). *Foursome* recycles key plot points from *Wild Things*. However, *Foursome* attempts to top the first film by adding one more participant to the previous ménage à trois. By turning the triad into a quad, *Foursome* makes good on the promise of its title.

Likewise, the fourth *Poison Ivy* film, which is subtitled *The Secret Society* (2008), is unrelated to the first film. The loose connection to the films is that the heroines of both films are named after plants. Drew Barrymore played Ivy in the first film and Shawna Waldron played Daisy in the fourth. The names of the female lead in the second and third films are Ivy and Violet, respectively. In the fourth film, the Ivy in the title is not the protagonist's name but is an elite society in a college.

Whereas few erotic thrillers have become series with four installments, there are many soft-core films that have, including *Emmanuelle*, an erotic-drama series that originated in France. Sylvia Kristel played Emmanuelle in five of the seven films, including the fourth, *Emmanuelle 4* (1984). In addition to the theatrical films in the *Emmanuelle* series, there were also seven television films, including the fourth film *Emmanuelle's Revenge* (1993); seven films in the *Emmanuelle in Space* series, the fourth was *Emmanuelle 4: Concealed Fantasy* (1994), and seven in the English language series, the fourth of which was *Emmanuelle 2000: Jewel of Emmanuelle* (2000).

Sex comedies have fared better at amassing sequels: *Revenge of the Nerds* (1984), about a group of misfits in college, *Meatballs* (1979), about a group of misfits in camp, and *American Pie* (1999), about a group of friends trying to lose their virginity, have all reached four or more offshoots. The *American Pie* series is the only one whose four films were all released theatrically. *Revenge of the Nerds IV: Nerds in Love* (1994) and *Meatballs 4* (1992), the fourth movie in the *Revenge of the Nerds* and *Meatball* series, were direct to video. But there is a thriving *American Pie* spin-off series, the fourth of which is called *American Pie Presents: The Book of Love* (2009), which co-stars Eugene Levy, who plays the part of a loving father in the theatrical series.

In Space!
The fourth film in a series can also be an opportunity to take the series to new heights, sometimes literally. *Critters 4* (1992), *Leprechaun 4*, and *Hellraiser IV* (2015), the BDSM-infused horror series, are all set in space. In *Hellraiser IV*, Pinhead, the killer Cenobite, has apparently killed so many people on Earth that he needs to go to outer space for fresh blood. The subtitles for *Critters 4* and *Leprechaun*, *They're Invading Your Space* and *In Space*, both make their celestial intentions clear, it would take Jason ten films and James Bond eleven films before they left Earth's atmosphere, in *Jason X* (2001) and *Moonraker* (1979), respectively. *22 Jump Street* (2014), a sequel to *21 Jump Street* (2012), ridiculed the very notion of sequels and made fun of the "in space"

phenomenon by predicting its future sequels in the end credits.

The *Critters* movies are knockoffs of the far superior and significantly wittier *Gremlins* films. *Critters,* like other *Gremlins* copycats, such as *Ghoulies* and *Munchies*, are about diminutive but lethal monsters. However, the film does feature an impressive cast. Future Oscar nominees Angela Basset and Brad Douriff play members of the crew of a salvage ship that operates in space. Like the similarly space-themed *Leprechaun 4*, *Critters 4* owes much to Ridley Scott's *Alien* (1979). Terrence Mann, who played Rum Tum Tugger in the original cast of the Broadway musical *Cats*, plays a bounty hunter named Ug. *Critters 4* begins with a witty first shot. A planet appears to be floating through outer space but as the camera pulls back it reveals a young boy juggling three balls that look like planets.

When writing about the planned fourth film in the *XXX* action-adventure series starring Vin Diesel, entertainment critic Scott Wampler poked fun at the trend of upping the ante to ridiculous levels, "If this franchise's history of increasingly ridiculous entries is any indication, this film will end up being the most absurd, unbelievable, amazing, breathtaking thing ever to grace a silver screen. I'll bet you ten bucks right now that the motherfucker goes to space in this one. Watch."[5] A filmmaker from a different Vin Diesel series did not discount the idea. Five-time *Fast and Furious* writer Chris Morgan countered, "I would never shoot down space. Never, never. I would literally never shoot down anything, as long as it hits the parameters: 'Is it badass? Is it awesome? Will the audience love it? And will it not break faith with the audience as they're watching it?' I'm down for whatever."[6]

This Never Happened to the Other Fella

By the time the fourth film is made, the actor playing the lead character might be reluctant to continue with the series. Perhaps, they have grown tired of the role. Sometimes the studios do not want to meet the actor's growing salary demands. In those instances, the studio can either write the character out or recast the role. The fourth *Species* film is the sole one that doesn't feature Natasha Henstridge's space-vampire. And the fourth Blade film, *Blade: House of Chthon* (2006), is the first one not to star Wesley Snipes as the vampire with a black belt in martial arts. Instead, rapper Sticky Fingaz puts on the fangs for the fourth bite in the series.

In *The Magnificent Seven* (1960), Yul Brenner played the lead role of Chris Adams, the gunfighter who recruits six other gunfighters to help free a village under the control of Eli Wallach's outlaw, Calvera. But Brenner returned just for the first sequel *The Return of the Seven* (1966) and his character was subsequently played by George Kennedy in *Guns of the Magnificent Seven* (1969) and then by Lee Van Cleef for the fourth "Seven" film, *The Magnificent Seven Ride*.

Van Cleef, a widely beloved actor and a cult hero, was a welcome addition to the series. Sergio Leone once described Van Cleef's angular face as being like a Hawk's. And his sharp-edged characterizations earned him a loyal following after his appearances in such movies as Leone's *For a Few Dollars More* (1965) and *The Good, the Bad and the Ugly* (1966), and John Carpenter's *Escape from New York* (1981). However, the rest of the cast lacks the star power of the first movie by considerable wattage. In addition to Brenner and Wallach, *The Magnificent Seven* starred Steve McQueen, Charles Bronson, Robert Vaughn, and James Coburn. The fourth film in the series presented unfamiliar names, such as Michael Callan, Luke Askew, and Ralph Waite.

Each *Magnificent Seven* production was given less money and fewer resources to rival the thrills of the first. According to *The Making of the Magnificent Seven*, the first film cost about $3 million to make and the sequels were allocated $1.78 million for the second, $1.36 million for the third, and the fourth had a budget of just $1 million. Even though *The Magnificent Seven Ride* failed to break even in its theatrical run (by about $20 thousand), the initial network sale of $1.05 million ensured that the film would make a profit.

Yet sometimes the fourth film can be the one with the highest budget. The first film *Night of Living Dead* was made for a reported $114,000; the second film *Dawn of the Dead* (1978) cost $1.5 million, and *Day of the Dead* (1985), the third film, cost merely $3 million. But *Land of the Dead* (2005), made with financing from Universal Studios, cost about $18 million. With the biggest budget, the film stars John Leguizamo and Dennis Hopper. Worldwide the film took in about $47 million, making it the second most successful of George A. Romero's *Living Dead* films, based on its initial theatrical run. Romero said that *Diary of the Dead* (2007), the fifth film, was made for under $4 million. Given the success of *Land of the Dead*, it might be surprising to some that Romero's fifth *Living Dead* was made so inexpensively. However, Romero insisted that while his partners at Universal were supportive, he did not always think that the additional funds benefited the film. "Even though I liked the film a lot, it was like approaching Thunderdome, it was getting a bit too big. I felt that it had outscaled its origins in a certain sense. When we made the first film, we were just a bunch of young people in Pittsburgh, making a movie, and I really wanted to get back to that [for the fifth film]."[7] [Zombieologists might insist that the 1990 remake of *Night of the Living Dead* should receive an honorable mention here, even if the sequel was not directed by Romero.]

Sometimes a fourth film can feature the return of a cherished actor to the series. Kate Beckinsale starred as Selene in the vampire-vs-werewolf Underworld series. Playing a vampire, Beckinsale kicked butt and took down Lycans in *Underworld* (2003) and *Underworld: Evolutions* (2006). She took a movie off and did not appear in *Underworld: Rise of the Lycans* (2009), the least financially successful sequel to that point. Presumably, to work around Beckinsale's absence, the film is set before the events of the first two films, and it introduced a new character, Sonja (Rhona Mitra), a powerful but doomed vampire. That film chronicled the first human to become a werewolf. Despite scene-chewing performances by Michael Sheen and Bill Nighy as a werewolf and a vampire, respectively, the film made $92 million, about $22 million less than its predecessor.

To hedge their bets, the filmmakers brought back series star Beckinsale for the fourth outing *Underworld: Awakening* (2012). *Awakening* expanded on the previous film's dense mythology. In the first three films, the bloody and centuries-old vampire-vs-werewolf beef has gone undetected by humans. However, as the fourth film begins, in voice-over, Selene informs the audience that the existence of vampires and werewolves is now known to the human race, and they are now hunting them.

Not only did *Underworld: Awakening*, the fourth film, perform significantly better than the third one—$160 million vs $92 million—it outperformed all of the other films in the series. It surpassed the first film's box office of $95 million by $65 million. Even though Beckinsale donned the fangs for *Underworld: Blood Wars* (2016), the $81 million return, suggests that audiences found the series to be a little long in the tooth.

Hammer Film Productions, the UK film studio known for its horror films, produced nine Dracula movies from 1958 to 1974. Christopher Lee played the vampire in seven films for Hammer. But the fourth Hammer film, *Dracula Has Risen from the Grave* (1968), is just the third time Lee played the role for the company. Lee did not appear in their second Dracula film *The Bride of Dracula* (1960). Lee's fourth performance in *Taste the Blood of Dracula* (1970) was Hammer's fifth film in its vampire series.

Happily Never After
Sometimes additional installments change a character's heroic arc. The horror film series *Scream* was conceived as a trilogy by writer Kevin Williamson. In *Scream* (1996), *Scream 2* (1997), and *Scream 3* (2000), Sidney Prescott (Neve Campbell) is terrorized and nearly killed by a revolving series of killers who assume the secret identity of "Ghostface." In a twist, Sidney's friends and her boyfriend are revealed to be Ghostface. As a result of this constant betrayal, Sydney is understandably distrustful of those close to her. By the end of *Scream* 3, she has finally vanquished all her enemies. In the last shot of *Scream 3*, security-conscious Sydney deliberately leaves her door open. The implication is that Sydney has finally found the peace that she deserves. But the filmmakers continued the series and Sydney's serenity was short-lived. A part four (*Scream 4*, 2011) and part five (simply titled *Scream*, 2022) followed and new killers threatened Sidney. As Vox writer Emily VanDerWerff posits, "Sidney will forever be trapped in a maze of knives because we don't want to see the *Scream* formula shaken up all that much. Sidney's a great movie character, one of the best in the slasher genre, played brilliantly by Campbell, so it makes sense we'd want to spend time with her. But the price of getting to hang out with her is also having to watch her nearly die, over and over again."[8]

"I thought you were dead."
Continuing the series when the main character has died in the third installment can be a challenge. But it is not an insurmountable one. Instead of creating a new lead for the series, filmmakers sometimes bring their heroes back to life. Take Ripley. At the end of *Alien 3*, Ripley is dead. But because Ripley had become the central figure of the series, she is brought back to life in *Alien: Resurrection*.

After watching a cut of *Alien: Resurrection*, Joss Whedon, its writer, was gutted. "It never was interesting to me as an idea to continue it," he said. "Then something really hard happened: Both my parents got ill. My dad first got ill, and my wife and I went home to take care of them, and we were really close to them. And also a good friend died in this very short period... It was just this constant grief. My dad died, then this friend died, then my mom died. I didn't really know how to process that kind of grief. I hadn't experienced it that closely."[9]

But Ripley is not the only hero who is resurrected for a fourth film. The Wachowski's *The Matrix* sci-fi spectacle was originally designed to be a trilogy. But eighteen years after the saga concluded with *The Matrix Revolutions* (2003), Lana Wachowski brought the franchise back to life with *The Matrix Resurrections* (2021). Wachowski faced a significant challenge in that Neo (Keanu Reeves) and Trinity (Carrie Ann Moss), two of the trilogy's three central characters, died in the third film. Yet they appear in *Resurrections*.

Spin-Offs

A handful of fourth films are spin-offs from the main series. Those fourth spin-off films include *Men in Black: International (2019)*, *Penguins of Madagascar* (2014), *Ocean's 8* (2018), and *Sharpay's Fabulous Adventure* (2011), a musical spin-off to the *High School Musical* series.

Passing the Torch

Instead of continuing the story of the protagonists of the first three films, fourth films can introduce new characters who are created to be the stars of a new franchise. To ease audiences into the new direction of the series, legacy characters also appear. For instance, in the first three *Karate Kid* films, Mr. Miyagi (Pat Morita) trains Daniel LaRusso (Ralph Macchio) in the art of karate. In *The Next Karate Kid*, Morita takes on a new student Julie Pierce (Hilary Swank). Similarly in *Ghostbusters: Afterlife* (2021), Peter Venkman (Bill Murray), Raymond Stantz (Dan Akroyd), and Winston Zeddemore (Ernie Hudson), the original Ghostbusters, appear in the fourth movie to help the granddaughter of the recently deceased Egon Spengler (Harold Ramis), banish poltergeists.

The fourth *Peyton Place* and *Texas Chainsaw Massacre* films look at the next generation of characters. The fourth *Transporter* film chose *Refueled* as a subtitle to indicate that a new actor is sitting in the driver's seat of the car-chase actioner. Whereas the first three *Omen* films told the story of Damien, the son of the devil, *Omen* IV: *The Awakening* (1991) introduced Delia, Damian's daughter. Technically speaking, *Jaws IV* could fall into this category because the killer shark is not the same shark from the first film. After being blown up by Martin Brody, that shark is sleeping with the fishes.

After Jason Bourne (Matt Damon) discovers his identity in the Bourne trilogy, there was an attempt to reboot the series with *The Bourne Legacy* (2012) and to focus on a new operative (Jeremy Renner), who was conditioned in the same program as Jason Bourne. However, after that fourth film failed to launch a new series, the series returned to its roots: Matt Damon's Bourne was recruited for one more mission in *Jason Bourne* (2016).

The subtitle of the fourth produced film in the *Barbershop* series, *The Next Cut* (2016), seems to suggest the story of the next generation of haircutters. Although the children of Ice Cube's Calvin are characters in the film, the protagonist of the earlier installments is still a central focus of the film.

Halloween 4 and *Friday the 13th Part IV* were to be "passing the torch" films, in which the main characters' evil transfers to new villains. Both films end with children who seem to now carry the evil that fueled Jason and Michael. But subsequent films did not follow through with those plans. *Highlander: Endgame* is also a movie in which the death of the main character was meant to set the stage for a new hero, a new, younger immortal swordsman. However, disappointing box office returns ensured that there would be no *Highlander 5*.

Similarly, the fourth *Shaft* feature film stars Samuel L. Jackson as John Shaft II, the nephew of Richard Roundtree's John Shaft. Roundtree played Shaft in three feature films and seven television films from 1973 to 1974. In 2019, the filmmakers passed the torch yet again in *Shaft*, the third feature film in the series. This time, Jessie T. Usher plays John "JJ" Shaft II, the son of Jackson's Shaft II. All three Shafts appear in the film.

The makers of the *Saw* franchise had to figure out how to incorporate Jigsaw into the fourth film, even though he died at the end of *Saw III* (2006). The film's problem became the mystery at the heart of *Saw IV* (2007). At the conclusion of *Saw IV*, Jigsaw has figured out a way for his murder games to kill long after his death. "I promise that my work will continue. That I have ensured. By hearing this tape, some will assume that this is over, but I am still among you. You think it's over just because I am dead. It's not over. The games have just begun." With these words, Lt. Mark Hoffman has taken over his grisly assignment. In *Scream 4* (2011), the cousin of the heroine of the first three films, turns out to be the new killer.

A noteworthy subset of passing the torch films include movies in which the torch is passed to relatives of the characters they played in the first film. In *Tremors 4: The Legend Begins*, Michael Gross plays Hiram Gummer, the fussy greater grandfather of Burt Gummer, the folksy character he originated in *Tremors*. In *The Planet of the Apes* reboot, Andy Serkis plays the son of Caesar, the protagonist of *Rise of Planet of the Apes* (2011), *Dawn of Planet of the Apes* (2014), and *War for Planet of the Apes* (2017). While not quite a relative, in *Alien: Resurrection*, Sigourney Weaver returns as a clone of Ripley.

Franchise Maintenance

Poorly received sequels to classic films can sometimes negatively affect the reputation of the franchise. For instance, *First Blood* is a taught thriller. But the following Rambo films strained credibility. Moreover, John Rambo, a victim of post-traumatic stress and an exemplar of the cost of war on the soldiers who fight it, became a meme for American imperialism. As a result, the original film's status is diminished. As writer Geoff Boucher observed, "*First Blood* gets respect from film fans who see it, but I wonder how many are motivated to take on that mission. It's a credibility prisoner to the Rambo sequels, which dwarf its commercial firepower while also diminishing the franchise's service record."[10] Still, Stallone stands by the film; he considers *Rambo* to be "the best action film I've ever done."[11]

Jaws is undisputedly a bravura piece of filmmaking. In his second theatrical film (after 1974's *The Sugarland Express*), director Steven Spielberg elevated what could have been a routine killer-animal horror film into an exhilarating film, which is anchored by three powerhouse performances by Roy Scheider, Richard Dreyfuss, and Robert Shaw. *Jaws II*, which is directed by Jeannot Szwarc and without Spielberg's involvement, is entertaining, but it is a pale remake of Spielberg's masterpiece. *Jaws 3-D* fell flat and *Jaws: The Revenge*, as noted, is universally derided (but perhaps unfairly so.)

The *Jaws* franchise might have been more fondly remembered if Universal had gone forward with Spielberg's original concept for the sequel to his taut and terrifying movie. In the original film, Quint, the shark hunter fiercely played by Robert Shaw, tells a chilling story about the USS Indianapolis, a World War II ship that sank in shark-infested waters in the South Pacific after successfully delivering the atomic bomb to Hiroshima. "Eleven hundred men went into the water. 316 men came out, the sharks took the rest."[12] Spielberg's original idea for the sequel was to depict the events that Quint described in harrowing detail.

And if making *Jaws* had not been so difficult, Spielberg might have overseen its sequel. The director stated, "I would have done the sequel if I hadn't had such a horrible time at sea on the first film. I would have absolutely jumped at the chance to own the sequel because I knew that when I was walking away from the sequel, I was walking away from a huge piece of my life that I had helped to create, but it wasn't a hard decision to walk away from it. I just could not imagine going back out to the ocean and sitting in a boat for 9 months. I just couldn't imagine it. So, I was happy and relieved not to have made the movie, but also, I wasn't happy with the sequel, and I realized I had let a franchise go that I could have made a good contribution to."[13]

Spielberg's regrets about the *Jaws* franchise led to his continued involvement in the *Jurassic Park* sequels, a group of films that has sometimes been described as *Jaws* on land. After directing the first film, Spielberg returned for its sequel *The Lost World: Jurassic Park* (1997). He has had a hand in selecting the directors for the follow-up films and in overseeing the direction of its sequels. Spielberg's strategy has paid off. *Jurassic World*, the fourth film in the series, earned a colossal $1.6 billion at the box office. Upon its initial release, the Colin Trevorrow-directed and Spielberg executive-produced film became the third highest-grossing film ever.[14] At the time, only James Cameron's *Avatar* (2009) and *Titanic* (1997) have so far earned more.

Sometimes a fourth entry can ruin the reputation of a franchise. The *Indiana Jones* series seemed to end after the third film *The Last Crusade*. As a way to signal to audiences that there is no more story to tell, it ends with Indiana Jones literally riding off into the sunset. A wonderful ending to a series that elevated action films. Yet, Spielberg and Lucas decided to make another film. The fourth *Indiana Jones* film was met with such derision that the phrase "jumping the shark" was replaced with "nuking the fridge," a reference to the moment in the movie where Indy narrowly avoids being nuked by jumping into a lead-lined refrigerator.

Christian Bale, star of Christopher Nolan's Dark Knight trilogy, said that he and the director refused to continue the story, which had a conclusive ending. Bale remembered, "Chris had always said to me that if we were fortunate to be able to make three, we would stop. 'Let's walk away after that,' Then when [Warner Bros.] inevitably came to us and said, 'How about a No. 4?' I said, 'No. We have to stick to Chris' dream, which was always to, hopefully, do a trilogy. Let's not stretch too far and become overindulgent and go for a fourth.'"[15]

Nolan and Bale understood that, generally speaking, as the number of sequels goes up, the quality goes down. Entertainment critic David Hochman wrote, 'Call it the *Friday the 13th* principle: For some reason, even the most well-intentioned sequels tend to peter out after three. Remember *Rocky IV*? (No? Two words: Dolph Lundgren.) What about *Death Wish IV*? …. Unless you've got a *Bond* or a *Star Trek* series, it's three times out before self-parody sets in." As *Jaws* and *Jaws* 2 producer David Brown said, "There comes a point with most sequels where it becomes about milking and milking something until it ceases to be worth it."[16]

Still, there are a few exceptions. It seemed that the *Mission: Impossible* spy series would be yet another example of the diminishing returns of a once-popular series. *Mission: Impossible*, directed by Brian De Palma, is a great spy film. *Mission: Impossible II* (2000) and *Mission: Impossible III* (2006) were inferior sequels. But, as previously noted, *Mission: Impossible: Ghost Protocol*, the fourth film in the franchise, is where the series found its stride, thanks to Brad Bird's direction, the film's visual inventiveness, and impressive stunt work by the series' star Tom Cruise. Writing for *Esquire* about the fourth *Mission* film, Chris Nashawaty enthused, "After the kinda disappointing [*Mission: Impossible III*], director Brad Bird gives the franchise the reboot it needs. I've got just two words for you: Burj Khalifa. Everything about this sea-sick skyscraper-scaling sequence on Dubai's tallest building in the world is so goddamned perfect it's like huffing laughing gas. In fact, it may be the defining action scene of the 21st century so far…"[17]

After *Ghost Protocol*, the series would be defined by Cruise's death-defying-stunts, including Five's affixing Cruise to the outside of a plane and Six's stunt-gone-wrong, where Cruise jumps from one building to another, breaking his ankle in the process. *Ghost Protocol* also stopped the downward trend of the series, and its next films, *Mission: Impossible: Rogue Nation* (2015) and *Mission: Impossible: Fallout* (2018) were equally strong.

Box Office
The diminishing returns of quality can also result in diminishing returns at the box office. Take the case of the *Police Academy* series. Although the total box office take for all seven films is an impressive $239,643,235, much of that haul derived from the first film's hefty box office take of $81,198,894. Each subsequent film performed less than the previous one. Films two through seven brought in, $55,600,000 (two), $43,579,163 (three), $28,061,343 (four), $19,510,371 (five), $11,567,217 (six), and the anemic final entry $126,247 (seven). Nevertheless, the first five films all made money at the box office; and I estimate that part six either made a little profit or broke even and part seven lost money.

Because the cost of releasing a film theatrically is so high, some fourth movies skip the movie theater and go straight to DVD (*Dr. Dolittle 4* aka *Dr. Dolittle: Tail to the Chief* (2008), *Scorpion King 4: Quest for Power (2015)*, *Wild Things: Foursome* (2010), *Substitute 4: Failure is Not an Option* (2001), and *Tremors 4* (2004). Fourth entries can also be made-for-TV films: *Psycho IV*, *The Omen 4*, *The Marine 4: Moving Target* (2015), *Home Alone 4* (2002), *Return of the Living Dead: Necropolis* (2005), *Shaft: The Enforcers* (1973), *Lake Placid: The Final Chapter* (2012), *Omen IV* (1991).

The fourth Harry Palmer film *Bullet to Beijing* (1995) is a TV movie, which aired 30 years after *The Ipcress File* (1965), the first film in the Michael Caine spy series. The *Hellraiser* and *Highlander* franchises faced similar box office challenges. The fourth *Hellraiser* and *Highlander* movies were the final entries in the series that were given a theatrical release. Subsequent films were straight to video.

However, the fourth film in the series can sometimes set box office records. The fourth modern *Transformers* film, while bombastic, made over a billion dollars. *Jurassic World* is the highest-grossing film of the series. *Fast and Furious* made more money than the three films before it and $150 million more than its second most successful film at the time, *2 Fast 2 Furious* (2003). While not beloved by fans, *Indiana Jones and the Kingdom of the Crystal Skull* (2008) was the most successful film of the series, earning $300 million more than the second most successful previous entry *Indiana Jones and the Last Crusade* (1989).

Fourth Time's The Charm
In the chapters that follow, I talk to filmmakers about the creative and practical challenges of making the fourth film in a series. These conversations take place with the creators of many of the world's most popular franchises, including *Star Wars, Star Trek, James Bond, Batman, Superman, Spider-Man, Psycho,* and *Halloween*. As you read the book, you will find an eclectic group of fourth films—from *Die Hard* to *Dirty Harry* to *Police Academy* to *Planet of the Apes*. I am very grateful to all of the filmmakers for taking the time to share their memories about their work with me. I am equally appreciative of you, the reader, for giving this book a shot. I hope you enjoy it.

SECTION 1
Superhero Movies

SUPERMAN 4

Superman IV: The Quest for Peace

Superman (1978), starring Christopher Reeve and directed by Richard Donner is widely considered to be one of the best superhero movies ever made. *Superman II* (1980), which was directed by Richard Lester after Donner was forced by the producers to abandon principal photography in order to complete post-production work on the first film, is a fun and exciting follow up. *Superman III* (1983), which was directed solely by Lester, is a disappointing effort in which the comic genius and dramatic talent of Richard Pryor is wasted. Pryor was unartfully shoehorned into a Superman movie, further helping to derail it. Still, there are a few standout moments, such as when Superman battles his evil doppelganger. *Superman IV: The Quest for Peace* (1987), directed by Sidney J. Furie, once again starred Reeve, Gene Hackman returned as Lex Luthor, and Mark Pillow played Nuclear Man, a muscular villain created by Luthor out of a strand of Superman's hair.

Despite some memorable moments, the film did not come together in a way that pleased anyone. While Christopher Reeve defends the script in his autobiography *Still Me*, the actor writes, "The less said about *Superman IV* the better."[18] For his part, Furie told his biographer, "I never saw the final version of *Superman IV*, nor will I ever."[19] Whereas *Superman* remains a high-water mark of the superhero genre, *Superman IV* is, along with *Batman & Robin*, generally thought to be one of the worst. *The Quest for Peace* routinely shows up on "the worst movies of all time" lists, and it nearly derailed the Superman franchise. Nearly 20 years passed before Superman returned to the screen in *Superman Returns* (2006), which ignored the events in *Superman III* and *Superman IV* and functioned instead as a sequel to the first two films.

What is often overlooked in considerations of *Superman IV* is that it is an earnest attempt to return to the roots and charm of the first film. It's a heartfelt effort to treat the character seriously and to avoid the campier touches that have ruined other superhero films. Despite its failings, there are some memorable moments in the film, including a poignant scene in which Clark visits the farm that once belonged to his now-deceased parents. The once-productive homestead is now near foreclosure and Furie's camera frames the landscape with appropriate bleakness. Clark won't accept an offer from a developer who wants to turn the land into a shopping mall; he wants to sell the land to a "real farmer." A family friend, who is also a real estate agent representing the developer, warns Clark to be careful in the big city because, "You're a long, long way from where you were born." Although the real estate agent was referring to Kansas, where the Kents raised him, Clark's birthplace is, of course, the distant and doomed planet Krypton. A wistful Clark replies, "I never forget that sir." As the script indicates, with his adoptive parents gone, "He's for now just an orphan boy from the Midwest."[20]

The highlight of the film is a comic double date involving Superman and Lois Lane and Clark and Lacy Warfield (Mariel Hemingway), whose father purchased the

Daily Planet. In the scene, Clark, moving faster than a speeding bullet, maintains the illusion that he and Superman are two separate beings while simultaneously entertaining both women. In another scene, Clark employs a power that was introduced in *Superman II*, a kiss that makes Lois forget the recent past. In *Superman IV*, Clark is conflicted about an important decision—should he rid the world of nuclear weapons or should he follow Jor-El's solemn admonishment that it "is forbidden for you to interfere with human history." Unsure of what to do, Clark visits Lois, reveals that he's Superman, flies her around the world, and finds comfort in her companionship. He then kisses Lois and makes her forget their encounter and his secret identity. The sequence is a romantic callback as well as a touching character moment that conveys that even Superman sometimes struggles with self-doubt and needs a loved one to help shepherd him through his troubles.

Working from a story idea by Reeve, Mark Rosenthal wrote *Superman IV* with his longtime collaborator Lawrence Konner. They also wrote *The Legend of Billie Jean* (1985) starring Helen "Supergirl" Slater, the sequel to *Romancing the Stone*, *Jewel of the Nile* (1985), *Desperate Hours* (1990), directed by Michael Cimino, and the Tim Burton remake of *Planet of the Apes* (2001). However, the movie based on their script was not produced by Alexander and Ilya Salkind, who had produced the first three films in the series, but rather by Cannon Films**,** known for cranking out second-rate action films. While the Salkinds weren't renowned for protecting their filmmaker's vision, they did have a reputation for making extravagant, big-budget films. In *Superman II*, as a romantic gesture, Superman flies to a remote rainforest to pick a rare and beautiful flower for Lois Lane. While shooting the Salkind-produced movie, Reeve and the crew flew to St. Lucia to film that fleeting moment. Cannon, on the other hand, was known as a penny-pinching production company. *Superman IV* suffered dearly for this change in stewardship.

Further, many scenes in the script were either not shot, or were shot but were later cut, because they would have been too expensive to convincingly produce. In the shooting script, Nuclear Man has the power to change shape, and, in one scene, he turns into a nuclear missile and launches himself at the Kremlin. In this instance, because he is both "man and missile" he is the "nightmare of the nuclear age."[21] Instead, Nuclear Man who is occasionally referred to in the shooting script as a "beast" is a poorly rendered villain, dismissively described by Rosenthal as "looking like a member of the Disco-era rock group the Village People."

Although he doesn't appear in the film, Rosenthal and Konner wrote the Jor-El character into the script. I suspect the writers hoped to entice Marlon Brando back into the part that he memorably established in *Superman*. Instead, Jor-El's intended dialogue is voiced offscreen by Susannah York who reprises her role as Lara, Superman's birth mother. *Superman* scribe, Tom Mankiewicz told me that Susannah York is a fine actress but she's no Marlon Brando.

There's another nice character-revealing moment, which was shot but did not make the final cut. In it, Clark has a nightmarish dream of Krypton "erupting in fire" and then exploding "in a hellish apocalypse."[22] It's a brief but essential scene that establishes Superman's fear that his adoptive planet will befall the same fate as his

Christopher Reeve as Superman
Illustration by Pat Carbajal

birth planet if he fails to rid the Earth of nuclear weapons. The nightmare would have helped move the film beyond well-meaning political rhetoric and would have given Superman a personal investment in preventing the looming catastrophe.

Shoddy special effects, a rushed shooting schedule, massive budget cuts, and capricious script changes sabotaged the filmmaker's original intentions and undermined the merits of the script. Still, I have a soft spot for the film. For all its failings, I choose to see the film's unrealized potential, and what it might have been under different circumstances.

Interview with Mark Rosenthal

Someday I hope to write a book called *In Defense of Superman IV*.
You and I will be the only people who buy it.

What are your thoughts on the franchise before your involvement with *Superman IV*?
Warner Bros hired us specifically to restart the franchise. They felt that with *Superman III*, which was the Richard Pryor film, they had taken a misstep. Not only was it not successful commercially, but it was also not successful critically. Perhaps the biggest issue was that Cannon alienated the cast. Despite his misgivings that he didn't have more opportunities in his career, Christopher Reeve was very invested in the series. He certainly didn't want the series to end that way. The cast didn't like the experience of making *Superman III*. Warners said that if they couldn't get Gene Hackman and Margot Kidder interested in doing it again, they wouldn't do another film. When we were hired that was our specific task.

Where did the story come from?
That was Chris. That just shows how much Christopher did not want the series to end on *Superman III*. He generated everything. With some consequences. He had an idea about Superman, hearkening back to Siegel and Shuster's original concept, which has an inherent flaw: if you are a superhero, this allegorical divine figure, why can't he just stop war? You can't address that question in a comic book, otherwise, the whole superhero premise doesn't make sense. In most comic books the superheroes fight one thief, one madman, or one conspiracy. But the superhero doesn't go to a country and say, "Hand over all of your nuclear weapons."

Chris felt that he had to do something very dramatic and perhaps even come up with a meta-story. I spent a couple of days with him in New York and he said he had this idea. What if Superman goes to the United Nations and says I'm going to stop war on the planet? Subsequently, there was a lawsuit, when somebody came forward and said that they had pitched that idea to Chris. If that's true or not I don't know. [Pediatrician, Kenneth Stoller, and Biomedical Researcher and Parapsychologist, Barry Taff claimed they submitted an unsolicited treatment to Reeve in which Superman rids the world of nuclear weapons.[23] The case was dismissed.[24]]

When Chris shared his idea of Superman ridding the world of nuclear weapons, what was your initial reaction?
When I first heard Chris's idea, which was to go to the heart of what Superman is, I

loved it. I grew up in an era where there were no film production classes. There were no screenwriting classes. There were only film appreciation classes. I was an English major. I have a doctorate in English literature, with a specialization in Chaucer. [Geoffrey Chaucer, the poet, is sometimes referred to as the Father of English Literature.] So I'm a literary guy. I loved hearing Chris's idea. I thought it was a chance to deconstruct the concept of Superman itself and look at what would happen. I was very enthusiastic.

Do you remember any ideas or variations on this idea that were discussed but not used?
That goes to the heart of the question of how the movie turned out. Warner's, and the cast, had to be convinced to do this approach for another Superman movie. The script we wrote was different from what ultimately got made after Cannon [which bought the film rights to *Superman IV*] came in and the director came in. It's a question of what they changed. There were differences in tone, in incident, and in the villain. It was wildly dumbed down.

We were going to have Superman take on the issue of nuclear war, which [in 1987] was certainly on people's minds. In our third act, Lex Luthor causes a panic and New York City is essentially evacuated. The reason Luther did it was so that he could loot the city with no one there. It was a very different third act from what they shot. It was more about what if they followed through on the premise? If you try to stop war, then there will be other people who are very interested in making sure that it doesn't go away.

The idea that Luther just wanted to evacuate Metropolis is an interesting one because it's a twist on the audience's expectations of Luther's actual plan.
Right. And one of the things that we wanted to do was to write to Gene Hackman. In some ways that was our single biggest call. Our marching orders were, "You've got to convince Gene Hackman." Gene Hackman is no fool and he's a great actor and there has never been a better Lex Luthor than him. I remember that we came up with an image first, which is to imagine that you see a line of cars on the George Washington Bridge and through the tunnels. It is one of those *Fail Safe* (1964) scenes where winds are blowing down the streets of Manhattan. Then you hear somebody singing. And around the corner is Gene Hackman with a shopping cart with paintings from the Met in it. We just thought that was funny. There would be paintings from the Met in it. That was our "what if." What if they shot that?

What was important to Chris in terms of how Superman was portrayed?
It goes back to that meta-question of what if Superman tried to stop war around the planet. And we also wanted to go at the big romantic implications. Since then, superheroes have been deconstructed in everything from *Smallville* [the 2001–2011 television show that depicted the exploits of Clark Kent's life before he becomes Superman] to their various reboots. But in those days the approach was very sacrosanct, and DC made sure that it was. Given the limited wiggle room we had, we came up with the double date idea to move the romantic side more to the center of the story.

After the third movie, a lot of the cast felt like it wasn't their movie, so we also wanted to show that they were all really good actors. Chris is a very talented light comedian and we kind of wanted to make a romantic comedy. To show a Myrna Loy and William Powell storyline and get to a classic English farce and get him to play both Clark Kent and Superman simultaneously. In some ways that's the only area of the movie where Sidney [Furie, the director] got close to it. We wrote it and we thought we needed to have a much more slam-bang director. Someone who could move the camera and pace the scene faster. We wanted it to be like one of those English farces where one character closes the door and another character steps back. He's Superman and he's Clark Kent. I think you could feel a hint of it in the air of the movie.

What guided you as you were writing the Superman character and Clark Kent? Now if you're going into the studio to pitch a superhero, you're almost always pitching a non-traditional version of the character. So today it doesn't seem surprising. The Clark Kent and Superman double life is a classic trope in literature and theater. It's the man in disguise. There are a million examples of it. For example, *A Tale of Two Cities* and *The Scarlet Pimpernel*. With *The Scarlet Pimpernel,* which is a famous novel set around the French Revolution, you have someone who to the public seems to be a fop but in actuality is a heroic undercover agent who rescues Aristocrats from under the nose of the terror.

That idea of someone being so courageous and so dashing and risk-taking that his masculinity is not threatened by playing a milquetoast character just so that he could further his good deeds. It's something that has been part of the narratives and the way we tell stories. Disguise in Shakespeare is a huge thing. There are so many fairy tales where a character will show up as an old woman or a decrepit old man but is actually a powerful witch or wizard in disguise protecting someone. I don't know if Siegel and Shuster were ever interviewed specifically about it, but it gets to the core of how we create characters. Certainly, you can link it up to these two poor Jewish kids in Cleveland creating Superman during World War II. It's hard not to imagine them thinking, "Yeah, we're just a couple of kids in the garage but we're smart and talented and have something to say."

I think an audience is predisposed to have certain tropes playing out with Superman and Clark Kent. They want Clark Kent to be picked on. They want Clark to push his glasses up and not react when he's threatened. I think it's for the audience's pleasure, for them to think, "Hey bully, hey criminal, do you know who you just picked on?" There's a scene in *Superman II* where Clark is on the barstool, not fighting back when he's picked on. I remember reading an article about why Superman was catching on and it pointed to that moment. At first Clark Kent doesn't fight back and then he returns later in the movie, and he does. You could argue from a feminist view that maybe that's what's wrong with masculinity. The need to show that well maybe I look like a smart and passive guy but I'm an incredible crusher. You must deal with that when you're writing Clark Kent and Superman.

I like that you try to bring the romance center stage. While seeing a man fly and witnessing his great strength is the spectacle of the movies, what gave them their

heart is the romance between Clark and Lois. That romance was the power of the first two movies.
The romance was important to us. What I was saying about Clark Kent physically is also true in the romance. In the comic books, Lois Lane is always telling Clark Kent how wonderful or essentially sexually attractive Superman is. "You're not the kind of guy I want to sleep with. I want to sleep with a guy like Superman, a real man." If you look at it in terms of male psychology in its most simplistic way, every guy likes to think that while he might look like Clark Kent there's Superman underneath.

As a sidebar, that's one of the psychopathic aspects of our president, Donald Trump. He's somebody who can never be Clark Kent because he needs to be told that he's Superman all the time. In order to be Clark Kent, who is teased all the time, you need to have a very well-formed ego and have confidence. I'm sure there's a very interesting essay to be written about why Trump violates the Superman-Clark Kent rule. While he is the most powerful man in the world as president, he needs to be told it all the time. Trump said he was the most presidential president since Lincoln. But Clark Kent would never boast about how powerful he is.

You need a little humility.
Clark Kent's humility comes from tremendous strength and self-confidence. It's the classic truism that a real man does not have to brag.

What's interesting about that double date concept is that in some ways Superman is teasing Clark by doing the opposite of what Clark would do. For example, there's a moment where, after prodding from Lois, Clark lamely compliments Lacy Warfield's dress. Then when Clark leaves, Superman arrives and gallantly remarks, "That's a lovely dress you're wearing."
Right, an original concept had much more of that. It's a convention that comes not specifically from Superman but from theater and opera. It's the back-and-forth of farce. There's always eavesdropping and disguise and people knowing things that others don't know that they know. We wanted to take advantage of that. With Superman's super speed and hearing, he could know things that were said even if he wasn't in the room. But the two couldn't be there at the same time back then. If we were to shoot it with today's special effects, it might be possible to have Superman moving so fast that it could create the illusion of him being in the same room as Clark. So by the time Lois and Hemingway's character Lacy Warfield turn their heads from one end of the table, where Superman was seated, to the other where they would see Clark. They could all be part of the same conversation. They would both seem to be there. It had real potential, but the level of filmmaking just wasn't up to it.

The way it could be staged is that first, the audience sees the mechanics of how Clark is tricking them. But once that's established and the audience is clear about the rules of how it's done, you could then see the date from a woman's point of view and experience it the same way they would.
That's right. But it didn't go anywhere. It didn't build. If it were shot right, there would be a little mistake in the quick-change and Superman could turn that into something cool. So that it didn't seem like a mistake. But the budget was slashed, and everything

was rushed through. And the truth is that the sequence needed more days to shoot. It should have been storyboarded much more meticulously and given him more to do, but it wasn't.

But the other great thing about the idea behind the scenes was that at the heart of the Superman story is a love triangle between Clark, Superman, and Lois and you found a way to dramatize that.
Absolutely. And that's because this was supposed to be the meadow movie where all those underpinnings of the story were addressed head-on. That's why we created the Mariel Hemingway character. To let them not just be allegorical rivals but to let them be actual physical rivals.

Along those lines, you can't make a superhero movie about nuclear war. The idea is too amorphous. You need a physical manifestation of it. Thus, Nuclear Man.
Yes. Remember the whole thing started with Chris's idea of what if Superman decided to bring about world peace? We knew it couldn't be just any old villain. And in those days, it was sexy and new to talk about clones. Even though the comic books had various permutations of Superman, including in parallel universes, we thought that Lex Luthor needed to create a villain that was as powerful as Superman and let's do it by cloning. There were a lot of problems with the execution of the concept. Nuclear Man was never meant to look like a member of The Village People. Instead, it was meant to be an outgrowth of the question, If Superman is powerful enough to save the planet, then shouldn't Lex Luthor be powerful enough to kill the planet. So we needed to show the potential for the holocaust of the planet. It was meant to be an aspect of Superman himself.

How did you want to see Nuclear Man rendered?
We originally wanted Chris to play him.

That harkens back to *Superman III* where Clark Kent and Superman literally fight each other.
Yes.

Which was the best part of that movie.
Yes.

Do you remember what you originally called Nuclear Man?
No, I don't. We probably went through 10 drafts before everything went south and I don't have any of them anymore. I moved so many times that I've whittled my 50 boxes of scripts and projects for all my movies down to just two. And then to one, and I can't find it now. I literally can't find it. It's unfortunate because one of the scripts was a Xerox copy of Chris's handwritten notes on it. Obviously, for emotional reasons, it would be nice to have it.

So he wasn't supposed to be a Bizarro figure like in the comics?
No. There are different characters like Bizarro in the comic books, but Nuclear Man wasn't supposed to be Bizarro. He was supposed to just be a clone of Superman. Lex Luthor saw some sort of demonstration about the power of Superman's hair, which is

holding up a weight and Lex can clone Superman using that hair through science that we never exactly explained. But Lex is using Superman's DNA to create a Superman clone.

In *Superman IV*, Superman is given a new power, the ability to move objects using his mind. He uses that power to rebuild the Great Wall of China after Nuclear Man destroys it. Was that your invention?
I don't remember exactly but I don't think we wrote that. The collapse and the budget problems started before they started shooting the movie. For all I know, Menachem Golem [co-owner of Cannon] was also writing the script at that point. I don't know. It was chaos. [According to a script dated October 30th (1986), it does not appear that Rosenthal and Konner gave Superman the power of telekinesis. In this draft, Superman reassembles the wall in a "blur of motion." Given that description, it appears that he rebuilt it using his already established super-speed.][25]

What was Chris's relationship with the character at that point? As an artist, he was probably eager to try new things. However, in interviews that were conducted during the promotion of *Superman IV*, he was talking about the idea of making *Superman V* sometime down the road.
I stayed in touch with Chris even after the movie. Another movie of mine that went south, and I didn't like the way they did it, was *Desperate Hours*, which is a remake of an old Humphrey Bogart movie. They put Michael Cimino on it as the director and the same thing happened, the script got changed. We were going to have Chris play the role that Anthony Hopkins ultimately played. Hopkins wasn't a star then. I used to have a place in Vermont where I would write, and Chris would call from his home in Massachusetts. The thing about Chris was that he was a very well-adjusted guy. He was very bright; he was educated. He was able to understand that the character of Superman was able to take an unknown actor and give him world renown. But at the same time, he wanted to show that he had the great ability to play other roles in other genres and other capacities. So while he could go back and forth at any given moment about being typecast, he wasn't a tortured soul. He was a very upbeat, very charming guy who was enormously fun to be around. He used to have this great apartment on the upper west side, and we would have story meetings there and he would say, let's go get some lunch. We would just walk down Columbus Avenue. Now keep in mind that things were a little bit different then and seeing a movie star in the street was still a big deal. So he was still Superman, he was still Christopher Reeve. And you could kind of feel when a star is uncomfortable about being recognized. It's a kind of brittle energy around them.

Not with Chris. He was upbeat. We would go down the street and find a place to eat and if someone stopped him or if they didn't stop him it didn't matter. If someone would say hi, he would say hi. If someone needed a hug, he would give it. He was funny. He was calm about the dichotomy of his career. I'm not saying that he didn't consider it and that he didn't wish that he had more power to do lots of other things, but he didn't writhe in bed or kick himself into a stupor because of it. Instead, he did what smart actors do, which is to exert some control. And to find the material. When he read about *Desperate Hours* in the trades, he called me out of the blue and said

Mark Pillow as Nuclear Man
Illustration by Pat Carbajal

he'd like to play a role. We thought, what a great idea. He wasn't passive about it.

The truth of the matter is that his heart and soul were in the theater. That's where his training was. This is a generalization, but it's often a lot more fun to hang out with theater actors than film actors. Theater actors are of course comfortable with words and it's not about power and celebrity, it's about ideas, and Chris was very charming.

Were you around for discussions about what would be done for *Superman V* if *Superman IV* were successful?
No, because we never got to production before the chaos happened. But remember that *Superman IV* was, in and of itself, an existential moment in the series. If we pull this off, the series might come back and if we don't, it probably won't. We weren't in that type of mindset to be thinking about down the road. The discussion was really, will there even be a road?

I think that's true of some fourth films in general. Look at *Star Trek IV*, a film that you had a hand in. *Star Trek IV* is very well-regarded but *Star Trek I* and *III* aren't as much. Also interesting, if *Superman IV* is the nuclear film, then *Star Trek IV* is the environmental film. Both *Star Trek IV* and *Superman IV* took issues and dramatized them.
Narratives are interesting things. It's not an accident that *The Amazing Spider-Man* went back to the beginning, rather than try to extend itself, to reboot the franchise. It's so much easier to establish the elements of a myth than it is to tell just another chapter in the story. It's hard to say what Zeus does in the 70th Adventure of the Gods? There are certain elements of telling a story that gets eroded by familiarity.

So you look for variations in a story and eventually, you get to the pop-culture idea of Jumping the Shark [where the quality of the series sharply declines]. And it means how many ways can you show the behavior of your main character? The audience expects certain behaviors. And movie sequels are like continuing episodes of a TV series. The audience does not want the central character to have an essential change. The first job I ever got was writing a TV show [*Cassie & Co* (1982)] for Angie Dickinson where she played an ex-cop [who opens a detective agency]. As I said, I came out of school with a doctorate in Chaucer. But I was a pop culture kid, and I grew up with comic books and horror movies until about age six. I was hired, and I had to write this one-hour script. I came up with a good idea and they loved it. At that time there was a big thing in the news because Norman Mailer had befriended an ex-con who wrote a book. [Norman Mailer wrote the introduction for Jack Henry Abbott's book *In the Belly of the Beast: Letters From Prison*. Mailer, with support from a few others, helped to get Abbott's sentence commuted; and when Abbott was released from prison Mailer helped him find a job.] They helped get him a job, but then he killed someone, and Norman Mailer and everyone who championed his writing, felt humiliated by not understanding how dangerous he was. So I took that idea and applied it to this story.

I had the Angie Dickinson character fall in love with a guy who gets out of prison, and she seems to be helping him, but he commits this terrible crime, and it breaks your heart. After I wrote it the producers said, "This is the best first script we ever got. And we're going to throw it out. We cannot have our lead character go through this crisis of who they are." On a TV series, you can't change the character in an ongoing narrative to a point where their essential dilemma has changed. Given that, you're always just looking for weird variations on the same story. That tends to lead to less-than-elegant plot devices.

You had to confront that when you wrote *Jewel of the Nile*, the sequel to *Romancing the Stone*. For *Jewel of the Nile*, you raised the bleak question of what do you do after you've had your big adventure? Can you sustain the romance?
That was part of the script discussions with Michael Douglas. What happens after you ride off together in the sunset and get married? And Michael said, "Will you try to kill each other?" Kathleen Turner had a lot of problems with the bickering, and Michael had to do some convincing to let her know that it was okay. The other idea that we explored a little bit there was that she married down. We wanted to play that dynamic too. She was a well-known book writer, and he was essentially unschooled. He's just the hunk she marries. It's like a man who marries the blonde bimbo and when the conversation replaces sex at some point you start to think this person isn't as much fun as I thought they were.

While we're talking about continuing stories let's touch upon *Star Trek VI: The Undiscovered Country*. [Along with Leonard Nimoy, Rosenthal and his writing partner have a story credit on the film.]
That started with a conversation with Leonard Nimoy who said what if Captain Kirk tried to make peace with the Klingons? And these are all indications that, at some point, the essential tension of a story has to be pulled apart. If you can't keep the narrative going, you have to question the essential. Look at the *Twilight* series. I'm not a fan of that series. I was probably too old for it when it first came out. But in that series vampires are allowed out during the day. Once you do that, you lose the metaphor, you lose the allegory about the other side of humanity. But once a story has been told a hundred times like with vampire stories, it's the thing that you do. Think about it in terms of Martin Scorsese. When he made the Nikos Kazantzakis book *The Last Temptation of Christ*, people went berserk. But he didn't change the Christ narrative, he just imagined what if he didn't die on the cross. I imagine that Kazantzakis was sitting around and thinking I'd like to write about Christ, but that story has been done and that other story has been done. "Oh, I know. I'll make it that Mary is sitting around at home happily, but I'll get killed if I do that, so I'll make it imaginary." Writers do this all the time. They think, "Let me take this well-known story and come up with a completely different take on it." That's the bread and butter of cable. They're just taking popular movies and reimagining them.

This brings us to your *Planet of the Apes* movie, which was billed as a reimagining of the *Planet of the Apes* saga.
It's the same thing. The new reboot is very good. And it's being reimagined in a more literal way and it's using the lack of sophistication of the previous movies as part of these new movies' narratives. [The reboot includes *Rise of the Planet of the Apes* (2011), *Dawn of the Planet of the Apes (2014),* and *War for Planet of the Apes* (2017)

and is set before the events of *Planet of the Apes* (1968). The recent films create a dialogue with the original series, incorporating and amplifying the older film's plot into their narrative. In this way, the reboot is both a prequel and launches a fresh beginning.] Tim Burton's *Planet of the Apes* movie was a little bit different because he has a slightly different agenda. He's making movies about the way he saw movies as a kid. We came into the project after there was already a first draft and after they were already in production. So we tried to jerry-rig a new story and clean up plot inconsistencies and we also tried to go at the Meta ideas in it to give it a sense of urgency. Because it included time travel, we thought why not go back to when the Apes were first taking over. And that's also part of the end of the movie which people remain endlessly puzzled about. [In the end, the astronaut leaves the relatively primitive planet of apes and returns to Earth only to discover that what he assumes is the modern Earth is actually a sophisticated, industrialized society being run by apes. The figure in the Lincoln Memorial has been replaced by a chimpanzee that looks pointedly like Abraham Lincoln.] Ironically, it hinted at what the series is doing now, which is going back and showing different points in the story's evolution and showing how things came to be.

Getting back to *Superman IV*, the most effective scenes are those without special effects. There is a very lovely scene at the beginning of the movie in which Clark goes to visit his family's old farm after his mom has passed away and someone wants to buy the land to industrialize it.

For us, it was a matter of trying to think through the logical implications of a story further along than you normally see it. So if you're going to confront everything, you're going to confront the mortality around him, the sense of loss. So you take characters through their normal paces the way that you would usually do in storytelling rather than in the frozen moments in the way comics tell stories.

What's also interesting about that scene for me is that we get to see a version of Clark Kent in which he seems at least at the moment to be authentic, where he is fully Clark Kent, rather than the alias that Superman adopts. He is without artifice. There's also a striking image of Superman who, after having his skin pierced by Nuclear Man's claws, is gravely ill. In the heightened AIDS-conscious era of the late '80s, it was alarming to see Superman looking as gaunt as someone with the disease.

I don't think that choice was intentional. The reproduction of Clark's sickness was not ideal, and everything was being jerry-rigged, and they fired the special effects artists on staff and brought in other, cheaper people. Sidney Furie was a nice guy, but this was just a gig for him. If you look at his career you can tell that he had no interest in Superman or comic book stories. He didn't bring any of his inner self to the story. As is often the case, not all directors are very inclusive with their writers. But Chris would always call me and keep me in the loop. But before Furie was hired, I remember Chris called me and he said that Warner's was thinking about either Sidney Furie or Wes Craven. And I thought that Wes Craven would be a very interesting choice. While Wes Craven has been typecast as a horror filmmaker, he is also a very bright guy. I thought Wes would bring an edge to the project and thought that Chris should go talk to him. But they went in the other direction. Maybe they were afraid.

You wonder who is going to show up. Is it going to be the Sidney Furie of the Michael Caine classic *The Ipcress File* (1965) or is it going to be the Sidney Furie of the Chuck Norris B-movie *Iron Eagle 2* (1988)? When you see *Superman IV* maligned, on these worst films of all time lists, what do you think? Does it bother you?

The truth of the matter is that it doesn't bother me. If the movie turned out the way we wanted it to or if I had directed it and then people thought it was terrible, then I would take it to heart. But it was a transmogrification of our script and our ideas. Warner essentially bailed out of the project and turned the production over to Cannon, who acknowledged that they were going through a financial free fall, and "we're trying to make it cheap…" Then yeah, duh, of course, it wasn't going to turn out well.

How would you characterize your experience working on the film?
I'm not writing novels here. I'm in the movie business. Each project is enormously collaborative, and you don't have full control. You rarely even have part control. It's not the writer's medium. As much as I would argue that the writing is the most important thing and gets the movie created. Everyone working on the movie reacts, but the writer is the creator. Just because everyone else is reacting to something in the material doesn't mean it's not important. I rarely look at the final product but instead, I focus in the end on the amazing journey of the process. Sometimes it's years. Sometimes it's much quicker.

For Tim Burton's *Planet of the Apes* (2001), we were hired on July fourth, and they were shooting in September and that felt like overnight. You look at the people that you're involved with, and the events that seemed bizarre at the time later become funny stories. Even the anger in retrospect changes into something where you go, "Wow, I went through that." I look at it as a chance to get to know Christopher Reeve. I was a kid who bought every DC Comic with every penny I had them lined up in my room as a boy in Philadelphia. So the idea that I was seeing my Superman movie was good enough. Even if it turned out the way it did, I went from living in a row house in Philadelphia, collecting obsessively, and lingering over every page of DC Comics, to sitting with Christopher Reeve and writing Superman. You must put a perspective on your life in the movie business because it's not predominantly a writer's medium, and you can't look at the finished film and think, "Oh man, they didn't do a good job with my script." But usually, they do a good job with your script.

You also revived a power that was introduced in *Superman II*, one that I suspect was widely forgotten by the time *Superman IV* was released. In *Superman II*, Clark makes Lois forget that he's Superman with a mesmerizing kiss, and you used that power cleverly when Clark, who is troubled, confesses to Lois that he is Superman. By opening up to Lois he can work through his distress, and then kisses her so that she will forget.
This came from the notion that if everything is on the table well then let's put everything on the table. We were talking about how sometimes the strong man is weak in real life like Donald Trump must get credit for everything. Similarly, Clark Kent in

Superman legend never really gets Lois to look at him differently. Let's do the moment where you finally say, "No, look at me." It is the tension inside this guy. What would happen if you finally said, "No, it's me"? I remember talking about this with Chris, the idea that we as a species cannot go up to someone you like and say, "I like you." Culturally, it's not done. But we've also sort of convinced ourselves that it would turn them off. Part of the romantic convention is not revealing your heart. It's something Shakespeare wrote about. Instead, for example, if you meet someone at a bar you should casually make conversation in the hopes that maybe in the future it could lead to something. But if you are more direct, it's considered weird. And that's inherent in the Clark Kent and Lois Lane relationship.

If part four had been successful, what would you have liked to have seen in part five?
I'm not the same person I was back then, so I don't know what I might have thought. I'm not even sure what Warner Brothers or DC would have allowed. I like using *The Last Temptation of Christ* idea and I'm not sure why. I would open in a suburban house with Clark and Lois, married with three kids. Then you figure out how they got there, I don't know. And one of their kids not knowing they inherited superpowers trying out a bong or something, I don't know. Who knows what you have to do to make Superman relevant today? The recent reboots have been incredibly unsatisfying.

Does he hang out in his house as Superman? Does he make breakfast in the Superman costume?
I don't know. I don't want to seem like I'm obsessed with this but in a world where Trump is President what constitutes a cartoon and what doesn't? Maybe it's about the fact that the public can't tell what a superhero is anymore. In *Batman v Superman,* they were trying to explore the public's inability to figure out who is in their corner. I would take it more deeply and make it much more of today's world. Given what's happening in the country you don't need a supervillain. The villainy is in the public temperament now.

BATMAN 4

Batman & Robin

Nipples, it almost always comes down to the nipples. When discussing Joel Schumacher's *Batman & Robin* (1997), critics invariably snipe at the nipples that adorned the Bat suit. It's easy enough to criticize the fourth Batman movie without this frivolous fixation, as even its stars often do. George Clooney confessed that his bad performance nearly "destroyed" the once-thriving Batman franchise.[26] Chris O'Donnell lamented that while shooting *Batman & Robin*, he felt like he was making a "kid's toy commercial."[27]

Joel Schumacher directed two Batman movies, *Batman Forever* (1995) with Val Kilmer as Batman/Bruce Wayne and *Batman & Robin* with George Clooney in the dual role. Because some advertisers and easily offended parent groups were outraged by Tim Burton's *Batman Returns* (1992), Warner Bros. instructed the filmmakers to make *Batman Forever* a stylish entertainment that would appeal to an all-encompassing demographic. They wanted to avoid a repeat of *Batman Returns* where its Penguin chews on raw fish and drools black bile, and its sultry Catwoman dons a form-fitting, S&M–tinged costume.

Schumacher successfully followed Warner's directive. *Entertainment Weekly*'s Owen Gleiberman wrote that "Schumacher directs [*Batman Forever*] like a musical, turning each image into eye candy, weaving one lush set-piece into the next, as if he were the Vincent Minnelli of blockbusters."[28] *Batman & Robin*, on the other hand, with its campy sensibilities and over-the-top performances by Uma Thurman as Poison Ivy and Arnold Schwarzenegger as Mr. Freeze, put the franchise on ice for ten years. The failure of the excessive *Batman & Robin* helped pave the way for Christopher Nolan to take a darker, more realistic approach to the superhero in his multi-billion-dollar-grossing Dark Knight trilogy.

It is not often noted that other than changing the lead actor, *Batman & Robin* was essentially made by the same creative team as *Batman Forever*: director (Schumacher), writer (Akiva Goldsman), producer (Peter Macgregor-Scott), composer (Elliot Goldenthal), cinematographer (Stephen Goldblatt), production designer (Barbara Ling), editors (Mark Stevens and Dennis Virkler), and the same costume designers (Bob Ringwood and Ingrid Ferrin). Schumacher also retained some of the key cast members including, Chris O'Donnell (Robin/Dick Grayson), Michael Gough (Alfred), and Pat Hingle (Commissioner James Gordon).

Yet responses to the films were utterly divergent. One film was a commercial success, the other was a box office failure. One movie is widely thought to be entertaining; the other is just as widely ridiculed. There are also vast tonal and stylistic differences between them. The question of how to account for these differences was foremost in my thoughts when I spoke with Joel Schumacher.

Joel Schumacher Interview

The book is called *Fourth Times's The Charm* and it's about the creative decisions

filmmakers make while working on the fourth film in an ongoing series.
I wouldn't say that *Batman & Robin* was charmed. I think the third time was a charm for us. I did the best I could with the fourth.

Before we get into *Batman & Robin*, let's talk about *Batman Forever*. How did you come to take over for Tim Burton, who was the natural choice to direct a third Batman movie?
I had done two films in a row for Warner Bros. and for my great bosses Bob Daly and Terry Semel. I did *The Lost Boys* (1987) and then *Falling Down* (1993). Both of those movies were considered risk-taking movies at the time. So I already had a relationship with them and fortunately, both of those movies turned out okay. But that was just luck. I was preparing *The Client* (1994), the John Grisham bestseller, in Memphis, Tennessee. We were about two weeks away from filming and I got a call saying my bosses wanted to see me in LA. I thought, Well I'm either going to be fired or something big is happening.

They had a few jet planes and they sent one for me. So it seemed important. I met with Bob and Terry in their office, and they explained to me that they had a lot of problems with parents complaining about *Batman Returns*. They said kids got scared and the parents also complained about Michelle's fabulous bondage costume. They claimed to have a great many letters from families complaining about it. They asked me if I wanted to do a Batman movie. I said, are you sure that you want *me* to do it? They said, yes. I grew up on Batman comic books, so I said, Wow, okay.

I then said that I needed to talk to Tim. I said I can't do this if it's not okay with him because it's his franchise. Tim and I have known each other for a long time. I had lunch with him, and Tim said, do it. Take it, please. He said that while *Batman Returns* was such a sensation, inside it was too much for him. I thought maybe he feels that way because Tim is an artist and he's a lot more sensitive than I am. At the time, I didn't know what he was talking about. But I did know that he had no interest in doing another Batman film. It also felt like the studio, for whatever reason, didn't feel like working with him. I only know what I was told, but it's none of my business. But because Tim said, please take it, I did.

You had a new Batman. You didn't use Michael Keaton, Burton's Batman.
For many reasons, we had to say goodbye to Michael Keaton. One weekend my friends and I saw *Tombstone* (1993) and Val Kilmer was so great as Doc Holiday. Every great western seems to have a shot of men walking down a dirt road, all spread out. In *Tombstone*, they had such a scene, with Val Kilmer walking in this long coat. I turned to my friends and said, "He'd make a great Batman." So I went to talk to my bosses, and they thought it was a great idea. There were other circumstances, but Terry Semel went over to where Michael was working at the time, and he told him that he was no longer Batman. Fortunately, Val wanted to do it. It was a younger Batman than I had originally planned.

Robin Williams wanted to play The Riddler but, for a year, he would not commit. I wanted Jim Carrey to play The Riddler. Robin never committed and fortunately, Jim wanted to do it. Warners met with Jim at Nate'n Al Delicatessen, and they made a deal to do it, on a napkin in about five minutes. I asked Nicole Kidman

George Clooney as Batman
Illustration by Pat Carbajal

to play Dr. Chase Meridian (Bruce Wayne's love interest) and I had worked with Tommy Lee Jones on *The Client*. I asked him to play Harvey/Two-Face and he wanted to do it.

What about Val Kilmer was closer to your idea of Batman than Michael Keaton?
I thought he was a younger and sexier Batman. Since I'd been asked to reinvent it a little bit I thought, Let's go that route, which had certainly been successful for me on my other movies. I knew that Val Kilmer would look great in the costume. Bob Ringwood, who also did the costumes for *Batman*, did the costumes for *Batman Forever*. Rubber had been reinvented at that point in the sense that you could do body-contouring Batman suits. If you look at Tim's first Batman movie, you could see that it was a much larger suit because they didn't have the technology to do this as form-fitting as we later would.

What else informed your approach to *Batman Forever*?
I also thought the movie should be a lot of fun. And maybe, if we were lucky, it would be fun for both kids and adults. Bob [Daly] and Terry [Semel] were stressing to me about families' disappointment with the previous Batman film. But it was a different time then.

Your Batman wasn't a complete reboot. You retained some of the elements from Burton's.
Right, I used Michael Gough, the same Alfred who was in Tim's two films.

There's also a similar aesthetic. It's a similar world even if there's a different Batman.
That's because Batman is just Batman. And Bruce Wayne has always been rich. But Barbara Ling, the production designer, and I fell in love with the idea of doing buildings like human beings. And there are a lot of human figures in the architecture, and I don't remember that in Tim's.

What was the general feeling at the time about the state of the franchise?
Because theater owners and distributors had been burned by *Batman Returns*, I had to travel the world trying to convince them to carry another Batman movie. They didn't want another Batman movie. Because licensing makes so much money, I also had to go to Toy Fair (a trade show) and get them on the bandwagon too. It was Warner's biggest franchise at the time. So much of the studio revenue depended on it. I'm not bragging or complaining, it was just my job. I was glad to do it. I'm sure it was the least expensive of the Tim–Joel–Chris–Batman movies.

***Batman Forever* came out and it's a huge hit.**
It was one of the biggest hits of the year. I think it was the highest-grossing film of the year, behind *Toy Story* [Pixar's first feature film]. We got lucky that it worked. It was fun to entertain so many millions of people. I had never done a blockbuster before. I had success with my smaller films, and they made enough money so that I could get the next one made. I was working freelance, and I just hoped that I'd do a good enough job that I'd get to do the next one. I don't think anyone expected *Batman Forever* to be as big as it was. And the companies who did sign on were very happy campers. I'm

talking about companies like Hasbro, who make the plastic figures that go with the movie, and Walmart who buy so much of the merchandise. They were willing to throw their hat into the ring with us. My goal was not to sell plastic figures, but sometimes it seemed like it was. We all see good movies every year that very few people also see. A lot of it has so much to do with being in the right place at the right time with the right movie. Hopefully, some talent helps too. And hopefully, there's something good in the movie. But there is a zeitgeist and we just got lucky. *Batman Returns* has a lot of terrific talent and invention in it but *Batman Forever* seemed fresh and the cast were all quite dazzling in it. The sets, the costumes, the music. And we had a blast doing it.

So Warner's asked you to come back and do another one.
I had never wanted to make a sequel before. *Batman Forever* came out in the summer of 1995, and I was in a small town in Mississippi getting ready to shoot John Grisham's first novel *A Time to Kill*. Once you finish a movie you hand it over. It's yours while you're making it. It's like raising a child that you're not the parent of and eventually, you have to give the child away. It's something that you have to get used to. That's the way it goes. Success happens without you. It's somewhere out there. It's usually just numbers. The studio will advertise and brag about how much money you're making. Friends will call you and tell you that a theater is sold out. And it's all very exciting. Then you hang up the phone and go on with your life. But there was a great deal of expectation and pressure to do another Batman right away. But I am the only person in charge of myself. I chose to do *Batman & Robin*. I had never done a sequel before. Columbia wanted to do a sequel to *St. Elmo's Fire* and Warner's wanted a sequel to *The Lost Boys*. There might have been talk about a *Flatliners* sequel, but I can't remember. [A *Flatliners* remake, directed by Niels Arden Oplev, was released in 2017.]

With *Batman & Robin*, you had much of the creative team returning.
Exactly.

One might assume that *Batman & Robin* would turn out just as well as *Batman Forever*. After all, there would be less to figure out because you've already established the world of Batman.
On the surface, perhaps. But I don't always think it works out that way. It is a different movie. It isn't the same movie. You can't repeat anything and think that'll work out. So while the creative elements were the same—the cinematography, the production design, the costume design—that is not going to make a great movie. It only makes it more visually fascinating. But there are so many talented people involved both on-screen and behind the camera that I don't think they ever got their due. But it made a lot of money and sold a lot of toys.

The tone is also very different from the previous film.
I think it is over the top. I think it is *too* over-the-top. I think with *Batman Forever* we sort of maintained the right balance on the tightrope. Maybe it worked because we didn't know what we were doing, and I just did what I thought I would like. But with *Batman & Robin*, it just felt like it needed to be bigger and better. And more. I don't

remember exactly, but it was expected to be a hit. I thought, you just never know. I had been working in Hollywood since 1970, and I knew nothing was predictable.

Where are you aware at the time that the tone was different?
I got carried away by the whole thing. No excuses. But there's a French expression that I will not do justice to, but I never got my ass in the seat right. Maybe it was too much too soon. But the film looks gorgeous. There's a lot of amazing talent in it and I've made so many movies since then. It came out in 1997 and *A Time to Kill* came out in 1996. I was making a movie a year. Sometimes two movies a year. I never had much time to look back. I couldn't get my ass in the seat right. There's no one to blame but me. I'm a big boy and I went in with my eyes wide open. I don't know. I think it just got bigger and louder. I think *Batman Forever* was a lot about less is more. I think *Batman & Robin* was about more is more.

In terms of the screenplay, all the characters have their arc. Alfred is dying, and as a result, Bruce Wayne is preparing to mourn his father figure. Bruce is also fighting with Dick Grayson over Poison Ivy whose magical spell they're both under. Barbara is becoming Batgirl. There is a lot of story there.
[Somewhat hushed] Maybe too much. Some fans were dying for a Batgirl and maybe that was too much story. Akiva Goldsman, who rewrote *The Client* and *A Time to Kill* and is such a brilliant writer, rewrote *Batman Forever* and then wrote *Batman & Robin*. Maybe we just overloaded it. But that all comes back to me. I'm the person who gets to say yes or no. Maybe we were trying too hard. I don't know. That's an interesting point that you bring up.

In the first two movies, Batman's a loner and then in the third movie, Batman teams up with Robin. In the fourth film, Batman is dealing with the repercussions of opening up emotionally.
I thought we would try a less brooding Batman. I remember that conversation very well. There was an attempt to be family-friendly and maybe we went too far towards the end. I don't know. It's so hard to analyze your own work.

There is one overarching story that's told over four movies. But there are three different actors playing Batman who are serving that story. I wonder if that confuses an audience.
The audience gets used to another Batman. It worked with Chris Nolan. His first film *Batman Begins* didn't have necessarily such a big audience. It wasn't until the second film [*The Dark Knight* (2008)], with the brilliant Heath Ledger, that his Batman took off. His second film was the billion-dollar Batman movie.

What qualities did you want with Clooney?
When Val dumped us at the eleventh hour and ran off to do *The Island of Doctor Moreau* (1996), Bob Daly, in tandem with Terry Semel, suggested George Clooney. I went to meet George—and to know him is to love him. He's such a sweetheart. Val has a very disturbed psyche, and George does not. And that shifted the tone too. It's funny looking back on it. I love that I'm learning more about it from you than I know myself.

I was a production assistant for the New York unit of your first Batman movie. One of my jobs was to hold up a big sheet of cardboard…
To hide the costume.

That's right. That also shows you how long ago that movie was made, when a piece of cardboard was thought to be an adequate security measure. But my point is that I was just mesmerized by the suit. I would stare at it.
It's a work of art. It's just beautiful. And powerful. Bob Ringwood designed it, and the wonderful sculptor named Jose Fernandez worked on it. The references were Greek statues and the incredible drawings that you see in medical books and sometimes on doctor's walls. Those were the books and the models that Bob Ringwood had brought into the sculpting room. And Jose was a brilliant, brilliant sculptor. It was beautiful. We were only able to do it because the technology for making the rubber suit had changed.

In the opening sequence, you have close-ups of bottoms and crotches on the suits.
Oh yes. What worked in *Batman Forever* was that it is so funny and the relationship between Val and Nicole is quite aggressive. There was a lot of tongue-in-cheek in that movie and it was fun. So I thought, Let's make *Batman & Robin* more fun.

When did you realize that it wasn't going to come together quite the way that you envisioned?
That's a good question. I was already preparing *Runaway Jury*, which would have been my third Grisham novel. I was so deep in casting. Gwyneth Paltrow had said yes to being in it and I was going to ask Edward Norton to be in it too. I was going around the world doing press junkets for *Batman & Robin*. You do these press conferences and all these one-on-one interviews. The press is very quick to tell you that everyone else hates you and wants you dead. And even though I've never been the critics' darling I never had that reaction before. And I was traveling all over the world selling my wares, which was part of my job at the time. I was in Rio, and I had half a day off. My assistant said to me, "You're kind of like a rock band. You fly to a city; you do a premiere and then you fly off again." If it's Wednesday, I must be in Belgium. We had a half-day off and I remember lying on the beach with a beer and my assistant. We were going to cut ribbons at a toy store that night. I kind of thought, what am I doing with my life?

I've always wanted to just tell stories. I grew up behind a movie theater and as a kid, I loved them. As great as it's been, what am I doing cutting ribbons at toy stores? Not that there was anything wrong with it, but I had one of those real soap opera moments. I went back to the hotel looked in the mirror and said, "What the fuck are you doing?" I called John Grisham and I called Bob and Terry and I said that I couldn't do another Grisham book.

Was there a talk of a *Batman 5* at this point?
There were plans for me to do another Batman. I met with Nic Cage to play the Scarecrow. But personally, I was just lost in translation. So I decided to do *8MM* (1999), which was as far from a summer movie as you can get. [Cage plays a private eye who is hired to find the truth behind a snuff film.] I think it was one of my best.

But the situation had all just gotten too much, with the private planes and the handlers. I wasn't that guy. I'm a New York street kid. I started in Hollywood for two hundred bucks a week. And I was glad to have any job in the land and the industry of my dreams. I kind of had it coming.

Nicolas Cage is an interesting choice to play the Scarecrow.
I think he can do anything. And when you need crazy, he's a good crazy.

What do you remember about his approach to the Scarecrow?
I'm over getting a call from his agent saying that he wanted to do the film. Very briefly, I don't know if you've ever seen *Vampire's Kiss* (1988), but I judge people on what they think of Nic's performance in that because it's brilliant, it's quite brilliant.

Nic was shooting *Face/Off* (1997), and I went to have lunch with him at his trailer. We talked, but you don't have long lunch hours when you're shooting. So we only talked a little bit. It was more of a getting-to-know-you conversation. But it hadn't been planned out yet. The Scarecrow is a fascinating character. And that's as far as we went. We hadn't worked it all out. But I had a great time with him on *8MM*. What Nic said to me about *8MM* is, I want to do a very reserved performance. I want to do an internal performance like I've seen Robert De Niro do. I remember saying, if that's what you want to do, we'll do it. I'll help you in any way that I can.

There were rumors that Nicholson would appear as Joker.
I wanted Batman to wind up in Arkham Asylum. [The Gotham prison for the criminally insane, which is populated by supervillains.] I thought Batman could be haunted by all the villains from his past. But I never mentioned Jack's name.

In theory, maybe put Jim in a scene as the Riddler?
It felt like whenever we burped or farted, it became huge news. It was leaked that we were spending 80 million dollars on the cast. It felt like people were gunning for us and I don't know why. I felt like we were a target. I was getting too much press. I never had a presentation in my life. But the studio did, and I was getting too much press. George Bernard Shaw said, "I want my friends to be successful, but not too successful." It became overblown.

Was there a finished script?
Not yet. But I wanted to do a very dark one. I used Arkham Asylum at the end of *Batman Forever*, and that's where the Riddler wound up.

Was it going to be called *Batman Unchained* or is that just a rumor?
Not to my knowledge.

Did you go to directors' jail for a while after *Batman & Robin*?
Directors' jail?

Yes, it's a euphemism for what happens to some artists if they make a film that underperforms. I know you continually worked but were there any repercussions?
After that, I think I made some of my best movies, including *8MM*, *Tigerland* (2000), *Veronica Guerin* (2003), and *Phone Booth* (2002). If I went to directors' jail, I wasn't

aware of it.

Did *Batman & Robin* change the kinds of films that you wanted to make?
Yes, I went back to the way I started. That's how I started. I was doing costumes for Woody Allen in 1973 for *Sleeper*. Woody encouraged me. Woody said if I wanted to be a director, then I would have to write. I said, "But I'm not a writer." Then he said, "Oh, just write something, but you have to finish it and people have to read it. If they don't like it just write another one." I said, "I can't write like you." He said, "Don't. Just be you." But then *Sparkle* (1976) was made and then *Car Wash* (1976), and then *The Wiz* (1978). [Schumacher wrote the screenplays for that trio of films.] Then a woman fought for me to write and direct television movies. The second one [*Amateur Night at the Dixie Bar and Grill*, 1979] was well received and I got to direct my first feature, *The Incredible Shrinking Woman* (1981). People actually went to see it. And then the second one [*D.C. Cab*, 1983] and then *St. Elmo's Fire* and *Lost Boys*, which were back-to-back. That opened doors for me in Hollywood that I had never seen. It was all just rolling. After *Falling Down*, I was considered to be a director to be taken seriously whether you like the movie or not. *The Client* was so popular and had such a great story, but it was made with a very modest budget. And then *Batman Forever* and then *A Time to Kill*, and it was just building. But then *Batman & Robin* and I was scum. But I can't have any regrets about it. I really can't.

I've been whoring around New York, this muddy island, ever since I was a teenager. I went to art school. I always ask people, "Did I ever say to you once that I want to be rich and famous?" No, never. I've always just wanted to tell stories. The movies had such an impact on me because I grew up before television. And I had comic books, which as you know are like storyboards. The Sunnyside movie theater was literally the back door to where I lived. My father died when I was four. My mother and I lived on the first floor and our windows looked across the street to the back door of the Sunnyside Movie Palace. I was always working since I was nine, I was delivering meat for the butcher. I would take the pennies, nickels, and dimes and go to the movies. And I would sometimes see the same movie over and over again. I also went to other movie theaters in our neighborhood. When I wasn't getting into trouble at school or in the street, I just lived at the movies.

I wanted to tell stories ever since I was seven and saw *Great Expectations* (1946). At the time, I didn't know that there were directors or that David Lean made that film. I didn't know who those actors were. I didn't know anything. But I just knew that it started with a little boy and a graveyard. And I was a little boy who had been in the graveyard, and it made such a visual impact on me. And then of course there's a story about a boy with *Great Expectations*. I couldn't sleep for a long time after that movie. I kept rerunning that story over and over in my head. I would toss and turn. I just wanted to tell a story like that. I don't know if I have reached Dickensian levels. [Laughs]

We're now 20 years past the initial release of the movie and I would imagine it's no longer a raw experience for you. How do you process it in your life?
That's such an interesting question. When I do interviews there is never a puff piece,

Arnold Schwarzenegger as Mr. Freeze
Illustration by Pat Carbajal

God forbid. So someone, having read everything about the movie, will ask, what happened with *Batman & Robin*? There is judgment within the question. I don't have a charge on it. I can't give them what they would like, which is to indignantly say, how dare you ask me that. I can't even fake it. I don't have it in me. Of course, it's not journalism if they can't ask tough questions, and they should. I just wish it wasn't the same question all the time.

It always gets reduced to the nipples.
And somehow you have to explain yourself. They present it to you like you killed babies. Nobody sets out to make a bad movie.

You tried to make a good movie and it didn't work out quite the way you had hoped.
Yes, and some people love it.

Have you seen it recently?
I don't watch my movies. However, if my significant other wants to watch one, then I watch it with him. Or if one of my friends wants to see a movie that I made, I can tell them anecdotes. I always leave the TV running in every room, and if I come home late, sometimes one of my movies is showing. For me, it's like a home movie. For a while, TNT and another channel were playing *The Client* and *A Time to Kill* all the time, which was lovely of them. I remember coming home late one night and *A Time to Kill* was on and I watched it thinking, that was the day that so and so was sick, or the camera broke down. It all comes back to me. And at a certain point I go, God, they're fucking *gorgeous*. I think that about a lot of my movies.

You tend to cast good-looking people.
I've been criticized for it. I remember one journalist said to me your films objectify men and women sexually. I said, "Well I like that." I grew up on movies that had great actors and actresses who are gods and goddesses. I grew up on Elizabeth Taylor, Paul Newman, Rock Hudson, Grace Kelly, and Ava Gardner. When you went to a movie, you got to see great stories with great people in them, gorgeous people. And if they weren't gorgeous, they were still bigger than life. Then I said to her, let me ask you a question if I may, "Where is the bad part? What's bad about that?"

Alicia Silverstone played Batgirl in your movie. She's great in *Clueless* (1995). I saw her years ago in a Broadway show written by Donald Margulies called *Time Stands Still* and she stole it. She was very funny.
I ran into her last winter. She looked gorgeous and seemed very happy.

But when *Batman & Robin* came out there were a lot of comments about her weight and a lot of comments that we would now call "fat-shaming."
I know, and it was horrible. I had never experienced anything like that. I thought it was one of the most loathsome things in the world. And I don't remember that being as common before then. Joan Rivers used to make fun of Elizabeth Taylor, but Joan Rivers is Joan Rivers, and you expect that out of her.

The newspapers would write derogatory comments about her body type in the

Jeep Swenson as Bane
Illustration by Pat Carbajal

title of the article. Instead of Batgirl, they would call her "Fat Girl." It's alarming that writers, editors, and publishers thought it was appropriate to do that.

It's much worse now. But I think Alicia came through it beautifully. She's happily married, and she has wonderful children. I ran into Alicia one winter's day and she was more beautiful than ever. In the movie business, like politics or any business where you have a high profile, you have to have the hide of a rhinoceros, or you won't live through it. There's that phrase, "That which does not kill us makes us stronger." What Nietzsche wrote is true. Some of us are destroyed by it and some of us are survivors. It's a rough life and it's especially rough when minors get into it. Because it's such a fragile time in the growth of a human being. But the girls are better than ever. I'm afraid that compared to now, it seems like a drop in the bucket. But it will never really be a drop in the bucket. When you think of the hate that spews through the electronics at every moment and on television and in print, then I'm afraid that some young people will be afraid to put their ass on the line. They'll be afraid of all this hatred and all this insanity that is going on. Besides the personal pain that this causes people, some people will hesitate about putting their ass out there. They'll be afraid that they will just get creamed. And that will be a shame.

Does all that negative attention affect you as an artist?
I don't think of myself as an artist. I hope I told my stories artistically. But I know what I consider great art on film and I'm not that guy. But I'm another kind of guy, and I try to be the best storyteller that I can be. I love visuals, I do. I do like it to look a certain way, to be lit in a certain way. I want the actors to smoke in a certain way. But if *Batman & Robin* had surpassed *Batman Forever* and had been a gigantic hit then, I don't know what would have happened next. There is no way I will ever know. It is just like what if my father had lived? I don't know what my life would have been like. I didn't have a father. It's not that I heard anything negative about him, I just didn't know him. I didn't live that life. We didn't have any money. Well, we did have some money because my mother worked six days a week and three nights a week to support us. I'm not telling you a sob story. I'm just telling you what happened. But if we hadn't lived behind the movie theater, I don't know what would have happened. In everyone's life, there's an *if*. If you've ever been in love, you know all the things that had to happen for you and your partner to be together. But if many things didn't happen, you wouldn't be. I have no idea what path that would have been. Looking back, I think that level of success would have been very dangerous. But that's just a guess. I don't know what would have happened then.

In the beginning, when I was making smaller movies, I didn't even know that there was going to be a career. For me, there was no career. It was always, where is the next job? I love making movies, so my question is always, when do I get to make another one? Before I became a director, there was the rise of Steven Spielberg, George Lucas, Francis Ford Coppola, and Billy Friedkin. I hate sports analogies, but they were hitting the ball out of the park. Not only did I love those movies, but I was in *awe* of them. But I never planned on being the blockbuster king. That was never the plan. The delight that I had when they said, "We'd like you to do the next Batman." I was immediately a little kid again.

With all that's going on in the world right now who could believe that a Batman movie could cause so much controversy at one time? What halcyon days. Like the international news was the new Batman movie. It was such a different time. Christopher Nolan's Batman movies got darker and darker. And his last one, *The Dark Knight Rises,* is definitely about where we are now politically. The battle between the one percent and everyone else. I think it's a good metaphor for where we are. But we have to have hope for your children and for you. You have to hope, we're never lost.

SECTION 2
Horror Movies

JAWS 4

Jaws: The Revenge

When *Jaws* was released in the summer of 1975 audiences were warned, "You'll never go into the water again" and "See it before you go swimming." The trailer for *Jaws 2* (1978), the entertaining if unnecessary sequel, famously cautioned, "Just when you thought it was safe to go back in the water." *Jaws 3-D* (1983) lamely promised "new depths of terror" and, playing off of the film's use of 3D, "the third dimension is terror." The tagline for the widely and perhaps excessively ridiculed fourth installment, *Jaws: The Revenge* (1987), bizarrely and confusingly proclaimed "This time it's personal." The ominous declaration that "this time it's personal" has since become shorthand for "this is a bad movie." However, at one time, *Jaws* was synonymous with great filmmaking.

Steven Spielberg's *Jaws* is a lean, propulsive, irresistible machine. With a script by the novel's writer Peter Benchley and Carl Gottlieb, a co-writer of Steve Martin's ebullient celebration of idiocy, *The Jerk*, and uncredited additional writing by John Milius, *Jaws* is part horror movie, part thriller, and part adventure film, grounded in intense performances by Roy Scheider and Richard Dreyfuss, and a wonderfully colorful one by Robert Shaw. In the movie, police chief Martin Brody (Roy Scheider) faces a killer shark that is dining on the inhabitants of Amity, a small New England island. It's a gripping and scary movie, with muted echoes of *Moby Dick* and *The Old Man in the Sea*.

Jaws was the first summer "blockbuster." Released in only 645 theaters, the movie had legs (or fins) that were eye-popping at the time. It played throughout the summer and earned an estimated $472 million worldwide. Twelve years and three sequels sans-Spielberg later, *Jaws: The Revenge* earned just under $51 million worldwide—about a tenth of the original film's total box office. In the end, the $23 million movie probably made a slight profit on the costs of production, distribution, and advertising. However, because it irrevocably tarnished the brand, *The Revenge* would be the final *Jaws* movie.

In *Jaws 2*, the residents of Amity are initially skeptical of Brody's claim that another shark is feeding on humans, but it wouldn't be a *Jaws* movie if their doubts weren't dramatically dispelled. Brody doesn't appear in the forgettable *Jaws 3-D*. Instead, the movie focuses on his sons Sean and "Mike" Brody (a young Dennis Quaid), who are battling a third shark at Sea World in Orlando, Florida. In *Jaws: The Revenge*, Brody is now dead, killed by a heart attack brought on by the stress of dealing with too many killer sharks. ("He died from fear. The fear of it killed him.") After Sean is eaten by a great white shark, Brody's grieving wife, Ellen (Loraine Gary) leaves Amity to visit her son, who is now referred to as Michael and is working as a marine biologist in the Bahamas. The unforgiving shark follows her and unsuccessfully tries to get "revenge" by eating her family. Lance Guest, who starred in the cult classic *The Last Starfighter* (1984), plays Michael, the son who initially thinks his mom has gone around the bend but soon comes to accept her tall tale.

The premise of the movie—a shark with a grudge—is more than a little absurd. But even if we accept the conceit that "this time it's personal," given that Brody killed the sharks in the previous movies, then this predator's motivation for revenge is still murky. One might suppose that it is somehow related to the previous great whites and feels a sense of anger or loss by their deaths. But even that rationale doesn't quite explain the creature's excellent sense of direction and its ability to track a single individual roughly twelve hundred miles. Moreover, for all its unwavering tenacity and supernatural abilities, this "eating machine" is the least effective killer in the series. With only two on-screen deaths, this shark is a guppy compared to the number of on-screen kills of its predecessors—six, six, and five—in *Jaws*, *Jaws 2*, and *Jaws 3-D*, respectively.[29] Maybe Jake, Michael's friend and coworker was right when he dismissively referred to the once-feared shark as an "overgrown goldfish."

When *Jaws: The Revenge* aired on television, some versions added a prologue spoken by a narrator whose primary goal was to deflect these kinds of questions. The speaker gravely intones, "Since time immemorial, events have taken place with no evident reason for their happening. Such phenomena have been man's dilemma and the subject of constant philosophical discussion. When there is no factor motivating an event, no case of cause creating effect, what triggered the action—fate or circumstance? What you are about to see concerns such an event. Maybe you can determine whether we are dealing here, with circumstances or fate." The inclusion of the narration, a desperate and feeble attempt to offset the absurdity of the plot, is also at odds with the film's title and its storyline, which strongly imply that the killer beast purposively seeks retribution.

Working from a script by Michael de Guzman, Joseph Sargent, who directed the New York City heist film *The Taking of Pelham One Two Three* (1974), produced and directed *Jaws: The Revenge*. In an interview with the Archive of American Television, Sargent candidly explains what went wrong. "It's a preposterous premise. But at the time we were kind of fired [up] by the possibilities...It's amazing when you make that choice [about a revenge-seeking shark], artistically...you can fall into a sort of romantic love affair with a notion that is so far out that actually feels right...or feels challenging. We felt that way. We actually thought this just might work."

What makes *Jaws: The Revenge* interesting to me is the challenge faced by Joseph Sargent and his collaborators: to accept the film's zany premise and to approach the material earnestly rather than condescendingly. They tried, not entirely unsuccessfully, to make it a character-based shark movie. Despite its shortcomings, the movie is not camp. It is an irony-free consideration of what might happen if a revenge-seeking shark terrorized a family.

Due to the moviemakers' mishandling of the *Jaws* franchise, Steven Spielberg retained tighter creative control on the sequels to his *Jaws*-with-dinosaurs film *Jurassic Park* (1993). He directed its follow up, *The Lost World* (1997), and served as an executive producer and oversaw the selection of the directors for the movies that followed. Unexpectedly, the fourth installment *Jurassic World* (2015), was the most financially successful entry in the series, and, at the time, became the fourth top-grossing film of all time. Conversely, if perhaps unfairly, *Jaws: The Revenge* routinely appears on lists of the worst films ever made.

Lance Guest Interview

What was your first exposure to *Jaws*?
I read the original book in a doctor's office. I must have been in around seventh or eighth grade and it was before the movie came out. I picked it up and started reading it. It's bizarre because I would not normally have done that. But I didn't see the movie when it originally came out. I'm a big ocean guy, I love surfing, playing in the waves and I just didn't need the notion of a killer shark in my head. There was a lot of shark-phobia going on and I didn't want to worry about that. We used to go to Monterey Bay, which had one of the highest concentrations of great white sharks and I thought maybe I don't need that in my head. I thought, maybe I'll just have fun in the ocean and not worry about sharks.

When did you wind up seeing *Jaws*?
I ended up seeing it eventually when I was about eighteen or so and it was on TV. It's a great movie. Still to this day, when it comes on, I'll just sit there and watch it all the way through.

What was your reaction when you first heard about *Jaws 4*?
When the fourth one came along it was originally called *Jaws '87* and I was a little disappointed. At the time it was uncool to do the sequels. Especially if you were in the original movie, you didn't appear in the sequel. Usually, sequels weren't as good as the original. *Godfather Part II* and *The Empire Strikes Back* are notable exceptions. Nowadays, sequels are a huge business. But then, by the time you get to Part Four, you're just like, Ay, yay, yay.

But I needed a job. And the part was really good. In the original script, you could follow the character through the script, and it all made sense to me. Sure, it was an outrageous premise but the way it was written made sense to me. I really liked the character, director Joe Sargent, the cast, and I agreed to do it.

You must have been a little surprised that they got Michael Caine.
It came as a surprise. I thought, "Wow, Michael Caine's going to do this? Great."

What was your relationship like with director Joseph Sargent?
I auditioned for him once for this TV movie [*Choices of the Heart* (1983)] about the missionaries who were killed in El Salvador. But I didn't get the part, Peter Horton did. Joe remembered me and when I met him for *Jaws 4*, he offered me the part. I didn't have to audition for it.

Once you were cast, how did you prepare for the role?
I had just finished performing in a couple of plays that I was doing, and those plays required a lot of homework, so I was in preparation mode. I did a lot of research, nailed down every scene, and figured out the ins and outs of each scene. Because the premise is so outrageous, you want to figure out what you want to do to justify such an outrageous premise. As an actor, you want to make it believable. You have to nail down the connective tissue to how your character behaves from one situation to the

Jaws seeks revenge
Illustration by Pat Carbajal

next. I had nailed that down. But on the first day of shooting, they rearranged the order of my scenes. I'm not quite clear why that happened, it might have been a technical problem with the shark, but it completely freaked me out. It didn't make any sense. I was really worried, and I started harassing Joe about it. I'm sure it was a pain in the ass for him. But it was troubling for me because I wanted to make it as believable as possible.

Before that happened, you felt that despite the strange premise the approach to it was sound and the film was going to work?
Right. Michael de Guzman wrote a coherent script. He's a good writer. But it's as if they changed the game plan a second before they even hiked the ball. It was very unsettling.

They weren't simply changing the shooting order, they rearranged the script itself?
Yes, they were changing the scenes so that certain developments would happen before they were originally planned, and it made less sense. We were creating a roadmap of fear but that was all changed. My character, Michael, had to make all these decisions based on what he knows about the shark, but if he knows too much, too soon in the story, and makes a stupid decision, he stops being the sympathetic character. Then he's just not behaving in a way that makes any sense.

Do you know why they did that?
There were all kinds of reasons. Sometimes a writer will write something, and a director will have an idea of how to pull it off. But then along the way, there can be a technical problem, something like a special effect or an action sequence, and then they realize that they can't do that. Then everything has to change.

But let's face it. It's a shark movie. People aren't coming to the movie because they are fascinated with the characters. They want to see people getting eaten by sharks. And that's what we were constantly reminded of while we were shooting the movie.

But the first movie was much more than that. That's why I like the original movie. I like the original *Jaws* because of the characters. I loved Robert Shaw, Richard Dreyfuss, and Roy Scheider.

So we didn't end up making the original script and that never happened to me before. When I made *The Last Starfighter,* the script was nailed down and nothing changed. We did a couple of reshoots and added a couple of scenes, but the script was locked during the shoot. When we started shooting that movie, we knew everything that was going to happen in advance.

The final film has a few subplots that are alluded to but are never fully explained. In one, Michael Caine's character, Hoagie, turns out to be not just a mysterious airplane pilot but a money launderer.
Yes, originally, he was a money launderer for drug dealers. At the time there were a lot of drugs passing through the Caribbean and the Bahamas and his character was going to be part of that. I'm not sure why that was downplayed. My character is very suspicious of Michael's. If Caine was a money launderer, then Michael's suspicions

would have been proved correct. But with it gone, my character is just being an overprotective son who is overreacting to this guy.

Was any of that shot?
We shot a scene where Caine is handing something to a guy who was renting a boat or something. But when they removed that subplot from his character it had a big impact on mine. But I wasn't a big star, so I don't think anyone gave it much thought.

The producers had hoped that Richard Dreyfuss and Roy Scheider would make a cameo appearance.
They wrote a scene where Richard Dreyfuss would have called Lorraine Gary, who played my mom, Ellen. But Dreyfuss didn't want to do it. [In the scene, Matt Hooper, who is "still chasing fish" calls the family to offer condolences for the death of Ellen's son, Sean.[30]] Roy Scheider would have been the first victim. But he didn't want to do it, so they had Michael's brother [Sean] be the shark food in the first scene.

When did you start to get a feeling that it wasn't coming together as you had hoped?
Immediately—as soon as they changed the scenes in the script. As soon as they did that, they lost their believability. I was about twenty-six years old, and I had over-prepared for the part. So I freaked out. Now, I would have handled it differently, but I didn't want it to be hokey. But it was not in my control. We were supposed to be there for ten weeks, but we shot for almost five months. Because of that, I was able to buy a house. That's what Michael said too. Michael was a great sport. He was so cool. He was nominated for an Academy Award, and he stayed down there with us. He didn't fly to Los Angeles to be there. He said, "No, no, no. I'm here." [Michael Caine, who didn't appear in person to accept his Best Supporting Actor award for his work on Woody Allen's *Annie Hall*, said *Jaws: The Revenge*, "will go down in my memory as the time when I won an Oscar, paid for a house and had a great holiday. Not bad for a flop movie."[31]]

Why didn't he go to the Oscars?
He wasn't thumbing his nose at it. His attitude was, I'm working. We might have watched the awards with him. I could be wrong but that's how I remember it. We were working, and it wasn't easy for him to get to LA and back. He was so cool about it. He was criticized for doing a movie like *Jaws: The Revenge* but he liked working.

Do you recall if it was the reshoots that kept him from attending the Oscars or was it part of the original production?
I think it was part of the original production because the Oscars were in March [March 30, 1987]. After the movie opened [on July 17, 1987], Universal wanted to change the ending. I got a call from Joe saying, "Lance, we're going out there. We're going back in the water." I said, "Joe you can't do that." He replied, "Yeah? Watch this." That was his favorite thing to say, "Yeah? Watch this." There were some plans to shoot it in Malibu, but we wound up shooting in the tank at Universal. There, we shot the alternative ending. Which one have you seen?

Lance Guest on the set
Photo courtesy of Lance Guest

I've seen both. In the original ending, Mario Van Peebles' character dies, and a jagged portion of the damaged boat skewers the shark. In the new ending, Peebles' character survives, and the shark explodes when the boat skewers it.
Yeah, the shark blows up, that's right. In the original script, the shark was in breach and then Lorraine runs the boat into him, basically stabbing him with the boat, and then he blows up. But it was a hard thing to convincingly do. They didn't have computer-generated effects that were as sophisticated as they are today. *The Last Starfighter* was an early instance of CGI. But back then they didn't have the ability to do it effectively. For *Jaws*, we finished most of the shooting of the dialogue scenes in just a few weeks. But we spent months working on the action sequences and trying to get the shots right. We must have been shooting in the tank at Universal for a month—going there every day and trying to make it work. But it didn't work. Then we'd go home, come back the next day and try again. We did a lot of that in the Bahamas too. We'd go out on the water and wait for the shark. The shark wouldn't work and then we'd go home. But Universal kept the production going because they knew they'd make their money back, and I guess they did.

Do you remember the first time you saw the film cut together?
I saw scenes while we were doing ADR, looping lines. I was pleasantly surprised. I remember the editor came up to me and said, "I liked what you did. You made an effort to string it together and that wasn't easy to do." That was the greatest compliment that I could get. I was happy that someone noticed. Because my main objective was to string it together so that it made sense. But after they scrambled the script, it didn't make any sense to me. But I did the best I could.

You walked away with a good feeling?
Yeah, I was surprised that it was as good as it was. And I felt kind of good about it. There were some things that I wished we didn't do or that would have been better if we handled them differently, but that's the way it goes.

What about the premiere?
I had my family down here and we took pictures. I was going out with this girl and I'm like, "Do you want to come to my premiere?" [Laughs].

What was your feeling when you saw it at the premiere? It's sometimes hard to accurately judge a film when you're seeing it with a receptive audience of family, friends, and crew.
I was prepared for it to be much worse than it was. But then the horrible review came out and people made fun of the tagline, "This time it's personal." It became this huge and ridiculous thing to say. But over the years people have come up and told me that it was great and that they liked it a lot. I'm like, "Well, I'm glad you liked it."

Not everyone loves it. The film appears on some fairly notorious lists.
Oh, sure. I think it is number nine in the twenty-five worst sequels of all time. I remember these things, it's like if you're gonna believe the good reviews, you gotta believe the bad ones.

How does that feel?

I don't care. I'm review proof. The first thing I ever did was I was in a play, and I did this one thing that the director wanted me to do but I didn't want to do it. The entire review centered around that one thing I didn't want to do. I don't get my feelings hurt. I think they think it sucks. I think that I can see how you would say that.

Another criticism of the film is that the shark is motivated to travel from Amity Island off Massachusetts to the Bahamas to stalk and kill the Brody family.
Yes, I could not fathom that, so I did not. I only dealt with me and my motivation. Mario and I have some lines of dialogue where we discuss whether that's possible and why would he be coming after my family. Lorraine's character brings that up and it's shot down like it's crazy talk. But that's what happens in the movie. Maybe it's like in Moby Dick, where Captain Ahab has this strange connection to the whale, but no one knows why it happens.

Not only does the shark have a motivation, but Lorraine's character can sense its presence. She "feels" when it arrives in the Bahamas.
She's set up as this person who everybody is worried about, and they think she might have lost her mind. But, of course, she's right.

Another complaint is that Ellen Brody is having a flashback to scenes from the original movie that she could not have possibly witnessed. In one instance, she seems to remember the scene at the end of the original *Jaws* where Roy Scheider is out on the ocean in a sinking ship trying to shoot the shark. But he's alone.
That's true. That flashback wasn't in the original script, that was added in later in post-production. I think that was an attempt to beef up the last sequence and make it more exciting. They tried as hard as they could to make the ending work, but it never really came together. The ending was widely criticized. Audiences didn't buy the ending. But when I read it, I bought it. It was in the execution of the vision. I'm not saying that they didn't have the ability or that anybody screwed up, it was just a hard thing to pull off.

Trying to give the ending a greater impact is probably what led to their poor decision to have the shark roar loudly. Sharks don't roar. This one did.
That was a little weird to me. That was a little strange, but they were just doing whatever they could to make it work. Everybody makes a big deal out of Michael Caine's shirt. When he comes out of the water, he's got beads of water on his shirt, but he's not dripping wet. What people don't know is that Michael Caine requested a waterproof shirt. So that when he gets soaking wet, he's not walking around like a wet t-shirt girl. Those were not his words, but he was saying that it'll make things easier if you don't have to match how wet or dry your shirt looks at any given moment. He just said, "Why don't we just get a waterproof shirt?" So that's what they got for him. They were dumping water on him all the time, but you couldn't quite tell. It wasn't a lack of continuity. It was what happened. I was there. It wasn't phony at all. Sticks in my craw. Sticking up for Hugo [Peña], the costume supervisor [Laughs].

When you're on the fourth film of a series and each film is centered on the same family, you try to come up with logical reasons why the story keeps repeating

itself. **Bad luck isn't an explanation that satisfies our curiosity about why one family is continually terrorized by sharks. There must be a reason, even if the explanation is a little bonkers.**
The original script was presented in such a way that the explanation didn't seem hokey. You could follow the reasoning for why every character behaved a certain way. But the problem is what's on the page is not always what's up on the screen. You're faced with the problem of what you can do. When I read the original script, I bought into it. I never did projects that I didn't want. I wasn't working a lot but even then, I would only do stuff if I liked it. The original script was carefully engineered. It wasn't hokey. It wasn't unbelievable.

You have a funny line. After a heated argument, Michael tells his blowtorch-wielding wife, "I've always wanted to make love to an angry welder. I've dreamed of nothing else since I was a small boy."
Michael de Guzman came up with that line. He wrote it. I love it too. That was my favorite line. There were some other fun things we did. There's a scene where I play guitar. Joe wanted to learn how to play guitar, so I taught Joe some blues. There's this great picture of me showing Joe how to play guitar.

When I reached out to you, I wasn't sure that this would be something that you would be open to talking about.
The movie didn't make any money at the time and the reviews were terrible. But what are you going to do? You do the best you can. I was known at the time for being very selective about the work I would do. And when it came out, people would say [derisively], "Great, Lance. *This* is what you're doing?" But *The Last Starfighter* didn't make any money and that's fondly remembered. I'll meet people and they'll say, "I used to watch you every day when I was ten."

What's your go-to *Jaws 4* horror story?
I always say Michael Caine saved my life. And it's a totally over-dramatic and overblown version of something that could have been disastrous. We were doing a scene in the climax of the movie where my character is afraid that my mom is going to kill herself by confronting the shark by herself. So Michael Caine, Mario Van Peebles, and I are in a dinky little boat and we're after her. I'm in the back of the boat and they're in front. But I weighed about 160 pounds and they're on the other side of the boat. So what do you think happened? We start to go over and the whole front of the boat is just submerged in the water. The battery pack that's running the boat was huge, it's about the size of a chessboard. As the boat goes down, the cameraman throws the camera on the barge, which is about five feet away and somebody catches the camera. Mario jumps overboard and the boat fills with water. So I'm sitting in a bathtub with a toaster. I feel this hand behind me, and I heard Michael scream, "Get the fuck out of the boat." With one hand, he pulls me out of the boat and onto the board because he didn't want me to get electrocuted. So that's my great *Jaws: The Revenge* story.

Lance Guest teaches director Joseph Sargent how to play guitar
Photo courtesy of Lance Guest

[Playing along.] He totally saved your life.
There you go. I have Michael Caine to thank for my life. But like I said, it wasn't unsafe working conditions or anything like that. It could have been a twelve-volt battery pack and it was covered in plastic, I have no idea why, but it's just kind of funny.

Part of my impetus for talking about this film is not to pretend that it's an overlooked masterpiece but rather to understand why smart, thoughtful people who make good movies could make one that goes off the rails a bit.
They've made movies based on flimsier premises. I keep going back to the original script because Michael De Guzman concentrated on the relationships between the family. There was blood and gore, but we wanted to make a movie that was about something else. It sort of had a TV movie kind of vibe in its structure and maybe it's a little sentimental, but he presented it in a believable way. So when that happened, I feel like I kind of saw it coming.

But really what is at the heart of why this movie didn't do so well is I think they just had a hard time selling the idea that the shark is going to travel all the way down to the ocean to the Bahamas and follow this family. That was just a little too far-fetched.

It wasn't the same shark from the previous films, those sharks are dead. So what is motivating the revenge?
Right. It's just a family that has bad luck with white sharks. But in the '80s, plenty of films were made on similarly non-substantial premises. But Michael de Guzman was able to weave a story that accommodated the premise, took the emphasis off the shark, and put it into the family. But then they realized that if they didn't get the shark

Michael Caine as Hoagy Newcombe
Illustration by Pat Carbajal

sequences right then the audiences would be disappointed, and the film would be lame. So they concentrated on making sure that the shark stuff was shocking, violent, and scary enough to appeal to the base of the people who go see *Jaws* movies. But there were a lot of things that had nothing to do with a killer shark that were nice, but they weren't getting the right amount of attention because they had to prioritize and focus on why people are going to see this movie.

Do you get a little bit of a tickle out of the fact that you were in an infamous film?
At the time it was my worst fear to be in something that was going to fall apart like this. But every actor has that fear. But it didn't affect me as much as I thought it would. Filmmakers who grew up with *The Last Starfighter* appreciate it. I would rather be in a cult movie than be a big deal. I would rather be in a movie where people had to find it. It makes it feel special when people discover it.

PSYCHO 4
Psycho IV: The Beginning

When Norman Bates is asked in *Psycho IV: The Beginning*, "How did you kill your mother?" his dry response is, "Slowly." Norman was referring to his mother's agonizing death by strychnine. But slowly also applies to the pace of telling Norman's complete story, from his cinematic entrance in Alfred Hitchcock's *Psycho* in 1960 to his exit three decades later in the 1990's made-for-cable movie *Psycho IV*. Thirty years would seem to be more than enough time for Norman, memorably played by Anthony Perkins, to resolve his mother issues. Unfortunately for his victims, he couldn't.

Norman is remembered for his split personality. He is both a dutiful son and a vicious, knife-wielding killer. *Psycho IV: The Beginning* also has a dual identity as both a sequel to *Psycho* and to a lesser extent *Psycho II* (1983) and *Psycho III* (1986), and a prequel to Hitchcock's original black and white masterpiece.

Most later films in franchises are either sequels or prequels. They either continue the story from where the previous film concludes or they depict the events that precede the earlier movie, often as an origin story. However, *Psycho IV* tells two different stories set in two different time periods. In one, a middle-aged Norman must decide if he's going to surrender to his darkest impulses and kill his wife, a psychiatrist who has tried to cure him and who is pregnant with his child, or spare her life and risk the chance that his offspring will inherit his murderous urges. In the other story, told through flashbacks, Norman (Henry Thomas) is a young boy struggling to resist his incestuous attraction to his emotionally abusive mother Norma (Olivia Hussey) as well as his murderous rage at Norma's physically abusive boyfriend. The prequel sections dramatize Norman's backstory, which is alluded to in *Psycho*, including his decision to kill Norma, to wear a wig and woman's clothing, and to speak in his mother's voice, effectively becoming her.

There are both practical and creative reasons for making *Psycho IV* a prequel-sequel, instead of choosing one or the other. Practically speaking, a Psycho film in which Anthony Perkins doesn't play Norman is bound to disappoint audiences. Creatively, *Psycho IV* would seem stale if it were just a retread of the first three films, with a succession of unwitting guests checking into the shabby Bates Motel, where Norman kills them. Placing the timeline before the events of the previous movies opens up new story-telling possibilities.

As a prequel, *Psycho IV* charts unexplored territory and offers explanations for why Norman "goes a little mad sometimes." To no one's surprise, his mother drove him to it. *Psycho IV* paints Norma as an overbearing, needy, cruel mother. Norma rages at her son, "I was fine until I gave birth to you. You caused a lot of damage… I should have killed you in my womb. You sure as hell tried to kill me getting out of it!" In another scene, after rolling on the floor with Norman and inadvertently arousing him, she punitively puts a dress and lipstick on him and demands, "You are going to forget once and for all about that filthy thing of yours! You'll forget that you even have one of those things!"

In the sequel portions of the film, Norman offers his perspective of his younger years. The adult, in-denial Norman cautions, "If the doctor's trying to turn this into some kind of an incest tragedy, tell him to forget it." For Norman, not all of the attention his mother gave him when he was a young boy was negative. He elaborates, "I know that in the cosmic scheme of things, little boys are small, but some days they can be...some days little boys can be giants." Screenwriter Joseph Stefano, who also wrote the screenplay for Hitchcock's *Psycho*, spoke of his approach to writing the sequel version of Norman, "The question might be asked why, if Norman is cured, does he revert to his old ways? I think he explains when he says, "I'm cured, as I'll ever be, but I'm still me." No matter how cured we are of certain psychoses, we revert when the chips are down. The film couldn't just be about Norman getting cured. It had to be about that cure coming undone."[32]

Before helming *Psycho IV*, Mick Garris's scarce credits included working as a writer and, in one episode, a director on the Steven Spielberg-produced anthology series *Amazing Stories* (1985-1987), as a writer-director of the *Gremlins* knockoff *Critters 2* (1988), and as a co-writer of *The Fly II* (1989). Since then, he has directed and written many horror and fantasy films, and he has been a prolific interpreter of Stephen King's work, including the three miniseries *The Stand* (1994), *The Shining* (1997), and *Bag of Bones* (2011), the TV movies *Quicksilver Highway* (1997), which he also adapted, and *Desperation* (2006), and the feature films *Sleepwalkers* (1992) and *Riding the Bullet* (2004), many of which were adapted or written by King.

Psycho would not seem to be franchise material. The original is a brilliant horror film about a motel owner who represses his own identity and assumes his mother's personality when he commits brutal murders. But *Psycho* has been a surprisingly durable concept. In addition to three sequels, there was the TV movie *Bates Motel* (1987) about a new proprietor of the motel, a Gus Van Sant remake also called *Psycho* (1998)**,** and a TV series *Bates Motel* (2013–2017), which focused on Norman's teenage years and his life with his mother Norma. *Bates Motel* became A&E's longest-running original scripted drama series. Despite these other iterations, at the center of the franchise is a riveting performance by Perkins who pulls off the high-wire act of drawing audiences into Norman's deranged mind without entirely losing their sympathy, even as he performs unspeakable acts. For Perkins, "Norman is, at heart, a benevolent soul with a dark side."[33]

Mick Garris Interview

Do you remember your first exposure to the original *Psycho*?
I went to see *Psycho* as a child. I saw it when I was seven or eight years old. There were four kids in our family, and we went to see it at a drive-in theater in the San Fernando Valley. In those days, horror films were thought to be kid's films. But *Psycho* turned everyone's heads around.

[Laughing] It was *not* a kid's film.
No, it wasn't. But I loved it anyway. There was never a moment that I looked away. We watched it from the back of our '57 Chevy station wagon. We used to tease our little sister mercilessly. We'd say, "Ms. Bates, Ms. Bates," and then [mimicking an unforgettable moment in the film] we'd turn back around with our eyes rolled into our head.

Was *Psycho* what set you on your career path as a horror and fantasy director?
Absolutely. But it wasn't my first exposure to horror films. I was already a lost cause to the horror genre from watching the Universal classics that were playing on television. The first movie I ever remember seeing on television was *Son of Kong*. The clarion call of the genre was implanted at a very early age. I heard the notes coming into my mind then.

***Psycho* came out in 1960 and it's become a classic. *Psycho II* was released 23-years later, and audiences and critics were pleasantly surprised by its quality. *Psycho III* wasn't as successful. What do you remember about those films?**
Around 1982, I was doing specialized publicity for genre films at Universal. So When *Psycho II* came out in 1983, I used to see Hitchcock being pulled up to his office by his chauffeur and helped into his offices, and I worked with the *Psycho II* director, Richard Franklin, on the press kit for that film. It was a connection that I never thought would later connect me to the series. But with *Psycho III*, Tony Perkins has certainly the best connection to the original movie, and he had a really clear vision for his sequel, but the movie was not financially successful or well-received. He wanted to direct *Psycho IV*, but because of how *Psycho III* was received the studio wouldn't let him. So as you can imagine, [his initial interactions with me] were a tangled web.

Psycho IV was made for Showtime by a brand-new division of Universal that was intended for cable as opposed to network television. Cable was nascent at the time and the Universal cable division was run by Ned Nalle. He also ran a division of MCA Television Entertainment. They started with a reboot of *Leave it to Beaver* for TBS, the Turner station. Ned, a brilliant guy, saw the future of cable television. With a partner of mine, I created a series for them called *She-Wolf of London.* They were happy working with me. I had also written a couple of screenplays for the studio. I had worked on *Amazing Stories* at Universal for Steven Spielberg and as a writer and director for my first feature *Critters 2*. John Landis was a good friend of both Perkins and Ned Nalle, and he recommended me wholeheartedly to direct *Psycho IV*. So they were all for it.

Then I had to have a lunch meeting with Tony, who had director approval, to make sure I was OK. I'm sure he had second thoughts about me. He must have thought, *Do I want the director of Critters 2 to be directing Psycho IV?* So he had his defenses up. But we had a very good lunch, and we went over the script page by page. He agreed to take a chance on me directing the film.

What was most important to him about how the character of Norman Bates was portrayed?
Well, it was interesting. We had long discussions about that because in *Psycho III*

Anthony Perkins as Norman Bates
Illustration by Pat Carbajal

there was a tendency to turn it a little more toward camp. There were a few reasons for that, among them, the ending of *Psycho II* being what it was, the character of Norman Bates had become so iconic that it was being spoofed all the time, and due to the popularity of Freddy Krueger, there was a tendency to play things a little camp.

I had the conversation with Perkins that we wanted to go back to the roots of the original *Psycho* and act as if there had never been a *Psycho III*. We would keep the progression in line with what had been in *Psycho* and *Psycho II*. So it was a matter of playing it straight and playing the era straight, and when I used the word "camp" it initiated a 35-minute conversation about camp. He became very obsessive about it. I wasn't intending to imply that he had gone that route in his direction of *Psycho III*. But there was more obvious humor than the kind of flat humor that Hitchcock had in the first one, which was under a couple of layers.

I think what was important to him was that we did treat Norman seriously. He's an iconic character, that we should not treat disrespectfully, and we should be true to what Hitchcock was trying to do, even though it was very challenging sometimes. Perkins and I did not come from the same direction in how to approach it, but he had much more experience than I in every regard, especially in knowing Norman Bates. However, he couldn't have been happier with what we ended up with. His way of getting into a role can sometimes take a lot more time and energy than you might have in the tight schedule that we had, but ultimately it paid off in spades.

He approached it analytically. Is that a fair assessment?
I would say that's true. He was a writer himself. He and Stephen Sondheim wrote a movie called *The Last of Sheila* (1973), which is a brilliant Agatha Christie-esque murder mystery. *The Last of Sheila* has a lot of humor and a lot of twists and turns and cleverness. He was very well-read; he was a very serious guy. He also had a sense of humor, but it took time to dig down to get into it. But yes, he was analytical and extremely verbal so any discussion that would come up often lasted forty-five minutes, for better or for worse, but ultimately for better.

In interviews regarding *Psycho III*, Perkins seemed to indicate that he wasn't well-prepared for the demands of being a director and that he wished he had more support and knew how to fully utilize the support he did have. What do you think about that?
That may well be the case, I don't know. I wasn't around during that period. However, I can't imagine a guy who had worked with Alfred Hitchcock and Orson Welles, these great directors, and who was so committed to becoming a director, not being impeccably prepared. Just in knowing him from my experience with him on *Psycho IV*, he was the guy who did his homework and was extremely conversant in the language of cinema. He talked a great deal about how Welles and Hitchcock would approach filmmaking. So I would be surprised if he was not prepared for the movie.

Were there times when Perkins would tell you Norman wouldn't do that?
That may have come up when we were going through the script, but the good news was that Joseph Stefano, the writer of the original *Psycho*, was the screenwriter for *Psycho IV* as well. But there were a couple of times, usually in reference to the teenage

Norman more than the adult one, when that occurred. There may also have been a couple of times during the development process or the pre-production process when Tony and I would discuss those things. This isn't an example of "Norman wouldn't do that," it's more about the most trying scene we had regarding a point in the script. Throughout the film, Norman is on the phone with the talk show host Fran Ambrose. In the script, it indicates that Norman gets furious and slams the butcher knife into the butcher board. So we talked that through, and we were setting it up to light the scene. We're getting ready to shoot it, the camera was ready, and Perkins said, "Mick, don't you think this is whoring, cheesy, old fashioned?" He offered something like thirty kinds of adjectives to describe what a bad idea it was. Then he said, "Don't *you* think that?" I said, "Well, I kind of like it." As he's going through that analysis of the situation, sixty crew people are standing around waiting to shoot a scene that we have to get in on a twenty-four-day shoot for a feature-length film. So I said, "Everybody keep setting up, get ready to shoot, and Tony and I will work this out." So we stepped aside and came up with the idea that he gets so angry that he twists an apple that he's holding in half. It's a very effective replacement. It's something that we came up with together. I think it's much better than jamming a butcher knife into a butcher block. But our conversation lasted at least half an hour before we got to a solution, while everyone was waiting to find out how to set up the scene.

That's a good illustration of how working together you took a conventional idea and twisted it? As he literally did with a piece of fruit.
Right, it's a great idea. It shows how thoughtful he was. He didn't notice it so much in the script stage but when we're putting it on its feet, it's like, wait a minute, let's talk about this! He was committed. He knew Norman Bates better than anybody else including Joseph Stefano. This was his fourth time playing the character, and obviously, he was called upon to spoof it [as in a 1976's *Saturday Night Live* skit] or do things inspired by it [like 1989's *Edge of Sanity*] many times during his career.

Was he conflicted at all about the idea of playing the character again? Did he have mixed feelings?
I think that might have happened before I became involved. But we had Joseph Stefano, who wrote the original movie, write this sequel. It was being produced by Hilton Greene, Hitchcock's first AD on the original *Psycho* and throughout the TV series *Alfred Hitchcock Presents*, and Hilton had produced parts *II* and *III*, as well. The fact that they were taking it seriously and that Tony would have some creative involvement in it probably assuaged any concerns he might have had. By the time we made *Psycho IV*, I don't think he was hesitant to make it. If a hack had come to make a quick buck off the name, then he would have dug in his feet. Even though the film was made on the low-budget arm of Universal and intended for cable, I think he was happy with how it was being treated. At the time, there was some concern that it was made for cable rather than broadcast television, but that ended up being a saving grace because the film ended up being released theatrically in other countries. With Showtime, there were no commercials and no censorship issues.

Getting the look of the house right was important.

We had mother's bed shipped out from Universal City to Orlando. We used the same blueprints for building the set. We had a lot of the props and set pieces there.

How did you go about preparing your approach to the film?
There's a necessary balance in making sequels in that you want to deliver what the audience loved about the original without doing the same movie over again. You want to bring something new to it, and I put a lot of thought into how to visually handle Joe Stefano's approach to narrating the story—the idea of flashing back to how Norman became Norman and depicting Norman today with his inner struggles. Hitchcock shot it in black and white for a reason and I didn't want to emulate that. Mine was the only sequel that went back and used the Bernard Herrmann score. I wanted to retrieve and retain those elements, but since we were shooting in color, I wanted to take real advantage of it.

For the flashback scenes, I wanted to create a sense of nostalgia, with heightened color and heightened memory. I wanted to supersaturate those flashback scenes and use a lot of primary colors, the blood-red, the yellows, the green of the grass, the bright, bright blue of the sky, and the neon lights. Everything would be hyper-real. Not surreal but exaggerated. In a sense, I wanted to make it *not* look like Hitchcock. I'm not Alfred Hitchcock and nobody was Alfred Hitchcock except Alfred Hitchcock. I certainly didn't want to try to imitate or emulate the great director. However, I tried to bring something to it that would make it as cinematic as what he did. I was trying to tell a time-honored story in modern terms. I also added some theatrical touches, like putting different ages of Norman together in a dream sequence. Moments like that. I had been working for Steven Spielberg for a couple of years on *Amazing Stories* and learning the language of cinema.

There were a few moments where you could have copied a Hitchcock shot but deliberately chose not to. For example, when Norman's looking through the hole in the wall, the framing is slightly different from Hitchcock's. When Marion Crane is driving in *Psycho*, the camera frame is dead-on, but when characters drive in your film although the camera is still in front of them it's slightly off to the side. It seems like you deliberately avoided quoting from it cinematically.
Gus Van Sant quoted the original when he replicated it shot-for-shot in his version. I didn't intentionally go out of my way to avoid giving homages to what Hitchcock had done because, frankly, he invented much of the language of suspense cinema. Not to learn lessons from that is to not be a good filmmaker or a good student of film. Having said that, I wanted the film to have its own style, to have its own validity. There's a little more camera movement than there was in the original. We could be a little more explicitly sexual than the original film. When you've got somebody like Olivia Hussey involved, there's a source of heat that you didn't have in the original film. So I played up those primary colors, for instance when he's applying the orange flower water to his mother's legs. They end up rolling on the floor and she reacts because she feels young Norman's erection. I wanted that to get kind of giddy. He's kind of losing control, as a sixteen-year-old boy would under those circumstances. So the camera rolls with them across the floor and frames them in this rug of flowers and romantic images and has her dress much more feminine than the mother that we all think of

from the original. You only hear her voice in *Psycho*. You don't realize that at one time she was this vital, beautiful woman.

So there were a lot of reasons to treat it differently. I had a different cinematographer, and obviously, my eye is different from Hitchcock's, so the attempt was to try and make *Psycho IV* on its own terms. It was about respecting its past without trying to ape it.

Some of the more unsettling aspects of the film are not the murders but rather the interactions Norman has with his mother.
When she throws the dress on him and puts the lipstick on him, it's a totally disturbing kind of thing that might have been in Hitchcock's mind in 1960, but that was not on the screen.

You mentioned the dress. In the original film, Norman wears a dress to become his mother. In *Psycho IV* a different reason is given for wearing the dress, which is to emasculate Norman.
Exactly. In writing those scenes in *Psycho IV*, Stefano was giving further background as to why Norman would have been moved to become his mother. Stefano had Norman's mother dress him in this way to emasculate him. So we were trying to give a context and maybe another motivation for why he adopts her persona later in life.

I guess that some people would call *Psycho* a slasher film, but I think of it as a psychological thriller.
I think you could technically call *Psycho* the first slasher film. But "slasher film" has become a derogatory term in that the movie's *raison d'être is the slashings*. In *Psycho*, they are just a part of the story. The slashings are crucial, but the film is not *about* horrific, gory murders with a butcher knife. That's unlike the slasher films of the '80s. What that term came to mean is gory, gruesome murder movies. So technically, it's a slasher movie, but I think it's disrespectful to call it that because the slashing scenes are such a small but potent part of *Psycho*.

To that point, I think that one of the reasons that *Psycho II* was probably allowed to be made was because of the popularity of slasher films.
It was still early in the cycle because it was '82 when *Psycho II* came out. Well, maybe.

It came out in '83 but that means it was made in '82 as you were saying.
Right, it was made in '82. *Halloween* was '78, and I guess the slashers kind of slopped over from the late '70s until the late '80s. *Halloween* is another example of a movie that is much more than a slasher movie, but it is put into that slash pile.

When we think of *Psycho*, a giant blade is one of the images that come to mind. Was there any pressure to up the killings or to include more violence than you intended?
Well, it was already there. It was in the script, but I don't think it's overladen with it. There are only a handful of violent scenes, but the set pieces with violence have long build-ups, and they are justified by who Norman is and what he's becoming. It's a

The *Psycho* House
Illustration by Pat Carbajal

psychological thriller, which is usually a copout term for a horror movie. I don't think there was any real pressure because we were making a movie with *Psycho* in the title starring Tony Perkins. That was a coup for Showtime. It was an afterthought that it was released theatrically overseas. They thought, maybe we can make some more money from it. Even though this was closer to my Steven Spielberg period and before any of the Stephen King movies, I also think that they were pretty sure that the horror elements could not be bypassed. It was already becoming a part of what I was known for.

I think Stefano would probably call both *Psycho* and *Psycho IV* psychological thrillers, as you were saying. For Stefano, those two movies are rooted in Freudian analysis and his feelings about psychotherapy. Through his art, he is exploring the questions, what turns a person into a madman, and can insanity be cured?
Yeah, I think you're exactly right. *Psycho IV* was a psychological thriller character study. We're looking at the questions, what does make a madman, and are you born that way? We were looking at the whole nature versus nurture debate. It was certainly addressed in the movie without giving an answer. But when you combine those combustible elements, it's like a match to gasoline. You've got nature and nurture shaking hands in a way that ends up putting a butcher knife in it.

In the end, Norman runs through his burning house and "sees" his now-dead mother and his victims. He's literally confronting his past.
Exactly, literally confronting his past. There was certainly a lot of thought put into the psychology of who Norman Bates was.

How would you describe Stefano?
Joe was very serious about that, and he had studied psychology. But Joe was also a very fun-loving, funny guy. He was serious when he needed to be but at the same time, he had created and was running *The Swamp Thing* TV series in Orlando, where we shot *Psycho IV*. *The Swamp Thing* was a hundred-and-eighty-degree departure from what we were doing.

Was there any talk of killing Norman?
No, not when I was involved. The script had been developed before I was brought onboard. We made some tweaks afterward, which Joe and I did together. But those changes were not structural. When I was involved, I never heard anyone talk about killing Norman.

One of the things that makes the ending of the original *Psycho* so powerful is that superimposed the shot of the car being dredged out of the swamp over Norman. The shot suggests that Norman's madness can't be contained and it's going to continue. *Psycho IV* ends similarly. Norman burns down the house, leaves with his wife, and says "I'm free," which suggests a happy ending. However, the next shot is mother's empty chair, which is rocking by itself. The camera tracks backward, through the basement and the storm doors seem to shut themselves. I wouldn't call it a supernatural touch. I interpreted that as representing the

basement of his mind.

Yes, it's Norman's point of view. It's how Norman sees it. The rocking chair is just the activation of a mind that is overly engaged.

My impression of the child crying over the credits is it's not meant to suggest there's going to be a part five (although theoretically there could be), but it's that same idea.

That's exactly right, I don't even remember if it was in the script or not, but as you say, it was never intended to imply a *Psycho V*. But it was intended that these genes will continue and that they will be contaminated by nature or nurture, or not. Is this a chance at a fresh new life or is it going to perpetuate madness? It's meant to be a question mark.

Do you think that *Psycho IV* was meant to be the last film in the series?

I think every one of the sequels was meant to be the last one. I think with *Psycho II*, they probably thought, this is great we've got a sequel and it's got an ending and great. I'm sure they thought *Psycho III* was going to be the last one. *Psycho III* could have been the nail in the coffin for interest in a *Psycho IV*. *Psycho IV* again came from Ned Nalle, I think it was his idea that there was room for another one due to cable TV. Because of cable and Ned Nalle, I think the idea was resurrected to be a one-shot affair. Showtime was not nearly as big as HBO at the time. It was, by far, the also-ran pay-TV network. They thought that if it was good people will be happily surprised and if it was not good no one will see it, and no one will know. I don't think it was ever intended to kick off another series of *Psycho* films.

You've worked in the playground of a couple of classics, *Psycho* and *The Shining*. Your approach to *The Shining* was that you were not translating the Kubrick film to TV but rather that you intended to create a fresh adaptation of Stephen King's novel.

Exactly. Stephen King wrote the script so that certainly has a lot to do with that. There was a certain amount of bravery or confidence in both acts.

Or foolishness. I was very naive about the whole thing, and I didn't even think about it because King and I had worked so well together on two previous projects. *The Stand* [the 1994 mini-series based on the book by King] was the most successful miniseries in history, so they asked Steve what he wanted to do next.

He had never been a fan of the Kubrick film, which left out many of the themes that were most important and personal to him. I had never before thought about [the legacy of] the Kubrick film. When we started to think about casting, I gave Gary Sinise a call since we'd had such a good time together on *The Stand*. When I asked him if he would consider playing Jack, he said to me that he would be a bit hesitant to step into Jack's shoes, meaning Jack Nicholson. Here's how naive I was, when Gary brought up his concerns, that was the first time I even *thought* about it. And then of course it became quite controversial. When *The Shining* happened everybody said, "Oh no, Mick Garris is going to do *The Shining*. Kubrick's film is a masterpiece." I love it as a Kubrick film, but not as an adaptation of King. It was the movie I was most forward to seeing in my life. I saw a screening of it at Warner Bros. a couple of days before it came out, and I was so crushingly disappointed because I loved the book so passionately.

People who met the movie first loved that movie and especially if they were of a certain age when it came out. If they were kids or teenagers or something, there's something incredibly resonant about the father-son relationship that is terrifying and iconic. But what people don't remember is that virtually no critics liked the film or the book at the time. King didn't like the film, and the opportunity that King had after the success of *The Stand* was to choose what he wanted to do. He's the one who said I want to do *The Shining* and do it properly, to tell the story of the book. So my naiveté was completely masked by my enthusiasm to work with King again on one of my favorite novels. I've gotten to direct my favorite Stephen King books and I never thought about it having anything to do with the Kubrick film**.** I didn't watch the Kubrick film again and again as research the way I did with the *Psycho* movie because it was exactly what we were looking *not* to do. Later, I appreciated it for what it is. It's a great Kubrick film and an amazing exercise in cinematic language, but as an adaptation of the King book, it doesn't tell the story that King was telling and wanted to tell again when we made the movie. So there's a long answer to your question.

As a side note to that. I worked for Gary Sinise as his assistant during the Broadway run of the play *One Flew Over the Cuckoo's Nest.* **Of course, Nicholson played the lead in the film. So by then, Gary was apparently more comfortable taking on a part that Nicholson previously established.**
Wow, I didn't know that.

Do you have a sense of what place your film has in the many different *Psycho* **films?**
I can't really say**,** but I can tell you what Tony Perkins thought of the four. We screened it for him at the Hitchcock Theater on the Universal lot here in LA. At the end of it, when the lights came up, he could not stop, he went on literally and somewhat embarrassingly for ten minutes saying how wonderful it was, that it was by far the best of the sequels including his own. And it was great, great justification, and I felt exonerated. Especially after what we went through to make our little movie in four weeks in Orlando. For him, it was by far the best of the sequels. And for Hilton Greene, who had produced the three sequels, this was the one he was most proud of as well. And yet it is probably by far the least seen of the sequels because it was not a theatrical release.

It's called *Psycho IV,* **and though it deliberately doesn't pretend the events of the second and third film never occurred they are largely ignored. I wonder if the film would have been better remembered if it hadn't been called** *Part IV***?**
The film references *II* a bit, but it ignores *III*. Although it is the fourth one, it could have been called *Psycho: The Beginning*. But I think the value of the numbers was still there. And at that time if it had a number in it, I had something to do with it. It was a time of Roman numerals.

HATCHET 4

Victor Crowley

When a *Star Wars* or *Avengers* movie makes over a billion dollars at the box office, it's easy to understand why the studio would want to make sequels. But what does it take for an indie-horror film franchise, like Hatchet, to reach four installments? The series is not as well-known as the *Halloween, Friday the 13th*, or *Nightmare on Elm Street* franchises. Yet, the series, created by independent filmmaker Adam Green, is going strong with four films, a comic book series, and merchandise such as action figures and Halloween masks.

Adam Green's *Hatchet* (2006), touted as a celebration of 1980's horror movies didn't make a killing at the box office. The movie grossed about a quarter of its $1.5 million budget. But through strong word of mouth, the film did well on home video, built a loyal fan base, and *Hatchet II* (2010) and *Hatchet III* (2013) followed.

The Hatchet series is known for its mix of horror, broad comedy, and effective use of horror icons in key roles. The films feature appearances from actors who play Freddy Krueger (Robert Englund), Candy Man (Tony Todd), Leatherface (R. A. Mihailoff), and Michael Myers (Tyler Mane). Angela Rose, the killer from *Sleepaway Camp* (1983) appears in a supporting role in the fourth film. Danielle Harris who played Jamie Lloyd, Michael Myers' niece, in *Halloween 4: The Return of Michael Myers* and *Halloween 5: The Revenge of Michael Myers*, plays Marybeth Dunstan, the heroine of the series, in the second, third, and fourth films.

But arguably, Green's most shrewd casting decision was enlisting Kane Hodder to play Victor Crowley, the hatchet-wielding killer who lives in the Louisiana swamps. Hodder, the actor-stuntman-fan-favorite played Jason Voorhees in four films *Friday the 13th Part VII: The New Blood, Friday the 13th Part VIII: Jason Takes Manhattan, Jason Goes to Hell: The Final Friday,* and *Jason X*, as well as in the video game *Friday the 13th: Friday the 13th: The Game*.

But unlike other horror franchises, the first three Hatchet films tell a complete story which *Hatchet III* seems to definitively conclude. In the final moments, Marybeth Dunstan kills Victor Crowley, blowing him to bits with a shotgun. The series was over. But Hatchet fans didn't see the next twist coming. At an anniversary screening of the first Hatchet film, they were treated to a surprise screening of the fourth Hatchet entry, *Victor Crowley* (2017), a film that was made in secret. Adam Green, the writer and director of the series, somehow managed to write, cast, shoot, edit, and complete a feature film without word getting out.

Green is the writer and director of *Frozen* (2010), the horror film primarily set on a broken chair lift where, in the dead of night, three stuck skiers, must contend with frostbite, wolves, and each other, in their desperate hope to survive the night. Green also co-hosts *The Movie Crypt,* the podcast with Joe Lynch (director of *Everly* (2014) with Salma Hayek) and created and co-starred with Lynch in a TV series about struggling filmmakers. The engaging podcast features candid conversations about the challenges and pleasures of making horror films with notable horror filmmakers, including Jordan Peele, Roger Corman, Joe Dante, John Landis, Chris Columbus, Abel Ferrara, and James Gunn.

Adam Green Interview

How did you decide it was time to make another *Hatchet* film? The series could have ended after three.

The series was supposed to be only three films. That was how I had set it up from the very beginning. The third film came out in 2013. Then, I ended up going through a series of personal tragedies in 2014. I slipped into such a terrible depression that I couldn't leave my house. Then I got a call to moderate a panel with George Romero [the legendary director of *Night of the Living Dead*]. I could not say no to that. So I went, and I did the panel. There were 800 or 900 people in the audience. When the panel was over, George got this huge standing ovation. He put his arm around me, turned me around from the crowd, and said, "Do you see this?" I said, "Yeah, congratulations." George said, "No, look." The audience is all wearing *Hatchet* and *Holliston* shirts and hats. He says "I know you're going through a hard time, but you got to get back up. You have got to give these kids what they want. When are you going to do another Crowley picture?" I said, "I'm not. It's over. I finished that." He said, "It's not over till they say it's over."

The next day, a fan came up to me and handed me an 8x10 photograph. I asked, "What is this?" and he replied, "I don't know what was being said. But it seemed important, I wanted you to have this." The fan had taken a picture of that moment, from the back of the auditorium using a telephoto lens. You can see that I'm crying, and George has his arm around me. That really did it. The photo has been hanging over my desk since.

Hatchet might not be *Star Wars*, *Harry Potter*, or even *Saw* but it's mine. They do want more. And with these slasher movies, if they hit, they get bigger every year. So I decided that I'm going to do it. But I got to do this for me as well. I didn't want anyone to know. So we made it in secret, which we didn't think would work in this day and age with social media. But I explained to every crew member why I was doing it in secret and who we were doing it for. I showed them fan mail from soldiers and burn victims. I said, "These are the people who are going to be excited when this takes them by surprise. So if you say anything, this is who you're taking that away from." Everybody kept it secret.

At the 10th-anniversary screening of *Hatchet*, I surprised everybody by showing *Hatchet 4*, and then immediately went on tour with it. It was a huge success. I can't think of too many series where the fourth one rivaled the first one in terms of success and reception. So it all worked out for the best. Sadly, George died 37 days before the night of the surprise screening. He was supposed to be there. The whole thing was dedicated to him. He's the reason I did it. I'm glad I did.

Now there are two Victor Crowley action figures from NECA in Walmart and Target, and the comic book series is going strong. There are Halloween masks, and, at some point, there's going to be more *Hatchet* movies. I just have to do other things in between making them. I can't just keep doing *Hatchet* movies or I won't love it anymore.

Once you decide that it's time personally and professionally to make the fourth film, how do you begin?
Creatively, it all hit me at once exactly what I was going to do. One of the things that's very special about this series is that the same core creative team has stayed with it. You don't see us leaving and passing the torch to other filmmakers. We did try to bring in another director (BJ McDonnell) on part three, and I ended up needing to be a lot more involved than I thought it was going to be.

But they wanted to kill me because they're like, why are we doing this again. This isn't a series that you do for the paycheck, the budgets are really small. The floor of the industry kind of fell out around 2010 when streaming became a big thing and physical media started to die. Then, video stores went away. The budgets for these indie things just keep getting smaller.

But the films become more popular every year. So why can't we get more money to do it? Because they know, if we're not willing to do it, then they'll find somebody else who is. It's a bittersweet thing.

Whenever a new one comes out a critic will call it a "cash grab." But most times, filmmakers don't see the money until way later, when the remakes and merchandising happen. I wish I could say that I was motivated by money, but I'm not. I'd be a happier and more financially set person if I did make decisions based on money. But I just don't.

But creatively, I immediately knew what I needed to do and how I was going to jumpstart it again, and also change the rules a little bit. If you have a slasher franchise, it's all centered around the villain. The villain is who everybody's going to the movies to see. They'll tolerate the rest of the cast for that movie. I usually interject a lot of comedy because I think it just makes the characters more likable. But the audience is there for the villain. If you start changing the rules of the mythology, the audience will turn on you so fast.

But with part four, I wanted to do something so that in future movies I could take Victor Crowley out of the swamp [where all three previous films were largely set]. I was able to pull that off and people accepted it. Because it's indie, I don't have to hit the nail on the head so hard.

Let's talk about the economics of the film business. It's the fourth film but the budget was less than the second one. You shot it at a breakneck pace of just 11 days. Is there a financial incentive to make a fourth film?
There certainly is one for the distributor. They're going to make a killing. But they'll never admit it. They never say how much money a film makes. They always play it down. But after downplaying it, they keep asking for more movies. They don't ask for more unless the last movie made a lot of money.

But for those of us who work on it, it's more artistic than financial. I have a little bit more at stake because I have a piece of merchandise. I'm invited to go to conventions and festivals. Although, I've never charged a fan for my autograph or my picture in my life. I just don't like doing that. But for the actors that are in them, for the rest of their life, there's going to be people paying you to sign something. The actors know that so they might work for SAG [Screen Actors Guild] minimum, but they know that in the long term, they're going to make a lot of money at the conventions. So I think there is money to be made for everybody involved. The crew is paid fairly based on the budget. In most cases, I think if they had something else that they could go do for those 11 days that paid more, they would.

But it's hard to say that it's financially lucrative for everyone. Because it's not. But it's just enough. But the distributors are the ones who make money. Eventually, there's going to be another strike for streaming revenues and hopefully, then we're going to find out how much these movies are making. Everyone claims there's no real money in streaming, but more people are watching these movies than ever before. They're everywhere now. Somebody's making money. Otherwise, they wouldn't keep making them. It's a mystery to me. But the distributors are definitely making money. The toy companies are making money. I don't.

What about the decision to call it *Victor Crowley*, as opposed to *Hatchet IV*? You could argue that it's almost a stand-alone film. But it's a continuation of the story. Was there a lot of debate about that?
There was a lot of debate about the title. But I was okay with the decision because I felt like *Hatchet IV* was starting over. The first three movies could be cut together as one. Each new movie starts on the same frame as the last one. But *Hatchet IV* starts 10 years later. The reason for the title is that distributors feel that if you have a movie with a number four after it then anyone who wasn't already a fan of that series isn't even going to consider watching it if they didn't see other ones. I don't know if that's true.

I remember when I was a kid and first getting into horror, going to the video store, I would always reach for the last one in the series, thinking it would be better than the ones before it. But you learn that lesson the hard way. Once you start watching, *Hellraiser 4* or *5*, you're like, "Ohhh..."

But the main reason was that the distributor wanted it to have the broadest appeal possible. I think their strategy worked because I did hear from a lot of new fans that *Victor Crowley* was the first one they watched. Then they saw the other three. But they didn't even realize it was the fourth movie when they saw it.

In other countries, they released it as *Hatchet IV*. In America, it was *Victor Crowley*. It didn't matter to me. I understood where they were coming from. I have to hope that they know what they're talking about. I want it to be as successful as possible. I didn't see the harm in calling it *Victor Crowley,* but fans are always going to call it *Hatchet IV.*

When you are ready to make the fifth one, what would you call it? *Hatchet 5* or *Victor Crowley* 2? Or maybe *Hatchet*, colon with a subtitle?
I think it'll be it'll be *Hatchet 5*. You can't call it *Victor Crowley* 2, because it's the fifth movie. I think that that works maybe once [where you call it by the character's name], but we'll have to wait and see. Ultimately, I don't get to make that decision. I hope they will call it *Hatchet 5*. I think by now the name means something. Fans are going to call it *Hatchet 5* and that's what they're going to call it internationally. So I hope that that's what it's called. Or maybe it will be *Hatchet 5* colon something. I

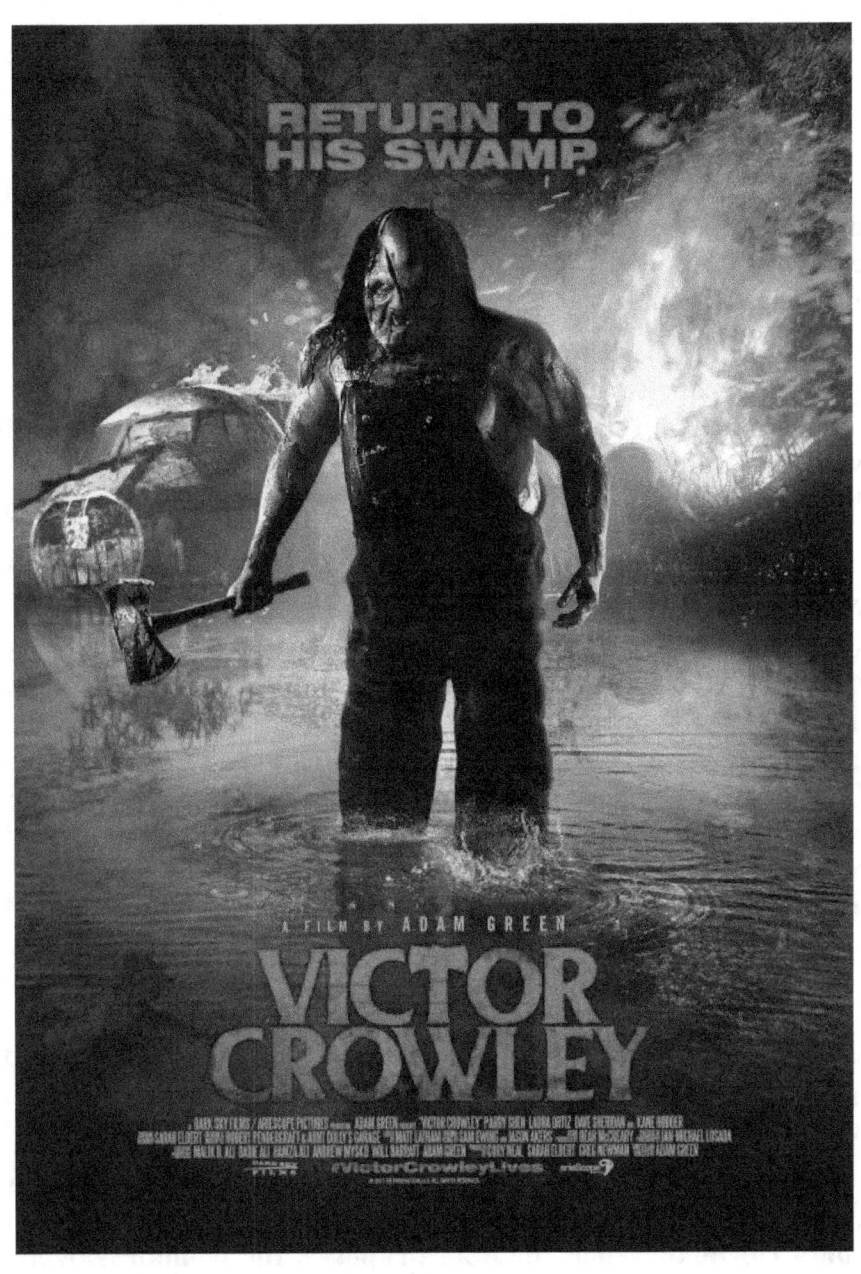

One Sheet poster for *Victor Crowley*
© ArieScope Pictures and Dark Sky Films

don't know. We always refer to them as *H1*, *H2*, *H4*.

I'm not going to be able to pull off making the next one in secret again. I think that only happens once in a lifetime. I think had Covid not happened, we probably would have at least been talking about starting the next one by now. But unfortunately, Covid killed all the projects that we all were working on. It's a little bit like back to the drawing board now that the pandemic is winding down. It'll probably be a while before we do the fifth one. It's also not lost on me that Kane Hodder is like 100 years old. I know I need to hurry up at some point.

How did you market *Hatchet IV*?
There's never been marketing for one of these films, it's always just been me. It's not like they don't know that. That's one of the reasons why I wanted to end it after the third movie; I just felt so taken advantage of. It can't be about money. It's about making the best movie you can make with what you have. The fans always make it worth it.

The release of *Hatchet IV* was more like a [music] tour than a typical theatrical release. We did about 56 dates across the country and a couple overseas [including the UK and Germany]. When I was in a band, we were in a different city with a different crowd every night. Sometimes doing multiple shows a night, based on demand. People drove six or eight hours to watch. And that's for a movie that they know that they're going to be able to watch and stream in a matter of weeks, with just a click of a button. But the fans come out. You don't see that with romantic comedies or action movies. There's something special about horror fans. They make it worth it.

I wish I could tell you all these secrets about money that's being made. It's not. Honestly, it's kind of embarrassing. Friends I grew up with say things like, "You must be so rich." They will walk into Walmart and see action figures based on that character that I created. They see kids come to their door dressed as Victor Crowley for Halloween. They'll say, "Are you loaded?" No. And my agents always say, "Don't admit that. Success breeds success," but I think, "Let people know the truth." So no, I haven't gotten much money off of this. At least, not yet. Maybe when it gets remade, that's when I'll settle up.

Tonally, the fourth movie is different than the first one. The first one had humor, but it was more of an homage to 1980s slasher films. The fourth one starts with a couple on a rowboat. When the man proposes, the woman is overcome with emotion, and she starts crying. But in no time, an excessive amount of music spews from her nose. It's very gross and borders on satire. *Victor Crowley* is not straight-up horror.
I think that was my response to the fan's reaction to *Hatchet 3*. The first three movies are supposed to serve as one long film. Each movie is a different act and *Hatchet 3* is the third act. In this case, the third act has a lot of action. But fans said, "I don't want to see explosions and gunfire in a *Hatchet* movie. If I want to see that, I'll go see a *Die Hard* movie. I don't need that in a slasher movie." But we knew we had to go out with spectacle, so we did. But the response from fans was that it was a satisfying ending, but it wasn't as fun as the other two movies. I listened to that. That opening scene was a way to tell the audience, "I hear you."

But this movie was, for me, purging all the tragedy that I went through. When my friend Joe Lynch read it, he said, "Well, there's your divorce movie." I was like, "What do you mean?" He's like, "Are you kidding? This whole movie is about your divorce." I didn't see it when I wrote it. But now I do.

After the plane crash, [the main characters are trapped in the plane] but if they stay on the plane at least one of them is going to die. Then, I raised the stakes by revealing that Casey is pregnant. When she drowns, the audience went silent. During the third night of the tour, some people in the audience were crying. I wanted people to feel something, but I didn't want anyone to cry. Then it started happening every night. It was not until one of the Q&As after the movie that I realized that I worked out a lot of dark personal shit in this one. It was me saying that I'm not going to get to have kids. I was in a place where I felt that marriage had been such a lie and that there was no love. Several reviews said that the movie was about this couple trying to get together but being forced apart. That is what I wrote. I wasn't [consciously] trying to say that, but it's what I said anyway.

I don't that people will expect that a "slasher film" series would be as personal for a filmmaker as it is for you.
You just hit the nail on the head. That's what it is. These are very personal films for me. All my friends are in them. All my friends are behind the camera. I pour my heart out into them. Because they're *Hatchet* movies, that might sound weird, but I care. I think that the core fan base is very connected and in tune with that. If you're not willing to put yourself into your scripts, the audience knows that. You can't just write something that you think that people will want to see. You have to be willing to give up something of yourself in everything that you write.

I think this fourth movie is the most personal one of them all. It's unexpected for a slasher franchise to have deeper stuff in it or for it to have heart, especially in part four. I think that all just goes back to the fact that it was made for the right reasons. It wasn't made because we said, "I guess we can, so let's do another one." It was made because it was time and I wanted to make it. I needed to make it, even if George had to point that out to me.

I sometimes wonder if there weren't sequels to *Halloween*, *Friday the 13th,* or *Nightmare on Elm Street* if those films would somehow be elevated in some ways. Did the lesser sequels, albeit sometimes fun, negatively, impact their legacy?
Wow, I've debated that with so many other writers. Some people think that when you make sequels, you stain the purity of the original. I don't think so. However, they've been asking me to make a sequel to *Frozen* since the first one came out. There shouldn't be a sequel. It's right the way it is. *Frozen* was designed to stand alone. But anytime a movie is successful, they immediately say that we need more now. For years, I was scared that if they could find any type of skiing thriller, they would buy and rename it *Frozen 2*.

I had a question about maintaining a franchise. From a story point of view, part four ends definitively. Victor Crowley is sucked into an airplane engine. He's diced up; bits of Crowley everywhere; victory for our heroes. The story is over.

But then, Danielle Harris, who was in *Hatchet 2* and *3*, but hasn't appeared in all of *4*, shows up after the credits. Is Harris' cameo designed to keep fans engaged? So that they continue to talk about the series and keep it alive? So they can speculate about what happens next.

From a personal standpoint, it would make my life easier if Danielle had not been in the movie. Because now, I have fans asking, "When are you going to take part five?" But even without her showing up, fans know that Crowley is a repeater and that as soon as the sun goes down, he's going to come back to life again.

But even if we never make the fifth one, I needed the audience to know that she survived and that she was OK. But I also know that the chances are strong that we're going to make more and that Crowley isn't done. The fans didn't want him to go. At a certain point, that's what I listened to. But I also have to be prepared for the "*Hatchet* army," the hardcore fans, to say, "That's enough now." But you want to be the one to make that decision. Hopefully, I'll be able to make the decision, but you never know.

I have to get a couple of other things out of my system and then I'll come back to it. I'm so lucky that the fans have embraced it the way that they have. I never take that for granted. There are so many movies out there that were made for the right reasons. But many of those movies never get seen. Maybe they didn't get the word of mouth going. It usually starts at festivals when people talk about their favorite movies and post about them on social media. When you go to conventions, people thank you for the art you made, you can't even put that into words.

At the end of the day, we're all going to die, and you can't take the money with you. So if you can make people's lives a little bit better while you're here, that is the greatest thing you could ever hope for. Not to get too deep about *Hatchet* movies, but that's what these are to me. I'm very grateful for every moment I've gotten to spend with it.

HALLOWEEN 4

Halloween 4: The Return of Michael Myers

The *Halloween* series serves as a vivid example of how *not* to manage a successful franchise. To be clear, I'm not suggesting that the individual films aren't scary. On the contrary, I'm a fan of the series. They remain chilling because of the enduring power of John Carpenter's creation Michael Myers, the unstoppable boogeyman in *Halloween*. *Halloween* (1978), which at the plot level is about a babysitter who is terrorized by Myers, the masked, knife-wielding killer in overalls, is a transcendent horror film. Shot inventively on a shoestring budget, the movie is a master class in how a filmmaker can create terror with a gliding camera, a pulsating synth-based music score, and actors, like Jamie Lee Curtis as Laurie Strode, who know how to scream, and Donald Pleasance, who as psychiatrist Dr. Sam Loomis, brings the film gravitas and additional urgency ("Death has come to your little town").

However, the *Halloween* franchise seems to consistently lack internal logic and consistency. *Halloween* and *Halloween II* (1981), which picked up immediately after the first film ended, told one unified story about Michael Myers' quest to kill Laurie Strode. *Halloween III: The Season of the Witch* (1982) told a different tale, without Myers or Strode. *Halloween 4* (1988) marked the welcome return of Michael and ended with the implication that his niece Jamie had assumed his evil spirit. *Halloween 5* (1989), marketed with the subtitle *The Revenge of Michael Myers*, ignored the previous film's chilling conclusion, and instead introduced the mysterious Man in Black, who has an unexplained link to Myers. *Halloween 6: The Curse of Michael Myers* (1995) posited that the Man in Black is connected to an ancient cult, which is the source of Myers' supernatural powers and of his need to kill his family members. *Halloween H20* ignored the events of the previous four films and featured the return of Laurie Strode. *H20* ended with Strode victoriously chopping off Myers' head and ending his reign of terror. But in its sequel, *Halloween: Resurrection* (2002), Myers, who is still alive, tracks down Laurie and kills her at the start of the film. For the rest of the movie, he kills a bunch of foolish teenagers who have dared to spend the night in his childhood home. The next film, Rob Zombie's *Halloween* (2007), is a remake of Carpenter's film; its sequel, *Halloween II* (2009), is a strange departure from the rest of the series. The eleventh movie *Halloween* (2018), serves as a sequel to the first film and, ignoring her senseless death in *Resurrection*, features the return (again) of Strode. It's also the third film in the series to bear the title *Halloween*. Its sequels *Halloween Kills* (2021) and *Halloween Ends* (2022) round out a trilogy.

Given how the series willfully flouts continuity, it's easy to see how moviegoers might be confused. The *Star Wars* and Marvel movies are carefully managed to ensure that continuity is assiduously maintained from film to film. The producers of the Bond films usually make sure that there were no glaring continuity issues between installments. (Ernst Stavro Blofeld's failure to recognize James Bond in 1969's *On Her Majesty's Secret Service*, after they had already met in the previous film, 1967's *You Only Live Twice*, was a notable exception.)

Although the *Halloween* franchise is invariably identified with its masked killer, that was not John Carpenter's original intention. Carpenter wanted to turn the series into an anthology where, save for the October 31st date, each film would tell a new story that was unconnected to the previous film. However, Moustapha Akhad, the financier, wanted the sequel to continue telling Myers and Strode's story, so, as its posters promised, *Halloween II* became, "*more* of the night that he came home." [Emphasis mine.] The scary sequel provided a reason to justify Myers' vendetta against Laurie Strode. *Halloween II* revealed that Strode is actually Myers' sister and he's come back to kill her.

For the third film, Carpenter finally got his wish: *Halloween III: Season of the Witch* is a Myers-less sequel. In *Season of the Witch*, an evil corporation makes Halloween masks, equipped with a secret microchip designed to brutally kill those who wear them. Although *Season of the Witch* has since gained a passionate cult following, audiences originally rejected the notion of a *Halloween* film without Michael Myers. If the series was going to continue, the masked serial killer needed to return. The result is *Halloween 4: The Return of Michael Myers*, one of the standout films of the series.

Directed by Dwight H. Little and written by Alan B. McElroy, with a story credited to Dhani Lipsius, Larry Rattner, Benjamin Ruffner, and Alan B. McElroy, *Halloween 4* is set 10 years after the events of *Halloween*. In it, Myers awakes from a coma and escapes from psychiatric care at Smith's Grove Sanitarium so that he can kill Jamie Lloyd, the orphaned daughter of Laurie. Donald Pleasance returns as the now disfigured Loomis, who remains singularly focused on stopping Myers before he can kill again. ("We are talking about evil on two legs.")

Some of the *Halloween* sequels rob Myers of his powers by offering unambiguous explanations for his motivation. In *Halloween 6*, he is possessed by a curse and in Rob Zombie's remake, Myers is the victim of an alcoholic and abusive father. These pedestrian motivations demystify Myers and rob him of his potency. *Halloween 4* avoids these traps. The film is wisely unconcerned with explaining away *Halloween*'s intriguing mysteries. Instead, *Halloween 4* is primarily concerned with examining the nature of good and evil, and it suggests the apparent futility in hoping to defeat relentless and ever-spreading evil.

Interview with Alan McElroy

What do you remember about seeing *Halloween*?
Many moons ago I saw the original *Halloween* and it was a great experience for me. I was in college at the time, and it had been in theaters for quite a while. So when I went to see it, there were only a few people in the audience. I loved the simplicity of it. John Carpenter was very smart about what you did and didn't see. He also built up the legacy of Michael Myers by having the Doctor Loomis character talk about why you needed to be afraid of Myers. Loomis explained the history of Michael Myers. So when Myers came on screen, you were terrified of him. Without having to rely on gore, Carpenter used Loomis to create suspense and terror. I thought that was fascinating. Of course, *Halloween* also has a brilliant ending. You think Laurie Strode

has shot him dead but by the time Loomis goes to inspect the body, Myers is gone. He seems to have disappeared. But it wasn't a cheap twist. It came from what we already understood about his character.

Then *Halloween II* comes out and it picks up moments after the first film concludes. *Halloween III: Season of the Witch*, despite being an interesting film, was a commercial disappointment because Michael Myers doesn't appear in it.
Right. *Halloween III: Season of the Witch* was an attempt at making the series into an anthology, but it failed at the box office. Producer Moustapha Akkad decided if they wanted to make another film, they needed to bring Michael Myers back. Dwight Little, who I was working with on other projects, was hired to direct *Halloween 4*. There had been three other scripts for the movie, but they weren't working and there was a writers' strike coming up. Dwight came to me and asked me if I would be interested in writing it and, of course, it was something that I loved, so I said, yes. I loved the character of The Shape, as Michael Myers is referred to in the scripts. So it was a chance for me to step into this franchise that I knew was going to be a part of cinematic history.

At the time, I had been reading a lot of Stephen King, so my writing had been influenced by his work. There's a Stephen King-like quality to my script, especially the way the townspeople of Haddonfield play out in the story. I wanted to base all the characters, their decisions, and the story, in sound logic. I had to come up with a rationale for how Doctor Loomis survived the explosion that seemed to have killed him at the end of *Halloween II*. I also wanted to make sure the characters in the film weren't the typically dumb characters that you usually see in horror films. In horror films, these characters are generally so stupid that audiences hate them. I wanted to create a scenario where the characters made all the smart choices and *still* ended up dying.

Ridley Scott's *Alien* (1979) is one of my favorite movies, and in it you see the characters making smart decisions, but they die anyway. It's much more interesting that way. I wanted the characters in *Halloween 4* to make equally smart choices. For example, there's a scene in the sheriff's office when the phone lines get cut off and Doctor Loomis comes in and says that Michael Myers is on the loose. The sheriff doesn't dismiss Loomis. After talking to him a bit, he knows that Loomis is telling the truth. There's another scene with Rachel [Jamie's foster sister] in the alleyway, and she sees a shadowy figure. Rachel doesn't walk toward him to investigate; instead, she turns and runs away. But that doesn't always happen in most horror movies. So making them do the smart thing was always important to me.

I also wanted to create a sense of legacy, a history for Loomis and Jamie, who Michael Myers is trying to kill, and a connection to the first film. It didn't necessarily come through in the finished film, but I also wrote little details for the characters, like the way Michael Myers would tilt his head to the right [when he's curious about something]. I thought fans would enjoy little details like that and I wanted to pay homage to the first film. It wasn't about me just putting my stamp on it. I wanted to honor John Carpenter and his creation. I just wanted to extend what he did and honor the way he was trying to create elevated horror.

Michael Myers played by George P. Wilbur
Illustration by Pat Carbajal

How did you come up with a logical explanation for Michael and Loomis surviving the big explosion in *Halloween II*?
I wrote a scene that would have been set during that moment at the end of *Halloween II*, which would have shown how he survived. It would have been like we were watching that same scene but from a different angle. The audience is looking down a hospital corridor and it's quiet. Then there's this loud explosion and the wall blasts out. Then you see Loomis' body, which is in flames, coming right at the camera. Then you cut to black. The audience would see that he survived the explosion [because his body was thrown clear]. Then we would cut to ten years later, where *Halloween 4* picks up. I can't remember if we filmed that scene or not, but I see it in my head. We may not have shot it.

For Michael Myers, it was different. Based on what we know of his character already, we know that he is capable of surviving that explosion. He's embodying the spirit of Samhain. [In *Halloween II*, Loomis explains that Samhain is the "lord of the dead." But Loomis also warns, "Samhain isn't evil spirits. It isn't goblins, ghosts, or witches. It's the unconscious mind. We're all afraid of the dark inside ourselves."] So Michael has been subsumed by Samhain in the first two movies. At the end of four, after Michael's been shot and he's lying on the ground, he touches Jamie, and the spirit passes from him into her. She's destined to become like him. My goal was to connect the first, second, and fourth films. To me, they are a trilogy.

Do you think of Michael Myers as a man?
No. In the first film, Loomis talks about looking into the eyes of Michael Myers when he is a boy. ("I met this six-year-old child with this blank, pale, emotionless face, and the blackest eyes—the Devil's eyes.") But Loomis realizes that he didn't see a boy anymore. He tried for years to cure this boy and says, "I realized he couldn't be cured because all I saw in his eyes was evil." He described it as a darkness, a force that should never be released. So Loomis devoted his life to making sure that Michael is not released from the sanitarium. Nobody believes Loomis when he says, "Michael is not a man, it's a creature." Michael is the spirit of Samhain. He's not a human being anymore. So blowing him up doesn't kill him. Shooting him in the eyes doesn't blind him. Michael Myers is just a vessel for this evil spirit.

That's how I came up with the character of the preacher, Jack Sawyer, who has also been pursuing Michael Myers. [Sawyer refers to Michael Myers as the "Apocalypse, End of the World, Armageddon. It's always got a face and a name. I've been huntin' the bastard for 30 years, give or take. Come close a time or two. Too damn close! You can't kill damnation, Mister. It doesn't die like a man dies."] That's the purpose of the preacher in the story. He serves to ask, what does this evil represent? Where does it go? What is its purpose?

If I had the opportunity, I would have told the prequel story about that preacher character pursuing another individual who was sort of the precursor to Michael Myers. Almost like what happened at the end with Jamie touching Michael Myers and having Samhain entering her, I would have told the story of this creature inhabiting another character. I would have possibly even shown the moment when the young Michael Myers is transformed by the evil force. We would have seen how that little boy ends up killing his sister. I would have loved to see that happen.

You also had to come up with a logical reason for Michael to be wearing his famous costume. After all, when the movie starts, he's a patient and a ward of the state so he's not wearing it yet.
Right, he's wearing a hospital gown until he reaches the gas station. There he kills the mechanic and takes his overalls. When he gets in town, he goes to the store and takes his Halloween mask.

Michael Chabon says that superhero costumes are the outward manifestation of the heroes' inner character. Is that true of Michael? That he needs that outfit for him to feel complete before he continues his mission? Or is it just for the audience?
I think it's for the audience. Once an audience has identified a character's outward appearance then, to them, that's who the character is and that's what they want them to look like. They want the status quo. They want to see the characters depicted the same way and they don't want any change. That's true for television, as well. Even if the character isn't wearing a uniform of any kind, they do have a certain look, an established color scheme. Of course, with *Star Trek*, they are wearing a uniform and it makes them look timeless. It's true of Westerns like *Bonanza* and *Gun Smoke*; all the main characters wear the same outfits each week. Even though *The Simpsons* is a cartoon, they wear the same clothes and have a consistent color scheme. Of course, superheroes like Superman and Wonder Woman have a certain outfit that they wear continuously and are most associated with. The same is true for Michael Myers.

Having said that, you can also say that the blankness of the mask and the clothing, which is an all-encompassing look, helps define his character. The look becomes the manifestation of The Shape, as he is called in the script. Because it's blank, it's not specific. He's a blank figure that is a representation of death moving through society. He moves through society and goes unnoticed. He's invisible. John Carpenter was very smart with that uniform for Michael Myers. Now people want to see him just like that, unchanged.

What about the motivation? As you said, he's evil, so that's what motivates him. The Rob Zombie remake suggests that his behavior was rooted in abuse. The sequels to *Halloween 4* introduce the idea that Myers was cursed and controlled by an ancient cult. But Carpenter maintains that Michael's absence of a clear motivation is what makes him terrifying.
In horror movies, audiences respond to something that *represents* death. It's death itself that we fear. We're afraid of the unknown, our mortality and, as a writer, you look for something that represents that. You're always looking for a new version of that. In *Jaws* (1975), the shark is a representation of death. The alien in *Alien* is a representation of death. The robots in *The Terminator* are death. When their skin bursts, and you see their metallic exoskeleton, you see that they are grim reapers. The only thing they are missing is the sickle.

Michael Myers also represents death. Once you start trying to create justifications for his character and motives that are beyond the mystery of what lies in the darkness, then you minimize him. Cults and physical abuse just minimize what he represents, and then he becomes less scary. Then we can find a way to explain away his behavior. But when he's something that you can't explain away, then he's terrifying.

So the notion of Samhain is scary because it's a version of death, a world beyond our comprehension. That was the only justification that I incorporated into the script. For me, there's some connection to Michael's family line that matters and there's a mystery to uncover. Why would Michael Myers want to kill his sister Laurie Strode? Why would he want to kill Jamie, his niece?

For that matter, why was young Michael Myers cursed? Was it in his family line? Was it something in their line that made them susceptible to Samhain? You could say that Michael was trying to destroy his family line because his family line was evil. Did his family need to be destroyed because they're not innocent? Do we need to be afraid of them for some reason? Is that what's going on?

There are many ways that you could deal with that idea. In a sense, Michael is the hero because he's wiping out a line of evil that might stretch back to the early days of the founding of America. Perhaps the Strode line goes back to Roanoke, the mysteries of Jamestown, or to the Salem Witch Trials. Maybe we're just catching a glimpse of that in *Halloween* and the Strode family needs to be stopped because they're perpetrating evil from generation to generation. Maybe that's why evil continues to live. Or maybe Michael Myers had to go to Jamie so that he can pass his legacy forward, which is what we see happen at the end of *Halloween 4*.

These mysteries make it fun for an audience. They can ask themselves these questions and try to figure out the answers themselves. When they do, the movies live beyond the ninety minutes of celluloid that they experience in the theatre.

If you were to go with the first explanation, which is that Michael is trying to get rid of the evil that's in his family line, then he becomes the protagonist and everyone else becomes the antagonist.
Yes, he becomes the hero of his own movie, which could be a fascinating twist on the story.

It seems that you created Laurie Strode's daughter Jamie to keep it in the family and made her a 10-year-old child instead of a teenager, which makes it scarier. How did you come up with that approach?
The answer is twofold. One, I wanted to mirror the idea of a young Michael, who we see at the start of the original *Halloween*. Throughout *Halloween 4*, we see that she's haunted by visions of a young Michael, as if it's her. There's a beat where she looks in the mirror and sees herself as a young Michael Myers. There's this slow character arc where she will take up the mantle of what he was. I wanted to explore the idea that she's being haunted by her uncle and that he was going to force this legacy upon her. I wanted to explore the notion of how innocence is corrupted. The audience wants to protect her; they don't want to see her corrupted.

Having Jamie being a child allowed me to cover another area and it has to do with her older foster sister Rachel, a teenager. Not only is Rachel trying to save her own life but also more importantly she's trying to protect someone else's. It's more interesting to watch a character putting their own life on the line to save someone than to just watch them try to save their own life. That's what I love about *Alien*. In the first act, Ripley is just trying to escape but, in the third act, she's trying to save the cat and we love her for that. In the second film *Aliens* (1986), she's trying to protect Newt. At the start, Rachel doesn't even want to babysit Jamie but by the film's end, she's putting her own life on the line to protect her sister.

At the end of the film, it is suggested that Michael Myers did pass the evil on to Jamie. If you wrote *Halloween 5*, would you have explored Jamie being evil?
That's a good question. I hadn't thought beyond our movie because I loved the ending and because the story came full circle. I loved that Loomis, who thought that he finally purged the world of Michael, would now see this girl right back where it all started. It's the ultimate nightmare. The evil continues, and the legacy starts over again. The image of her standing there in a bloody clown costume was the same image at the beginning of the original *Halloween*. So I don't think I would have brought Michael back. If you were to follow the logic of the progression of the story, there's no logic to his inclusion in the next story. The spirit was passed to his sister. That would be the story and you would follow it forward. So Michael is no longer The Shape; Jamie is the new Shape. Then the questions would become, what would Loomis do? How would she be contained? What would happen to her next?

That's an interesting question. In *Halloween 5: The Revenge of Michael Myers*, which you did not write, Jamie suffers from post-traumatic stress and is not a force of evil. Instead, Michael Myers comes back and it's more of the same. *Halloween* is interesting because, as Loomis keeps reminding us, it's about the concept of an unknowable and unstoppable evil.
I agree, that's what interests me about *Halloween*. It's the battle between good and evil. Given my druthers, I would have gone back and told the story of what happened in Haddonfield in the '50s. That would have been interesting.

The preacher is an interesting character because he shows up and he suggests that the kind of evil we see in *Halloween* isn't limited to Haddonfield. The preacher also sees Loomis as something of a kindred spirit who could see evil. Why is Loomis able to see evil where others can't? Was he touched by it? Did something happen to him before the events of *Halloween*? I think there's more going on with Loomis than simply that he was Michael Myers' psychiatrist.
I agree. I think, in the universe of *Halloween*, that's another tributary of a story to tell. In another story, you can ask, what happened in the life of a young Loomis that set him on this course?

At some point in his formative years, had he crossed paths with The Shape? Perhaps he saw something in The Shape that he couldn't explain, and this led him to a search for science, logic, and psychology that he could use to explain away evil. So maybe, when he heard about Michael Myers, he sought him out. Maybe Myers represents something that Loomis saw when he was young.

Loomis comes to realize that the answers to his questions cannot be explained by psychology; they can only be explained by something which lies in the world of true evil, which is real. It is beyond our ability to truly understand and explain. It is a spiritual or metaphysical force that we must confront as a human being, and we need to destroy it if we can. That would have been a fascinating story to tell in the universe of *Halloween*.

When I was watching the movie, I was thinking that whoever wrote it must have had strong religious beliefs or was struggling with their beliefs. It seemed that the film was taking that aspect very seriously.
I don't know John Carpenter's background, but you come across a lot of people who seem to struggle with their Catholic background. They are always battling it, and you see movies like *The Exorcist* (1973) that seem to come out of Catholicism. I have a very strong religious background and so it's important for me to tell these kinds of stories and to show the battle between good and evil and show that God can triumph over evil. Although, in *Halloween 4,* evil passes to this young girl.

In *Halloween 4*, good does not triumph over evil.
I would have told this story differently today. I would have taken a different tack now that I'm much older. Whether you're religious or not religious, trying to understand more about the nature of good and evil is something that we see every day. We see it in the news and we're always asking the question, what would I do if I'm confronted by it? Do I defeat it? Will I have the willpower and the strength to overcome it? Where do I find my strength when I need it? There is no mention of God in the landscape of *Halloween.* But you do see the characters drawing from something greater than themselves to face and defeat something that otherwise seems overwhelming.

You were saying that Donald Pleasance helps create fear in the audience in *Halloween.* I think Robert Shaw has a similar function in *Jaws*. They are also both heavyweight actors who command dialogue that might come off as a bit silly uttered by actors not of their caliber.
You always need a character like that in these movies. It's what horror is built on. I was working on a project, and I just told a director about this because he asked me, what is horror and how does it work? I said that horror is built on legacy. When writing horror you always must continually build the legacy of what you're facing. In *Jaws,* Robert Shaw gives you that because he tells you about what a shark is. Shaw is constantly reminding you that a shark swims and it eats, and in his eyes, you can see his soul. He tells you about the destruction of the Indianapolis. He tells you over and over again that a shark is an eating machine. In *Jaws*, you have two characters building the legacy. You have Shaw and Richard Dreyfus. The Richard Dreyfus character, an oceanographer, gives you a scientific understanding of the horror of the shark. But Robert Shaw gives you the nuts and bolts of the physical terror and legacy of the shark.

In *Halloween,* Loomis tells you what Michael Myers is and what he represents. He explains the evil that he is, that he's not a man. He is always telling you the legacy. Ghost stories are built on that principle. They say, "In this house, these terrible things happened, and this family was murdered." Then, when you send your characters into that house, it's scary. Because you know the legacy, you're terrified. *Alien* works in that same manner because you're told right from the start that the crew of the ship got a distress call and that means something bad happened. Then they land on this horrifying planet. Now the crews are on their way to answering the distress call. Soon, they discover that it wasn't a distress call, it was a warning. Now someone's telling you whatever you're facing is bad. Then they get to the alien ship and find an alien navigator with his chest and inner bones broken out. It's again reminding the audience of legacy and that something bad happened here, something horrifying.

In most horror movies there is someone to remind us of the legacy. Even in *Terminator* (1984), which is not strictly horror, Kyle Reese serves that purpose. Reese tells Sarah Connor that the Terminator can't be bargained with, it can't be reasoned with, it doesn't know pity or remorse, or fear and it absolutely will not stop ever until you are dead. Well, that description of a relentless force also describes death itself.

In recent years, horror movies have been built on shock and filmmakers are now fighting their way out of this period of torture porn (the subgenre of horror in which characters die in progressively more gruesome ways). They're not built on anything, except the next shock, the next shock, and the next shock. The problem is those movies have no long-term effect because people don't care. Once you've felt that shock or seen that moment of gore it doesn't stay with you when the film is over. We have to find our way back to the legacy kind of filmmaking.

You're talking about legacies within the film but you're also describing the legacy of the franchise itself. When you were making the fourth film, you couldn't have anticipated that seven more films in the series would follow.
Dwight, the director, and I often lament that we didn't do the fifth movie, which we were offered because we were working on other projects. Gosh, I wish we had done the fifth one so that we could set the series on a course that we think would have been a better way to go.

Did you experience a sense of special challenges in writing the fourth film in a series?
For me, it wasn't a challenge so much as an opportunity that I appreciated. I was being allowed to bring The Shape back to life and that was fantastic. I felt like a kid in the candy store. I was 27-years-old, and it was going to be my first feature film credit. I was excited to do it. I only had a short period to do it because of the impending writer's strike, but I wrote it at the speed of light. I stayed up all night and wrote it in 11-days. We broke [outlined] the story in advance and we knew what we wanted to do, but it poured out of me because I was so excited. I loved those films, so I didn't feel at all challenged but more excited and enthused and wanted to do them justice.

I imagine that if you were hired to write *Halloween 5*, then the producers would have insisted that Michael Myers come back. Do you have a battle between the girl and Michael, or does he try to stop her and make her good?
Interesting. They started Part Five with a scene from the end of *Halloween 4*. In it, after Michael Myers gets shot multiple times, and falls into the abandoned well, the police throw in dynamite and blow it up. At the time, we thought it was overkill. So

Donald Pleasence as Dr. Samuel Loomis
Illustration by Pat Carbajal

they cut it out of *Halloween 4*, but they used it at the start of the next movie. There are many ways you could go with the story. I'd have to think about it. But you could have Jamie imprisoned and held in containment. Maybe Michael needs to unearth himself from his buried tomb so that he can become Jamie's protector. Then he frees her. Now you have the visual of the small girl in a clown costume and Michael Myers standing over her like a supernatural bodyguard. This way you don't have a little girl murdering people throughout the film. Or do you have to find a way to free Jamie from the evil? Does it pass back to Michael? But if you do that, you're just having evil pass back and forth and you're not moving the story forward. I'd have to put some thought into it because what you always want is to be able to move the story forward somehow.

Or you can expand on the legacy of Samhain and discover where this evil came from in the first place. I'd want to give the audience new information, so I might have brought the preacher back into it. If you have to bring Michael Myers back, then you'd have to find a smart way to unearth his character and bring him back either as Jamie's protector or to pass it back to him.

For this thought experiment, there are three story threads leftover from *Halloween 4*. One, Jamie is now evil and will continue with Michael's goals. Two, Loomis has already decided to kill Jamie. Three, Michael is putting an end to his family line.

There's no question that there's something there. I think the great question to ask is why is Michael trying to kill off his family line? I think that's where it's starting with that idea and the question, what is it that Michael's trying to do? Well, Michael is trying to kill off his family line but now that the evil's passed to Jamie does Loomis need to kill her so that evil doesn't pass into someone else? But he wouldn't want to kill Jamie, so he exhumes Michael's corpse. So the only way to save Jamie is for the evil to transfer back into the vessel of Michael Myers. Loomis becomes instrumental in trying to make that happen. I don't know what choices I would ultimately make, but it's an interesting conundrum.

Where do you think *Halloween 4* lies in the *Halloween* franchise?
Moustapha Akkad loved *Halloween 4*. He loved the structure of it, and he even openly admitted that he took the structure of *Halloween 4* and used it in *Halloween H2O*. There was a scene in the script of *Halloween 4* that wasn't used but he used it in *H20*. In it, Jamie hides in the school. She enters a classroom and hides under the desks. Michael enters and makes his way through, just stabbing through the tables, trying to get her. We didn't have time to shoot that, and Moustapha used a scene similar to that in *H20*, which is funny. So he loved *Halloween 4*. I view *Halloween, Halloween II,* and *Halloween 4* as a trilogy. I look at Part Four as almost an unofficial *Halloween III*.

In some ways, you owe your career to *Halloween 4*.
I love the film and it'll always hold a warm place in my heart. Usually, writers are moved off the set quickly, but I got to spend two weeks on the set and hang with Donald Pleasance. I was there when they were picking locations. I was part of the

casting process, and it was a great experience for me and made me feel like, oh, this is what filmmaking is. This is awesome, I love this. Never happened again. I'd work on other films and think, isn't it always supposed to be like *Halloween*? It has never been that good again. In thirty years it has never been as positive and as rewarding an experience as it was in *Halloween 4*. It was a great start for my career, it made me love filmmaking, but it also set me up for like, "Wait, aren't all things supposed to be like this?" *Halloween 4* is the film that people still reach out to me over and want to talk about. I love that people love the film and that it was a good experience for them. I'm glad that they took away something from it that they enjoyed and that's what it's all about. Even though it's escapist entertainment, you want people to hopefully take something away from it that enriches their life. Even if it's a horror movie, you want to create something that somehow makes their lives a little better. Or maybe they think, I can face evil and defeat it. Or maybe it makes them think about the nature of evil and good.

FRIDAY THE 13TH *4*

Friday the 13th: The Final Chapter

Whereas the *Halloween* series has tried to navigate a complex narrative linking each film, the *Friday the 13th* franchise largely tells stand-alone stories, with little connective tissue linking each successive film. In place of complex mythology, *Friday the 13th* offers an uncomplicated, but equally lethal villain, Jason Voorhees, the hockey-masked, machete-wielding killer. Scant familiarity with Jason's origin is required to understand his motivation or to follow the plot. Audiences only need to understand that Jason, like the shark in *Jaws 4*, is out for revenge.

For the uninitiated, in 1958, Jason Voorhees, the eleven-year-old son of Mrs. Voorhees, drowned in the lake while his counselors, who were charged with keeping him safe, were satisfying their carnal desires. Twenty-one years later, Mrs. Voorhees, who then works as a cook at the camp, attempts to kill a brand-new batch of libidinous counselors. But before she can kill 'em all, Mrs. Voorhees is beheaded by Alice, a resourceful counselor and one of Mrs. Voorhees' intended victims. Enraged by his mother's death, Jason rises from his watery grave. In all the sequels that follow, in zombie-like fashion, Jason hacks away at other camp counselors and just about anyone else he encounters. But the series can be further reduced to its most basic component—undead killer slaughters teenagers.

What started as a *Halloween* rip-off has become an established series with a rabid following. The original 1980 film cost a scant $550 thousand but grossed nearly $40 million. To date, the box office total for all the films is about $466 million. The haul is significantly more when aftermarket revenues, such as DVDs, Blu-rays, cable, premium channels, and merchandise such as toys and video games are accounted for.

Given the subtitle of *Part IV—The Final Chapter*—one can be forgiven for believing that the film was intended to be the last one in the series. Yet, including the spin-off movie *Freddy vs. Jason* (2003) and the 2009 remake, eight films followed. In the following interview, Barney Cohen, who wrote the screenplay, looks back at the franchise that, like Voorhees, just won't die.

Barney Cohen Interview

How did you attempt to make *The Final Chapter* different from the previous films?
I thought we had to "humanize" Jason before we killed him, which is why we flipped his mask off in the final hugger-mugger. Once you see his Quasimodo-like face, you kind of get a feeling for the poor guy. Quasi nothing! He's all "modo!" And then some. But the point is he looks more like a human being than an undead thing in a hockey mask. That means more emotion when we kill him. And the possibility that he really is, finally, dead.

What do you have to keep in mind when writing the Jason character? How is Jason different from other modern horror icons, like Michael Myers?

Jason Voorhees
Illustration by Pat Carbajal

Initially, I wanted to make Jason more human right from the beginning, rather than the shark-like killing machine we'd come to know in his first three visits. But a filmmaker diverges from the canon at his peril and people love/hate the killing machine, so it's wise to stick with it. That's why we left the "humanizing," such as it is, until the climax.

Were you writing the script as if it were the last film in the series or did you intentionally keep the door open for future installments?
There were long arguments about this. I was hired to end it. Really end it. Kill him in a way that says, "That's all folks!" it's over, *no mas*, finished! In fact, I humanized him to finish him off. But because of the endlessly Talmudic arguments over this, I left it open just a crack. As it turns out, it did really well at the box office and human nature took its course. A sequel franchise was reborn.

I was hoping the sequels would spin off nine-year-old Tommy Jarvis as a child version of Jason. Corey Feldman was twelve at the time of the shoot, but he played Tommy as a nine-year-old. I suppose that's why I always snarkily suggest the Jason vs. Tommy rematch whenever someone asks me for a sequel idea. I just loved that kid character; hell, I created it. Tommy did appear in several subsequent Fridays, just not by me, and not as the main character.

Why has the series endured while other slasher films, which try to copy the formula, are largely forgotten?
I reject the premise that Jason has endured while the other body count archetypes have faded. As with Dr. Frankenstein's monster, I'm expecting to see him reborn more than once. If you're asking how he differs from Michael and Freddy, I suppose it's twofold. Jason never gets a chance to explain himself, which means he's trapped in his own horror without any chance of exculpation. Also, because he never gets to explain himself, the audience can see his pain in any way they like. Jason is a blank face beneath a mask on which we can project anything we like, including ourselves. What has happened lately though is the growing number of low-budget and under-low-budget body count villains whose sequels are about to run to double digits.

What would you have liked to have seen happen in *Part 5*?
Part 5 is a funny story, at least for me. They asked me to write it, of course, and I wanted to base it on Tommy Jarvis (Corey Feldman did, too, still does, of course), but when I met the director, Danny Steinman, he had other ideas. "Creative differences," they call it around here. I'm not disappointed. I'm happy to have done my part in the history of Jason. To have done more might have made me his slave.

But I'd like to sequelize other characters along with Mr. Voorhees. Assess their growth; what has happened to them over the years. For instance, what about a rematch with Tommy Jarvis [whose mother and sister were killed by Jason], now that Tommy is all grown up and something of a monster himself?

Who should audiences root for in a well-made Friday film—Jason or his victims? Why?
Jason's victims are basically jerks. Remember, "in the beginning," the camp counselors were screwing around (some literally) while the boy Jason was drowning.

Jason is all of us punishing the various jerks in our lives. Yes, he always dies in the end, the hero often does in the classics. That's Greek classic, not horror, don't be dim. But look, we're all going to die, you know? How cool is it to die to the sounds of a cheering audience on their feet, if we're lucky? Of course, we root for Jason! We even root, each time, for his ever more spectacular demise. But when the time comes for me, I don't want to be buried in a hockey mask. Just remember me fondly for 90 minutes of fun in a movie theatre.

What place does *Part 4* hold in the series?
It's the best! No, really, lots of the later reviews of the series call it the pick of the litter. Look it up. [Note: When ranking each film in the series, *Entertainment Weekly* writer, Kyle Anderson contended that "the fourth film in the series is its absolute peak."[34]] When people in the business, particularly in the horror genre, want to butter me up, they always tell me they like *Final Chapter* the best. It doesn't work; I've moved on.

NIGHTMARE ON ELM STREET 4

A Nightmare on Elm Street 4: The Dream Master

When it comes to the icons of horror, Freddy Kreuger has something that Jason Voorhees and Michael Myers lack—a killer personality. Jason Voorhees, the hockey-masked killer, and Michael Myers, the knife-wielding murderer with a grudge against babysitters, are more symbols of evil than they are fully dimensional characters. When John Carpenter and Deborah Hill wrote the script for *Halloween* (1978), they utilized the intentionally oblique descriptor "The Shape" to refer to Myers.

Freddy Kreuger has them all beat. But it might not be a fair fight. Freddy has a trait the other slayers do not—he speaks. Whereas Jason and Michael are mute, Freddy is a bit of a chatterbox. Moreover, as the series progressed, Freddy, as played by Robert Englund, spoke more and more. And when he does, he's often spouting killer quips. In *A Nightmare on Elm Street 4: The Dream Master*, when one of Freddy's victims is pulled into a waterbed, Freddy asks, "How's this for a wet dream?" In *A Nightmare on Elm Street 3: Dream Warriors*, when a character is tied to a bed with tongues, Freddy questions, "What's wrong, Joey? Feeling tongue-tied?" Later, Freddy smashes another character's head into a television set and wisecracks, "Your big break in TV." In *A Nightmare on Elm Street 5: The Dream Child*, Freddy channels his inner superhero, "Faster than a bastard maniac, more powerful than a loco madman, it's…Super-Freddy!" And in *Freddy vs Jason*, where the two titans face-off, as Freddy props up a dead victim, he observes she's "dead on her feet."

The *Nightmare on Elm Street* films are divided up into two categories—the scary ones and the "funny" ones. In the first few films, Freddy Kreuger is depicted as a dark force of evil, who kills teenagers in their dreams. With his brown fedora, red and green sweater, a glove with blades attached, and severe burns on his face, Kreuger is very much the vision of nightmares. However, in the later films, Freddy more closely resembles a Borscht-belt comedian, who spouts one-liners after dispatching his victims. For his part, Englund acknowledges that the "Freddy punch lines were used as a kind of punctuation mark, a way to end the scenes with a filmic rim shot. Had we kept Fred Kreuger strictly the incarnation of pure evil, things might've become boring and predictable, but we also had to be careful that we didn't turn him into a Catskills comic."[35]

But Freddy's origins aren't decidedly less light-hearted. Craven described to *Vulture*, Freddy's surprising origin story, "I'd read an article in the *L.A. Times* about a family who had escaped the Killing Fields in Cambodia and managed to get to the U.S. Things were fine, and then suddenly the young son was having very disturbing nightmares. He told his parents he was afraid that if he slept, the thing chasing him would get him, so he tried to stay awake for days at a time. When he finally fell asleep, his parents thought this crisis was over. Then they heard screams in the middle of the night. By the time they got to him, he was dead. He died in the middle of a nightmare. Here was a youngster with a vision of a horror that everyone older denied. That became the central line of *Nightmare on Elm Street*."[36]

Depending on the horror franchise, fourth films can serve different functions. *Halloween 4* was supposed to reintroduce Michael Myers, who was absent from *Halloween III*. By contrast, *Friday the 13th 4* was intended to end the series. The fourth *Child's Play* film *Bride of Chucky* was a tonal departure, while *Nightmare on Elm Street 4* was designed to expand the mythology. In the first three films, Freddy is seeking revenge on the parents who killed him by murdering their children.

For the series to continue, Freddy's victims could not be limited to the finite number of children who did him wrong. But after making minced meat of teens for the first three films, by *Elm Street 4* there were only three "Elm Street kids" left, including Kristen Parker, Joey Crusel, and Roland Kincaid. In the film, he makes quick work of Roland and Joey. But if Freddy dispatches Kristen, the sole survivor of the Elm Street kids, Freddy will become powerless. So Freddy tricks Kristen into utilizing her dream power to pull her friends into her dreams. During the process, Kristen unwittingly passes her power on to her friend, Alice. Now, Freddy's prey isn't finite. The plan to expand the mythology worked. Alice would become the protagonist of *Elm Street 5*.

For Englund, the fourth Freddy film was one of his favorites. In his autobiography *Hollywood Monster,* Englund writes, "*Nightmare 4* contains my favorite sequence in the entire franchise and I'm not even in it! Alice is locking up for the night at the Crave Inn diner…then she and Rick walk out to his truck, open the doors, and get in, and then the sequence repeats and repeats and repeats in a time-disorienting, continuous loop. The first time I saw it, I was spooked because it reminded me of how my nightmares tended to function. That repeating exit was the most hypnotic, disturbing, and accurate depiction of a dream I'd ever seen."[37]

Dream Master, the fourth Freddy film was based on the story by William Kotzwinkle, and it was written by Brian Helgeland, who would later write *LA Confidential* (1997). and Ken and Jim Wheat who wrote *Ewoks: The Battle for Endor* (1985). Ken and Jim Wheat would later go on to write sequels to classic horror films by David Cronenberg and Alfred Hitchcock, *The Fly II* (1989), *The Birds II: Land's End* (1994), and the Vin Diesel horror-sci-fi movie *Pitch Black* (2000).

Ken Wheat Interview

How did you become involved in the fourth *Nightmare on Elm Street* film and what were your marching orders?
We had just done a pressure cooker rewrite of *The Fly II* that took it from dead in the water to an official green light, at which point they brought in Frank Darabont to do the final polish. Bummer. So we got an urgent call from our agent in late January 1988 about a *Nightmare on Elm Street 4* rewrite. A meeting was set for the next day, and we read the two scripts that night. Oh, and the whole thing revolved around the fact that they had a mid-August theatrical date set, so they had to start shooting by the first week of April.

There was an initial script by William Kotzwinkle [who wrote the novelization for *E.T. the Extra-Terrestrial* (1982)] and another by Brian Helgeland. Brian had, quite appropriately, used nothing but the names of the lead character—Alice—and of

Robert Englund as Freddy Krueger
Illustration by Pat Carbajal

the film—*Nightmare on Elm Street 4: The Dream Master* from the Kotzwinkle draft. I have zero memory of that first script, other than thinking WTF? the whole time I was reading it.

Brian's screenplay had some good scenes and was in no way bad, but it wasn't anything close to a shooting script. I've searched my garage, where I think there's a box with copies of those earlier scripts as well as our outlines, but it remains hidden. For that matter, printed copies of our drafts aren't on my shelves of scripts, which is very weird, but I did find some 3 1/2-inch plastic floppy disks that apparently included *Nightmare on Elm Street* material.

Minor detail, I don't have a computer that'll play these ancient discs. So I found a USB drive on Amazon, with which I could open them up. Problem two: Microsoft Word for DOS circa '87 did the formatting by using an attachment called a style sheet, so all I could bring up was a totally unformatted version of our stuff. But thank goodness some geek at some point devised a program that could convert old Word for Dos documents into Word for Windows 97 with proper formatting, which in turn could be converted into a semi-normal screenplay.

Anyway, my memory of what Brian had done is less than precise, but as I recall, he started, I believe, with Kincaid in the auto graveyard and had a Bull Mastiff doing the peeing fire bit.

But I'm jumping ahead. I'm supposed to be talking about how we got the gig. So to backtrack, when we heard about the job, and read the scripts, we had a couple of hours to drive around and brainstorm the next morning before we had to show up for our pitch. We were not happy about the time factor and how much work would be needed to turn it into something that could be shot very soon. About an hour before the meeting, we decided that there was no way we could come up with a good pitch because our feeling at that time was that they needed more than we thought we could repair under the circumstances. So we pulled over to a payphone and put in a call to our agent. We told him we needed to cancel the meeting because we had no idea of what to say other than that the script required more work than they seemed to have thought was needed. Our agent said it was too late to cancel and said that if we didn't like what they had, we should just say so, and take it from there. Which is what we did. We said that Brian's script had some good scenes but would require a total overhaul. They said fine. We said we didn't know exactly what to do with it, and they said, "That's okay. Just go for it and get us a script within three weeks."

Can you talk about the evolution of the script?
Our first draft included several of Brian's Freddy sequences and some of the characters. Alice, of course, was part of it from the beginning. Whether there was a brother Rick before us I can't recall. I do know that the opening ten minutes at the Elm Street house was ours. He might have had a boiler room scene, but the first thing I remember in his script was the auto graveyard scene with Freddy's resurrection and Kincaid's death. In our first draft, which makes me imagine it was based on Brian's version, the dog was more horrific and wasn't Kincaid's pet.

So the evolution of the script was getting it whipped together as quickly and creatively as possible. They were happy with our first draft when we turned it in on

February 18th, and we were ready to move forward with the next one. A few days after we finished the script, they hired Renny Harlin to direct. [Harlin would go on to direct *Die Hard 2* and *Exorcist 4*]. So we had a chance to kick a few ideas around with Renny. A problem was that they were also designing sets and effects, casting, hiring crew, etc., so Renny's time was limited. A much bigger problem was that a strike by the Writers Guild of America was set to start on March 7th. We worked on a detailed outline and pushed to get started on the next draft. Finally, about a week before the strike, we explained that we wouldn't be allowed to work on the script once the strike was called. So they let us get going. We finished about half of it—which was used with no changes other than extraneous dialogue revisions—and I believe the second half was based pretty closely on our outline, which I can't find.

There was extra writing by Renny, Rachel, and others after the strike started, which didn't matter at all to us. Our problem with that was that they kept putting out new drafts with our names and the current dates on them. We were super paranoid about breaking guild rules (although almost no one ended up being punished) so we weren't thrilled about the way they were handling it. That was why we used a pseudonym, which turned out to be unnecessary. Such is life.

Oh, other things about the evolution of the script...The Roach Motel was another sequence of Brian's, although it was a jock guy who remained in our first draft. She became female in our second draft, although we saw her as being tougher. The beach sequence? I have no idea which of us developed that. The movie theater was definitely ours, since we're huge fans of the Buster Keaton movie *Sherlock, Jr*. In our first draft, the one sucked into the screen was a female character dropped from our final draft. She was the girlfriend of the bodybuilder guy who was also dropped, and the movie she became part of involved her giving birth to Freddy. That was changed in the outline for our second draft with Alice being sucked into a movie of the run-down Crave Inn. Oh, and we can take credit for the Diner's name, [a reference to Wes Craven, the creator of Freddy Kreuger].

What makes a good *Elm Street* sequel?
What makes any kind of movie good? Compelling situations. Appealing characters. Surprises. Great effects. Good use of Freddy.

How did you want to distinguish part four from the previous films? What did you want to bring to the series?
Well, Part 3 was a very tough act to follow. It had a creative setting that got everything away from Springfield, and high school, and average teens. The decision to return to the hometown elements was a given, so we just did the best we could with that setting.

In the first three films, Freddy is seeking revenge by killing the children of the parents who caused their death. However, there are only so many of those children to kill. So, in part four, it was necessary to expand the lore and have him want to kill teens who were not the descendants of the parents who murdered him. How do you expand the lore without invalidating the rules established in the previous films?
Every film that's a fourth or later in a series is going to have to expand the lore to a

degree, especially when the entire concept of the stories is that some of the lead and secondary characters get killed off in each one. Calling friends into the nightmares may have been Brian's idea or could have been ours. Or could have been Bob or Rachel's before we got involved. I can't remember. In any case, it was a reasonable solution to the dilemma.

While some might characterize the film as a slasher film with fantasy elements, there are always mysteries that run through it. One, how is Freddy back? Two, how can the teens stop him? Incidentally, the characters in the story faced the same questions that the filmmakers did. Can you talk about how you tried to answer those questions?

Boy! That's the question you could ask of any horror series that kills the villain/monster at the end of each one! Dracula, Frankenstein's Monster, Bruce [the shark from *Jaws*], The Alien, and so on. One of my favorite resurrections was in *Taste the Blood of Dracula*, the fourth Christopher Lee Dracula film. If you've never seen that one, give it a shot. Ralph Bates plays a degenerate young Lord who promises some older sleazeball "gentlemen" that he can share with them the ultimate thrill. Using Dracula's powdered blood left over after his most recent death, Bates mixes the powder with his own blood, but the other three gents are afraid to drink it. Bates does and gets wacky, and the others kill him. After they take off, the young Lord's body turns into Christopher Lee, who is pissed off at the others. Most of his dialogue in the movie is "That's one." "That's two" after he kills each of them. The device worked superbly, and this was one of the last top-notch Hammer horror films.

Often, getting rid of the monster has an element of "is he or isn't he" surrounding his death. As I recall, the *Creature from the Black Lagoon* kept getting shot at the end and sinking into the water. But it turns out he wasn't dead!

With *Friday the 13th*, Jason wasn't the killer, he was dead. But in all the sequels he became more-or-less supernatural, a la Freddy, so bringing him back was more-or-less straightforward. In several, he wasn't really dead at the end of the previous one, and later he's brought back by lightning, then telekinetic powers, etc.

In Universal's first *Frankenstein*, the monster is burned to death, but by the beginning of *Bride of Frankenstein*, he's just kicking back in the ruins of the burned-up windmill. At the end of Bride, the monster blows up himself and his bride. In the next one, he's found in a crypt and revived. At the end of that one, he's dissolved in molten sulfur, which in the next one turns out to have preserved instead of destroyed him.

To me, the *Halloween* movies are about the nature of good and evil. What would you say the *Elm Street* movies are about?

Teenagers are just dreamers. They deserve to die! No, not really. It's about teenagers who wouldn't have nightmares if they only took more drugs! Oh, that's not it either. Okay. I think what the *Elm Street* movies are about is the nature of good and evil.

There are two distinct kinds of Elm Street movies, those where Freddy Kreuger is scary and those where he is mostly funny and dispenses quips. Can you talk about the balancing act?

Well, by the time *Nightmare on Elm Street 4* came along everybody was expecting quips from Freddy. I still like to consider him being scarier than "mostly funny." His quips are verbal jabs at dying victims, which makes Freddy cruel in that sense, too. Plus, audiences like for Freddy to do that. In any case, I was fine with having a bit of humor in it, but I consider the film to be pretty serious for the most part. I was not wild about some of the "teen humor" that was added after we left. There was a bit of that in our drafts, but I thought it got a little too loose at times.

What do you need to keep in mind while writing the character of Freddy?
Since most of his lines are "punchlines," I guess it made me think about the James Bond films. "She's just dead..." as his dance partner is shot. "Shocking!" after he kicks a heater into a bathtub. "I think they were on their way to a funeral," after a hearse filled with killers goes over a cliff. "I think he got the point," after he shoots a guy with a spear gun. etc. I can't remember which of us came up with which Freddy lines. I know Brian did "You can check in, but you can't check out." And I seem to recall that Robert ad-libbed some lines here and there.

But there was also the question of how to bring Freddy into scenes. He couldn't just walk through the door. So there were things like the nurse at school, and the bathroom stall elevator, both of which were ours. Oh, we also had a martial arts fight in the elevator shaft instead of the Dojo.

Where did the "Dream Master" master concept come from? The professor, who is played by New Line studio head Robert Shaye, says the Dream Master is both a person who controls the dream and someone who guards the positive gate of dreams and protects the sleeping host. There is also a nursery rhyme about the dream master that becomes the key to defeating Freddy.
"The Dream Master" was introduced as a title in Kotzwinkle's draft, but I have no memory of whether or how it was mentioned from there on. So we knew we were dealing with a "Dream Master," and we had various lines to set up and explain the dream master in our scripts. The lecture by Bob Shaye and the "Dream Master Nursery Rhyme," on the other hand, were both added after we were gone. I was fine with Bob's scene, although it laid it on a bit thick, I didn't like the nursery rhyme at all. It felt far too convenient and not at all believable as a children's rhyme. [The rhyme is "Now I lay me down to sleep. The master of dreams, my soul I'll keep. In the reflection of my mind's eye, evil will see itself and it shall die."]

By the time a series gets to the fourth film, there is often a lot of lore that audiences need to retain. That can make for more satisfying stories that need to be told over multiple films. If you do not expand the mythology, then the films just become quasi-remakes of the first film. And that gets old, fast. But the danger in expanding the lore is that it can also mire down a franchise, where only the most devoted fans can follow along and are emotionally invested. What are your thoughts on how *Nightmare 4* dealt with that issue?
That's a tricky one because I agree with all that you just said, contrary as it sometimes was. In a film series, the audience potentially has a lot to hang onto by the fourth episode. And yeah, Netflix and the other streaming services show us that audiences

enjoy a story that's told progressively over eight hours or so. And those shows aren't like network series, where 12–20 episodes are done on the fly as mostly self-contained stories.

Relative to sequels becoming quasi-remakes of the first film, it's almost impossible to see any studio or independent producer approaching them any other way. It can be a blessing or a curse whichever way it's handled.

The second *Halloween* and second *Elm Street* films were both disappointing, but not far enough off to kill the series. *Halloween III*, on the other hand, tried to be independent of the original story and bombed pretty badly. Tommy Wallace, the director and writer of *Halloween III*, is a talented guy, and he and John Carpenter took a courageous step by using the title but creating a mostly new mythology. Which left audiences confused and annoyed.

Nightmare on Elm Street 1 was pretty hard to top. It was simple and efficient and created a mythology that was easy to buy. While they were filming, Bob Shaye must have seen the potential of a sequel, because the ending certainly makes one uneasy.

I haven't seen *Nightmare on Elm Street 2* since it came out, but I do remember being less than thrilled by it. Which was tough, because [actor] Clu Gulager, who is a friend, did things that changed the mythology, some of which was pretty odd. But that was just a blip for the series because it wasn't as though it was *bad*, and the mythology was relatively faithful to the first film. Then director Chuck Russell brought the series back to life with *Dream Warriors*.

As far as how we dealt with the script? Our only interest was in creating the blueprint for a movie we'd like to see. We weren't concerned about the previous ones because Parts 1 and 3 were really good, so it was a matter of being faithful to them. As far as what they would do in the next one? That never entered our mind for a split second. You could strap Freddy to a nuclear bomb and atomize him, but there would be a way to bring him back. A new Atomic Centrifuge has been installed at Springfield College, and when they test it, Freddy's atoms re-fuse. Uh oh!

Oh, I just remembered a brilliant horror film that was followed by a whole bunch of lame sequels. *The Omen* showed what a low-budget studio film could do in that genre, and none of the writers and directors of the sequels had a clue.

The *Elm Street* films were crucial to the success of New Line Studio. In terms of the direction of the film and continuing the franchise, what was important to them about what they wanted part four to be like?
They just wanted a script that could go before cameras in a few weeks.

Dream Master is considered to be a highlight of the series. Looking back, what is your assessment of the film. What does it do well? Where could it have been better?
I consider the first and third to be the best, but maybe that's just me. Considering how quickly they put that film together, I have nothing but admiration for all of the creative artists involved. I think it was only Renny's third film, and he was certainly the right guy at the right time. I think Renny did a great job with the visuals. To do a film with that many effects in just a few months? That amazed me. I think the look throughout

is solid. Freddy's makeup is great. Englund hits a home run. It does suffer from that late 80s hair problem. Especially Sheila and Rick. But I was sorry they couldn't think of a better way to show that their dad was a drunk than to have him carry around a bottle in a bag. That seemed super on-the-nose to me, and when I mentioned it to Rachel Talalay after she sent me their first "rewrite," she was furious, and never spoke to me again. I guess it had been her idea. And it still bugs me when I see the film.

In addition to *Elm Street*, you are no stranger to working on other beloved properties. You also wrote and directed the 1985 TV movie *Ewoks: The Battle for Endor*. While *Battle for Endor* was the sequel Ewok film, it was the fifth *Star Wars* film. Can you talk about the challenges of working on a wildly popular series like *Star Wars*?

Well, it was sixth if you count the *Holiday Special*. That eight-month period making *The Battle for Endor* was as much fun as movie-making can possibly be. Not that it wasn't also a huge amount of work, but the environment and crew were the greatest. We shot at numerous places around the ranch, and its environs, and quite a bit on ILM's biggest stage. It wasn't really a sequel to a *Star Wars* film as much as it was a sequel to *Caravan of Courage*, [the first made-for-tv set in the *Star Wars* universe]. Decisions had been made on that one both because of budget and the young, intended audience to create a slightly different Moon of Endor. So that was the world we fell into. Admittedly, when we first met with George, we told him that we had been big fans of Disney's *Swiss Family Robinson* when we were kids and suggested having pirates for the Ewoks to go up against at the end. He was fine with that as long as they were 7 feet tall and ugly. And he had just watched Heidi with his five-year-old daughter, so he liked the idea of the little girl from the first one becoming an orphan and hanging with grumpy hermit Will Brimley.

When talking to me about *Caravan of Courage*, screenwriter Bob Carrau told me that George Lucas made that film to show young children that they could be self-reliant and that they did not always need an adult to help them. What was important to Lucas about what he wanted you to convey with *Battle for Endor*?

Well, from our first talks with George about making it just about Cindel, the little girl, Jim and I suggested that the parents and brother could be frozen in carbonite or whatever, so they could come back to life later on. But George thought it was important for kids to learn about death and grieving. My wife used to work at *Sesame Street*, and a friend there got us various documents from child psychologists about dealing with death with a child.)

In our email exchanges, before the interview, you brought up *Concorde: Airport 79*, a rare disaster film that hit the four-film mark. Most disaster movies are not turned into sequels, and if they are, they usually stop after the second one. *The Birds 2: Land's* End, a film you wrote, is an animal disaster movie, and a sequel to Hitchcock's classic. Can you talk a little about working on that film and the challenges of continuing that story?

Must I? [Laughs.] That was our super quickest. It was produced by Showtime, and they had a script and a director. Perfectly good director, but the script was not even fair. And it was another "have to shoot now" situation because their location in North Carolina would no longer be available after the 3rd of July. And this was maybe on June 10th? So we flew back to NC with the director, scouted locations with him, and worked out a story. As much as possible it had to use the same locations as the previous script, but otherwise, it was just doing whatever you can do in a week or so.

Why do you think *Elm Street* made it to part four, and beyond, but other properties like *The Birds* and *The Fly* stopped after two movies?
Elm Street is a natural for a series because it has a very strong central, recurring character. He happens to be a villain, but so was Arnold in the first *Terminator*. Maybe they should have done a *Nightmare on Elm Street* where there's evil Freddy up against his good guy ancestor who was burned at the stake as a heretic back in the day. Hitchcock's *The Birds* was one of a kind, and the idea of a sequel was a bit lame. But then, isn't there a reboot floating around out there? The same goes for Cronenberg's *The Fly*. Talk about a movie that had a conclusion that didn't invite a sequel.

In the end, the heroes seemingly win. Freddy is defeated and the souls of his victims have been set free. There is a slight tag at the end suggesting that Freddy is still out there, but the ending feels somewhat conclusive. Can you talk about the ending? Was this intended to be the final film?
When is the ending of any film like this ever conclusive? "Series villains" can be crushed, fried, exploded, dropped from 60,000 feet, and they'll be easily resurrected if the producer wants to do another one. There isn't the slightest chance in the world that they intended this one to be the last. All it had was a tiny tease at the end, and that was plenty. I don't think any viewers walked out saying, "Well, that was the end of Freddy. They won't be able to do any more with him."

SECTION 3
Action Movies

JAMES BOND 4

Thunderball

The posters for *Thunderball* accurately boast that it's the "Biggest Bond of All!" Six decades into the series, *Thunderball* has sold more tickets in the United States than any other film in the franchise.[38] Many Bond aficionados prize the movie, as do I, for its wit (Domino: "What sharp little eyes you've got." Bond: "Wait until you get to my teeth."), its eye-patched villain (Emilio Largo), its memorable stunts (Bond's jet pack), the sumptuous John Barry score, and the thunderous theme song delivered by a forceful Tom Jones ("He looks at the world and wants it all."). In his book *The Battle for Bond*, Robert Sellers writes that Sean Connery is "operating at the peak of his powers, turning in his best-ever performance as 007."[39]

Bond experts John Cork (*The James Bond Encyclopedia*), Jon Burlingame (*The Music of James Bond*), Lee Pfeiffer (*The Incredible World of 007*), Graham Rye (*007 Magazine*), and Steven Jay Rubin (*The James Bond Films*) told journalist Michael Coate that they count it among their favorites.[40] Rubin said that *Thunderball* will always be the 'big one,' when Bond was bigger than anything on the planet, except maybe the Beatles."[41]

Some fans subscribe to the theory that each Bond film is, in some ways, a reaction to the previous one. If *Goldfinger* was big, then *Thunderball* was bigger, more spectacular. If audiences missed Connery in *On Her Majesty's Secret Service*, then *Diamonds are Forever* satisfied that need. If *Moonraker*'s outer space premise was too outrageous, the *For Your Eyes Only* plot about a stolen encryption device brought the series down to earth.

For some, the sex and violence in *Thunderball* seemed to be more intense than it was in its three predecessors, *Dr. No*, *From Russia with Love*, and *Goldfinger*. The British Board of Film Censors, as the United Kingdom's film rating agency was called at the time, was concerned that filmmakers were in danger of going too far. In a 7-page memo, board member John Trevelyan cautioned the producers that *Thunderball* was in peril of being assigned an X certificate, which would have prevented children under 16 from seeing the film.[42] After he "studied"[43] a draft of the screenplay, the censor cautioned the film's producers that the script was "too hotted up"[44] and "seems to us rather less-light hearted than that of the previous Bond pictures."[45] Trevelyan took issue with the script's depiction of "sex, sadism, and violence."[46] (Amusingly, after advising the filmmakers to "take serious notice of these comments" and detailing the script's many suggestive scenes, the solicitous Trevelyan offered to "keep a copy of the screenplay in my office for the time being.")[47]

In many ways, the depiction of women in *Thunderball* is a reaction to the first three Bond movies. The early Bond films, in particular, have been criticized for their depiction of female characters as sex objects, who too easily fall for 007. Consider the plot of *From Russia with Love*, in which a Russian clerk pledges to deliver a decoding machine to the British government on the condition that she can deliver it directly to Bond, whom she claims to have fallen in love with while looking at his photograph.

The movie hinges on Bond's vaunted sex appeal. (Bond's reaction to the demand: "The whole thing's so fantastic, it just could be...true.") Although the villainous and, it is hinted, lesbian Pussy Galore initially claims that she is "immune" to Bond's charm, by the end of the movie Bond's irresistible magnetism (and brute force) has not only turned her to his side but has also caused her, at least briefly, to redefine her sexuality. (Bond: "I must have appealed to her maternal instincts.")

The introduction of Luciana Paluzzi's character Fiona Volpe is a deliberate attempt to redress the depiction of some of the women in the series. Paluzzi is a powerful Italian actress who has also been directed by Fritz Lang and Roger Vadim. It would be a misnomer to dismiss Volpe, an agent of the criminal organization S.P.E.C.T.R.E., as a "Bond girl," a phrase which has come to mean a bikini-clad innocent who coos, "Oh, James" and then falls into 007's outstretched arms. Unlike other women in the series, Volpe is not charmed, rescued, or reformed by Bond. In fact, Volpe delivers a stinging retort that skewers the trope, "But of course, I forgot your ego, Mr. Bond. James Bond, the one where he has to make love to a woman, and she starts to hear heavenly choirs singing. She repents and turns to the side of right and virtue. But not this one!"

Paluzzi's Volpe doesn't intimidate easily. In one scene, Volpe scares the normally unflappable Bond. "You look pale, Mr. Bond. I hope I didn't frighten you." It is also significant that she's not the villain's underling or moll. She doesn't take orders from Largo. She is his superior. When Largo tries to eliminate Bond without her authorization, Volpe admonishes him, "If Bond had died last night as a result of your hastiness, his government would have known for certain the bombs are here. When the time is right, he will be killed...I shall kill him."

When Volpe eventually does join Bond in bed, she is not helplessly succumbing to Bond's seductive powers like "a Bond girl," and their post-coitus scene is one of the most intimate in a Connery-era Bond film." When Volpe asks if Bond likes "wild things," he replies, "You should be locked up in a cage." Volpe purrs, "This bed feels like a cage. All these bars. Do you think I'll be...safe," But it's not Volpe's safety that's in jeopardy, it's Bond's.

Interview with Luciana Paluzzi

How aware were you of James Bond before you were cast in *Thunderball*?
I didn't know much about it. But as you say in the title of your book, the fourth time was the charm. The Bond movies really exploded in popularity because of *Thunderball*. Even today, *Thunderball* is still the biggest grossing of all the Bond pictures, if you translate from yesterday's money to today's money. I had worked with Terence Young before I was cast in *Thunderball*. I made two other pictures with him. [*No Time to Die* (1958), released in the U.S. as *Tank Force*, produced by Albert Broccoli. And after *Thunderball*, Young directed Paluzzi in *War Goddess* (1973)]. I knew that Terence had directed the first two Bond pictures, but I didn't know that they would be as big as they would become.

What was the casting process like for you?
I originally went to London to perform a screen test for the role of Domino [Vitali,

the villain's innocent girlfriend]. Terence had recommended me to the producers. So I went to London, and it seemed like 200 girls were also auditioning. It might have only been 50 but it felt like hundreds. I did the test and went back to Rome where I was residing at the time. I didn't hear back from anyone about it for a long time. Then one day I got a call and both producers, Cubby Broccoli and Harry Saltzman, were on the line. One of them said, "We have good news, and we have bad news." I always like to hear the bad news first because I always like to end up on a happy note. So I said, "Well, what is the bad news?" They said, "You didn't get the role of Domino." I was silent for a moment. I said, "I am really sad about that. But what is the good news?" They said, "The good news is that you were so good in the test that we decided to change the role of the villain to an Italian girl, and you are going to play the villain." I said, "This is not just good news is fabulous news. It is more fun to play the villain than to play an ingenue." So that is how I was cast in the role.

What was the test like?
They put me on film. These days they don't have the patience to put you on film. Instead, they just have you read. I was so lucky because I don't even know how I did with the reading.

Did you read with Sean?
No, Sean wasn't there. There were so many girls who were testing for the role. So they wouldn't have asked Sean to sit behind the camera to read the lines.

Did they give you the actual script or did you perform scenes from a previous Bond film, as has become an informal tradition?
No, they gave me the script.

After you were cast, did Terence Young talk to you about his ideas for the character?
No, I didn't see him until I got on set. He never even called to congratulate me. While he was the one who suggested me for the part, it was up to the bosses about whether I was cast or not. At the end of the day, they are the ones who decided that I should do the part.

What did you like about the character of Fiona Volpe?
It allowed me to do something that I don't do in real life, like being a bad girl and shooting rockets out of a motorcycle. That was a lot of fun for me.

Terence Young gave you a memorable introduction. You are on a bed. The camera starts on the back of your head and your fiery red hair. You twist around, and we see your face, but it's upside down. Then you turn right side up and we finally see your face clearly for the first time.

It was a great introduction. The movie was made many years ago and many films from that time seem old-fashioned. But Terence knew how to create great moments so that it still feels fresh and new. I think Terence really was James Bond. He was the one who injected all those moments of humor. One of the things that I wasn't crazy about when Daniel Craig first started playing James Bond was that he was so serious, so intense. Always with the long face. His Bond originally didn't

Lucianna Paluzzi as Fiona Volpe
Illustration by Pat Carbajal

seem to have much of a sense of humor and slowly that has changed. But I think that that could be the fault of the director because the director could come up to you and say, put a little twinkle in your eye as you said this line. But Terence was the one with all the right touches. As you say, the introduction was terrific. He had this great idea of filling the screen with my red hair.

Then the camera holds on your face for a while, and it says here's a character that you're going to need to watch and pay attention to it for the entire film.
I was very lucky at the time. Today they develop much bigger roles for women. But at the time, women weren't given as many chances in the Bond films and the villains were just men. I think my role was excellent.

Fiona is not the traditional Bond girl. She is a very different character from the women who preceded her. She isn't there for Bond's pleasure. She is driving the plot.
I'm very feminine and sweet but I also have a strong character and I'm not wishy-washy. I've been through a lot in my life. After having gone through a divorce when I was very young, I raised my son alone. And I supported my mom. It was just us—my son, my mom, and me. It was just the three of us. I went through a lot. But I've met Mr. Wonderful, my husband [Michael Solomon]. We've been married 38 years—happy, happy years. I'm a very lucky, content human being.

Do you think they responded to your power and that's why they thought you were better suited to play Fiona and not Domino, who is manipulated by Largo?
I don't know. That is a tough question. I should have asked Terence before he died.

Tell me about your relationship with Terence.
He was like my father. When I got married to Michael in New York, Terence was shooting a movie in Rome. Because my father had been dead for many years, he came in on a Saturday morning to give me away. Then he walked me down the aisle and then the next morning he got back on the plane and went to the set. That is the relationship we had. Terence was like a dad to me. He was one of the most wonderful human beings that I have ever met. Generous to a fault. Intelligent, funny. He had a great sense of humor. When we were working on *Thunderball* we would stay in many different locations between shots. Sometimes in a hotel, sometimes in the trailer, or sometimes in the back of the bar if they didn't have any other place to put us. He had a yacht anchored at the port in Nassau and we would go there and relax there between takes. That was Terence.

***Thunderball* was the fourth Bond film. The previous three films became progressively more popular, yours became, and remains, the most popular.**
Yes, I'll tell you what happened. I can't tell you why, but the fact is people liked it; it was just a question of luck. But everybody knew that by the time we got to making the fourth one, it would be a success, money-wise. We knew that people were going to see it no matter what. You felt it on the set. We were on location in went away, then you had to wait two hours for it to clear to match the preceding shot. the Bahamas for three months. If we were shooting and the clouds appeared, or the sun.

Sean Connery as James Bond
Illustration by Pat Carbajal

When that happens on most film sets, people get nervous. And the producers usually get upset. And everybody is cussing. But on *Thunderball,* everyone was so tranquil. Time is money when you shoot a picture, and you have a whole crew that you're paying. Every day that you lose, millions of dollars go out the window. But not here. It was the calmest atmosphere. Nobody worried when that happened. Instead, they said, "It's fine. We'll wait." Nobody was worried about waiting because they already knew that they were going to make their money back. I've never seen that happen on another film, and I've worked all over the place for what seems like 270 years. But when we were shooting *Thunderball,* there was a security in knowing that the film was going to make a huge amount of money. It was going to be the pinnacle. If the other three films went from zero to 20 to 50, then they knew that this one was going to be a 100.

Was Sean as relaxed as everyone else?
Yes, yes.

Was he still fully engaged in the part?
He was very engaged. He liked it. The part of Bond propelled him into stardom and that's what an actor wants. Later, maybe he wants to go do King Lear, but this part is a way to command your own future. By arriving and having such stardom. He seemed very grateful.

In 1971 Sean said, "I don't think a single other role changes a man quite as much as Bond. It's a cross, a privilege, a job, a challenge, and as bloody intrusive as a nightmare."
[Laughing.] He said that? He probably did. Of course, it's because everyone recognizes you. Let me tell you a story. There is a friend of ours who was the president of Emerson College. He called me and said, Listen, Luciana. I have a young man here who wants to talk to you because he knows everything about James Bond. This young man, with his English accent, was so adorable and, to make a long story short, I said that I will meet him when I come to London. He organized a Bond Club at his school. I went in and talked to the kids. These children are about 11 years old, and you know how old I am. [Luciana Paluzzi was born in 1937.] The kids were in this huge room and there must have been 50 of them. All the questions that they had asked me, from the most tired like, "What's it like to work with Sean Connery?" to "Did you still have to stay on the set after you died?" which I thought was very cute. But all 50 of them raised their hands and had two different questions to ask me. I was so impressed. Why did I bring this up? It's because all these kids seem to know everything about what I did, and they were so young they were obviously not even in the womb when *Thunderball* came out. They're just little kids but they know Bond. Bond propels you to such notoriety that you go out and people know who you are, and they ask for your autograph. It doesn't die because they show the films on TV continuously. It's like a cult. But it's also very nice, it's very rewarding.

There's a very interesting scene with you and Sean in bed. It's sexy but it's also very intimate. However, from photos taken at the time, I gather you and Sean had a lot of company that day.

That is very correct. They decided to have all the photographers from all the magazines and the newspapers on the set that day. But all through the day, besides the crew, we had about 30 extra bodies on the side shooting away in between takes. They would only go silent while we were shooting, but that was only for about a minute. It was fun even though the sex scenes are never really sexy. You're never really naked. Thank God it was not in fashion at the time. Even when I appear to be naked in another scene in the tub, I still had my underwear on. I wasn't totally naked.

Speaking of that scene, Bond enters the bathroom, finds Volpe in the bathtub, and tries to intimidate her so that he can see her bare body. But Volpe refuses to be dominated.
That's why the character was fun to play. I know after so many Bond films that it all becomes like a blur, but I think all the villains and the Bond movies are always interesting and motivated. You can't play a villain as a weak or feeble character.

What are your most vivid memories of making the picture?
There are so many. One on top of each other. The test, the moment they told me that I was going to get the part, Nassau, Pinewood—it's tough to pinpoint just one. But I would say the most vivid memory is when I arrived on set to shoot the scene with the motorcycles. [Fiona assassinates a fellow S.P.E.C.T.R.E. agent with her rocket-firing motorcycle.] It was seven in the morning, and they gave me an instructor. I'd never been on a motorcycle before, so they tried to tell me how to brake and how to accelerate with the handles. If you know what you're doing, it's very good. But if you don't, it's not so good. They said action and I get on the motorcycle and suddenly, I don't know what happened and I see this wall coming at me. Is it breaking or accelerating? And the wall is coming fast, and I went sideways, and I let go of every handle. I let go and I fell with the motorcycle. My leather outfit was shredded, and my underwear was shredded. But my skin was fine. I'm under the motorcycle and I see people running. I hear Terence running towards me and yelling at me. Yelling, "Look what you did." Instead of asking, Are you okay? Instead of saying "poor girl," he was screaming at me. He yelled, "What did you do to the motorcycle?" It was a very expensive motorcycle, and he was very upset. I said, "Why did you yell at me? Why didn't you have me come in before and take lessons instead of just giving me a motorcycle an hour before filming?" I was very upset by that. Then everything was rearranged, and they got a stunt person to do it. That is all so clear in my mind.

What do you remember about your death scene? Your character dances with Bond. She gets shot. He props the dead body on a chair, and quips to a partygoer, "Do you mind if my friend sits this one out? She's just dead."
It was a long night. Especially because there were a lot of extras. All the Junkanoo [a street parade with music, dance, and costumes] scenes were done at night. The floats were real. They have a carnival in the Bahamas at a certain point of the year. So for filming, they had to close down a long street and had the floats circle around again. They never stopped. There was no way to stop them. It's like Rio de Janeiro, once they start going there's no way to stop them. So we had to wait to get exactly the same people in the same float and everything. They were very long nights. And that was the

same thing with the nightclub scene. There are so many people there. It was fine though; it's part of working.

Once the film was completed what were the publicity demands for you?
Today actors go from one talk show to the next. But I don't think those days were as organized. I was only asked to go to the premieres in London, in Dublin, and in Los Angeles. But it wasn't that demanding. Once I was in a new city, they would ask to have an interview, but it didn't even seem like it was organized by the publicity department. It was more like if I were living in Italy, and someone would call me and make an interview request. They would ask to come to the hotel and do an interview. But it was very informal.

Is there a downside to being a Bond woman?
The downside came if I wanted to work on an upcoming film with directors who were very sophisticated, like [Michelangelo] Antonioni and [Federico] Fellini. These days even if you're Italian and have an accent as I do, they will change the role to fit you. But in those days, it was very rare. So I was relying primarily on working in Italy, I also worked in Spain and France. I went to Japan, came back to the United States—I worked all over the world. But the *inteligência,* the intellectuals, didn't want anybody who was in a Bond movie to be in their film. I knew them all. We were all friends and liked each other, but they still had this idea. You think that they would have cast Sean, but they wouldn't. It wasn't because of Sean's acting; he's a fabulous actor. They wouldn't use him because of the association with Bond. It's like having a girl from *Playboy* doing a movie on the Family Channel. It's not because she is not a good actress; it's because of what she's attached to. It's the association.

In the *Thunderball* remake, *Never Say Never Again* (1983), Barbara Carrera played a version of your character.
That film was so different from *Thunderball* that I didn't associate the two. She did a very good job with what she had to do. But it felt like it was different.

Do you keep in touch with other Bond women?
Oh, yes. I've been friends with Ursula Andress for a long time. But it's become more difficult to speak to her now that she lives in Italy. I saw her the last time I was in Rome. I invited her to dinner at a friend's house and she came, and it was wonderful. I'm also friends with Martine Beswick who's also in *Thunderball.* I just saw her. I'm also friends with Carole Ashby (who appears in *Octopussy* and *A View to a Kill*.). Maryam d'Abo (*The Living Daylights*), I adore her. We're very close friends with her and her husband. The four of us went out for dinner. I used to talk to Roger Moore [before he passed away in 2017]. I haven't spoken to Sean in a long time. The last time we saw him we went to his apartment in New York. We had a wonderful afternoon with his wife. But I haven't seen him or talked to him in a while. I'm also friends with Britt Ekland (*The Man with the Golden Gun*). That's more or less it.

Do you go to Bond conventions?
Yes, once in a while. I do that because it's really fun. I just came back from London and did one. I make money and I send it to my favorite charities. Most of my money

James Bond strikes like Thunderball
Illustration by Pat Carbajal

goes to dogs and animals and that kind of charity. There is one woman in Sicily who is an ophthalmologist who goes to work during the day, but she has like 1,575 dogs. People leave them at her house, and she takes them to the vet to be taken care of. So she needs help and she's grateful when she gets it. So I was in London last Saturday. I went to a convention for one day. From 10:30 am to 4:30 pm. There were so many people on the line. I didn't have a break the entire time. I never went to the bathroom or had lunch. I just didn't have the time. It was one after the other after the other. Everyone said something nice. They all have something nice to say to you. They would say, Oh you're my favorite. They might have been lying and they might say that to the next person too. But it makes you feel good. And they're nice. And they're so interested. So it's a big booster for your ego. It's a nice thing to converse with these people who have so much admiration for you. So I do it for these two reasons. I feel better when I walk out and do something good for someone else.

You helped chart a new path for Bond women.
You make it sound like I really thought about all this at the time. I worked hard when I was doing it. I did what I felt was best at the moment. And with the help of Terence who would tell me, you have to be in this spot by the end of this line or you can't stay back there. But I didn't overthink it. I just did it. I just got into the character, and I did it. Sorry to disappoint you.

How do you try to explain the Bond women experience to people?
It's a great ego boost. It makes you feel really good when you go around. I have the genes of my mom. I can still move, run, and walk. I'm blessed. I still look good. I was just saying to someone a few days ago that I've never really done anything with my life that was so fabulous. I never felt like I gave anything to the world that was meaningful. I didn't save any lives. I'm not in South Africa helping kids. I always felt humbled about what I *haven't* done in my life. Until this person said to me, "Don't look at it that way." They said, "Look at the fact that so many people have enjoyed your work and you have given them happiness and pleasure." I said, "Thank you for saying that to me. I've never thought of it." It made me think for a second. I've had so much fun being an actress. Yes, it was difficult at times but overall there is a great difference between being an actor and having to pick rice in China every day. I was really lucky. But as I say, I now have a new way of looking at it.

DIRTY HARRY 4

Sudden Impact

Harry Callahan is miffed. Sure, he's annoyed that a group of punks are robbing his regular diner and taking his favorite waitress Loretta hostage. But what's really sticking in his craw is that there's too much sugar in his coffee. Inspector Callahan explains to the crooks in *Sudden Impact* (1983), "Every day for the past ten years, Loretta there's been giving me a large black coffee. Today, she gives me a large black coffee only it has sugar in it. A lotta sugar. I just came back to complain. Now, you boys put those guns down."

The punks don't comply.

Callahan, or Dirty Harry as he's known among his colleagues, calmly continues, "Well, we're not just gonna let you walk out of here."

A confused criminal, who has the drop on Harry, wants to know who's the "we?" After all, Harry's alone, outnumbered, seemingly unarmed, and still holding his mucked-up cup of coffee.

Putting his cup down slowly, Dirty Harry replies, "Smith…and Wesson…and me."

Before they can react, Harry Callahan draws his gun and fires, making good on his promise.

The Dirty Harry movies, in which the hero repeatedly violates the law, uses excessive force on suspects in his custody, and does away with due process, all in a bid to protect the innocent, are controversial. In a review of Don Siegel's *Dirty Harry* (1971), the first film in the series, the renowned and influential film critic Pauline Kael called the movie "fascist."[48] While praising the filmmaking as a "stunningly well-made genre piece," Kael observed that the movie "proceeds to offer a magically simple culprit for [police officers'] deaths: the liberals."[49] Kael also argued that "*Dirty Harry* is a deeply immoral movie" in which the "evil monster represents urban violence, and the audience gets to see him kicked and knifed and shot, and finally triumphantly drowned. Violence has rarely been presented with such righteous relish."[50]

Roger Ebert, an acolyte of Kael, echoed her thoughts in his review, "The movie's moral position is fascist. No doubt about it."[51] (A 2008 post on Ebert's website may have signaled a change in his views. The post was a letter from a fan, Scott McCrea, who argued against Kael and Ebert's similar views. McCrea countered that not only did the critics misuse the word fascism, which is a form of government, but they disregarded the implications of their position: namely, that "the criminal's rights trump all" and that the "rights of Scorpio's victims, and potential victims, are trampled."[52])

While sympathetic to Callahan's disdain for bureaucracy and sense of justice, *Dirty Harry* was deliberately messy about the challenges police face when protecting citizens. In the interest of pursuing public safety, Callahan sometimes steps over the line and violates due process. Within the context of the story, Callahan might be forgiven for shooting and torturing a serial killer who has terrorized the city of San Francisco, murdered an innocent swimmer, kidnapped a teenage girl (who dies before she can be rescued), and who will later threaten to kill a busload of school children. For Callahan, torture was the only way to get the criminal to *immediately* disclose where the teenage girl had been buried alive so he could get to her before she suffocated. In this context, Callahan's choice to use excessive force could be understood. The movie ends with a frustrated Callahan throwing his badge in the river. Fed up with the entire system, Harry quits his job and walks away. The implication was that since Scorpio has been killed order has been restored to society. Therefore, Callahan is no longer needed as a cop and consequently, there would be no further need for him to violate other suspects' civil liberties.

However, because of the film's success, Callahan's self-imposed retirement became temporary. He was back on duty in *Magnum Force* (1973), which addressed the uncomfortable questions that *Dirty Harry* raised. In *Magnum Force*, a group of police officers follow in Harry's footsteps. Unlike Callahan, they are corrupt and unrestrained in meting out their brand of vigilante justice. When the cops invite Callahan to join their team, he firmly rejects the offer, "I hate the goddamn system! But until someone comes along with changes that make sense, I'll stick with it." The third Dirty Harry film, *The Enforcer* (1976), is where the series started to tire. The weak premise of the film is that the misogynist cop is assigned to work with a female detective. ("She wants to play lumberjack; she's going to have to learn to handle her end of the log.") In the fourth film, *Sudden Impact*, Jennifer Spencer (Sondra Locke), a survivor of a violent gang assault, seeks revenge on her attackers. Callahan has been ordered to track her down, and as he does, he develops romantic feelings for her. Like Callahan, she is acting outside the confines of the law, but unlike Harry, she does not have a police badge to insulate her. *Sudden Impact* is the highest-grossing film of the five-film series, which also includes the final and least financially successful Dirty Harry movie, *The Deal Pool* (1988).

Sudden Impact is the only film in the series directed by Eastwood; Joseph Stinson wrote the screenplay with a story credit by Earl E. Smitha and Charles B. Pierce. Stinson also co-wrote the Burt Reynolds and Eastwood crime-comedy *City Heat* (1984) with Blake Edwards, the Reynold's crime drama *Stick* (1985) with Elmore Leonard, and he did an uncredited rewrite for Eastwood's war movie *Heartbreak Ridge* (1986).

Unlike Eastwood's taciturn character in the *Man with No Name* trilogy, Stinson's Callahan is a talker. In one scene, Harry literally talks a mob boss to death. After, crashing the wedding of the mobster's daughter, Callahan threatens to prosecute him and expose the details of his relationships with prostitutes. The embarrassed and enraged criminal has a heart attack and dies on the spot. Stinson relishes writing the tough-guy dialogue for Callahan, often with a satiric edge. In another scene, a fellow detective observes that the job is getting to him. Callahan ruefully explains, "No, this stuff isn't gettin' to me. The knifings, the beatings, old ladies being bashed in the head for their Social Security checks, teachers being thrown out of a fourth-floor window because they don't give a shit. That doesn't bother me a bit... Or this job, either.

Having to wade through the scum of this city, being swept away by bigger and bigger waves of corruption, apathy, and red tape. Nah, that doesn't bother me. But you know what does bother me?" His colleague inquires, "What?" Callahan responds, "It's watching you stuff your face with those hot dogs. Nobody, I mean *nobody* puts ketchup on a hot dog."

Sudden Impact is best remembered for Callahan's refrain, "Go ahead, make my day." The line caught on unexpectedly and became a national catchphrase. Even President Ronald Reagan, used the phrase as a challenge to Congress if it attempted to pass a tax increase. The American Film Institute determined that it was the sixth-best movie quote of all time.[53] The AFI placed Callahan's tough-talking threat ahead of "May the Force with you," "You talking to me?" and "Bond, James Bond."

Interview with Joe Stinson

Do you remember your first exposure to Dirty Harry?
Oh, yes! When I came to write *Sudden Impact*, I had a very clear idea in my head of how to write the film because of my feelings about *Dirty Harry*. I also had a very rare experience in filmmaking of getting a very clear idea of what you want to do and what everyone else wants to do. I saw *Dirty Harry* in high school or college, and I was blown away. I was a fan of Clint before that, from the Sergio Leone films. Clint had come back to America [after shooting the *Man with No Name* trilogy in Italy] and started doing American-made features like *Hang 'Em High* (1968). When I saw *Dirty Harry,* it was unlike any other crime story movie that I had ever seen. I have always been a fan of detective fiction and crime fiction. I cut my teeth on Dashiell Hammett, Ross Macdonald [whose work became the source for the Paul Newman film *Harper* (1966)] and Raymond Chandler, like everybody does. Police novels as well, including Joseph Wambaugh (*The Glitter Dome*). It was really startling and very different. It all came down to that scene when Harry does *not* put his gun down in that hostage situation with Scorpio. [Clint momentarily lowers his gun as Scorpio uses a young boy as a shield, but then quickly shoots Scorpio and the boy escapes, unharmed.] I didn't realize it at the time, but cops are trained not to put their guns down in those situations. The dramatic impact of it all struck me.

After that, I became aware of film criticism and it seemed that the vast majority of people were talking about movies as something other than entertainment, instead, they were looking at them as art. I didn't realize it at the time, but the French New Wave was happening, and Andrew Saris was talking about the auteur theory. I hate to do Pauline Kael an injustice because she was a great critic, but she and others wrote articles and reviews about the film in a way that I hadn't thought about. It really surprised me. I also disagreed with her theory, which was that there was fascism in the film.

To me, *Dirty Harry* was a story of one guy, a cop, who had a code. He had a very rigid code, and he would do whatever it took to maintain it. It was his Code of Honor. It reminded me of King Arthur and the Knights of the Round Table, and the knights-errant who would go out and travel the countryside opposing unjust situations and trying to put them right. That is how I saw Harry Callahan. He's an interesting

Clint Eastwood is Dirty Harry
Illustration by Pat Carbajal

character and not the two-dimensional cardboard creation that other people were talking about. To me, one of the most important factors in the movie, which I later used, is that he was a loner. He did not have a partner. In the films, they make jokes that no one wants to be his partner. All his previous partners wound up dead or wounded.

Harry had depth. A lot of that depth came from the fact that his wife was killed by a drunk driver. The film didn't explain it and I thought the mystery was more thought-provoking. It was mysterious to me. I wondered about this guy. It was a character that was unlike any other that I've ever seen.

The Leone movies were satirical, but there was no satire in *Dirty Harry*. The direction was blunt. It was a tight lean movie. Nobody was apathetic about *Dirty Harry*. But it didn't have any great insights in it. At the same time, it was just a movie that I enjoyed. But I don't want to paint the wrong picture and suggest that I was up all night reading reviews of the film and underling passages in it.

Dirty Harry didn't lend itself to a sequel. At the end of the movie, Harry essentially assassinates Scorpio and throws his badge into the water. And that was the powerful statement of the film.
A lot of people believe that the ending of the movie is when Harry Callahan doesn't put his gun down and instead shoots Scorpio [played by Andrew Robinson]. But that gets topped when he throws his badge away. But that film has story development right until the last shot. Traditionally, there's filler for the last two minutes.

What did you think about the two sequels?
Dirty Harry stood out for me. *Magnum Force* was really good as well, but it didn't have quite the impact that *Dirty Harry* had on me. I thought *The Enforcer* was entertaining and good but didn't have quite the impact of *Magnum Force*. My Pavlovian response to the sequels was that the bell went off and I was looking for the cheese. I didn't consider that we ate all the cheese [in the first movie] and now we're out.

How did you get involved with *Sudden Impact*?
I was doing theater for the better part of a decade and then I moved to Los Angeles in the early '80s. Over the course of a series of seemingly insignificant events, which later turned out to be significant, I wound up writing trailers. I thought trailers were the things that you hooked up to the back of your car. Although I didn't know what they were called, I always love watching trailers. I wasn't one of those people who would shop right before the movie started. I wanted to arrive five minutes before the trailers started. I love them. There was a guy who had a company making trailers, and he was in partnership with his brother who had an ad agency in New York. I had a meeting with Charlie, who handled the trailer aspects for the business, and his brother Bill Gold handled the posters. Bill is a Hall of Fame illustrator. His first movie poster job right after he got out of the army was *Casa-fucking-Blanca*.

I was out to dinner with Charlie and my wife. He was explaining that he did the trailers and that he also did the copy lines. And I said what's a copy line? He said it's the line that goes on the movie poster. For some bizarre reason, I had always gotten a kick out of reading those one-liners. I said, "Oh you mean like 'We are not alone,' from *Close Encounters of the Third Kind* (1977), or "They're young. They're in love. They rob banks," from *Bonnie and Clyde* (1967). I let him know that I was in the theater, and that I had written some plays and some short stories. Charlie said, "You could make a pretty good living writing trailers. If you would like to see what it's like, I'll pick you up and you can see what's going on." I thought he would forget about it, but he didn't. Instead, he called me one morning and said I'm going to work on a trailer do you want to come, and I said "Sure!"

Charlie took me to his film lab in Hollywood. He brought me upstairs and set me down at a state-of-the-art KEM editing machine. It had three monitors so you could run all the master shots and all the pickup shots at the same time. He said, "I'm going to be cutting a trailer here. But over there on that rack, you'll see 26 reels of pictures and on that rack, you'll see 26 reels of sound. Get someone to show you how to work the machine and sync it up. Here's a grease pencil, make little marks, cut out any pieces of film that you want to use and make me a 90-second to a two-minute movie. You can write lines for it; you can move lines around. Do whatever you want with it." I thought, I can't do this. I had the impulse to leave but I didn't have any money for a cab and LA didn't have any good public transportation. The head of the editing department came over to me and said, "You look like you could use some help." He showed me how to do it and although I'm the least mechanically inclined person, I picked some of it up and I started to work on it. Then Bill Gold came back in, and he said, "Do you have anything?" My first thought was to say "No," but then I thought well, maybe I do. I showed it to him. And that became the trailer to Clint Eastwood's movie *Bronco Billy* (1980).

Charlie and his brother did all of Eastwood's pictures. Clint was completely involved in every aspect of it. He chose the poster. He chose the trailer. It. was part of his formal or informal agreement with Warner Bros., which was that as long as he made pictures for them that were profitable, he could have free reign. At the time, not that many actors were producing their own material. One thing led to another, and I wrote some lines for the poster for *Bronco Billy* A while later, Clint asked Charlie to "get that guy who wrote that one line to write another." I didn't think I was particularly good at it; I thought it was very difficult, but he picked my line again.

Then, one day out of the blue, Clint called and said, "Joe, it's Clint." I thought it was a friend and I said, "Stop fucking around I know it's you. I'm not in the mood." There was a pause on the phone, and he said, "No, it's Clint." He asked me if I ever thought about writing a screenplay. I said something absurd like, "I'm going for the record." He said, "The record?" I said, "Yeah, the only guy in Los Angeles without a screenplay." He said, "Why don't you come in, we'll talk things over, and we'll see if we could work together." I went in, we had a couple of get-togethers, and schmoozed.

In essence, this was the first step forward for the movie. Clint wanted to make a small film, which he would produce but not direct or star in it. He said that he would like to shoot it in the Monterey area because he grew up there and, except for *Play Misty for Me* (1971), he never really shot there. He thought maybe a town like Santa Cruz. He wanted to make a movie for Sondra Locke. They had done *The Outlaw Josey*

Wales (1976) and *The Gauntlet* (1977) together and they were together romantically at the time. Clint thought maybe we should do a movie with somebody coming back to avenge a wrong. The idea seemed like a natural for him because he had done a few of those kinds of movies and he certainly understood the genre.

Can you describe your research and writing process?
As a former method actor, I decided to go to Santa Cruz and do some research. I took a bus up there and spent the better part of a week wandering around, staying with people, talking to people, and I came back. I thought it would be a great place to set the movie because it has a lot of flavor, it had a very dark undercurrent to me. There were a lot of unsolved murders each year. It also had a big amusement pier. While lots of people associate that with kids' stuff and cotton candy, to me they're sinister. Especially at night with the fog rolling in. I was there in the winter, and I got this great, dark vibe from it. [Stinson would later set the brutal attack against Sondra Lock's character and the final shootout at the pier.]

I got back to Los Angeles, and Clint said, "Can you do it?" I said, "Maybe I should write a treatment," and he looked at me like I was insane, which of course I was. Nobody offers to write a treatment when they're offered a movie. A treatment is just a shortcut to bail on your work. He said, "Okay fine," and I went off to write the treatment. I gave it to him a couple of hours later. He called back and asked, "Can you write the screenplay now?"

It was a murder story. I figured if there's a murder there's going to be bodies and there's going to be a cop to investigate it. I called the cop Jack Donnelly [whose name echoes Harry Callahan]. I don't know if I was having flashbacks to the original *Dirty Harry* or if I was just talking to Clint but that's the name that I gave him.

I got the script back from the typist, and I didn't proofread it. I really trusted the typist to do a great job, but I also didn't want to read it because I thought, *God, I probably blew this*. I handed the script to Clint and for a second, both of our hands were on it. In one of my many unguarded moments, I started to laugh. He asked, "What are you laughing at?" I said, "It looks like a real script," and he said, "It is a real script." It felt like the Earth moved and I thought to myself, *can I have this back so I can go home and make it better?* And we had like this little tugging match over the script.

I went home and perversely read it. I had handed it in, but I also wanted to eliminate the suspense that it truly was awful. I started to read it and I thought some of this is not bad. I also realized that the cop character had sort of taken over the script. The balance between the cop and the woman avenger wasn't correct. I thought, *oh well*.

After he read the script, Clint asked, "Do you want to do this again and take another shot at it? But this time," he said, "make it from the cop's point of view. Make it the cop's story. Between you and me, we will make him Harry Callahan." I just choked. I was vapor-locked because it was Dirty Harry. It had been about seven years since the last Dirty Harry film came out. It was never in my mind that my script would become a cop story or would become a Dirty Harry movie.

It could have been the result of something else going on in my subconscious at the time. There was talk of making a new Dick Tracy film and people were speculating that Clint would play Dick Tracy. He made a statement to the effect that he wasn't going to play Dick Tracy and that if he ever did play another cop, it would be Harry Callahan. However, he added, those stories were done because he couldn't see any place else to take the character. In conversations with him, he did say that the studio would be above the moon to make another Dirty Harry movie, but he didn't see any place else to go with him. He told me, "I just don't want to do the same thing." So that all went into my thinking. I said to myself, "Forget about all those other movies, forget about the reality of the situation, working with Clint, and let's just think about the character himself."

How did you approach the character?
I asked myself what happened to the character in the seven years between the films? I kept going back to that scene where we learned that his wife had been killed by a drunk driver and that he's been alone. Sure, Harry's had temporary relationships and one-night stands but there's no real relationship in his life. He doesn't have close friends on the force, which you often see in buddy movies. Then, I recalled that great scene in *Magnum Force* when we saw Harry's apartment. It was bare, to say the least. He opens his refrigerator and there's nothing there except for a couple of empty beer cans and a six-pack of beer still in those plastic loops that hold them all together. He took a beer. Maybe there's a half-eaten cheeseburger and a single takeout container of Chinese food, which he opens, sniffs, and tosses in the trash. So he drinks the beer. That scene was incredibly revealing to me. I latched onto it like it was a Rosetta Stone that revealed where Harry is today. His apartment was bare-boned except for maybe a photo of his wife, and in my mind, he was eating at diners like the one in the Edward Hopper painting *Nighthawks*.

I imagined that he was just walking the streets doing his job, and that's all he had and that's all he wanted. There are some creature comforts here and there but that was it. There was nothing there but his job. His code had morphed itself into his life. It wasn't a code anymore it was his life. I also didn't like the running jokes throughout those other movies about how none of his partners wanted to work with him. I thought maybe he doesn't have a partner because no one will work with him and he's just out there alone like a knight-errant. That's how I saw the character and that's how I reworked him into the script.

My idea on how to try something new or different from the other films was best summed up in the scene where Harry is faced with the choice between handing the avenging woman over to the cops or not. He lets her go. There is a moment when the younger cop comes up and says, "Is that it?" Harry looks at her and he looks at the young cop and he's forced to make a choice. What will he tell the younger cop? Maybe it's the first choice he's had to make for years. Part of that is he'd just been going forward; he's always had this path to follow and that's it. This is the first time that he has been brought up short, and it challenges everything that he's devoted himself to, his Bushido [the samurai code of honor], and he says, "Yeah, that's it," and he lets her go. Then, they walk off together.

I very much had in my head the end of *Dirty Harry*, when he tossed his badge in the lake. At the time, I never really asked what happened next. Did he go in and did he really quit or did he go in and just say I lost my badge? Did he go on sabbatical, and they brought him back in? I didn't worry about any of that stuff. To me, it was enough that he was back for *Magnum Force*. Those concerns weren't as important as his emotional reaction to the situation. But for this new movie, I wanted a kind of symmetry with *Dirty Harry*, and him walking off with her at the end of *Sudden Impact* echoed tossing his badge away. That whole film was about setting the wrong to right, finding the killer, bringing the killer to justice, and returning the world to right. The natural order was out of whack but finding the killer returned the world to its natural order. But tossing the badge flipped that in a very subtle way. In the same way, having him walk away with her created that symmetry and it just felt right. I didn't really think all this stuff out. I just did it. But I was feeling it. It was my gut instinct.

How did it feel to write dialogue for Dirty Harry?
I felt like I had the rhythm of Callahan's speech down. Clint once said to me, "You write like I talk." It probably comes from my days in the theater where backstage we used to do imitations of Dirty Harry to amuse each other. I had his rhythm and that was not a small thing. Aside from all this artsy-fartsy stuff, I felt like I had a sense of what Harry sounded like. And what Harry sounded like revealed his character. There's a school of thought which believes the way people talk, the way people put their words together, is a huge insight into the way people are, and I certainly felt that. Especially for Harry because the way Harry talks *is* who he is.

What was Eastwood's reaction to your first draft?
A week after I gave him that draft, he called me and said that he had three points. He told me what the first point was, and I said, Okay I get it. The same thing happened with the second one, but for the third one, I said, "This is what I was trying to do, and this was the point I was trying to make." He said, "Oh, that's right, okay. I get it." It was an incredibly important and revealing moment for me. Clint Eastwood was arguably the biggest star in the world at that time and I was a completely inexperienced writer. I felt like we were at the old Hollywood bungalow, and someone made an appointment with a screenwriter and ordered a tuna fish sandwich. Here I am, and I'm the tuna fish.? But I got there first. The actual screenwriter had a flat and they thought *I* was the screenwriter. That's how I felt. So this idea that this fledgling young guy would say, "Well, you see, this is how it is," and he said, "Ah, yeah, you're right." It was amazing that he would listen to me.

Do you remember what any of those points were?
Clint wanted Callahan to find out things at the same time the audience does. That was a great note, and it just turned my head. I hadn't done that for the first two acts and part of the third act, but then I wanted to change it around so that the audience would be a little bit ahead of Harry. Of course, when the audience knows things that the characters don't it's called dramatic irony. I was using dramatic irony to kick things into gear as the film headed toward its conclusion. He said for these kinds of movies he likes the audience and the character to discover things at the same time. A bell went off for me. It was an important way to keep the audience empathetic toward the

character. It puts the audience and the character in the same head and heart. When they experience things simultaneously, it makes the audience and the character one.

In the ending Harry Callahan lets Sondra Locke go. Is Harry's decision solely based on Callahan's perception of the limits of the law or are we also seeing a change in the character?

Yes and no. I was saying that his code became his life and his code morphed into his life. It was based on justice and the rightness of the situation. At the end of *Dirty Harry*, when Harry takes the shot and kills Scorpio, that's what Harry felt he had to do. The thing about Harry Callahan is that he does see shades of grey and the complexity of certain dilemmas, but he sees his way through them. The conclusion that he comes to is the one that he sticks with. Even if the answer is difficult to pull off. The shot he took at Scorpio was very difficult but for him, he knew he had to do it. Why? Because it was the right thing to do. At the end of *Sudden Impact*, he lets her go and I thought that would be revealing about his character. It was a reversal of his code. She was a killer, but she was also a victim. The question became what is he going to do about it?

Having said that I don't want to lessen the second part of what you said which is yes, Harry was opening himself up to her. They walk off-screen together as the camera goes into a helicopter shot, but the implication is that he's not just going to take her to the bus stop. They were probably going to go somewhere and sit down and talk. Or maybe he would just take her back to her house and they would just sit and look at each other. Or if he took her home and left maybe he would return later, and they would examine their consciousness. But even if he did drop her off at home to recover, you knew that he would be back the next day. I don't think I thought of that in those exact terms but that was what was going on in my unconscious at the time.

Some of the criticism of the films was that he was a rigid, mindless character. They said he was too reactionary, and I thought it was all off base. I think there was a lot more going on there that had to do with the past events of his life and how that shaped his personality.

Harry Callahan and Sondra Locke's characters were developing a romantic relationship prior to him discovering that she was an avenging woman. Do you think that relationship continues? Or does that have to stop based on the revelation?

I don't know if I've ever thought about this before, but I think that they do continue, or they would at least try. I don't know if their history would allow it to continue. If Harry were with her every day, would he just let it go? But I never pictured him as a guy who would let stuff go. But then again, he was the kind of guy who once he makes the tough decision then he goes with that decision. He's not going to have second thoughts or whine about what he should have done. He'll take what comes.

You correctly observed that the first three Dirty Harry films are free of satire. I think that while you respect the character there is also satire in your approach to him. For example, he has a dog called Meat Head that urinates anywhere he wants. There's a car chase in which Callahan is driving a bus filled with senior

citizens.

[Laughs] That is partly reflexive and partly intentional. My first draft was way darker. But, in light of Harry's backstory and in light of what happened to the Sondra cookbook character, it needed some humor. To see the true darkness of something, you need a little light for contrast. You need some light to see how dark something truly is. Even in the darkest and bleakest of stories you need some character somewhere shining some light. You need that perspective. So he sees a crime and he jumps in the nearest vehicle. In a different movie, he would have grabbed a car, but you have seen that 200,000 times. I thought, what would be bizarre and interesting? They did have those vehicles in Santa Cruz, so the answer revealed itself. So he's in this bus and he turns around and sees the senior citizens. But that's kind of Callahan as well. Harry reacts, makes a decision, and then he looks back. Sometimes that's quite dangerous. He will go for it because he's driven. But in this case, he was driving an old folk's bus and I thought that was funny.

But maybe what was then unconscious I'm saying now, but I don't know if I was thinking that then. But certainly, within the framework of the story, which was so dark, I knew I needed some light and humor to balance the rest of it. Stephen King says that in his writing he tries to balance a horrific moment with a moment of humor. It gives the audience a moment to recalibrate, or the audience can reach overkill and they don't feel anything. They just get overloaded, and nothing means anything. That was just good energy to me. I thought at the time, and I still do, that it didn't cross the line. You can't burlesque burlesque because then you just have a pile of shit. It wasn't parody; it was lightness.

But the other thing in terms of spending time with him and talking back and forth is that you realize he's funny. We would laugh a lot. I knew that he had a sense of humor. It was dry. We'd be having a meeting or talk, and he'd start laughing. I hung out on the set. He was also generous. He was always looking for me and when he spotted me, he'd bring me over and say, look through the camera, this is what I'm trying to do.

Let's talk more about the dialogue because there are a lot of great speeches in this movie. The most famous one is "Go ahead, make my day."

After I turned the script in, I didn't work on any more trailers. I didn't work on the trailer for *Sudden Impact* either. But when I saw the trailer, I noticed that the line was in there twice. And that's because Clint said to Charlie, "This is the line. Make sure it's in the trailer." So Charlie put it in the trailer twice. Clint was so right from the get-go that that line would resonate. I didn't think it would. I thought it was a good line absolutely, but I thought there were other good lines in there too. But Clint knew it was *the* line. Everything that I thought about his character went into that line.

I do remember that line. I have a total recall of the afternoon I wrote the line. That line has everything that I've been saying, everything that I felt that I had to do in the script that people wanted to see in a Dirty Harry movie. By people I mean me, if I were sitting in an audience, I would want a confrontation scene [where Harry faces off with a bad guy with a gun and makes a threatening speech]. Okay, have to have a confrontation scene. After the first movie, it became part of the heart of a Dirty Harry film. I thought I wanted to get it out of the way early in the movie so that people wouldn't sit through the whole movie wondering when it was going to happen.

They would be looking ahead; I couldn't have that. I thought I had to be realistic about the viewer's experience and expectations because if I were in the audience, I would look for that. So I had to write one. Short of cutting to black and having a sign come up saying there will be no confrontation scene. I had to write one. I wanted it early on so that we could have it and it would be great but then we can move on. That afternoon I thought, well who is Harry? I spent all afternoon thinking about that, trying to understand his character and who he was, and I wrote it. Clint delivered the line perfectly. He goes up to the last man who's holding the waitress hostage. He's got his gun by his side, and he says, "I know what I'm going to do. So, decide what you're doing to do." All of that is what "go ahead, make my day" means. That was the sense behind it. That was the thought process.

There were other good lines. Perhaps not for the ages, not for Bartlett's, but I always got a kick out of the conversation between Harry and the punks that took place in the elevator after the trial, when the punks are taunting Harry. [Callahan says, "Listen, punk. To me, you're nothin' but dogshit, you understand? And a lot of things can happen to dogshit. It can be scraped up with a shovel off the ground. It can dry up and blow away in the wind. Or it can be stepped on and squashed. So take my advice and be careful where the dog shits ya!"] I got a kick out of that scene.

I also like some of the stuff with Harry's friend Horace, including the line, "You need to strain the remains for fingerprints." There are a couple of good lines. [In the scene Callahan gives Horace's gun faint praise. Horace replies, "Not bad, my ass! You've got to strain the remains for the fingerprints." Callahan coolly counters, "Well, this is the .44 Magnum Auto-Mag and it holds a 300-grain cartridge. And, if properly used, it can remove the fingerprints."] The "strain for remains" line is good and it's there for an impact, but it doesn't have the same effect as, "Go ahead, make my day." I wasn't trying to come up with a buzz line. I wasn't trying to come up with a line they'd use in a trailer or that would be repeated in 20,000 commercials and that Reagan would say. That was a character line. To me, that was all about revealing the character. He was saying you do whatever you want to do because I know what I'm going to do. You could die, I could die, we could both die, you could give up. You've got a lot of choices. Make a choice.

How did it feel when Ronald Reagan, the President of the United States, quoted lines from your movie?
Absolutely weird. Completely weird. I didn't hear it initially, but many people called me and said, "Put the TV on!" When I originally wrote it, I was just a guy in my apartment. At the time I think we were working on something else, and Clint would come over and pick up pages. I was in my cave. Just you in a room by yourself. You just sit in a room by yourself, and you work a certain number of weeks or months. In the old days before the internet, you'd work in your little room and you'd take a draft to another a little room, maybe the agent's little room, or the studio, and give it to the studio executives or give it to Clint. But they're all in little rooms, so you go from one little room to another room. If you're lucky everybody gets to go away on location for

a couple of months and shoot a movie. They're having fun but where are you? Well, you're in your little room working on the next project.

Clint had invited me to the dailies. He said, "Come up to my room and go to the dailies." I just thought of this now because you're bringing me back into it in a very visceral way for the first time. I remember the first scene I saw at dailies, and I'm thinking wow this is good. But it felt weird because I wondered who wrote this? Did he get another writer? Did he write this himself? Did they improvise this? Well, this is good. Okay, that's okay. But it took me another 90 seconds to realize I wrote it. It was so otherworldly to me. I thought I could see these scenes in my head, but I had no idea. It was such an out-of-body experience watching the dailies that I thought somebody else wrote it.

I was there at the very last scene at the rap of the whole movie. I said to Clint, "I've never been on a movie set. This is my first time. For what it's worth I think you did a hell of a job." He said, "I just shot it the way you wrote it." That's the best thing anybody's ever said to me about my writing. "I just shot it the way you wrote it."

Of the five Dirty Harry films, why was *Sudden Impact* the biggest commercial hit?
I'd like to think because it was good. I also think it was stripped down; it had the essential elements. I think all of the things that we talked about play their part. But I don't think anyone who saw the film as an audience member thought about any of the things that were talking about right now. That's not their job. They should just watch a movie and react to it. That's their job. But this one had a lot of stuff that was clear in my head, and I got it down on the page. And it was tight. I also think that time had something to do with it too. There had not been a Dirty Harry movie for seven years. That could also have been a disaster because while there are big fans of the character, if you take a seven-year break people are not always going to embrace you. I think there was a little more attention to it and a little bit more of, " Let's see what you've got." So the focus and the scrutiny were stronger. People would say, "Harry's back. I wonder what this is going to be like. Is it going to be awful?"

What is the appeal of Harry Callahan?
The appeal of Harry to me is the same as it was when I first saw the first movie, which is that he's a character who lives by code and doesn't deviate from it. He makes decisions based on this code. He acts based on this code regardless of personal expense. Are you going to say all that to your boss even if you think it? Are you going to call him an asshole? Who gets to do that in real life? Being able to see through to the essence of the situation and to be able to handle it in the best way that you can and to stick to the decision. It's his decisiveness.

I didn't think about it then but it's also the knight-errant. But it's Westerns as well. Even though Clint put on a sports coat and a tie, the image is Clint from the Westerns. And the characters that he played like Josey Wales. Orson Welles has said that it's one of the best Westerns ever made. [Welles said: "I suppose Clint Eastwood is the most underrated director in the world today...They don't take him seriously...an actor like Eastwood is such a pure type of mythic hero-star in the Wayne tradition that no one is going to take him seriously as a director. But someone ought to say it. When

I saw [*The Outlaw Josey Wales*] for the fourth time, I realized that it belongs with the great Westerns...of Ford and Hawks and people like that."⁵⁴] It was Clint's first directing job because he took over during production.

I don't normally talk about this stuff but because you asked, I'll answer. Maybe the times also played a part. There was a sense then that an individual could make a difference. I wonder if the audience thought, "If Harry can make a difference, maybe we can make a difference." Harry's surrounded by bureaucracy. Harry's surrounded by criminals. Harry's surrounded by a shabby personal life, but he's doing things. He's doing something because he thinks it's right. He's trying and, in the end, he is persevering. On a very subterranean level, I think that's what's going on. If you just go back to the Greeks and Aristotle, it's the idea of catharsis. You see Oedipus go through his journey and you may feel one way or the other, but regardless you are certainly wrung out emotionally. And you might feel a little bit better about things because it can't get any worse. There hadn't been anything else quite like that then. Subsequently, there have been a billion imitations. If I had to write Dirty Harry right now, I'd have to figure it out and ask myself who is Harry now? I think that people could connect with a character like that because the character was out front. I also want to tell you that it was shot terrifically by Bruce Surtees, who is an artist, edited by Joel Cox, and had music by Lalo Schifrin. Clint was what he always is, which is present. He was clean and there wasn't a wasted gesture. He was spot-on. There was no indication that he was acting. He was just being. Sondra was terrific. I think a lot of it just came together. The elements were so mixed. The same guy who said, "Thy eyes see not thyself but by reflection" also said, "But the elements were so mixed."

If one were now to make a Dirty Harry film, where is Harry now in his life?
Oh, boy. That would take some thought. You know I wrote another one.

Did you?
Yes, I wrote another one and Clint said, as he sort of does with everything, "We will do this when the time is right."

What's the backstory of the unmade sixth Dirty Harry movie?
I was hanging out with Clint, and he said, "Can you read a couple of scripts and tell me what you think?" We used to have a phrase that you need a friend in court. He said, "Just tell me what you think, and we'll go from there." I said, "Okay, fine." Sometimes he would like the character but not the rest of the script. He would say, "Tell me if you think the character is good and the right way, we could rework the rest of the script." We were doing this a lot. He said, "Let me show you this," and he took out a copy of *Unforgiven*. This was several years before he made it. I was a big fan of Clint doing Westerns, so I said, "I can't wait for that." He said, "Well, when the time is right. It's not right now. I want to make it, but we'll see when the time is right. " It was always about the timing. This is also why I say that timing had a lot to do with the success of *Sudden Impact*.

So I wrote this other Dirty Harry movie. I did it with a friend of mine. I told you that the first trailer that I did was for *Bronco Billy*. Well, the writer of that picture was Dennis Hackin who is a terrific screenwriter. From time to time, Clint would say,

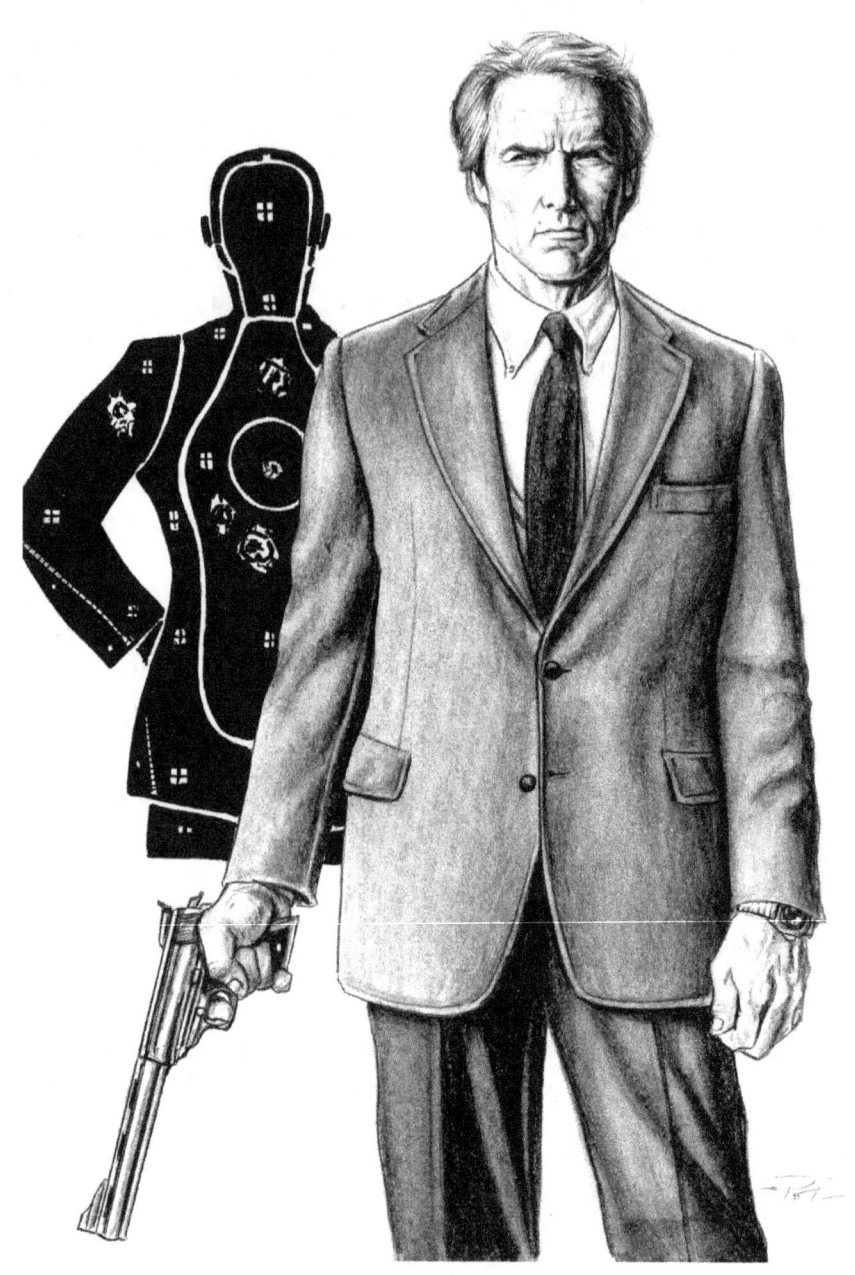

Go ahead, make his day.
Illustration by Pat Carbajal

"You've got to meet Dennis. He's a great guy." I subsequently learned that he would say similar things to Dennis about me. He would say, "You guys would get along." He said it a couple of times. I remember one afternoon the phone rang and it was Clint. He said, "I'm down in the bungalow with Dennis. We're just chewing the rag." I remembered that phrase because my father used to say it. He said, "Do you want to come over and chew the rag with us?" I came over and we were making a lot of jokes and having a great time. And somehow doing another Dirty Harry came up.

It was all silly stuff, wouldn't it be great if Dirty Harry does this or just that? It was ridiculous stuff. Suddenly, he said, "You two guys can get something together and I'll call business affairs and make the deal for you." Suddenly, he's walking us to the door, and he says, "Let me know when you come up with something." I'm looking at Dennis who I just met a half hour ago and vice versa. As I recall, I said "Are we writing another Dirty Harry picture? Are we partners in this?" He said, "I guess we are." I said, "This is just crazy." He said, "Let's see what we come up with." Then we went somewhere else and got more coffee and we were thinking about outrageous things. It started to become real. Then we went to San Francisco, and we drove around, and we talked. We came up with a Dirty Harry movie. We used to joke that it was the ultimate Dirty Harry movie. When we turned it in Clint said, "If and when the time is right." That was his whole thing, timing. For someone to have something that they loved and not want to do it immediately was unique to my decades of work in Hollywood. Usually, it's the opposite. They're all rushing toward something.

What do you remember about the premise of that script?
This might have been about ten years later, so maybe it was the early '90s.

So that's post-1988's *The Deal Pool*, the final Dirty Harry movie?
It was several years after *The Dead Pool*. I'm guessing about '93 or '94. Harry was even more solitary. I remember less about the actual script than I do thinking about it and figuring it out. I think it had to do with the police, government corruption, and the San Francisco Police Department. I remember saying, it would be interesting if he goes up against the San Francisco Police Department. Or part of it. We were purposely trying to make it as out there as we could. We were trying to make it as bleak as possible. It was set in the city of San Francisco and we're trying to make it a corrida [a bullfight]. Think of *The Good the Bad and the Ugly* and the circle with Eli Wallach, Lee Van Cleef, and Clint. And the Sergio Leone film with Charles Bronson, *Once Upon a Time in the West* (1968), was very much in my head. But I'm bad at coming up with a synopsis of it. If you were to ask me how to explain *Sudden Impact,* I'd say Harry tracks a killer. But I wouldn't even know how to finish describing it because it would sound so stupid to me.

Based on what you're saying about *Once Upon a Time in the West*, how about this? Harry tracks the killer who winds up connected to the upper echelon of the police department?
Yeah, something like that. This was Harry investigating his own department. There it is. Harry senses that there's something rotten in the state of Denmark. He just has an instinct, and everybody turns on him, even the good guys, just because he's Harry

Callahan. They think he's a wacko. There is no port in the storm. That was where we started. Horace, or a character like him, would say something like, "Harry, you've been at this too long. You're seeing ghosts where there are none. You're seeing shadows and the sun is shining." That might have been a line.

Whew, that's a good one.
I should go write that down. I've got to ask Dennis if I came up with that one.

It's interesting that you mention *Once Upon a Time in the West* because that film depicts the end of an era. Were you thinking of it as the final Dirty Harry film?
I don't know if I ever thought of it exactly that way but yes. After they did *Once Upon a Time in the West*, I was never interested in another one of those kinds of films.

It was the end of the Western.
It was the apotheosis. That's what we were going for.

***Once Upon a Time in the West* was about the formation of a modern America and the end of a certain kind of man, the loner. So maybe this Dirty Harry film would be less about fighting an individual bad guy and more about the system.**
Yes.

The villain is larger than anyone one individual.
The larger villain is the shadow bureaucracy.

Do you recall what you would have called it?
No, and I'm not even sure we gave it a name. As it turned out, Clint didn't make it. Maybe other projects were better, or they needed another pass. Who knows? It just never came about.

I'm trying to think of what an old Harry Callahan would be like. You might say that Eastwood explored that territory in *Unforgiven* (1992).
That's a good point. I hadn't thought of that. Maybe by making *Unforgiven* another Dirty Harry wasn't necessary. Certainly, there were large differences between Harry Callahan and William Munny [the aging gunfighter who has renounced violence but finds himself drawn to it nevertheless]. William Munny was an evil man; he was a killer. He had a sense of good, but he was a ruthless, bloody killer. Which Harry never was. But what is important are the aspects of coming to grips with everything.

There is a line in *Sudden Impact* when a colleague asks Harry what's troubling him. Harry says that police work is like, "Having our fingers in the holes and the whole dike is crumbling around us." That's what your unmade Dirty Harry film sounds like.
That's a good way of looking at it. That's who Harry is. If there is a hole in the dike, then Harry's going to try to plug it. And if someone tells him you might as well give up, there are three other leaks, that doesn't matter to him. He sees a leak and it's his job to plug the leak. His character is such that he says that despite the societal war, this is my battle and I'm going to fight it. It's worth it.

RAMBO 4

Rambo

Some fictional characters have professions that lend themselves to continuing adventures. For instance, James Bond and Ethan Hunt can be assigned a new mission; Rocky Balboa can strap on his gloves another time and agree to fight another boxer, Dirty Harry and Sherlock Holmes can catch another case; James T. Kirk can land on another planet, and Hannibal Lecter can always get the munchies. But what does a franchise do when its lead character initially has no profession?

While John Rambo is a soldier who can be sent to different areas of the world to fight, that's not how audiences discovered the character in *First Blood*, the first Rambo movie. At the start of *First Blood*, Rambo, played by a doe-eyed Sylvester Stallone, has already put down his weapons. Rambo only becomes violent because he is harassed and physically abused by the sheriff's office while Rambo is only seeking peace and solace. But because the film was a hit, it was necessary to put the reluctant soldier back into wartime situations.

It's interesting to ponder whether telling serialized stories about the character changes his trajectory. Does it by its very nature make him the one thing, he doesn't want to be—a weapon. In the first film, Rambo's only goal is to avoid capture and stay alive. In that way, he shares something with similar heroes who, like John McClane in *Die Hard* and Ellen Ripley in *Alien*, are reactive heroes. They are fighting to survive. At some point, these characters either become figures of folly who attract violence and mayhem, or they deliberately choose to place themselves in harm's way, as the heroes that we believe them to be.

As such, Rambo cannot go from film to film, being a victim of circumstance. In *Rambo: First Blood Part II* and *Rambo III*, the Vietnam veteran accepts dangerous missions, which motivate the plot. In *Part II*, Rambo's mission is to rescue veterans who are prisoners of war and in *Part III*, Rambo must rescue his former commanding officer and father-figure Colonel Samuel Trautman (Richard Crenna).

Rambo, the fourth film in the series, picks up twenty years after Rambo saved Trautman. The script, written by Stallone and Art Monterastelli, describes Rambo thusly: "Though having matured, the long-haired outcast still resembles the one-time super-soldier, whose monastic lifestyle has kept his body strong."

In *Rambo*, John Rambo, living a peaceful life in Burma, makes a living catching and selling snakes, and transporting people and goods on his boat. Rambo is hired by a group of missionaries to aid Burmese victims of war. When those missionaries are captured by the brutal Burmese army, Rambo returns to his violent ways and rescues them. In a coda, Rambo returns to America and his father's farm.

As Rambo was essentially a nomad in the first film and a man without a country in the second, third, and fourth movies, Rambo's homecoming seemed like a fitting conclusion to the series. Yet, the unexpected success of *Rambo* led to another sequel *Rambo: Last Blood*, in which the injured veteran literally rides a horse into the sunset.

Art Monterastelli Interview

What are the most important things to keep in mind while writing a Rambo film?
I'd say the single most important thing you need to know when you're writing a movie like Rambo is that you're ultimately writing a "star" movie role. Rambo has become an iconic figure, and even though we went against the grain in many ways, especially compared to the two previous films, Rambo is still, by choice, a solitary figure. He's older and probably a little wiser, but at the very core of his being, he's still a warrior. In the movie, he's now a man in his 60s, or at least pushing 60, but he's still living by the same warrior code that he's believed in, and made his own, since the very first movie. Hand in hand with this realization is the fact that you're writing for an actual movie star. It could be argued that Stallone's star has to some degree diminished here in the States, but in the rest of the world Sylvester Stallone, definitely Sylvester Stallone as Rambo, is still a major star. He's even more than that. When you're talking about Stallone as Rambo, you're not only talking about an international movie star, but you're also talking about a truly iconic figure. And that's something you have to be aware of when you approach the script.

What was the hardest aspect of writing the fourth film of the Rambo series?
The most difficult aspect was finding a story that would do justice to the Rambo character. Over the years there had been a lot of attempts to come up with a script for the fourth Rambo. For whatever reason, the vast majority of those scripts recast Rambo as either an undercover cop or a disgruntled ex-cop who's hired to travel into Mexico to recover his best friend's daughter. I was working with Sly on another project, an HBO mini-series about the LAPD's Rampart scandal when he called me to talk about ideas for Rambo. The first thing we agreed on, and the reason I probably got the job, was that Rambo was *not* a cop. He was a soldier. A warrior. And so we needed to find a "soldier's or warrior's story" to make the screenplay work. Sly himself had already done some research on the political situation in Myanmar, formerly Burma. It made sense to both of us that Rambo was still living somewhere in Southeast Asia, so Myanmar made a lot of sense in terms of the world we were trying to create.

The next most difficult thing was the characterization of Rambo as a man who is still living by the warrior code but is almost sixty years old.

***First Blood* is an effective and taut thriller, in which despite his considerable skills, John Rambo is an underdog. In *Rambo 2* and *3*, he's a force of nature, a one-man army. *Rambo 4* returns the character to its roots and makes him more vulnerable. Can you talk about that approach and what decisions you made to make him more human?**
Your last question leads directly to this one. And to be honest, the most difficult thing was probably the characterization I was just talking about. Stallone liked the work I had done on a movie called *The Hunted* (2003), which starred Tommy Lee Jones. He appreciated the degree of realism that the film tried to achieve. *Rambo 4* wasn't going to be about a superhero shooting or pulling Soviet jets and jet helicopters out of the sky. There might come a point in the movie where he was forced to take on

an entire army, but we weren't as interested in the whole superhero complex this time out.

The movie is set in a war-torn part of the world, but Rambo himself is doing everything he can to avoid any new wars. He's not a mercenary for hire when the movie opens. Rambo's a former soldier who's made his separate peace with the world and is supporting himself by capturing and then selling highly poisonous snakes. An attractive woman in her mid-thirties approaches him with a small group of American missionaries. The woman wants Rambo to lead them "upriver" so they can rescue her sister, who happens to be another missionary. The other members of her group don't trust Rambo, they think he's nothing but a cynical mercenary, prepared to do anything for money.

But Rambo surprises them, and the audience, when he turns them down. The truth is, even though he still embraces parts of the warrior code, he's sick of war and he's sick of killing. On top of that, he's not particularly fond of suicide missions, and that's what he thinks these people are on. The woman goes to see him at his private quarters, later that night. She tries to convince him that he is their last hope. She knows they're entering an incredibly dangerous part of the world, but she has no choice: her sister is missing, and she has to find her. Since Rambo has no blood connection to the woman, he doesn't have the same imperative.

A few scenes later, when the woman's group is ambushed and taken prisoner, Rambo's emotions get the better of him. A part of him is angry with himself for not agreeing to be their guide from the very beginning, but an even bigger part is angry about the savage and incredibly violent world they all live in. We see that part of the "warrior code" re-awakening inside him. It's not a logical move—everything that happens tells him he was right all along. It would have been an insane choice to agree to take them "upriver," and it's an even more insane choice now. But the true warrior doesn't look at the world logically. The true warrior is always the servant of either a grandmaster or simply the greater good.

While he's not a superman in *Rambo 4*, Rambo remains a mythic figure. Can you talk about how you wanted to render those mythic aspects of the character?
Sometimes the simplest or most obvious choice is the most important. In *Rambo 4*, it was extremely important to find the right "job" or project that he had taken on. We know he's retired from the actual battlefields, but the actual job he had taken up tells us a hell of a lot about his character.

In an early draft, I had him working alone on a beach in India, salvaging scraps of metal from the biggest naval graveyard in the world. It would have been great if we could have shot at this specific location, but it simply wasn't in the cards. Stallone came up with the idea of "hunting snakes" during a location trip to Thailand. It turned out to be perfect for the character. It was exotic and wildly dangerous, and it was also something you do far, far away from human civilization. In both cases, we know the man wants to be alone. We know he wants to be as removed from what we think of as normal society as he can be. At the same time, he's not simply meditating and chopping wood, the more Zen approach. He still has the warrior spirit in his heart, which means he's still not completely at peace with himself. It's almost as if, even in

Sylvester Stallone is John Rambo
Illustration by Pat Carbajal

seclusion, he has to do some kind of penance.

What was most important to Stallone about how this character was portrayed?
The most important thing for Stallone was to find a way to keep it real. This brings up back to your question about "the most difficult aspect of writing the script." The expectations for a new Rambo movie—the first in about twenty years—were enormous. At the same time, because of a fairly limited budget, the general age of the character, and the actor playing him, we couldn't go in for the pyrotechnics of Rambo 2 and 3, which was fine by Stallone. He was always more interested in who this guy was now. Not only approaching sixty, not only living out in the jungle catching poisonous snakes but also the "soldier" who never went home.

That's the thing, I believe, that reawakened the warrior spirit in his heart. The female missionary was from "back home." Yeah, she was blonde and pretty, but she was also a little beat up. Her American idealism had brought her halfway around the world, in pursuit of a mission that was never *not* a suicide mission. Yes, it's illogical. But the warrior spirit isn't about logic, it's about "honor." At first, Rambo says no to her offer. But when a second opportunity presents itself, even though it's still a suicidal mission, even for him, he has no choice [but to accept the mission]. This is the "choice" he made a long time ago. That doesn't mean he likes it. He doesn't. He's no longer a young warrior. Nightmares plague his dreams, and he isn't interested in adding any new ones. But the young American woman's plight, and her sister's, stirs something inside him.

You pointed it out in one of your later questions. I forget the character's question, but Rambo's answer, later in the movie, is "There isn't one of us that doesn't want to be someplace else. But this is what we do. This is who we are."

In *Rambo 3*, Rambo's mentor Colonel Trautman tells him, "You're always going to be tearing away at yourself until you come to terms with who you are. Until you come full circle." As you just indicated, in part 4, Rambo says, "There isn't one of us that doesn't want to be someplace else. But this is what we do, who we are." Who is John Rambo? Is he a weapon? A victim? An instrument of peace?
John Rambo is a warrior. Was he always a warrior? No. He was drafted into the military and sent to Vietnam at a very young age (probably while he was still a teenager). Later on, he rose through the Special Forces ranks. It's not 100 percent clear, but the myth indicates that it was Special Forces training that turned him into the elite soldier, the elite warrior that he, in time, became. The mythic element in Rambo, I believe, begins in the first movie, and is cemented in the opening of the second, when Rambo realizes that no matter what he chooses to do, he was born to be a soldier. It's at this point that he fully commits to Bushidō, the Japanese Warrior Code, and makes his "separate peace" with the rest of the world. He's very much aware of the fact that he'll always be the bull in the china shop, a little bit too much for polite society. In *Rambo 4*, he hasn't forsaken the warrior code, if he'd done that, he would have been able to finally return to his home in the United States.

Deciding to rescue the missionary, knowing that it's pretty much suicide, going into that particular part of Burma, is not only Rambo coming out of self-imposed retirement but also doing it in a way that reconnects him with the "home" he hasn't seen in over 40 years. You could almost say he's "halfway home" just by deciding to rescue the missionaries.

Rambo is not a victim. Although he was drafted while still a teenager, and most likely trained as an elite soldier before he was able to fully understand the commitment he was making, Rambo is in no way a mindless killing machine. He embodies the Japanese Warrior Code in almost every way…making his separate peace with society in general; isolating himself from that society when he decides to retire from the battlefield, even though there are still some things gnawing at his subconscious; and finally, making his own decision about when he's going to fight and, ultimately, when he's going to die.

The violence in *Rambo 4* feels very different than the violence in parts 2 and 3. *Rambo 2* and *3* feel like "action movies," *Rambo 4* feels more like a "war movie." The violence is also tougher, more graphic.

It was important to Stallone, right from the beginning, that the violence, the story itself, be as real as possible. It was Stallone who wanted to tell this man's story. He wasn't interested in any kind of superhero gags or set pieces. He wasn't interested in telling another "action" story. He wanted it to be a war story from the very beginning. In fact, it took me a little while to fully grasp this, as I was extremely aware of the "expectations" many people would have for this film.

Rambo 4 ends with John Rambo finally returning to America and walking to his father's house. Can you talk about the significance of the moment and using it to give his story a little closure?

That very last shot, Rambo showing up on the highway outside his family's ranch or farm in Arizona, was not in any of the first few drafts. It was Stallone's idea. He knew, before any of the rest of us, that this was most likely going to be his last outing as Rambo. Can a character like Rambo ever be integrated back into society? It's a great question. I'm working on a script right now about a character like that. Part of it depends on what you mean by "society." I don't see Rambo or any of these characters ever being at home, or comfortable, in big-city America. That's why the stories that have worked the best, about attempting this kind of integration, usually take place, for the warriors, in extreme settings even in this country: i.e., Montana or Alaska, or northern Michigan, or even Key West and the islands going into the Caribbean.

A.O. Scott wrote: "To dwell on Rambo's ideological significance was (and still is) to miss his kinship with the samurais and gunslingers of older movies."[55] Do you think that's true? Can one strip away politics when discussing Rambo?

I think A.O. Scott got it exactly right. Rambo is not a political or ideological character. His kinship is definitely with the Japanese Samurais and the mythic gunslingers of the old west. I'm reminded of *Shane* (1953) in particular. A gunfighter who, for almost the entire picture, has hung up his guns and tried to make a go of it as a simple ranch hand. But when the ultimate bully blows into town, and begins hurting, and even killing, people he cares about, he has no choice but to finally put his guns back on and challenge the bully to a duel, a duel to the death.

DIE HARD 4

Live Free or Die Hard

Die Hard is considered to be one of the best action films ever made. It also established Bruce Willis, who was coming off of the comedy–mystery tv series *Moonlighting*, as a movie star. Willis played John McClane, a wise-cracking, off-duty cop, who must stop an apparent act of terrorism to save his ex-wife Holly Gennero, trapped inside a building with the terrorists. Out-manned, out-gunned, and without any shoes, McClane frustrates, irritates, and eventually kills his adversaries.

Willis's McClane isn't as chiseled as other 80's action stars like Arnold Schwarzenberg or Sylvester Stallone. Nor is he as book smart as Harrison Ford's Jack Ryan but he's street smart, defiant, and indefatigable.

Die Hard, written by Jeb Stuart and Steven E. de Souza and directed by John McTiernan, created a sub-genre of action movies, with a hero trapped in a confined area with a villain. Notable copycats included *Die Hard* on a boat (*Under Siege*, 1992), *Die Hard* in a hockey rink (*Sudden Death*, 1995), and, most absurdly but effectively, *Die Hard* on a bus (*Speed*, 1994).

Perhaps it's only fitting that its sequel *Die Hard 2*, (1990), *Die Hard* in an Airport, was also a copycat. In *Die Hard 2*, Bruce is back as McClane, and this time he's trying to save his wife who is on a plane that has been taken over by terrorists. The sequel was directed by Renny Harlin, who would go on to direct *Exorcist: The Beginning* (2004), the fourth Exorcist movie.

The third *Die Hard* film, *Die Hard with a Vengeance* (1995), broke the formula. McClane is no longer trapped in a confined space nor is he trying to save his wife. In fact, Holly Gennero doesn't appear in the film. Instead, McClane is running around New York City, while trying to solve a series of riddles doled out by Simon, who is later revealed to be the brother of Hans Gruber, the villain from the first movie.

In the fourth film *Live Free or Die Hard* (2007), a late but serviceable sequel, McClane is trying to save his daughter who has been taken hostage by a cyber-terrorist (Timothy Olyphant) who has unleashed an attack on Washington DC.

Even though *Die Hard 4* was a box office success, earning about $388 million worldwide, some fans complained that the character of John McClane changed from an all-too-human beat cop to a superhuman man who, in the film, jumps on top of a jet, and falls off, relatively unscathed. Other fans bristled at the PG-13 rating, the first in the series, which was known for bloody action and colorful language, including McClane's catchphrase, "Yippie Ki Yay, motherfucker."

In *A Good Day to Die Hard* (2013), the fifth and possibly final film, McClane goes to Russia to save his estranged son. Some fans felt that Bruce Willis, a charismatic and gifted actor, was not completely engaged in the material. Despite all the pyrotechnics and explosions, the spark was gone from the franchise.

To date, the last time that Bruce Willis played John McClane was in a commercial for DieHard batteries, which aired with much fanfare and a little derision during the 2020 Superbowl.

As I indicated, the fourth *Die Hard* film is a serviceable sequel but it's nowhere as beloved as the first film. Bruce Willis seems less invested in the part than in his previous performance. There are also subtle but significant changes to the McClane character. He's no longer an ordinary but highly skilled cop, he's not a bit of a superhero, able to perform near-super heroic feats. In one scene, McClane jumps off his semi-truck and onto a jet, holds on to it and is then thrown off, and survives. He's relatively unscathed. Now, compare that with the classic scene in the original where the shoeless McClane is sidelined after running over broken glass. In an effort to up the stakes, an understandable instinct, the filmmakers lost sight of what was appealing about the series.

For most of the book, I've interviewed the writers, directors, and actors who were involved in making the fourth films. However, because I don't particularly have an affinity for *Live Free or Die Hard*, I tried a different method. I decided to interview Doug Richardson, a screenwriter who was selected by Bruce Willis and hired by the studio to write the fourth *Die Hard* film. Richardson has also worked as a screenwriter on *Die Hard 2* and *Die Hard 3* and wrote the Willis thriller *Hostage* (2005).

Before the interview started, Richardson teased me that in devoting a book to the fourth film in a series that I was writing a book about movies that nobody cares about.

Doug Richardson Interview

How did you get involved with the *Die Hard* series?
I got involved when Larry Gordon, who produced *Die Hard*, secretly hired me to write the sequel. This is the smartest thing I've ever seen anyone do in showbiz. *Die Hard* had only been in theaters for three weeks. I got a call from my agent asking, "Do you want to meet with Larry Gordon?" At the time, I was just a baby writer. I worked a bit, but I hadn't got anything made and I had never written an action before. Leonard Goldberg, who was the head of the studio, was involved in all of this. So I met with them, and Larry Gordon asked, "Did you see *Die Hard*?" I'd already seen it twice. Larry said, "Here's the deal. The studio is going to want a sequel. But they don't know it yet. If they commission a script, it's going to be a giant cluster fuck. Agents will submit all their clients, you have to hear a lot of takes, and the studio is going to be involved. I want to avoid that."

Larry also said, "There's the Joel Silver issue. Once something is called *Die Hard* then Joel's contract kicks in and they didn't want to involve Joel in the process yet. Larry had already had his heart attack and he called it "Joel Silver." So he said, "I've got this book called *58 Minutes,* [which is unrelated to *Die Hard*]. I'm going to have you adapt it. To make that happen, it's just a phone call to the studio, saying, 'I'm going to hire this guy to adapt this book as a potential movie.'" Because you don't cost a lot, they're just going to say yes. And so you're going to get hired to write *58 minutes*. But between you, me, and Leonard, we know you're writing *Die Hard* 2.

One more thing by the time you get done writing it, they're going to want Steven de Souza [who co-wrote *Die Hard*] to do a rewrite. I said, "Sure, great. Sounds wonderful." So I wrote *Die Hard 2*. Then Leonard left the studio. Within days of me

Bruce Willis is John McClane
Illustration by Pat Carbajal

delivering the script, Joe Roth had come into the studio and said, "A new sheriff is in town, and I want *Die Hard* 2. Larry said, "Funny you should ask. We already have it." Larry gave the script to the studio, and it got a green light. Just like that. Pretty smart stuff.

What happened next?
As soon as they call it *Die Hard 2*, Joel Silver comes on, fires me, and brings in Steve de Souza. It sucked for me, but I knew it was going to happen.

When you were writing the secret draft to *Die Hard 2*, did you call the character John McClane?
No. They were all avatars for sure. I used different names, but it was about John and Holly [McClane's wife]. It took place around JFK and not Dulles Airport.

Why does *Die Hard* 2 feel like it, at least for me, it captures the spirit of the original, more so than the other ones?
I can only guess but, based on how well I know Bruce, I think he really didn't want to do more than two. When John McTiernan came back and did the third film, *Die Hard with a Vengeance*, I thought he brought back that same spirit. *Die Hard* is all about John McClane, it should be called *John McClane* and John McClane is Bruce Willis.

As a writer, you think about how this character is navigating the problem and, as a viewer, that's what is so much fun to watch. To me, that's one of the charming things about the first one. It was also the most fun thing about it, aside from the action set pieces, which were hyper-realistic for the time. There hadn't been a super hyper-realistic, superhero-esque character who wasn't a superhero. The second one was still somewhat contained within the airport, and, and the surrounding areas. He was the fly in the ointment. It was kind of close to the original in that respect.

As the series went on, they lost all the containment that, the *Die Hard* in a blah-blah had, right? So part of the appeal was the containment of John McClane and the villains in the same space. They became bigger and broader and, then it just becomes John McClane, and not *Die Hard*.

Tom Rothman wanted to make John McClane in *The Day After Tomorrow* [the disaster movie]. He wanted to make it for the trailer. That was what he wanted to make. That's a very cynical endeavor.

I got involved with *Die Hard* utterly by being a dumb ass. I made this mistake many times in my writing career because I like telling stories and I like solving problems. So, one day on the set of *Hostage*, Bruce dropped Mark Bomback's script to *Die Hard 4* in my lap. At the time was called *Die Hard 4.0*. Bruce said, "Would you mind reading this?" I said, "Do I have tonight? Or do you want me to read it like at lunch?" He said, "I want you to read it today at lunch, ASAP." So I kind of read it between setups, then read it over lunch, and went to his trailer. Bruce said, "What do you think?" I said, "I sort of shrugged, and I said, "I think I don't want to see *Die Hard* 4. That's what I think." He goes, "Well, neither do I." And I said, "Well say no." He says, "What would be a *Die Hard* for you to want to see?" Unfortunately, that's where I fucked up. Because I answered the question. I began running it around in my mind and asked myself, what would be the *Die Hard 4* that I would want to see?

At that point, Bruce went from not wanting to cast Ben Foster in *Hostage* to realizing how brilliant Ben was. Bruce had become like the biggest Ben Foster fan on the planet. I said, "Here's the *Die Hard* I want to see. I want to see *Die Hard: 20 Years Later*. I want to see John McClane old and in pain. Play him as Bruce's age. The *Die Hard* films work best as buddy movies. What if it was you and Ben Foster, and he's your son.

Remember all the things we've seen John McClane do that were just awesome and great. And the fictional world in the movie is a John McClane fan because he saved the Nakatomi Tower, and he saved Christmas. But he's a shitty dad. And his son hates him because he was such a shitty dad and because he's out saving the world. Now, it's a father-son story because, I said, I haven't seen that. The son gets to see his dad be great. That's a *Die Hard 4* I'd want to see." The conversation went on for about an hour. And then it was sort of like that's the *Die Hard* I want to see but that it has nothing to do with the *Die Hard* you gave me. So I don't want to see *Die Hard 4* and I left.

The next day or so, I see Bruce and he says, "You need to take Friday afternoon off because you and I have a meeting with Tom Rothman over at Fox." And I said, "What about?" Bruce says, "*Die Hard 4*. I want you to tell him what you told me." I'm going "Oh, no, this isn't good. I'm being brought in to be the guy who says "no." I've been in that spot before because the thought is that I'll fight with anybody.

So we met at Fox, and I had the same talk with Tom Rothman that I had with Bruce, Bruce says that's the direction I want to take. And Tom says, "Great, that's what I want to make, too." Because Tom needs to make a *Die Hard* that Bruce wants to be in. *Die Hard* is a money-printing machine. Years ago I asked Bob Semmel, former head of Warner's, "What do you say when Clint Eastwood comes to you and says that I want to make another Dirty Harry?" Bob says, "You say, 'Thank you.'" It's that simple. That's the business Tom was in.

Suddenly, I now had to go write the dialogue for *Die Hard 4* but I didn't want to see *Die Hard 4*. But my whole idea was, let's make it a really good movie, let's solve the problem and make a *Die Hard* that's interesting. Let's make a really good one because the fourth one sucks, almost all the time. That's what I tried to do. We went through a lot of trials and tribulations—finishing *Hostage*, then writing *Die Hard* and delivering it to the studio. Bruce was really behind the script. This is the *Die Hard* that he wanted to make.

But the studio had a release date in mind, which is an ass-backward way of making movies. if you have a release date before you have a finished script, you're just going to make a bad movie. You just are, but suddenly, I'm in that position. Tom Rothman says, "We have a release date, we need to get a director within so many weeks, so we can start prep on this thing." Of course, there are all these discussions about the director. And then there's a meeting at Fox with Bruce, me, Tom and Hutch Parker, and Jimmy Giannopoulos, who was the head of marketing. Tom was like, "I love the script. It's great. I just need some trailer moments. Blow up a cornfield. I've never seen that happen." Bruce would reply, "Great." So Tom would say something, and Bruce would say, "Great." Tom kept coming up with things he wanted in the movie. I had only weeks to get the script done and deliver it.

Anyway, we left the meeting, and I was pissed off about all the terrible notes. I thought they were going to ruin what we had worked hard to make work. Bruce said to me, "You don't have to do any of the notes if you don't like them. I said, "Dude, you just said yes to everything Tom said in the meeting. He's the CEO of the studio. He's my boss, you aren't. Now I have to go pound every one of those square pegs into a round hole and make it work for him. And I have like four weeks to do it. Because you said yes to everything. So unless you want to go back in there with me and say, "By the way, Tom, I didn't mean to say yes to anything." But Bruce didn't want to do that. He says, "Figure it out." Then he goes off to make another movie. I was trying to fix it.

While I was trying to cobble all these bad notes into this script I'd written, I had the studio in one ear and Bruce in the other ear. It was just disastrous. It was no fun. I realized that I was the only one who wasn't engaged in a cynical endeavor. At that point, I wasn't even sure what Bruce wanted, maybe he just wanted cash—that big check. But Tom Rothman wanted John McClane in *The Day After Tomorrow*, and I hadn't written that. Keep in mind that I'm the guy who Bruce dragged into Tom's office and told him this father-son story.

Then, we couldn't get a director. I didn't think the script was very good. Even though everyone's talking about how much they loved it, I thought it sucked. Then, I think I was fired or wasn't I fired? Bruce threw up his hands and said, I don't want to make *Die Hard 4* and left. I got the blame from the studio.

Once they got the director, it seemed like they went back to Mark Bomback's script.
Well, that's a long story. But CAA [the talent agency] was working very hard to divide Bruce from Arnold Rifkin, his manager and partner. They'd been together for years and Bruce is all about loyalty. I also knew that CAA wanted to stick Bruce in another *Die Hard,* and, without Arnold, Bruce didn't have anyone to go fight his battles for him, which Arnold did. So, yeah, they went back to Mark's script and that's the script they made. It had those "trailer moments" in it. They took bits and pieces of what I did and what other writers came after me, but the basis was still Mark's script.

***Die Hard* 4 and 5 both seem to have used elements from your script.**
There are some leftover parts of my thing. Instead of it being a father-son story, it's Bruce and Justin Long [who plays a hacker] story. That's a bit of a leftover. There are a few other little bits and pieces. There's one completely intact scene, which is this scene in that where they start the car with the OnStar [where Justin Long's character uses the security company to remotely start a stolen vehicle]. There are a few at-home action bits and a little bit of dialogue. But really, there's nothing left that I did.

They brought in a bunch of sequence writers, including Kevin Smith [who had a small part in the film]. At one point while they were shooting, Bruce was asking for every draft that I wrote, he was looking for bits of dialogue to use.

But when it comes down to arbitration [and who deserves on-screen credit], there was a list of people who ever worked on a version of *Die Hard*. It becomes a lottery, and everyone just throws in their name. I said, "This is Mark's script. This is when it comes down to it. It's still Mark's script, it's a lot of little bits of everybody else in it, but it's pretty much Mark's script. When I wrote my letter to the arbitration committee, I said, "This is the script Tom wanted to make. This is the script Mark wrote. At the end of the day, this is still Mark's script, and he should receive sole credit." It worked out for him. So that kind of launched him and his career too. He's been kicking ass ever since.

In your version of *Die Hard 4*, was John McClane fighting the same bad guy?
My villain was a little more like a comic book guy. And he wasn't Tim Olyphant. He was a mix between Stephen Hawking and Ted Kaczynski [the domestic terrorist]. He's a wheelchair-bound guy who was hell-bent on shutting down the world. The studio still wanted this catastrophic internet event to occur, and John McClane has to save the day. I never liked that. But I did keep it, so my villain is more of a comic book kind of guy who's angry at the world. He's an angry billionaire who just wants to shut down everything and take it back to zero. He's kind of a Ted Kaczynski sort, anti-technology, a guy who built his career around technology, who then wanted to end technology. That was sort of what I was going for.

Shutting down the internet seems like the wrong problem for John McClane to solve.
Right, it was the wrong thing to solve. The script I had was a father-son story in that he's a terrible dad. His son has become a dark hacker. And this story starts when his son gets out of jail. McClane is there to pick them up. The son's been in jail for doing all sorts of bad hacking things. And McClane is just a complete Luddite, and his son is a genius. So he needs his son to solve the problem. That was my take. The first movie had him doing everything to save somebody he loves. So they keep doing that. But then it comes, don't be someone this guy loves. In the third one, the villain wants revenge for his brother Hans. But it's kind of a silly story. It's, "I'm going to fuck with John McClane. But while I'm fucking with John McClane, because of what he did, to my brother, I'm going to rip off the Fed [Federal Reserve]." Stealing from the Fed was the only thing that they kept. In my version of *Die Hard 3*, there are no family members in peril. But it had the idea of ripping off the Fed, and they kept that. When they grabbed the Jonathan Hensley script, they shoehorned the idea of stealing from the Fed into me.

For me, *Die Hard* is about family and having his son in it made it about family. Even though it wasn't saving his son, his son was involved in it. But they're saving each other. Part five was also a father-son thing [with McClane traveling to Russia to save his son].

Sequels can sometimes change the basic nature of the character. Ripley in *Aliens* and Paul Hirsch in *Death Wish* are ordinary people in extraordinary situations. But by the fourth movies, they are no longer ordinary and in the case of Ripley, she's no longer a person. She's a replicant. Similarly, McClane becomes a quasi-superhero by *Die Hard 4*. He's jumping off of airplanes and surviving. Of course, you want to raise the stakes in each sequel but sometimes it comes at the cost of

character.

In *Die Hard 4*, he drove a car into a helicopter. I had him jump his motorcycle on top of a moving train. It's all about the trailers. The studio just wants bigger and bigger set pieces. It started with me saying, I don't want to see *Die Hard 4,* waxing on and being creative about it. And by the end of it, it broke my heart. It was just not fun. The whole process was a pain in the ass. The pressure was extraordinary. It's a big giant franchise. There are hundreds of millions of dollars on the line. People expected to make a lot of money from the movie. Some people treat it entirely like a cynical endeavor at that point. But I didn't. So I tried to be true to the character. And the character I was trying to be true to at that point was a guy who did all this stuff we've seen, which makes him [a great hero but] a terrible dad. That worked for me.

What does Bruce know about the character?
When you're trying to talk to him about the character about what John McClane would do and would not do, if he disagreed with you, he'd say, "Hey, if you know so much, you go play John McClane." But I'm trying to make this an interesting movie that people want to see, and that people say, "I can't believe this is the fourth movie."

***Fury Road*, the fourth Mad Max film, surprised a lot of people with its filmmaking and energy.**
What makes that a great fourth film is that it's not about Max. George Miller revived it. It's more about the Mad Max Universe but it's not about Max. Before Disney bought Fox [which owned the rights to *Die Hard*], Fox was going to try and pass the torch to somebody where they were going to do a John McClane origin story. Because Bruce was getting older and gets a check. I'm a movie fan. When I was writing my version of *Die Hard*, I wanted to do *Fury Road.* I wanted the audience to walk away from the theater going, "Wow. You figured out how to do a fourth one that's relevant."

What is important to Bruce Willis about how John McClane is portrayed and what his character should be?
Bruce is an actor and he's not necessarily an idea guy. He's also really smart. But he's doing it based on what I'm building. He really liked what I was doing. He did say, "I want you to kill the character. I want John McClane to die in this movie. Because I don't want to be put on the spot again."

Bruce and I had this joke that the movie wasn't called *Die Hard,* it was called *Die Really Fucking Hard*. I tried to write it like John McClane was older and in pain. He's got a bullet lodged in his skull, from something that happened in another film [that we didn't see]." The fun is seeing how bad things can get for him. In the first one, McClane runs across the broken glass in his bare feet. Bruce plays hurt well.

McClane is the guy who can get the shit kicked out of him but he's able to get back up. That's one of the things that Bruce loved in my version, there's a helicopter crash in the end. McClane has his hand stuck under a seat and he can't get out. But he's carrying a knife, a Boy Scout knife. We establish the knife at the beginning of the film. He wants to give it to his son. For McClane, it was the last time they were father and son. "We were in the Scouts together and I was a Scout dad." So he wanted to give it back to his son. But the son doesn't want it, so McLane has it the entire time.

Back to the helicopter. McClane is stuck and he can't get out. So he takes out the knife and cuts off his hand. He's bleeding. So he cauterizes the cut on the steaming engine block. That was really hard.

But Hutch Parker, who was President of Production told me, "That's badass. But we're not cutting off John McClane's hand because then we have to do all this expensive CGI work." He was trying to keep the cost down. He was complaining all the time about the cost of *Master and Commander*, [another Fox film] and he was complaining, "Do you know how much money [director] Peter Weir has spent digitally on the film?" Hutch tells us, "We're going to do nothing but practical effects on the movie. We're not going to cut off his hand because I don't want to digitally remove it. When I tried to get Bruce to fight for it, he didn't. But it was a fun thing to think about.

John McClane lives through the movie, I assume.
Right, but I was trying to make *Die Really, Really, Really, Really Fucking Hard*. So there was a darkness to it. If you're going to do a fourth one, you can't be shy. You've got to pull the trigger on it. During the process, Tom Rothman suddenly says, "You can't put that in. This is going to PG-13." I was like, "What about *Die Hard* is PG-13? I can only use one non-sexual use of the word "fuck." Have you ever heard John McClane talk? Have you ever talked to Bruce? Bruce puts the word fuck between every comma. You've got to stop him from saying it. It's pretty funny.

But Tom had an answer for it. He's planning an ad campaign and he wants to sell it during *The Simpsons*. Therefore, it must be PG-13. I said, "You realize you're going to get some slap-back from *Die Hard* fans. Tom said, "I don't care about [existing] *Die Hard* fans. I'm looking for new fans."

At the end of the movie, McClane winds up reunited with his son. He only has one hand left and it's his shooting [left] hand. You get the impression that he's done and that he's at the end of it. I wasn't allowed to write in such a way where he's definitively done. But you would walk away asking yourself, "Is he done?" You get the sense that he could leave it or not. But because it's a cynical endeavor, you know McClane is going to come back. If *Die Hard 4* makes money, there's going to be a *Die Hard 5*.

Did you have a director in mind for your version?
I didn't have a director in mind. The only reason that they got Bruce back for *Die Hard 3* is that they got John McTiernan. He originally said that he didn't want to do it. But finally, they got McTiernan and Bruce felt comfortable. For *Die Hard 4*, the studio wanted a journeyman director who would be in lockstep with everything they wanted. They didn't want auteurs or big names who had sway. They wanted someone they could control. I think Tom would have been happy with Roland Emmerich because of his love for *Day After Tomorrow*. [In the end, the studio hired Len Weisman, who directed the first two *Underworld* films.]

What did you do with the phrase Yippee Ki Yay? It's part of the plot of the first one and in the second one, it makes sense because he's saying it in victory. But by the third and fourth one, it becomes just a catchphrase that is divorced from

the story.
Right, it became ubiquitous. My idea is that everybody else is saying it to him. It's something that haunts him. He hates it. His son hates it. Then it became, how many times could I make the joke work.

I wanted the movie to have a lot of fun in it. But it's supposed to be comic and dark, at the same time. I had a line where McClane is getting so frustrated with the internet. He goes, "Where's the off button? Can we just turn off the internet?" His son looks at him saying, "This is my dad. This is my fucking dad." There was a lot to balance.

Certain movie characters lend themselves to additional stories. A cop can always catch another case and a spy can always be assigned another mission. McClane is a cop so ostensibly he fits into that word. But the fun of *Die Hard* was that he was off duty, he was out of his element, and he was just trying to save his wife. Stopping the bad guys was secondary.
The good thing about John McClane is that you can plug him in anywhere, as long as he isn't winning. He's that problem cop. He can't leave well enough alone. He's going to get himself into trouble. That's a deficiency in his character.

He's also very blunt. He wouldn't try to pick a lock. Instead, he'd try to kick the door down. But [there's a danger in] turning him into a superhero. It's important to keep it hyper-realistic and grounded.

There's an old Hollywood adage that asks, "How do you say no to a movie star?" The answer is, "You don't." You don't say no; you find a way to say yes. On *Hostage*, my relationship with Bruce is always right, because—and this is why he likes and respects me—I would just fight with him. I wasn't afraid to fight with him. He likes to fight. He likes that. I think McTiernan likes to fight with him. I think that's one of the things that makes him somewhat engaged in those films because McTiernan is a big dude. I could see him just, not taking Bruce's shit. I'm not a big dude, but I just am not afraid to argue with him. I was willing to have those fights with them all the time.

It's hard because you got to be willing to take the call at three in the morning when he's got insomnia. And he's thinking about what you're shooting the next day. He's got an idea and it's a bad idea. You have to un-ring the bell before you show up on the second the next day. It's tiring, but it can also be a lot of fun.

I'm sorry that your version of *Die Hard 4* didn't get made. Because it sounds engaging.
When I was just writing, and it was just Bruce and me, I think that was an interesting version. But when the studio got involved, they kept trying to make it familiar to them. Then we had to get the script into prep by a certain date so that we could make the July 4th release date and so that we could hire a director. I had Bruce calling me between takes on his movie and he was giving me notes. I'm trying to be constructive and he's tearing the script apart again. I said, "Dude you gotta stop calling me and let me try to do this thing for the studio." He would say, "I'm worried about this." I would say, "Stop worrying about this movie and worry about the moving you're doing right now."

It was hard. I had to go hide from him. He would find me everywhere I went. I checked into a hotel, under a different name. It's funny stuff now. But when you play a character that launches your career, you now have financial security and then some. But people want you to play the same part over and over again. For a creative person, that's not why you became an actor. You have a love-hate relationship with it, and it puts you in a box. That's not what people want. Generally speaking, people want to play different parts and that's how they imagined it for themselves. But nothing succeeds like success. That applies to directors and writers too. After *Die Hard*, everyone wanted me to write those *Die Hard* knock-off movies. When Steven Seagal was making *Under Siege*, he worked on the script and they said, "Why don't we call the *Die Hard* rewriter again. It's lucrative but it's not fun. But I'm very grateful for it. I'm grateful that my kids went to private school and college. So, I'm grateful for that box.

SECTION 4
Science Fiction Movies

STAR WARS 4
The Ewok Adventure

"What is the fourth *Star Wars* movie?" For most franchises, the answer to this question is straightforward. However, with *Star Wars* the answer is surprisingly problematic. For first-generation fans, the fourth movie is *Star Wars: Episode I - The Phantom Menace* (1999), the fourth *theatrically* released film. For younger fans, it's *Star Wars: Episode IV - A New Hope* (1977), the fourth *part* of the story. However, there is another candidate—*The Ewok Adventure*.

The Ewok Adventure is the fourth film set in the *Star Wars* universe. With a story by George Lucas and a teleplay by Bob Carrau, *The Ewok Adventure* is a made-for-TV movie that aired in 1984, a year after *Return of the Jedi*, the third film in the saga. Although it was released theatrically only overseas, it is possible that at least for those audiences the idea that *The Ewok Adventure* was the fourth film in the *Star Wars* series is somewhat less farfetched.

I realize that most moviegoers are unlikely to embrace this notion, and even die-hard fans don't often revisit *The Ewok Adventure*, but the muddy facts are what they are. The movie, which was directed by John Korty, lacks the scope and spectacle of the theatrical films, and perhaps further undermining the argument that it could be the fourth *Star Wars* movie, *The Ewok Adventure* was aimed specifically at children; so unlike *A New Hope* and the canonic *Star Wars* movies, it cannot be enjoyed on multiple levels by different age groups.

Befitting its target audience, the plot is deliberately simple: After their spaceship crash-lands on the distant planet Endor, the teenage Mace (Eric Walker) and his young sister Cindel (Aubree Miller) are separated from their parents. As they search for their parents and learn to rely on each other, they are befriended by the brave and resourceful Ewoks, who help them survive on this dangerous moon and rescue their parents who have been captured by a ferocious monster. Further signaling that it's a family film, *The Ewok Adventure* was narrated by Burl Ives, who is familiar to many as the narrator of the perennial holiday favorite *Rudolf the Red-Nose Reindeer* (1964).

Although *The Ewok Adventure* can be dismissed by some as "only" a made-for-TV movie, it is nevertheless a *movie*. It is also firmly placed in the *Star Wars* universe and draws on many of its most recognizable elements. Joe Johnston, the art director in the visual effects department for *Empire Strikes Back* and *Return of the Jedi*, was the production designer on *The Ewok Adventure*. *Ewok* scriptwriter Bob Carrau would later write 14 of the 35 episodes of the animated series *Ewoks* (1985–1987), as well as *Monsters and Aliens from George Lucas* (1993), which looks at the creatures from different Lucasfilm movies, and, with Terryl Whitlatch, *Wildlife of Star Wars* (2016), a field guide to the creatures in the *Star Wars* universe.

The Ewoks, a controversial but integral part of *Return of the Jedi*, are central to the *Ewok* movie. Reprising his role from *Jedi*, Warwick Davis plays Wicket, the curious and empathetic Ewok who befriends the Towani children. Logray and Chief

Chirpa, featured Ewoks in *Jedi*, also appear in the movie. Moreover, it probably isn't a coincidence that Mace Towani (Eric Walker) looks like a mini Luke Skywalker. Not only does Mace sport Luke's floppy haircut, but he also wears a similar orange jumpsuit. (Lucas would later repurpose the character's name as Mace Windu and give it to Samuel L. Jackson's Jedi Knight in the prequel trilogy.) Evoking the iconic moment when Luke and Leia swing across a seemingly bottomless shaft in *A New Hope*, there's a scene in which an Ewok also swings across a cavern. Instead of opening with the familiar "A long time ago in a galaxy far, far away," Ives narrates, "Our story begins in a time long, long ago, deep in an enchanted forest on the distant planet of Endor." In *A New Hope*, Leia calls Chewbacca a "walking carpet" and in *The Ewok Adventure*, Mace refers to the Ewoks as "walking hairbrushes."

ABC aired *The Ewok Adventure* against first-run episodes of the CBS mystery show *Murder, She Wrote*, the sitcoms *The Jeffersons* and *Alice*, and the NBC made-for-TV mob movie *The Vegas Strip War*, starring Rock Hudson and James Earl Jones (the voice of Darth Vader). Despite the competition, *The Ewok Adventure* attracted an impressive 36% of the viewing audience.[56] According to StarWars.com, the official Lucasfilm website, 65 million people watched the movie.[57] It is also worth noting that *The Ewok Adventure* won an Emmy for Outstanding Special Visual Effects and was nominated for an Emmy for Outstanding Children's Program.

As previously noted, *The Ewok Adventure* was released theatrically overseas. It played in various markets, including the United Kingdom, Italy, Australia, Japan, France, and Spain. In some countries, it was advertised with the branding: *Star Wars Presents*. The film, later retitled *Caravan of Courage: An Ewok Adventure*, was successful enough to prompt a sequel, *Ewoks: The Battle for Endor* (1985), which aired on ABC the following year and was released theatrically overseas in some territories, including the United Kingdom. Plans for a third film were abandoned. Lucas told *Starlog* magazine, "We made two and were going to do a third, but they became very expensive to make."[58]

The Ewok Adventure was made decades before the theatrical release of Disney-produced "non-saga" *Star Wars* movies, including *Rogue One* (2016) and *Solo* (2018). *Rogue One* and *Solo*, like *The Ewok Adventure,* do not employ the *Star Wars* logo in their opening credits, but they do use characters and situations from the original trilogy to tell new tales. *Rogue One* explores how the rebels obtained vital information about the vulnerability in the Death Star's design that enabled them to destroy it, a plot point briefly referred to in *Episode IV*, and *Solo* depicts the early adventures of the galaxy's most charismatic smuggler, Han Solo. Both *Rogue One* and *Solo* were advertised under the banner "A *Star Wars* Story," but *The Ewok Adventure* was the first non-trilogy film to fit the descriptor.

Like *Rogue One* and *Solo*, *The Ewok Adventure* is designed to broaden the audience's understanding and appreciation of familiar characters. The TV movie expands our knowledge of the Ewok's daily life, customs, and traditions. For instance, before the children and the Ewoks begin their journey, the narrator explains that "the adventurers gather for a traditional Ewok ceremony…[Ewok] Logray must bestow upon them the sacred totems of the legendary Ewok warriors." More significantly, audiences are introduced to what appears to be magic, a first in the live-action *Star Wars* universe. When Cindel falls ill, the Ewoks and Mace travel to the "one tree in the primeval forest" that "contains a special fluid, which only Ewoks know. They have used it for generations to cure their ills." Once fashioned into a medicine, Cindel's health improves almost instantly. In another scene, the Ewoks use a crystal image spinner, a top-like object that reveals the location of the children's missing parents. Later, when Mace is mysteriously trapped underwater, Cindel employs a "magic walking stick," to free her drowning brother.

Pop culture writer Luke Farr argues that *Caravan of Courage* should be held in high esteem by *Star Wars* fans. Farr believes that the Ewoks wouldn't be "dismissed so readily" if they weren't thought just to be "cutesy comic relief." He writes:

Very rarely are the Ewoks given the space and story to become anything other than endearing teddy bears, but it's not hard to see their potential…Ewoks are a hunter-gatherer war-like species, and they offer their lives to help win the Battle of Endor for the side of the Rebel Alliance [in *Return of the Jedi*], when they could not possibly have a very high stake in the outcome of the fight…*The Caravan of Courage* makes the Ewoks much more sympathetic. We see them die, and we see them mourn their dead. In particular, there is a scene where [Ewoks] Deej and Shodu, Wicket's parents, embrace sadly over baby Winda's cradle. The scene is not narrated nor subtitled, but the significance is clear. Deej and Shodu are embracing in fear, Shodu is worried that she will never see her mate and her sons again, that the quest they are embarking on will take their lives.[59]"

For me, the question of whether *The Ewok Adventure* is really the fourth *Star Wars* film is less about the merits of that playful argument than it is about the larger issue of how we categorize movies and how we judge which films belong without a qualifying asterisk to a filmmaker's canon or determine which films legitimately belong to a series. In his indispensable book *Discovering Orson Welles* (2007), the film critic and scholar Jonathan Rosenbaum grapples with the difficult issue of classifying an artist's work. Rosenbaum writes: "I can't pretend to any sort of completeness even in relation to the 13 features released during Welles's lifetime…such as *The Fountain of Youth* and *Filming Othello* that have eluded canonization simply because they aren't readily available."[60] He argues that because some of Welles's films are hard to find, they are often ignored.

In *Discovering Orson Welles,* Rosenbaum also cautions about the dangers of letting "video stores determine the Welles canon."[61] His warning also pertains to the availability of three different versions of *Touch of Evil* (1958). Not only did Welles not have final cut on *Touch of Evil*, but the released version included scenes that were directed by Harry Keller, a contract director for Universal Pictures. Decades later, a second version of the film was discovered. However, while this edition incorporates previously excluded scenes directed by Welles it also included more of Keller's work. Upon this cut's 1976 release, Universal misleadingly publicized it as the "uncut and restored version." In 1998, Universal commissioned Rosenbaum and editor Walter Murch to conform the second version of *Touch of Evil* to a 58-page memo that reflected some of Welles's notes, written after a single viewing of the studio's version.

For a while, this third version supplanted the first and second versions of the film. Rosenbaum persuasively argues that because none of the three versions of the film reflects Welles's unadulterated vision, all editions should remain available. But because Universal invested a considerable amount of money in the endeavor, it was in the company's financial interests to give the new cut preferred status. It wasn't until the 50th anniversary of the release of *Touch of Evil* in 2008 that Universal belatedly released all three versions together.

Determining which films merit inclusion in an established series is an issue that has also stirred controversy among fans and scholars of the James Bond movies. When considering the Bond films, should we include 1967's *Casino Royale*, a movie that was not made by Eon, the company that has produced all the "official" Bond films? Few serious Bond fans would consider the psychedelic film to be anything more than an easily dismissed spoof. However, *Never Say Never Again* is more problematic. Although it wasn't made by Eon and lacks iconic elements such as the James Bond theme, and the signature gun barrel sequence, it does star Sean Connery, the first cinematic Bond, and it is a remake of Eon's *Thunderball*. Moreover, *Never Say Never Again* is faithful to the spirit of the Bond franchise.

In the documentary *Everything or Nothing* (2012), Barbara Broccoli, who with Michael Wilson is best known for running Eon, suggests that fans shouldn't confuse *Never Say Never Again* with the real McCoy. Broccoli argues, "*Never Say Never Again*, I think, proved the point that a Bond film cannot exist with just one element alone. Just having Sean wasn't enough."[62]

Not everyone agrees with this esteemed producer. On the 50th Anniversary of the first Bond movie, MGM Studios and Twentieth Century Fox Home Entertainment released *Bond 50: Celebrating Five Decades of Bond*, a DVD and Blu-ray box set of 23 Eon-produced films to date. At least one persnickety fan was frustrated by the decision to omit 1967's *Casino Royale* and *Never Say Never Again*. Claiming false advertising, Mary Johnson initiated a class action lawsuit.[63] The case was settled and, without admitting any wrongdoing, MGM and Twentieth Century Fox agreed to give claimants digital copies of *Casino Royale* and *Never Say Never Again*. The suit was frivolous, but it calls attention to how business interests (and, in Bond's case, how different rights holders) can affect how films are categorized.

The question of which novels based on *Star Wars* themes, stories, and characters are "official" has provoked comparable debate. According to Lucasfilm Story Group member Pablo Hidalgo, some of the most "common questions about the spin-off novels are: How "real" are these stories? Do they count? Did they really happen?"[64] Likely taking the cue from Lucas himself, Hidalgo's ready response is: "The most definitive canon of the *Star Wars* universe is encompassed by feature films and television productions in which George Lucas is directly involved."[65]

Using that definition, it could be argued that *The Ewok Adventure* belongs to the canon.[66] Although Hidalgo is referring specifically to the original and prequel trilogies, as well as to the animated series, *The Clone Wars* (2015–2018), *The Ewok Adventure* should not hastily be dismissed from consideration. After all, Lucas *was* "directly involved" with it. Not only was the movie based on his story, but he was also a co-writer and executive producer (even allowing that sometimes the title is honorary), and Eric Walker said that Lucas directed some pickup shots for the film. It should be noted that Hidalgo was writing in 2012 before Disney acquired Lucasfilm.

Without Lucas's direct involvement in recent *Star Wars* movies and television series, new definitions of what belongs in the canon are evolving. Hidalgo has elaborated on his definition of the canon by adding that admittance requires that "other storytellers *need* to be beholden to it [its narrative]. That's it."[67] A statement, which echoes Hidalgo's (and presumably Lucas's) thinking, was issued on StarWars.com: "While Lucasfilm always strived to keep the stories created for the EU [Expanded Universe] consistent with our film and television content as well as internally consistent, Lucas always made it clear that he was not beholden to the EU. He set the films he created as the canon…These stories are the immovable objects of *Star Wars* history, the characters, and events to which all other tales must align."[68]

Even its star, Warwick Davis, is unsure of how to classify *The Ewok Adventure*, "They're in and out of canon every time you read something. I don't know what's what. Who knows? I'll have to talk to Pablo…at the Story Group and ask him."[69] Davis's confusion might stem from the complicated system for classifying *Star Wars* properties that Lucasfilm employed before the Disney purchase.

Broadly, Episodes I through VI were considered G-Canon (G for George Lucas). *The Ewok Adventure* was considered C-Canon (C for continuity), a lower level of classification that also included novels and comics. Other classifications included T for television canon and N for non-canon material, which included officially licensed stories that directly contradict the narrative continuity established by Lucas. In this instance, it was Lucas and Lucasfilm that set up these guidelines, and not an external agent.

However, what constitutes the canon even in Lucas-created stories is subject to change. Originally, Han Solo shot Greedo first. However, in the special edition of *A New Hope*, Greedo fired first, and Solo returned fire only in self-defense. In 2006, Lucasfilm employee Leland Chee, who maintains a database for all *Star Wars* stories called the Holocron, noted: "The only relevant official continuities are the current versions of the films alone, and the combined current version of the films along with whatever else we've got in the Holocron. You're never going to know what George's view of the universe [is] beyond the films at any given time because it is constantly evolving. It remains elastic…"[70]

Artistic intentions aside, the marketplace has a powerful sway on how art is viewed. This was brought sharply into focus when Disney acquired Lucasfilm. Before that purchase, *Star Wars* novels told stories that continued after Luke redeemed his father and killed the Emperor in *Return of the Jedi*. In these tales, Luke marries Mara Jade, an agent of the Empire turned Jedi Master, and fathers a son, Ben Skywalker (who is named after Ben Kenobi, Luke's mentor), and Han and Leia have three children, Jacen, Jaina, and Anakin Solo. In another, Han Solo's friend and everyone's favorite Wookie, Chewbacca is killed. However, when Disney started making its own feature films and publishing its own books, the company understandably wanted to control the narrative. Some of the major plot points in the pre-Disney stories, such as the death of Chewbacca, would be directly contradicted by the not-yet-released *The Force Awakens* (2015). Similarly, the Skywalker lineage would be completely revamped. In the Disney *Star Wars* films, Luke is apparently childless and Han and Leia's only offspring, Ben Solo, is seduced by the Dark Side and becomes the villainous Kylo Ren.

Perhaps even more jarringly, while Luke, Leia, and Han's adventures continue for decades in the novels, all three characters will have died by the end of Disney's sequel trilogy. In anticipation of these vexing plot discrepancies, in 2014 Disney began labeling many of the novels as "*Star Wars* Legends," a designation that removed those stories from cannon. The decision irked numerous fans who were emotionally invested in the novels and didn't want to be told that the events in them no longer mattered. *The Ewok Adventure* is now designated as a Legend. *Star Wars Rebels*, the Disney-produced cartoon that was made without Lucas' involvement, is not. In 2014, Leland Chee, a member of the Story Group, explained: "[The] Story Group has a hand in all facets of *Star Wars* storytelling, including movies, TV, games, and publishing."[71] He noted that the "primary goal" of the new classification was to avoid "setting hierarchy" among properties in different media.[72] Therefore, going forward, a narrative element of a feature film wouldn't directly contradict an event in a comic book, novel, or, say, in a made-for-TV movie about Ewoks.

For years, *The Ewok Adventure* hadn't been available on DVD, Blu-ray, or digital streaming. Instead, fans had to hunt for the film on the underground and second-hand market. Some might conclude that the decision not to make *The Ewok Adventure* commercially available was intended to minimize its significance in the *Star Wars* universe. To paraphrase Rosenbaum, it should not be in the hands of video stores and corporate interests to influence movie enthusiasts or movie history in big ways (determining what we can or cannot see) or in smaller ones, such as deciding which of the *Star Wars* movies is the fourth.

In 2021, *The Ewok Adventure* was finally made commercially available. It appeared on the streaming service Disney+. However, the television movie is not awarded the same status as the nine-film Skywalker saga, the spin-off movies, and the Disney-produced *Star Wars* content. Instead, it appears to be marginalized. The film is listed under the category "*Star Wars* Vintage," a retro-subheading that seems to give the film lower stature.

When considering which films belong to a series' canon, the artist's intentions and the relative quality of a movie are different but overlapping matters, which are linked to the thorny matter of classifying *The Ewok Adventure*. It is possible for *The Ewok Adventure* to be in (or out) of the story canon without considering it to be the fourth *Star Wars* film. The inclusion or exclusion of a work from a series' canon can invite debate, but the perceived quality of a work cannot be a determining factor.

Still, it would be an overreach to argue that the TV movie is a major work worthy of being judged against the original *Star Wars* trilogy, a once-in-a-generation work that created a new and engrossing mythology. *The Ewok Adventure* was never intended to occupy the same artistic space as Lucas's rich space opera. The scaled-down adventure should instead be viewed as another filmmaker's attempt to tell stories within the fertile and versatile universe that Lucas created.

Although George Lucas would reject the argument that *The Ewok Adventure* is the fourth *Star Wars* movie, others can reasonably argue the merits of that claim. There is no simple answer to the question, what is the fourth *Star Wars* movie? Is it *The Phantom Menace*, *A New Hope*, or *The Ewok Adventure*? As wise old Ben Kenobi might opine, they are all "true, from a certain point of view."

Bob Carrau Interview

How did you come to write *The Ewok Adventure*?
It was the first thing I ever really wrote, and it was 35 years ago. I had worked at Lucasfilm in a very gofer-level way, but I worked with George and his main office. He was married at the time [to Marcia Lucas, the Academy Award-winning film editor]. To make a long story short, I learned how to write with the support of George and his wife. George said if you write something that's good, maybe we could find something to do [with it]. When that happened, they were also thinking of doing [*The Ewok Adventure*], which started as just a TV special at first. George felt that was something he could handle with me because I hadn't written anything professional. I could handle that with him. [Laughs.] I am a little uncomfortable talking about this because George and I wrote this together and I talked to him now and then, but we haven't talked to each other for many years. I wish we were talking to each other more and I hope that I'm remembering it right. Of course, I don't know what he was thinking at that time, and I don't want to put words in his mouth.

It was originally intended to be a Christmas special, which is what they were calling it, with the Ewoks. They were also planning on doing a couple of animation series, one based on the Ewoks, and one based on the droids. George just said I think you would get involved with both of those. That's how it happened. Before I became involved with it, I think Lucasfilm and ABC decided it would be a nice idea to make a kind of Christmas special with the Ewoks. They probably figured that the Ewoks were the softer and more cuddly versions of all the *Star Wars* characters. That's how the idea came.

George and I developed the story part together. By the time we developed the story, he wanted to write it. George is really into mythology, and he wanted to write a myth for kids who were dealing with what happens when their families get a little disrupted. He wanted to show kids how they could work through their emotions. Even if the family is getting a little bit shattered, then the kids could be empowered, in their own way, to bring the family back together. He had a pretty general idea of what he wanted to do, and he and I kind of worked out the details of all that. He thought that the Ewoks could be a fairy tale and provide a magical element in a story like that. That's where that story came from.

While the children do reunite with their parents at the end, that's not what the film is really about. It's really about the sibling's relationship and how they protect and rely on each other.
It was an attempt to help kids find their own sense of empowerment in a world where

Warwick Davis is Wicket
Illustration by Pat Carbajal

their family life becomes a little shattered and it was a little scary out there. But to address that in a totally fairy tale way. So they did have to find a guy with some kind of magic. But fairy tales are all psychological. The impulse was to create a story that did exactly what you just described.

Lucas likes to experiment with genres. In *American Graffiti*, he told multiple stories simultaneously. It had its critics, but what interested Lucas about the fourth Indiana Jones film was the idea of inserting Jones into a 50's sci-fi movie. While *The Ewok Adventure* is set in the *Star Wars* universe, it's a different kind of story and in it, Lucas included more fantasy elements than before, including magic.

I wouldn't say that it was contradictory to the rules that were established in *Star Wars* films, but I will say that I was conscious that while we were in the *Star Wars* universe and working with Ewoks, who were in the main movies, we were also conscious that it wasn't part of the main storyline of those movies. *The Ewok Adventure* wasn't part of the main mythology. We knew right away that it wouldn't be about Luke Skywalker and that story. It was going to be about a fairy tale that happens on the Ewok's planet.

I know that George is really into genres, but it was my sense that he was attempting to keep the same genre with *Ewok Adventure*. My guess is the two things that were going through his head were that this is going to be for kids, and in a different way than *Star Wars*, which was for both kids and adults. Here we were trying to keep the level of storytelling kind of simple because it was for television and, at first, it was a Christmas special.

I keep going back to his interest in mythology and it was much more about using these characters to tell a modern fairy tale and to help kids. I remember more of that than discussions about genre. One of the things I used to do there was work as a projectionist, and they used to screen a lot of [film] dailies that were being made. I remember they were making *Raiders*. That was all about genre. And they talked all the time about how much fun it was to watch serials that felt more about the genre than what we were doing.

The Ewok Adventure also has magic, which isn't necessarily a part of the main series.
I would say that the Ewok culture is a primitive culture that practices magic, and they are intuitive with nature. It was a fairy tale, so in many ways, it was less science fiction and more of a fantasy. It had an in-the-woods kind of feeling.

Do you remember what fairy tales you were drawing upon?
Not really. There was a little Hans Christian Andersen, but it wasn't conscious. It was more like, here's the way we worked, and maybe this will help. George and I sat down together, and we worked out the story, beat for beat. It was great for me because I got a Master Class about writing while working with him. It was one of the great experiences of my life. I was about 23 or so. If my memory is right the movie was only going to be an hour, but ABC liked what we did and they asked if it could be an hour and a half, and that way they could release it in Europe as a movie. I don't remember all the details, but the story got expanded. When we first started with the

outline of the story George was calling on fairy tales and he was steeped in it, especially because of his interest in Joseph Campbell. He read a lot about the power of fairy tales and Bruno Bettelheim. [Bettelheim wrote *The Uses of Enchantment: The Meaning and Importance of Fairy Tales*.] I don't remember any specific conversations, but I remember from day one he said I want to write a fairy tale about kids whose parents get taken away. For George, setting it on the planet Endor was already sort of putting it in a forest. Right away, it felt like the right environment. As we beat it out, he had clear ideas there was going to be a crash. At first, we didn't know if it was going to be a monster or if the parents got trapped somewhere. So we had to work all that out.

I want to be sensitive about how I express this, but he had just gone through a divorce, and he wanted to write something for his daughter about what she was going through at this time in her life. It might have also been for kids elsewhere whose families were breaking up. He wanted to empower them so they could somehow find integration in their own lives in a chaotic family situation. I was around during that, and I thought it was beautiful that he wanted to take some of what was happening in his own life and use some of the skills and powers that he has to help others. It's one of the things I like about the movie. The second movie *The Battle for Endor* was more in the battle mode, and I certainly understand that people could have liked the second one more, but I like the one we did because of what it was about. It was about helping kids process their emotional turmoil.

In the sequel, *The Battle for Endor*, the brother and the parents are killed at the start.
I know, it's really dark. [Laughs.] But I think some audience members were missing the lightsabers and the guns in the first movie. I remember a lot of discussion about whether they should even use a gun in ours. But the second one was like Armageddon. In the end, they did use a gun briefly. But there was discussion about what we could and couldn't use from *Star Wars*. It wasn't a hard and fast rule, as I remember it. But there was a definite sense that it was not about the story of the main movie, and it wasn't about the characters of that movie. It meant staying away from all that stuff from the narrative point of view. To me, that also meant no lightsabers. But I do remember a lot more discussion about whether they should use a gun or not. The question was, do we even *want* a gun? Our discussions were not about the *Star Wars* aspect of a gun. Instead, we asked ourselves, should a gun be something that helps provide an answer? Ultimately, we thought the gun did bring a space element to it. Then the question became how often you can use it. The questions were from a place of guns having a certain symbolic and narrative quality of power. Once you shoot a gun it's very powerful, but there are other ways to express that. Can Mace be like MacGyver and build a slingshot? So there was a discussion about it. [In the end, Mace uses his blaster to shoot open a cave entrance.]

You briefly touched on the timeline element. Some fans argue that *Ewok Adventure* takes place before the *Return of the Jedi*. However, by the film's end, the Ewoks have acquired some language so they would have been able to use it to communicate with Leia in *Jedi*. To me, the film feels like it takes place after

Jedi.
To be honest with you Mark, I don't remember what we decided but I know we talked about it. I can't remember if we talked about if *The Ewok Adventures* takes place before Luke Skywalker goes to Endor. I don't get a sense that the Ewoks have a sense of that [story and those characters] yet. [In the Lucasfilm Holocron, the film is set before *Jedi*]

In terms of referencing the main trilogy, Mace is dressed exactly like Luke from *A New Hope*. He also has Luke's haircut. But that might have more to do with the execution than a script note. Also, Mace and then an Ewok swing over a chasm, as Luke and Leia do in *A New Hope*. Were you deliberately trying to refer to the original *Star Wars*?
We weren't trying consciously to reference *Star Wars*. I wish I could remember more clearly, but I could have imagined that Mace was a mini or archetypal version of Luke. But I know that we didn't say we need to have them swimming across the chasm, so it looks like a similar scene in *A New Hope*. That was more about how Ewoks would deal with the situation since they would only have vines. I'm sure Eric Walker was thinking, "I am Luke Skywalker." But you're right, he was dressed like Luke.

There's this little creature filled with light and energy who reminded me of Tinker Bell. Were you consciously drawing on Tinker Bell?
We weren't drawing on Tinker Bell, but we were drawing on those kinds of fairies and they are part of many fairy tales and mythology. It's coming more from that place. Tinker Bell is a version of those archetypal fairies. However, because George and I had seen Tinker Bell, I'm sure that's part of our unconscious. But it wasn't a deliberate reference point. We talked about it from a fairy tale perspective all the time. We talked about it with a sense of once upon a time without attempting to create characters who resembled classical figures. It was much more about how do we tell a fairy tale in this landscape with these characters.

In terms of trying to teach children...
We were not trying to teach them anything, but we were trying to help them understand the situation. Maybe help them feel empowered. We were not trying to be didactic.

Lucas gave Eric Walker and Warwick Davis a camera and told them to make a home movie on the set. So they interviewed the cast and the crew. Walker has subsequently edited that footage into a documentary called *The Making of Caravan of Courage: An Ewok Adventure*. In it, director John Korty talks about the scene where Mace is looking at his reflection in the pond and gets trapped under water, unable to escape. Korty's take on it was that it is a reference to the myth of Narcissus. It's the kind of story you would find in Greek mythology or a fairy tale.
Yes, I would say that. Yes. I'm a pretty unconscious worker and I don't always know where things come from but there is a sense of narcissism. That character was dealing with his own sense of ego, and he was a little boy who was thinking I'm going to take care of it. But there's also the sense of you shouldn't go near there. There are a lot of

magic ponds in fairy tales and creatures that would come out and grab your food. We thought that was an interesting idea to explore and it does have a riff on narcissism. And someone else has to save you from narcissism. That's how you get out of it. John Korty came in at the end of the writing process. He had a lot of input on how it was getting done and we changed a few things to accommodate his ideas.

Something unconventional about the film is that there's a lot of untranslated Ewokese, and the audience has to figure out what they're saying.
There were a lot of great things for me about that experience but that was one of them. We did decide to have them speak in their own language. There was already language in the movies. I do remember certain discussions where someone would ask aren't you going to translate it, and I would wonder why? When making that movie we created a glossary of language. It was not so that the audience could understand it but really to help the actors. But we did think of a language. We might even have had a linguist who was helping us with that.

The same thing bled over into the Ewok animation series, which I also worked on. But once it turned into animation the network was like, come on, what does that word really mean? We could kind of play that game where you could use one word, but it had to be in a sentence with enough context so that the audience could understand what it meant. You're making me remember that one of the things I liked about this movie is that the language is really real. It was a real language. It wasn't just sounds.

I was watching *The Ewok Adventure* with my child who was about ten at the time. Once it is established that there is an Ewok word for food, my kid would recognize its meaning when it was used later in the movie.
That's great. Part of it was what would it be like to be a human around these creatures, around these animals. They are smart, and how do you learn? It's great that you picked up on it. Part of the way it works is that we just wanted to be consistent so if they were talking about a certain something that word would always be the same.

When it first came out it was called *The Ewok Adventure* and then it was later retitled *An Ewok Adventure: Caravan of Courage*.
It was called *The Ewok Adventure* in the United States and then it got released internationally theatrically as *Caravan of Courage*. Now, it's called *Ewok Adventure: Caravan of Courage*.

The theatrical release was not part of the original plan. My impression is that once it expanded from a 30-minute special into a movie that the idea evolved to release it internationally.
I'm not sure how much of the decision to release it internationally was due to the quality of what we were doing or if the thinking was that since this is George Lucas and it's the first time he's coming to television, we can make something out of this. I'm sure it was a bit of both.

It was a challenge to take a fairly complete story and then expand it. That's one of the main reasons that there is a journey feeling to it, where first they meet a shaman character and then another character who feels like he's out of a [Akira]

Kurosawa movie. It was tight at 60-minutes but then it expanded to 96-minutes or so. It's easier to slim things down than to do the opposite. We had to try to keep the drama and integrity while opening things up. It turned it much more into a journey. If I remember correctly, originally after the parents were caught, the children and Ewoks found [the monster's lair] right away. Originally it was pretty quick. [But in the expanded story, the children meet and enlist additional Ewoks along the way.] I don't know how much of the decision to release it internationally was based [on the feeling that] this is cool and how much of it was a business decision.

What was your response to the news?
This was the first time I was doing something like this, so it was a thrill. Now I would have had a different reaction. I would be more amazed. But back then I just thought that's how these things work.

Okay, let's talk about the fourth-ness of the movie. While it is a TV movie it was also released theatrically overseas. For those international audiences, it was the fourth *Star Wars* film.
In terms of what you're trying to do it is an interesting idea because it wasn't perceived that way in my memory. It's an interesting thing because it's not, but it is. It's like what you said the other day in your email and that from a certain point of view it is the fourth movement. When I was thinking about this and talking to you while riding my bike the other day, I thought about comparing it with Beethoven's work. *Ewok Adventure* was more like a chamber piece that was done on the side and the movies are one of his symphonies. That's what it feels like to me. But I could see what you mean that someone in Barcelona would have thought that it was the fourth one. Even though in George's grand scheme it was never part of it, he had those nine-planned movies. From his point of view, it was integral to it, but it was never part of the main storytelling narrative push of the big overarching series. However, even though it was not consciously thought to be the fourth movie it was the fourth. Depending on when you came to it. If you watched *Ewok Adventure* as a kid, you could think it was the fourth. But if you're watching it as more of a *Star Wars*-savvy person, then you know that it wasn't. Like you said, if you were born now, you would think that *A New Hope* was the fourth one, although it was actually the first.

Sorry to bring up my child again, but my experience of the film changed when I was watching it with them, as opposed to when I was watching it alone. Anyway, my child thinks A *New Hope* is the fourth *Star Wars* movie.
It *is* from a structural place. I don't have the answer for you in terms of your thesis for your book. I'm not sure of the answer, but it's an interesting question. One of my favorite animals is a Euglena, which is a single-cell animal. The thing that defines animals is that they have cilia and the thing that defines plants is that they have chloroplasts, and the Euglena has both. But when I was there with George writing this, I got no sense that we were writing the fourth *Star Wars* movie. It was all about we were doing a special with Ewoks for Christmas. I would also think that George was thinking, how can I do something here without having it reverberate throughout the Wagnerian aspect of what I'm doing.

Margarita Fernández as Kaink, an Ewok on an adventure
Illustration by Pat Carbajal

And if we put ourselves back in 1984...
Yikes.

They have a completely different perspective than we do now. Take Marvel, for example. They have their major storylines that play out in feature films, but they also have TV shows on various platforms, including Netflix and Disney+. Some of the TV shows do more to integrate the film narrative and some do less. DC has a different philosophy from Marvel. The DC film and TV universe are separate entities. They have different actors playing Superman and Flash in films from those who play them in their television shows. To use your analogy, today audiences are expected to distinguish between what is a major piece and what is a minor piece.
I know this is kind of random, but when I knew George the trilogy thing used to interest him on a lot of levels. When we were doing the first season of the Ewoks animated series, we changed producers during the second season for various reasons. But in the first season, he wanted to bring the trilogy aspect to the cartoons. I remember thinking it was a challenging thing to write. On episodic weekly television cartoons, we were trying to write three-half-hour episodes where each had to stand on its own but like the movies, they were all connected. So every three episodes formed a trilogy. It was an interesting experiment to try to bring to Saturday morning television at the time. So if you watch one of the self-contained episodes it's interesting, but you can also package them as three. I remember one trilogy that I wrote had something to do with a group of gypsy-like characters who came to the Ewok village. Each episode with those characters was part of a bigger story. You needed to make sure there was an overarching story to the three episodes even though each episode told its own story. It's an interesting way of doing things.

You've written about 14 of the 35 episodes. What do you remember about the development of the animated series *Ewoks*?
The cartoon started developing right around when the development of *Caravan of Courage* was starting to wrap up. Miki Herman [who worked on various Lucasfilm movies and] who produced the first year and Paul Dini [later of *Batman: The Animated Series*] who was the writer at that time, and I would meet with George about once a week. George told us that he wanted to tell little fairy tales and have a trilogy aspect to them. He found it structurally interesting and there was nothing like that on television. At the time, they were selling video cassettes and George and ABC felt that these little trilogies would make a nice package [for marketing purposes]. Besides that, he wasn't so involved in the development process, but we would send stuff to him, and if he felt like we were getting too out there, he would say something. We were pretty free to make it into a Saturday morning cartoon. I like that in the series the trees could talk, and that water could turn into fire. I thought, wow, okay, let's go. I remember it being a real challenge to do this weekly, but we did it because we had to.

It's a very ambitious idea.
It was. If you watch the two seasons, you could see that the second season becomes much more traditional Saturday morning television. The characters are more appealing, but they are also more conventional. I worked on both, and I appreciate both styles, and I learned a lot working on both. But the first season is more in the old-school storytelling mode.

Where do you place *Caravan of Courage* in the franchise?
Are you trying to say that the production values aren't as high as the other ones or the storytelling isn't as dramatic, and it's a different kind of thing, so people can dis it a bit, and how do I feel about that? Or are you trying to say where do you place it?

Both.
I don't feel a need to place it. It's like that analogy that I thought of while biking. There are symphonies and there are also chamber pieces and they're both music even if the scale is different. For me, *The Ewok Adventure* is a little chamber piece.

As for people's reaction to it, I'm not unaware of what kind of movie it is. I would say that I'm proud of it because I think we were trying to tell a certain kind of story. I think little kids, who are the intended audience, like it. I might be biased because I worked on the first one, and I like it more than the second one. But I think people like the second more because it has more of the production values of the big symphonies, but to me, it's all about guns and war. On the other hand, I'm not militantly saying that the first one is great. I know what it is. Part of that was I was on the inside and I know that this didn't have the budget of the big movies.

We struggled over how to make it look like *Star Wars* when people expect spaceships and intergalactic flight, and this wasn't that. We thought about how to handle it and there was a lot of fanfare about "George Lucas is coming to television." So we weren't thinking strategically but there was an awareness that expectations were not going to be met and it was different than the *Star Wars* movies. Thinking about it now, I'm sure there was some concern that it wasn't going to be released in Europe. And it's not *Star Wars*, it's a different thing.

It's a double-edged sword. Because it's *Star Wars* and you could depend on an audience, you could explore something on TV that you couldn't have done theatrically, where the stakes are higher. But to use your apt analogy, you used just the brass even though the audience probably anticipated an entire orchestra.
It's also a very simple story. It's not a complex tale. There are not a lot of characters with different stories woven through the plot. It's not like a *Star Wars* movie in that way either. *Star Wars* had a lot of themes in it. There are all those characters and each of them had stories them and grander things were working and there was the force. There was a meta-narrative in a narrative. Even though it looks like a comic book, and it appears very simple there was a lot to it. But *The Ewok Adventure* story is, kids crash and how can they save their parents. It's a chamber piece in that way too. Just one theme. You're also using only young actors. We were trying to be unpretentious, and we got a lot of criticism for it.

STAR TREK 4

Star Trek IV: The Voyage Home

In the 13 *Star Trek* feature films to date, the Enterprise has been blown up three times. The franchise, like the vulnerable starship, has seemingly been under continual threat of annihilation. The first near-death crisis occurred even before the TV series' 1966 liftoff when, in the original pilot episode, a miscast Jeffrey Hunter sat in the captain's chair. NBC executives rejected the pilot, but instead of canceling the show, the network allowed the series' creator Gene Roddenberry, to reconceive the sci-fi saga. Among other course corrections, William Shatner was cast as James T. Kirk, the charismatic and exuberant leader of the Enterprise in the second pilot, which NBC approved.

The next red alert occurred when, due to the series' dwindling ratings and its high production costs, NBC considered canceling *Star Trek* after its second season. With the encouragement of Roddenberry, passionate *Star Trek* fans organized a letter-writing campaign to "Save *Star Trek*." NBC executives listened, and *Star Trek* was renewed for a third season.

It seemed to signal the end of the franchise when NBC canceled the show in 1969, ending its three-year run and the unrealized promise for the crew of the Enterprise to fulfill its 5-year mission. At the time, few fans would have expected to see the return of Captain Kirk and his trusted yet prickly science officer Mr. Spock. But thanks again to a group of dedicated fans, Trek not only maintained its popularity in syndication, but it also increased it. Capitalizing on the growing Trek fandom, Roddenberry attempted to turn *Star Trek* into a feature film and, when that failed, into a follow-up television series called *Star Trek: Phase Two*. Paramount, influenced by the unprecedented financial success of 1977's *Star Wars*, decided that it needed to enter the cinematic space race. So the pilot episode of *Phase II* was refashioned as a feature film, and Robert Wise was hired to direct *Star Trek: The Motion Picture* (1979).

While some fans responded to the central premise of the film, in which a computer becomes sentient, many felt that the film was dull, turgid, and bogged down by special effects. Some debated whether this movie adaption was mishandled or if *Star Trek* was better suited to television. The writer and director, Nicholas Meyer, answered the naysayers by turning *Star Trek II: The Wrath of Kahn* (1982) into a rousing adventure. With a bravura performance by Ricardo Montalbán as the titular villain, Shatner at his cocksure best, and an emotionally charged ending in which Leonard Nimoy as Spock sacrifices his life for the "needs of the many," *Wrath of Kahn* is a satisfying crowd-pleaser that also deepened the audience's understanding of these familiar characters.

Whereas *Wrath of Kahn* was a well-executed course correction, *Star Trek III: The Search for Spock* (1984) was perhaps a step backward. *The Search for Spock* was aimed too narrowly towards fans steeped in Trek lore and it served only to bring Spock back from the dead. Moreover, the movie squandered other storylines that seemed potentially rich. For example, Kirk's long-lost son David Marcus, who was introduced in *Wrath of Kahn,* was abruptly written out of the story, killed by "Klingon bastards." Kirk's relationship with his son was not sufficiently explored so David's death had little emotional impact on the audience.

Three films into the revival, the franchise was already on shaky ground. Although the movies were still profitable, they weren't embraced outside the fan community, and each film, as is often the case with sequels, grossed less at the box office than the previous entry. If the crew of the Enterprise had any hope of continuing to explore strange new worlds, it was critical for it to expand the audience beyond its diehard Trekkie base. However, after 79 television episodes and three feature films, it was fair to ask if was it possible to significantly enlarge the audience for *Star Trek*?

Thanks to *Star Trek IV: The Voyage Home* (1986), the answer, surprising to some, was a resounding yes. In *The Voyage Home*, the Enterprise crew must travel to present-day Earth to find and capture humpback whales, which hold the secret to neutralizing a threat that will otherwise destroy the planet. While remembered for its environmental message ("To hunt a species to extinction is not logical."), *Star Trek IV* is really a larky character study that gently pokes fun at the beloved heroes. When a marine biologist skeptically challenges Kirk, "Don't tell me. You're from outer space," he replies, "No, I'm from Iowa. I only work in outer space." In another scene, after engaging the cloaking device on their spaceship, Kirk instructs his crew, "Everybody remember where we parked." The film delights in subverting classic Trek tropes, such as the use of the Vulcan neck pinch. In this adventure, Spock doesn't deploy the technique to subdue a combative Klingon; instead, he uses it to neutralize an annoying punk whose music is too "damn" loud.

Star Trek IV earned raves and became the most successful *Star Trek* film in the original 10-picture series, prior to J. J. Abram's franchise reboot in 2009. Based on an idea by Leonard Nimoy and Harve Bennett, *The Voyage Home* was directed by Nimoy, with a script by the writing teams of Steve Meerson and Peter Krikes, and Bennett and Nicholas Meyer. The movie did more than revive a flagging franchise, *The Voyage Home* also paved the way for new Trek adventures, including the TV series *Star Trek: The Next Generation* (1987–1994). Featuring Patrick Stewart as Captain Jean-Luc Picard. *The Next Generation* lasted 7 seasons and produced over 178 episodes. In addition to the 13 original *Star Trek* films, 9 TV spin-off series have been produced, including 6 live-action and 3 animated shows.

The enduring success of *Star Trek* can at least in part be attributed to *Star Trek IV: The Voyage Home*. Although it is not necessarily the fans' favorite (that would probably be *The Wrath of Kahn*), *The Voyage Home* proved to the film and television industry that *Star Trek* could appeal to audiences beyond the franchise's passionate loyalists. In other words, you didn't have to know the difference between a Klingon and a Romulan to enjoy *Star Trek*. *Star Trek IV* also demonstrated that for a well-managed franchise to continue, it is sometimes necessary to try something new, to break the mold, to be daring. It is an overstatement to say that *Star Trek IV* "saved" *Star Trek*, but its success did a great deal to ensure that the series would live long and prosper.

Steve Meerson Interview

What was your perception of the franchise at that point?
I wouldn't say that it was in disarray, but it was lacking direction. We had heard no rumblings of them bringing back the television series, but they were trying to create a franchise that had some legs. I think there was a general feeling that the last few movies were not as exciting, not as revelatory, not as schematically interesting to people as they had hoped they would be. They were looking for some new blood to try to reach a wider audience. I think that was primarily the reason Peter and I were brought in to write the movie.

How did that come about?
Peter and I were relatively new to the business. We had been in the business for about four or five years. We had made a couple of deals at Paramount to write for them and we were working on a movie called *Summer School* with Mark Harmon [as a sarcastic gym teacher forced to teach unruly kids in summer school.] They probably had ten drafts of the script; they wanted to make the project. So they gave it to Peter and me to rewrite. Peter and I did two or three drafts. We were uncredited, but after we did the two or three drafts, the film got made. We were writing another project for Paramount, a sequel to an old movie called *Foul Play*. We also sold an idea to them after another company, Tri-Star, put it in turnaround [dropping the project from Tri-Star's slate but allowing the writers to sell the script to a rival studio]. Paramount bought it and we found ourselves at Paramount again. So they put our name on their list of potential writers. Paramount had also read another script that Peter and I wrote for Fox, which was called *The Long Way Home*. I think that had something to do with the title, *Star Trek IV: The Voyage Home*.

We weren't writing romantic comedies, but we were kind of in that world. We were known to be relatively funny. I think that Paramount wanted to inject the movie with a bit more humor and they wanted it to be a little more accessible to people so that the audience wasn't on the outside looking in. So we were put on the list of potential writers. Then we had a couple of meetings with the producers, Harve Bennett, and Leonard Nimoy, and we were hired for the film.

Based on your *Summer School* and *Foul Play* sequel credits, it seems clear that they were specifically targeting comedy writers rather than sci-fi writers.
Yes, I think it was an effort to expand their audience. They were thinking that they had to do something different. Those days at Paramount were pretty exciting. There were a lot of great movies getting made and Eddie Murphy was making movies for them. I don't know if you've ever heard the rumor that Eddie Murphy wanted to be in *Star Trek*, but it's true. The first couple of drafts that Peter and I did include a part for Eddie Murphy. The part Catherine Hicks ultimately got [Dr. Gillian Taylor, a Marine Biologist] was based, in part, on the Eddie Murphy character who we originally wrote in the script. Eddie was going to play an astrophysicist at UC Berkeley. It didn't happen for a lot of reasons. We were told that they were worried that Eddie would overshadow the *Star Trek* cast. I also think they got cold feet going in that direction. So we created the Catherine Hicks character in the subsequent draft. Then the idea

became that the Hicks' character would interact with the rest of the crew. I have to tell you that I haven't seen the movie in forever or read the script recently, and I've written so many things since then so my memory of this is a little vague.

At the time Eddie Murphy was one of the biggest stars in the world. He was also one of Paramount's most important actors. When you hear Eddie Murphy wants to be in *Star Trek*, what is your reaction? Is it good news? Is it bad news? Is it a mixed blessing?
At first glance, I thought it was a great idea. Peter and I went through the entire process. Even though Eddie was so big, I didn't worry that he would overshadow the crew. I never had those reservations. That's a little more about vanity. But what I didn't know was if, at that point in his career, audiences would have been able to see him inside a movie like this one without any carryover baggage that would impact the story. So I had some reservations about that. But I'm a hired gun and I try to execute as best I can the ideas that people have, work through them, and try to come up with decisions and an approach that best serves the story.

Eddie Murphy is a very talented performer. We've now seen him do drama. How would his alchemy mesh with the *Star Trek* crew, who were also fish out of water in the humor-infused story? Do you worry about that, or does that come down to performance?
It is a performance issue, but I'm also a big believer in tracking that character arc. You have to make sure who that character is. We spent a lot of time giving him a backstory and writing sort of a biography for the Eddie Murphy character. This way we would have a better understanding of who he was. We were trying to make him as authentic as possible. I think that's the only way characters resonate anyway. We wanted to give him a character arc with a beginning, middle, and end. We wanted to make sure that he changed within the story. Of course, we are also order takers, as all writers are when we're hired to do a project for a studio. In this case, there are eighteen different opinions, from the head of production to the two or three other people who are executive VPs in charge of production to the *Star Trek* machine. It's a difficult process when you step into something like that. In any case, you have to hit it straight down the middle of the fairway to make sure everyone gets satisfied. But for us, it was about defining who that character was, and I think it worked. It could have worked, but I go back to my reservations about it. I think you said it best, it's an alchemy issue. Do people buy him in that role? Or do they look at it as Paramount trying to exploit one of the biggest assets in the movie industry at that time by tossing him into another franchise? Would it have worked? I think the movie would have been very successful with him in it. It was certainly a different film with Catherine Hicks. But it was one that Peter, and I are very proud of.

What do you remember any of the early ideas that were floated at your first meeting with Nimoy and Bennett?
There is a lot of misinformation out there about who did what and how things developed. It's something I never really paid attention to until the last couple of years.

Leonard Nimoy as Spock
Illustration by Pat Carbajal

But I will say Peter and I were specifically hired to write a script based on a story by Leonard Nimoy and Harve Bennett. I'm going to be as delicate as I can, but there was no story. They knew they wanted to make a film that incorporated whales and environmental issues. But they had no idea how to get from here to there. They also had a notion about time travel, which obviously found its way into the film. But that was basically it. Peter and I set about writing about seven outlines. Each took the film in slightly different directions. The studio finally approved our seventh outline. So did everyone else. But in those early meetings, you're in search of the best direction to take the story.

I have to confess that when I was hired, I think I had seen only two or three episodes of *Star Trek*. I was not a Trekkie. Peter knew the material better than I did. In those days Paramount had a great library with all the TV episodes plus all of these scripts and manuals from the series. So they armed me with all this great material, and we watched the episodes. I educated myself as to what I was stepping into. But it was an arduous process coming up with the story. We were dealing with a big mix of people. So, on the one hand, it was very satisfying and on the other, it was a difficult experience.

What do you remember about those other outlines?
I don't know that the story varied widely from the first outline. What did change a lot was what I call the ornaments on the tree. At about the second or third outline, we hit upon the spine of the story. In our heads, we had come up with what we wanted to do with it, and then in subsequent meetings with Harve and Leonard, they would come up with how we do that. For example, in the final script, the spaceship appears in a park. In an earlier draft, it flew over the Super Bowl and that's when everybody saw it. So by that point in the process, it's coming up with different variations on the theme.

Everybody has an idea for a scene. What if we put a scene here or there? What if we do it like this? At the end of the day, everybody in the studio system has an idea. Producers always have an idea. Everybody thinks that their ideas are gold. There's always a lot of vanity involved, especially in projects like this. I go back to being a hired gun—you try to incorporate people's ideas. But structurally, I don't think anything changed at that point. After the decision was made to pull Eddie out, after the first couple of drafts of the script had been written, the question then became how do we slot in the Catherine Hicks character in those scenes without disrupting the structure of the rest of the script. We also had to figure out who the character was and what kind of character do we come up with?

Ultimately, adding Hicks benefitted the movie because it gave Kirk more business. He had to enlist her help. The crew as a whole has a main objective, getting the whales and going back to the 23rd century, but they also have individual objectives, and they face different kinds of obstacles along the way.
That's an interesting thing you're touching on because Peter and I consciously did that. We felt strongly that some of the characters had been used in lesser ways in the franchise. We felt that the other crew members needed more to do. To us, the theme was: out of many, one. We're better as a team, we have values, all of us do. We all

fight for what we believe in, and we felt that that needed to be expressed by everyone, not just by two people, Kirk and Spock. Ultimately, that's not the way they wanted that franchise to track, so the other parts were scaled back a bit.

Talk about writing the Kirk and Spock dynamic.
You have to understand the rhythm of it. Kirk always had to come up with the idea, but Spock sometimes would verbalize it. It came down to the question of who's driving the bus at this point? That was always the big question. Peter and I felt very strongly that the other characters needed to have something relevant, or at least more relevant, to do in a story like this. You have two hours to create an emotional ride for people and we felt the characters all needed to have a beginning, middle, and an end, they all needed to change. In fact, we had written more business for them than what wound up in the film, but we had to scale that back because, in their heads, it always had to be Kirk and Spock driving the bus.

Can you elaborate on the notion of who is driving the bus?
At that point in the franchise, there was always a delicate balance in how Kirk and Spock would overcome a challenge. Kirk had to have a fundamental grasp of the issue, but you had to bring Spock's perspective into those issues. It's almost like a Vaudeville routine and it's a matter of who gets the punchline. At the end of the day, the balance sheet has to be about equal. I think there's a certain dynamic that has to be preserved and a certain bottom line that has to be preserved in order for both actors to be pleased with the project. My perception was that neither of them wanted to be updated. It was always about finding the right balance and being conscious of that. By the way, we didn't discover that trick until we had finished the first draft. Then we said, Oh, that's how we have to handle that. Each character will take us through how to solve a problem in their own way. This way the punchlines, so to speak, are divided up in a way where everybody's happy.

Do you remember Shatner's direction to you about how he wanted Kirk to be portrayed?
We only met him once. That was it. His thoughts were relayed to us through Leonard. So I never really knew what prism Leonard was looking through when he relayed the information. The writer's meetings were always with Harve and Leonard. We had asked to meet the other cast members, so we could get a sense of them and so that we could incorporate our own observations about them and their characters. But that never happened. When you work on a franchise, at least on this one, people are very protective of their territory. Ultimately, this led to Peter, and I being let go and Harve and Nick Meyers saying, now it's time to "Trek this up." We knew that at a certain point, we were probably going to be disposed of and it wasn't even painful. We took a lot of pride in our work, and we always gave it everything we had. On some level, we found it amusing how possessive they were. They were changing lines so that if, for example, we wrote "let's go to warp eight," it would become "let's go to warp ten."

What do you think they meant by Trek it up?
What do I think it *really* meant? What I think it really meant is they wanted to get

some writing credit on this movie. That's what I think it meant. I know what was in the material we handed them, I know what was in notes and outlines and summary memos that were traded back and forth, and, in the end, it was a bloody battle for credit on the movie. I stand by the Writer's Guild and what they came up with. Peter and I got first position screenplay credit, which translates to we did the lion's share of the work. In those days for a producer to get a writing credit, he has to write more than sixty percent of the material. It wasn't necessarily that it had to be six pages out of ten. But, for example, it was for structural and character contributions as well. It wound up in an uncomfortable arbitration. If Harve Bennett and Nick Meyer wrote sixty percent of the film, they would have had first position credit. Instead, Peter and I get first position screenplay credit. Peter and I learned a lot about the business and the lengths to which people will go to get credit for things that aren't theirs. I'll leave it at that.

Bond writers are often told either by the Fleming estate or by Eon that 'Bond wouldn't do that.' Often their notes are very perceptive. It's a creative note, not a corporate one. You have to understand that you are writing their characters. They don't belong to any given writer.
I have to tell you that that's totally accurate because having been up to write a Bond movie and almost writing two of them, that's exactly how it went.

Tell me about that.
Well, I think you already know the end of that story. They are being very proprietary about these things, and they should be. As an outsider, regardless of whether you agree or not, that's the way they chose to view their franchise and you have to respect it. It's worthy of respect. Especially if upon reflection one believes that's what's created the longevity of the franchise. They live with this stuff day in and day out. It goes back to our *Star Trek* experience, and I think they wanted to break the mold a little bit. So there were a lot of comments about what they wouldn't do or what they would say. In *Star Trek*, they wanted it to be different. But in our experience with Bond, it felt very much like there were rules and that you had to accept and work with.

What did you want to do with Bond?
Our goal was to bring him back down a bit.

You wanted to break the Bond mold?
Well, yeah. We came up with about twenty pages of where we thought the Bond character should go. We thought we had to reinvent him a little bit because we thought he was getting a little old and stodgy. We thought that we needed to get Bond into the 21st century in a slightly different way. And I think we did. It was received well enough for them to talk to us three or four times and to hear everything we had to say. They did reinvent the franchise a bit. They did reinvent the character a little bit. He became a little rougher, tougher, more real, more edgy. I'm not saying that happened because of the information that we gave them. I think they would have gotten there themselves. With these assets that are so successful for such a long period of time, the question becomes how much change can we really make? How much can we actually change this and expect to keep our base? Do we need to gradually drag people into a

place where they are comfortable with the changes? They're machines and it's an interesting process.

Where did you get with the Bond writing, did you get to the phase of outlines or pitching story ideas or was it just sort of a general meeting?
No, it was my understanding that it came down to Peter and myself or another writer. I don't even remember which movie. But we were deeper into the process than a general meeting. We had presented them with two or three different stories for that film by that time. We were trying to break the Bond mold a little bit.

Getting back to *Star Trek*, when you did meet Shatner, what was his most important note on how Kirk should be portrayed?
It was always about strength. Strength of purpose, strength of leadership, strong moral foundation, and strong ethical foundation. It was about sacrifice. About a guy that brought the best of all his qualities to a situation, from physical skill to mental prowess. That's what Kirk is about. He's someone who tells the truth and someone who can be trusted.

Do you remember if there was any pushback about not having the traditional villain? Except for our own human arrogance, there's no villain.
Right, that's the villain. There was never any talk of a traditional villain. You said it best, humans were the antagonists. There's an overarching lesson and that's one of the reasons that the film was as successful as it was—it addressed a problem on Earth for humans that we could all relate to. It's an object lesson. I think it was a bit ahead of its time.

In terms of the movie's message?
Yes. Greenpeace was around in those days but clearly, people are a lot more aware of environmental issues and about the planet than they were then. Especially as it relates to our responsibility as humans to the greater good. That was the issue for us back then, at least for Peter and myself, and I think that was also true for Leonard and Harve.

You also had to deal with a lot of story threads from *Star Trek III*, including a newly formed Spock, and the destruction of the Enterprise.
There's a lot of baggage you had to deal with. But going beyond how to deal with the plot points from previous movies we wanted to figure out ideas for the future of the series. That was important. I think the scene is still in the movie where Spock is standing on a cliff and looking out into the distance. But you don't know why. It was our idea that Saavik was pregnant with Spock's child. But they didn't want to do that.

Thinking this through, if Spock has a child, it could create interesting story possibilities for later movies.
That was our idea. What would that be like for him?

Spock is half-human and half-Vulcan, and Saavik is all Vulcan. So their son would probably behave like a Vulcan. It would be fascinating to observe Spock attempting to draw out his son's humanity, much as Kirk has done for Spock.

William Shatner as James T. Kirk
Illustration by Pat Carbajal

Exactly. You obviously understand what we were going for. That was our hope too. It would have opened up stories for part five, irrespective of whether we or someone else wrote it.

Do you know why they didn't use it?
I'm not being flip, but I've given up trying to understand what goes on in other people's minds. That was our idea but for whatever reason, they didn't want to use it.

When people decide to make another Start Trek film, they often use *Star Trek II* as the template—Kirk against a villain who has a personal vendetta against Kirk or against the Federation. But *Star Trek IV* was the crossover hit. In some ways, it's the most unconventional *Star Trek* movie because it broke the formula. Do you have any thoughts about what lessons could have been learned from breaking the mold as you guys did?
I think people should be trying to do that all the time. It's a lesson that studios need to learn sooner or later, they need to do something new with the assets they have. When *Star Trek IV* came out, seventy-five percent of the box office was from domestic receipts, as opposed to foreign. Now the model has been flipped. That's because there are places in the world that haven't yet been saturated with our culture. But it will grow old and tired quickly. Especially now when everything seems to happen exponentially faster than it used to because of the technology we have that we didn't have then. There is a certain amount of fear on the part of the people who work at the studios and who are getting paid a lot of money to make decisions. So they usually make safe choices. People are afraid to stick their necks out. I appreciate why they don't, but we live in a world that thrives on invention and creativity. Rehash doesn't take us anywhere new, and it isn't food for thought. It's disposable entertainment, and that's troubling.

PLANET OF THE APES 4

Conquest of the Planet of the Apes

Few could have guessed that a series of movies with men in monkey costumes would be a beacon for innovative storytelling. Unintentional laughs? You bet. Bad ape puns? Sure. But laying the groundwork for the way cinematic stories were told? Sounds like monkey business. Most later films in franchises tell standalone stories. While there may be references to or lingering consequences from past exploits, sequels typically tell discrete stories that require little knowledge of the preceding films. The *Planet of the Apes* series took a different approach. While telling self-contained stories, each film also builds on the events from previous entries. The result is a sprawling, overarching storyline. Marvel Studios and the *Star Wars* and *Harry Potter* series have successfully adapted this ambitious tactic, but it was uncommon in 1968, when *Planet of the Apes* and its sequels were released. According to its star Charlton Heston, *Apes*, released nearly a decade before *Star Wars*, "created a new film genre: the space opera."[73]

In *Planet of the Apes,* Taylor (Heston), an astronaut, crash-lands on a planet with an upside-down society where talking apes' rule and mute humans are their slaves. In *Beneath the Planet of the Apes* (1970), another astronaut is sent to find Taylor and, in the process, discovers an underground city comprised of humans with telepathic powers. Heston, who makes a cameo, was reluctant to appear in *Beneath*. His feeling was, "[T]here is no sequel. There's only the one story. You can have another picture about further adventures among the monkeys, and it can be an exciting film, but creatively there is no film."[74] His observation was largely correct about the second film. The notion of the underground city was inspired by the iconic shot in *Apes* of the partially buried Statue of Liberty, but *Beneath* feels partially like a retread.

Beneath's ending, in which Taylor blows up the apes' planet, seemed to signal the end of the series. After all, it would seem unlikely for the tale to continue if there was no titular planet for them to rule. But the filmmakers found a way around this nit-picky problem. In *Escape from Planet of the Apes* (1971), we learn that before the ape planet's destruction, chimpanzees Cornelius (Roddy McDowall), Zira (Kim Hunter), and Dr. Milo (Sal Mineo), succeeded in using Taylor's spaceship to leave the doomed world and time-travel to then present-day Earth. On Earth, the talking chimpanzees are admired at first but are then imprisoned out of fear that their species will eventually rule the human race. While being held in captivity, Dr. Milo is killed by a guerilla. Cornelius and Zira give birth to a son and name him Milo, after their fallen comrade. Cornelius and Zira are assassinated by government agents and Milo, who is thought to have been killed, is taken in by the warm-hearted circus owner Armando (Ricardo Montalbán). In the last moments of the film, the baby chimpanzee speaks and heartbreakingly calls for his "Mama." Audiences are left to wonder what will happen when the baby chimpanzee grows up and learns that both of his parents were senselessly killed by humans.

Conquest of the Planet of the Apes (1972) is the culmination of the story told in the three previous films. In *Conquest*, set twenty years after *Escape*, humans are using apes as slave labor. Armando is still secretly looking after Milo, the son of Cornelius and Zira, now a guileless adult who goes by the name Caesar (Roddy McDowall). We are introduced to Governor Breck, played by the Academy Award-nominated actor Don Murray, who is the head of the local government and has unbridled contempt for the apes. Breck believes the government's dire warning that Caesar's parents have come from the future and that "their descendants will have all but exterminated the human race from the face of the Earth." The Governor is consumed by his fear that the apes are "burning with resentment. Waiting, just waiting for an ape with a new intelligence, enough will to lead them. Waiting for an ape who can think, who can talk."

Breck suspects that he's uncovered the truth of Caesar's lineage and tortures him on a futuristic "shock table." Later, when Caesar asks him why humans enslaved his species, Breck venomously spews, "Because your kind were once our ancestors. Because man was born of apes, and there's still an ape curled up inside of every man. You're the beast in us that we have to whip into submission…You taint us, Caesar. You poison our guts. When we hate you, we're hating the dark side of ourselves."

In the first half of the film, the humans beat the apes with billy clubs, discharge flame throwers at them, and torture them with jolts of electricity. So when a hardened and defiant Caesar leads the ape's revolt in the second half, the audience is rooting for the apes. After a violent and sustained battle, the apes are victorious. A triumphant Caesar addresses his simian soldiers, "My people will crouch and conspire and plot and plan for the inevitable day of man's downfall… And we will build our own cities in which there will be no place for humans except to serve our ends! And we shall found our own armies, our own religion, our own dynasty. And that day is upon you... now!" However, when the apes are moments away from tearing Breck apart, Caesar has a sudden change of heart. "But now we will put away our hatred. Now we will put down our weapons…And who were our masters are now our servants. And we, who are not human, can afford to be humane…So, cast out your vengeance. Tonight, we have seen the birth of the Planet of the Apes!"

In the original cut of *Conquest*, the apes kill Breck. But Twentieth Century Fox decided to blunt the chilling ending and constructed a new one in which Caesar spares Breck's life. The new finale was cobbled together by blending new dialogue, voiced by Roddy McDowall, with previously shot footage. Although Caesar doesn't allow his warriors to kill Breck in the new version, *Conquest*'s sympathies remain squarely with the apes and firmly support the idea that an oppressed people (or species) can and should take any means necessary to overthrow its oppressors. *Conquest* simultaneously argues that even though "Violence prolongs hate, hate prolongs violence" and that sometimes there is a "right" to "spill blood."

The ending of the fourth film, in which the apes rule earth, neatly sets up the events in the first one. The script for *Conquest* was written by Paul Dehn who also wrote or co-wrote all four Ape sequels and co-wrote *Goldfinger* (1964) with Richard Maibaum. Upon *Conquest*'s release Dehn told *Cinefantastqiue*, "Arthur Jacobs said he thought [*Conquest*] would be the last so I fitted it together with the beginning of

[*Planet of the Apes*], so that the wheel had come full circle and one could stop there quite happily."[75]

Conquest was directed by J. Lee Thompson, who has created some great entertainment, including *The Guns of Navarone* (1961) and *Cape Fear* (1962), both with Gregory Peck, as well as lesser fair like *The Evil that Men Do* (1984) and *Death Wish 4: The Crackdown* (1987), both with Charles Bronson. In addition to dealing with the artistic challenges of the film, Thompson felt added pressure, "[T]here's always the nerve-wracking possibility that the bubble of success may burst at any moment, and you will be the person handing in the one sequel which is the unsuccessful one."[76] He needn't have worried. *Conquest* is the best sequel in the original series.

Conquest concluded the story told over four separate films, but it is not the final *Apes* film. A year later, in *Battle for Planet of the Apes* (1973), also directed by Thompson, the apes and humans battle for "what's left of the earth" following a nuclear war. In the end, the surviving apes and a band of sympathetic humans decide to coexist peacefully. However, the film suggests that theirs is an uneasy peace, and the truce won't last.

The Apes saga continued in the television series *Planet of the Apes* (1974) with Roddy McDowall as Galen, his third role in the series, in 13 episodes of the animated series *Return to the Planet of the Apes* (1975–76), in a remake by Tim Burton *Planet of the Apes* (2001), and in a reboot film series, *Rise of the Planet of the Apes* (2011), *Dawn of the Planet of the Apes* (2014) and *War for the Planet of the Apes* (2017). Although it's not a remake of *Conquest*, *War for the Planet of the Apes* covers similar ground. In both films, Caesar again leads a revolt against human oppressors.

In addition to its bold storytelling approach, each film tells an allegorical story about a political or social issue. A wide range of topics are explored, including racism (*Planet of the Apes*), the dangers of nuclear weapons (*Beneath*), immigrant rights (*Escape*), race wars (*Conquest*), and humanity's seemingly endless inhumanity (*Battle*). As discussed in the following interview, the series' approach to these morality tales is what drew *Conquest*'s star Don Murray to the role of the sadistic villain Breck.

Interview with Don Murray

How were you cast in *Conquest for Planet of the Apes*?
The offer came through my agent. My agent told me that Arthur Jacobs, the producer [of all five *Apes* movies], wanted me to play Governor Breck, the dictator of the humans. I thought, "That's an interesting role. Normally I play good guys." So getting a chance to play the heavy would be an interesting experience for me. And that's why I was very happy to do it.

Did you audition?
No, I did not have to audition.

Roddy McDowall as Caesar
Illustration by Pat Carbajal

Were you aware of the previous other three films?
The only film that I had seen was the first one, the original *Planet of the Apes*. It was a wonderful movie. The fact that the first movie was so good was another reason why I was so pleased to be offered the role.

Did you immediately understand the serious tone of the picture and how you would approach it?
J. Lee Thompson, the director, spoke to us. He said, "Don't think of this in any way as a parody. Approach it as a completely realistic film about what would happen if the apes and humans were close enough in [genetic] makeup, that it could develop to this point." Everything was to be taken very seriously. And we did.

Beyond the idea of getting a chance to play a heavy, what else about the themes of the movie appealed to you?
I thought it was interesting, from the point of view of the film, that the apes were actually superior to human beings. It's their character that makes them superior. I thought that was very interesting. I thought the producers took a chance by challenging the audience and saying that they, as humans, were inferior, at least in this story. It was a bold choice, especially since the apes weren't paying to get into the theater. [Laughs]

The film suggests that left to our own devices the worst impulses of man will manifest.
Yes, absolutely.

It's also an anti-war picture.
I'm glad that you see it like that. I felt that there were elements of that too. And it's marvelous that you also see it that way.

You were a conscientious objector during the Korean War.
I became a conscientious objector even before the war because I didn't want to get drafted and be placed at a desk position, sitting around. You had to sign up for the draft even before people were actually being drafted. But then the Korean War suddenly broke out people were getting drafted. I wanted to get involved and help in a healing way. So I volunteered for service once the war broke out. I volunteered as a medic in Korea, but I was turned down for that because I didn't have the right medical training. I volunteered with United Nations Reconstruction Agency, which was rebuilding South Korea as our troops were reconquering the peninsula. So I volunteered to do construction work, but they were only hiring people who were advanced engineers. They weren't hiring people just for labor. So I volunteered for a group called Brothers and Service; they were doing post-war reconstruction work in Germany. I joined for two years, and I stayed for another six months. During the week I was a laborer, and on the weekends, I joined the German Sports movement trying to convert the young German athletes who were a part of Hitler's Youth into people with Democratic principles. Then I worked with refugees in barbed wire camps around Naples, Italy where they were being held. I stayed there an extra six months because I wanted to complete my work with the refugees. Later, I went back with my wife,

Hope Lange, and we made the down payment on some land in Sardinia with an American visionary named Belden Paulson. We built a free community for refugees and took them out of barbed wire camps and moved them to this free community. So that was my experience in the war.

I love your expression, you wanted to help in a "healing way." It's a beautiful sentiment.
I took the example of that from Lew Ayres's World War II character. That's what he did. [Ayres played the German soldier in *All Quiet on the Western Front* (1930).]

Was your anti-war experience a factor in working on the movie?
That was really the main feature of it. As a matter of fact, if it didn't have that message, I probably wouldn't have done the film. I was a salaried employee, the salary for *Conquest of the Apes* was below what I normally would get paid. But I decided to do it anyway because the film supported my beliefs.

I am impressed by the film's allegorical approach. On its surface, it's an action movie that pits humans against apes, but it conveys a serious message.
And what do you think that message is?

To misquote Caesar, violence begets violence. Hate begets hate.
Right, you stated that very well. That's the core of it.

Practicing your lines in German was a way for you to find the character. There's a lot of Nazi and police imagery in the movie.
There are a lot of parallels between the fictional world of *Planet of the Apes* to the real world of Nazi Germany. My character wore black and that's because the SS officers in Germany also wore black. The swastika was black against the red background.

The film also suggests that if you are a member of a group that has been oppressed, as Jews have been and as African Americans and as many other groups have been, that revolution is one alternative to accepting the status quo.
Yes, that's a very good point.

What was your approach to playing a sadistic villain? I imagine you wanted to try to find his humanity.
I think that's very necessary for an actor. You can't say, I want to play a villain, but I don't want the audience to hate me, so I'm going to compensate and force some humanity into the character if none exists. I didn't do that for Breck. I played what was written in the script. That's what I always did. If I accept the role, I don't try to change it, so the audience thinks differently of me. I submit myself to the role and to whatever the writer writes and that's what I'm going to say on the screen. I don't try to insert my own feelings, convictions, or personality to change the author's intention. The author is the one I serve.

From Breck's point of view, how is he right?
From Breck's point of view, he's absolutely right. He was convinced that the apes were dangerous. They did fight against us. In fact, they won. The ending of the movie proves that Breck was right. [Laughs] He was right all along.

Your character dies violently in the original cut, but he lives in the theatrical cut.
Right, in the original script, and as we first shot it, my character was killed by the apes. They changed it because they wanted to bring my character back. But they didn't consult with me before making that decision. They just made the change. Then they came back to me, and they said we want to bring you back as Governor Breck for the next sequel [*Battle for Planet of the Apes*]. I said, I've already done that I don't want to do it again as a series. I played that role, and I don't want to repeat it. So Mr. Darden ended up playing the new Governor and not me. [Severn Darden played Chief Inspector Kolp in *Conquest*]

Do you have a preferred version of the ending?
I like the new ending where the character doesn't die and the apes, thanks to a rousing speech by Roddy's character, show their moral superiority. Roddy says, "We're going to put away our weapons and end this war between the species." I like that ending. I think it is admirable.

***Conquest* feels like it should have been the final film in the series. On the set were you aware of any talk of extending the franchise?**
No, I was never involved in any discussion about that.

Roddy McDowall was in four *Ape* films.
I had been a friend of Roddy McDowall for years. We had been struggling actors together in New York. So it was a lot of fun to play opposite him in the role. He was magnificent as Caesar.

You must have been grateful that you didn't have to go through hours of makeup as he did.
Oh my gosh, every day I would thank my lucky stars that I was playing a human. I was very grateful that I was not playing Roddy's role. To watch him go through all those hours of makeup. At lunchtime, I could take a break and eat a sandwich and I would look over and see him sipping soup through a straw. That was practically the only food he was allowed to eat. [Laughs] I would always tease him about that during lunch. We had a lot of laughs about that. He had to stay in that costume all day. He couldn't get out of it. Even for a lunch break. He would just drink liquids all day. They would also put these cooling dryers in his mouth so that he wouldn't overheat. They had to do that with all the actors playing apes.

Could you hear the actors clearly when they were in their ape costumes?
Yes, I could. That wasn't really a problem. They would just rerecord their lines later in post. I had to do some looping but not as much as they did.

Did you get the sense that Roddy McDowall, who was in five of these films, enjoyed working on them? They seem grueling and easy for some to dismiss.
I think he really enjoyed the results and that he appreciated that he had made an interesting character. I think he enjoyed playing the character. One of my favorite scenes that I've ever played is a scene between Roddy and myself where we're choosing a name for his character. He points to a name in the book, he points to Caesar, a king. I thought that was a very interesting scene. My character Breck was

trying to figure out if this fellow had any level of intelligence. He's very worried that if Roddy's character had intelligence, then he might be a threat.

What was it like working for director J. Lee Thompson? Thompson has made some really good films, but he's also directed several exploitation movies. What was he like on set?
It was a very positive experience. He saw my preparation and interpretation of the role. I would practice the role just for him. Hitler is, of course, the epitome of a dictator. So I had my lines translated into German and I'm fluent in German. I practiced my lines in German. I also did the role for him in German, mostly for his amusement. It made him laugh and he appreciated it. He gave me a lot of freedom to do the role the way that I wanted to do it. As a director, he supported me in that.

He was a guy who would spend a lot of time thinking about the big picture and the overall impression that he was trying to make with the film. He did not spend a lot of time talking about characters and motivation. He didn't spend a lot of time talking with me about Breck or Roddy about Caesar. He had confidence in us. He saw that we understood how the parts should be played, and Roddy and all the actors were playing them as he wanted. So he spent most of his time on the action of the film and making sure that that was interesting and visually compelling. He wanted to make sure that the visual elements evoke an emotion in the audience. I don't remember a lot of character discussion at all.

Thompson used a lot of handheld cameras for the battle scenes to create energy and authenticity.
Yes, he did. Because of that handheld camera work, you got a visceral feeling of what it would be like to be in that battle. And at that time, they didn't do that very much in movies. It's much more common now.

What is your favorite memory of working on *Conquest*?
My favorite memory is working on that scene with Roddy where I'm trying to figure out if he has intelligence. I loved playing the scene. I love watching it because it came out exactly how the writer and director wanted it. It came out just the way I thought it would as I was playing it. That is also thanks to the editing. They cut it exactly as they should have. It's a very satisfying scene to watch.

Does the film come up at all in your life these days?
Yes, I get a lot of fan mail. I'm constantly getting pictures of *Planet of the Apes* for me to sign. I think I get as many pictures and mail about *Planet of the Apes* as I did as I do about *Bus Stop* (1956), which is a film I made with Marilyn Monroe. It's one of the best films I've ever done, and I was nominated for an Academy Award [and a BAFTA, the British Oscars] for it and I won other awards for it as well. I'm amazed and surprised that I get so much fan mail for the *Apes* movie, but I really appreciate it.

It's off-topic, but what do you remember about working with Marilyn on *Bus Stop*?
She was very, very frightened for some strange reason. The camera obviously loved

Preparing for the conquest
Illustration by Pat Carbajal

her. There was nobody better in front of a camera than Marilyn Monroe. Nevertheless, she was very frightened. She would walk onto the set with smooth skin like a baby's, and without any makeup on, and then she would get her makeup on and come back to the set. She would get so nervous that she would break out in a strawberry rash all over her body. It was just amazing to watch. She was so secure in front of the camera and yet she was so frightened. She was magnificent in it. I think she deserved an Academy Award for it. But she was never nominated for that film or any other. She never even received a special career award, and I think she deserves one. Her performance in *Bus Stop* was more deep, varied, and compelling than Ingrid Bergman's in *Anastasia* (1957). Bergman won the award. She was very good, but Marilyn was clearly giving a more distinguished performance.

Billy Wilder said that she required a lot of takes.
Yes, a lot of takes with Marilyn. She would constantly lose her concentration and have to start over again. It was frustrating because as an actor you had to be at your best in every way possible for every take because they would invariably use the take where she does her best work. So it was very difficult to work with Marilyn.

Any memories of working with Ricardo Montalbán, who played a human who was sympathetic to the ape's plight?
He was one of the kindest and most generous of actors. He was just ideal. He was a total gentleman. He was always very professional but also very warm, he was also helpful to everyone. For example, if you're doing a scene in there doing a close-up of you, he would act his scene off-camera at full performance. And that helps you with your performance. And he gave himself fully to his part and to the film.

Should I have asked you anything else?
No, I think we covered it. You really know and like your subject and that comes across in the questions that you've asked.

You are very kind to take the time to talk to me.
Well, when people get to be my age it's nice to be contacted and not forgotten. [Murray was born on July 31, 1929.] So I appreciate the opportunity to talk to you.

That's kind of you. I almost forgot to ask, do you go to science fiction conventions?
Not specifically science fiction conventions, but I do go to film panels where *Planet of the Apes* comes up.

What are the most common questions?
They want to know about how I fit into the entire *Planet of the Apes* series and why I didn't continue after my character survived. They also want to know if I understand the importance of the movies. And the answer to that question is yes. I do understand the importance, but I am still surprised by it.

HIGHLANDER 4

Highlander: Endgame

"There can be only one" is the oft-spoken refrain of the Highlanders, immortal beings who battle each other to claim The Prize, the power of all the Highlanders who came before them. At the end of *The Highlander*, Connor MacLeod (Christopher Lambert) chops off the head of the Kurgan, an evil immortal, assumes all of his adversary's power and knowledge, and wins The Prize. In doing so, MacLeod becomes one with all living things and will use his power for the betterment of all humankind.

Because there can be only one and because MacLeod is that one, we might wrongfully assume that there are no more stories to tell. However, because the film was a success, tales of the Highlander continued. In the further adventures, it was revealed that MacLeod was not the final immortal. In fact, scores were left. So Connor continued his quest in two sequels—*Highlander II: The Quickening* and *Highlander III: The Sorcerer*.

Between those films, the producers created a spin-off television series *Highlander: The Series* (1992–96) that ran for six years and that focused on Connor's countryman, Duncan MacLeod (Adrian Paul). Connor would occasionally show up in the series.

But as the series continued and as the lead actor became older, more expensive to hire, and possibly less inclined to endure repeated grueling film shoots, the producers decided to pass the baton to a younger generation and change the hero of the series from Lambert's character to Paul's. So the two immortals must join forces to battle Jacob Kell, an enemy with no respect for the Highlanders' sacred rules of combat. Calculating that it would take their combined energy to defeat Kell, Connor forces Duncan to kill him. As a result, Connor's power transfers to Duncan. When the two immortals battle, Duncan wins.

However, by the time the film was released two very different factions of Highlander devotees had emerged—fans of the film series, which was heavy on action, and fans of the television series, which leaned toward romance. Thus, admirers of the theatrical films, walked away from *Endgame* feeling disappointed that their hero fell.

Screenwriter Joel Soisson discussed his approach to setting these two heroes against each other.

Joel Soisson Interview

What makes a good *Highlander* sequel?
A good *Highlander* sequel is like a Bigfoot sighting—hardly anybody would say they've actually seen one. But if I were to guess, I would say you need, bodice-ripping romance, the ennui of immortality, and at least a half-dozen good decapitations.

What were your marching orders with *Highlander: Endgame*?

Although I was hired by the Weinsteins to write the screenplay, I worked closely with Bill Panzer and Peter Davis who produced the prior installments as well as the TV series. They had compiled a frighteningly detailed, annotated genealogy of all the characters, their psychological profiles, histories, and specific rules of engagement—like something Tolkien might have written if he was marooned on an island for thirty years with nothing to eat but coca leaves. Bob Weinstein told me to ignore all that bullshit and just write him a good movie. Nothing like having your bosses coaching from the same playbook.

Typical of serving different masters, Panzer and Davis insisted on creating a role for their favorite character from the TV series, a lovable Scottish rogue played by Roger Daltrey [of the Rock band The Who]. Daltrey had no place in the story, but I was happy to oblige. I spent several days getting the part right—a delicate balance of physical and verbal humor with just the right touch of pathos. Bob Weinstein threw it out. He had control over casting and wasn't interested in a Rock dinosaur-like Daltry. He wanted something for The Edge [U2 songwriter and guitarist, David Howell Evans]. Being a U2 fan, I was even happier to oblige. I banged out a whole new scene—an eighteenth-century Irish wedding, chock full of physical and verbal humor with just a touch of pathos. Plus, and this was truly inspired, I had him jump up with the fiddle band, grab a mandolin and rip into a blistering Celtic jam. The U2 fans would go nuts. I faxed the pages to Miramax, sat back, and waited for my attaboy. My Miramax exec, Beth Calabro, was very complimentary. Except she was a bit baffled how a World Wrestling Entertainment wrestler was going to master the mandolin and an Irish accent in two weeks. Fuck. Wrong Edge.

What are the biggest challenges of making the fourth movie in a series?
Sequel fatigue is unavoidable in all but a few franchises. In the case of *Highlander*, how many times can your immortal hero bed yet another super-hot mortal knowing that someday her looks will fade, and he'll have to move on to the next hottie? OK, in real life, the answer is probably, like, a lot. But in movie terms, the storyline had gotten kinda stale.

James Bond movies are sometimes said to be "the same, but different." How did you need to make *Highlander: Endgame* the same as the previous *Highlander* films and how did you want to make it different?
Romance and swordplay and time-shifting are all basic elements of a *Highlander* movie. So a lot of our story fit under the "same but different" heading. I didn't really get excited about the writing assignment until they let me kill off Connor McLeod. There is no greater satisfaction for a sequel-writer than killing off the original protagonist. It's often the only thing your episode gets remembered for. And here is where I think I was truly inspired by my complete ignorance of swordplay. I came up with a move where the combatants, once engaged, could not disengage without one severing the other's head. Kind of like a game of Twister where you can't quit unless somebody dies. Which, by the way, I now own the copyright too. To add maximum drama and pathos, Connor Macleod, the hero of the film series vs. Duncan MacLeod,

Christopher Lambert as Connor MacLeod
Illustration by Pat Carbajal

the hero of the TV series, the two combatants were lifelong friends and clansmen. And in the end, there could only be one. The TV guy. So yeah. Sweet.

Come to think of it, the film presages the ascent of TV and the decline of cinema. I expect that in years to come, *Highlander: Endgame* will be recognized by scholars as the cultural watershed that it was.

With *Highlander: Endgame*, you had to serve a lot of different masters, including fans of the original *Highlander*, starring Christopher Lambert and fans of the TV series with Adrian Paul. While there is some overlap, they are also two distinct groups. How did you try to address that?

I was told that the typical fan of the TV series was a 40-year-old overweight housewife. I know that's a pretty crass generalization, but it helped me visualize my target audience and try to imagine what was missing in her life that needed fulfillment. The movie side was a much more typical action-adventure demo anchored by young males drawn to blood and mayhem. I tried to create a balance of the two, making the endless parade of burnings, gorings, and decapitations a bit more sensitive and soulful. In addition, I created a special "sanctuary" where Connor could go to avoid being drawn into battle and instead spend eternity in a kind of comatose limbo. Because deep down, he does hate fighting. And speaking with a Scottish accent. Director Doug Aarniokoski definitely skewed to the action side at the expense of the "thoughtful" side. Which was not necessarily a bad thing. Unless you're the writer.

Passing-the-baton-movies are challenging for filmmakers. Often the beloved hero (and more established actor) has to die so that a new hero (and younger actor) can continue the series. Han Solo and Captain Kirk were killed off in *Star Wars: The Force Awakens* and *Star Trek: Generations*, respectively. In both cases, fans were disappointed by how they died. *Highlander: Endgame* had to conclude Connor's story and provide Duncan with a platform to continue the franchise. Can you talk about the decision and the challenges of killing off the main character who started the franchise?

Well, first off, immortality is a bitch when your number one immortal keeps aging on screen. So, in that sense, Connor's screen days were always numbered. The reasons for ending a beloved character are rarely just creative. In this case, I vaguely recall that Christopher Lambert was not too keen on doing any more *Highlander* movies (read: more money) so it seemed like a good time to kill him off. Whether creative or contractual, the hope is that the demise of the main character and the ascent of a new one will give a shot in the arm to a sagging franchise. It's no surprise fans get upset.

Fans have a huge investment in these characters. They're like family. Sometimes the change is successful. But in the case of the *Highlander* series, I think we merely sped up its demise. In the last-gasp installment, *Highlander: The Source* [the fifth film in the series], the whole storyline sank into a pit of conflicting agendas, bad writing, and horrific directing. If it had been seen by more people, it would definitely be on several worst-movies-of-all-time lists.

Full disclosure, I wrote the first draft of *The Source* and ended up taking a pseudonym because it was beyond lame. I came up with the idea that Duncan went in search of the wellspring of immortality—essentially a reverse "origin" story—mostly because I had always wanted to visit South Africa, so I Googled my Africa bucket list and strung it into a road movie. It was going to be the best location shoot ever. Note to self, if you write something that can only be made in South Africa, make sure the producers are committed to shooting there. Our producers, in their wisdom, wound up shooting in Romania instead. And everything just flowed from there.

In some ways, *Highlander* is particularly hard to sequalize. In the first movie, Connor becomes the last immortal. In other *Highlander* films, it turns out that there are other immortals. So on some level, each subsequent film must in some ways betray the basic premise of the first.
I think any change can be made as long as it's done boldly and with full commitment. I think Marvel grasps this every time it makes a sequel. Don't try to split hairs by explaining too much. That was then, this is now. If it works for the story, go for it. And try not to get hung up on details. Die-hard fans, in my experience, won't be happy no matter what you do. Because the perfect sequel has already been made in their heads. *Endgame* was basically the story of a warrior who grew tired of The Game. Maybe on some level, it was a metaphor for writing sequels.

The first two *Highlander* sequels contradicted the lore established by *Highlander*. Part 2 suggested that Connor was actually of alien origin. Part 3 suggested that Connor wasn't the last immortal. In some ways, Part 4 is a sequel to Part 1, but it also accepts the legacy of Part 3 and the TV series by acknowledging that there are more immortals left. Can you talk about the challenges of navigating a complex and contradictory mythology?
Greg Widen, who wrote the original *Highlander* is a longtime friend and collaborator. I watched the original when it first came out and really liked it. I heard *Highlander 2* and *3*, in which Greg was not involved, pretty much sucked so I never watched them. Still haven't. I guess you could say that's not doing my homework, but I just considered it a negative inspiration. So, for me, *Endgame* springs pretty directly from the original and what works best about it follows that pedigree. The whole Duncan side, and the TV characters that came with him, were a bit more problematic since I was never invested in the TV series. I treated Duncan as half of a star-crossed bromance. I did my best to shoehorn in a few of the TV characters, along with Bob's wrestler guy, without really knowing who they were or what they were doing in the film. And even so, I thought the script was coming along pretty nicely until some hack did a dialogue polish that dumbed the film down to a Saturday morning cartoon. Maybe I'm just resentful because that's usually my job.

Critics were pretty snarky as I recall. Variety noted that *Endgame*, released on a scorching hot Labor Day weekend, would be appreciated primarily by people who like air conditioning.

Accepting continuity from one film and ignoring it from another has become standard practice for many long-running series, including Superman and Halloween. But it can be confusing to an audience. Can you talk a little bit about audience confusion and how this impacts the overall perception of the franchise?
Once I heard that the second *Highlander* had something to do with aliens, I figured I

was home free. Kind of like when a quarterback sees his opponent commit a foul and knows he can throw the ball with impunity. I don't know if we would have fared better with *Endgame* if we had somehow amalgamated all that came before. I seriously doubt it.

Since sequels have now become the economic engine of the film business, a new language is emerging, a new set of rules. Sequels can be just sequels, or they can be reboots or they can be sequel/reboot hybrids. My one guiding principle of late has been that, whenever possible, go back to whatever began the series—movie, novel, short story, newspaper clipping—and ignore what followed because you'll avoid a whole lot of contradictory bullshit. For the latest *Children of the Corn* sequel—a franchise that is no stranger to sucking—I went back to the original Stephen King novella and took up exactly where the King story left off, completely ignoring the dozen or more sequels that preceded it, including mine. Liberating.

At the end of the day, though, it's still all about the "Big Idea"—that one alchemic element nobody has ever thought of before, or at least not in the last six months. Without it, you're just serving up leftovers with some spicy sauce poured over to mask the spoilage.

Once you've become so bereft of new ideas, big or small, that your franchise is on life support, a series will sometimes descend into self-parody. It never works but at least you can squeeze out one more sequel before fans run you out of town forever.

Can you talk more about how you killed Connor Macleod? His death needed to be heroic and meaningful, but you could have handled it in many different ways, including having the villain kill him. How was it decided that Connor's best friend would behead him?
I was always a big fan of gladiator movies, not just for the spectacle and all that great over-acting but for the one fundamental element they all seemed to embrace—the hero locked in an inescapable death match with his one true friend. And the ending was always, like, "If I have to die, I'm glad it could be by your hand." It just stands to reason that a richer, more complex emotion arises from killing your bestie than seeing him taken down by a monstrous cartoon villain.

Sacrifice and suffering are essential elements of any hero's journey and the more Christlike, the better. So I looked at Connor's death, and its empowerment of Duncan, as the catalyzing event in the film. Everything else flowed to or from that point. Without a defining moment like that, I think *Endgame* would have been rudderless, falling back on every worn-out cliché in the sequel playbook. I don't recall having to pitch the idea very hard. It came up in our preliminary story discussions and may have been the one—and only—story point that all the producers agreed on.

The one reliable thing that killing off an aging romantic hero like Connor McLeod does for a franchise is to clear the decks for a reboot. Fans get all the emotional impact of seeing their main man die—and then wait in restless anticipation for the thrill of seeing him reborn, young, and shirtless again, and supported by better visual effects. Although we had not discussed a *Highlander* reboot at the time, I embarked on the screenplay for *Highlander 4*, I could sense the end was nigh when one of the producers, Bill Panzer, unveiled his plans for *Highlander: The Musical* on

Adrian Paul as Duncan MacLeod
Illustration by Pat Carbajal

Broadway. It just seemed like the right time to kill Connor. In retrospect, there probably never was a bad time to kill Connor. I feel like I just kinda won the lottery.

TERMINATOR 4

Terminator Salvation

James Cameron's *The Terminator* movie is a lean, tough, action movie. It's about Kyle Reese (Michael Biehn), a soldier in the future, who is sent back in time to protect Sarah Connor (Linda Hamilton) from a cyborg (Arnold Schwarzenegger). The cyborg has been sent to kill Sarah in the hopes of preventing the birth of her son John Connor, the leader of a resistance that will eventually bring down the machine-led army who rule the human race in the future. If the soldier fails and Sarah doesn't give birth to the leader of the resistance, a nuclear Armageddon will take place and most of humanity will be wiped from the face of existence.

To date, there have been five sequels and a television series, all inspired by Cameron's 1984 film. Each film has incorporated the plot of the original and expanded the existing mythology. Because the series is fundamentally about the impact that time travel can have on history, there are three different timelines that a sequel can take place in. Subsequent films can be set in the aftermath of the first film (like *Terminator 2: Judgment Day*, *Terminator 3: Rise of the Machines*, *Terminator Genisys*, and *Terminator: Dark Fate*), in the far-future (*Terminator Salvation*), or in the past (the franchise has yet to explore this timeline).

Terminator Salvation, the fourth Terminator movie, tried to break free from the complex mythology by setting the film long after the events of the first three films have taken place. By breaking free of Cameron's tightly knitted and well-constructed plot, screenwriters Michael Ferris and John Brancato were tasked with writing the fourth film, the first of a planned new trilogy of films. However, *Salvation* wasn't as successful as anticipated and plans for follow-up films based on this new story fizzled out. Subsequent Terminator films, including the James Cameron-produced *Dark Fate,* returned to more familiar territory.

In the interview that follows, Michael Ferris reflects on the challenges of writing a sequel to a beloved franchise.

Michael Ferris Interview

What are the essential elements of a good Terminator sequel?
A good Terminator sequel has to feature strong female roles, of course. Give James Cameron points for that. Also, killer robots from the future were considered a pretty indispensable element in the first three installments. However, since *Salvation* was actually set in said future, our parameters were suddenly widened. My partner John Brancato and I felt the mandate to display the entire panoply of Skynet's technology.

What, while tempting to include, should be avoided?
What we were most eager to avoid was rehashing the phrases "Come with me if you want to live," and "I'll be back." Some things, however, are inevitable.

What were your creative marching orders?
The only criteria we were given at first was that the story should be set in a post-

The Terminator
Illustration by Pat Carbajal

apocalyptic landscape. This was fine with us since it had been our notion to end the previous film with the bombs falling.

What were the biggest challenges of making the fourth film in this series? Conversely, purely from a story point of view, were there any benefits in making a fourth film?

When we came aboard for *Rise of the Machines*, the third film in the series, we saw it as an opportunity to bring closure to the series. The Terminator movies seemed to work quite well as a trilogy, with something of the trappings of Greek tragedy. In the first film, an oracle from the future speaks of an unavoidable fate. In the second film, it seems fate has been cheated. In the third film, we find out, oops, not happening, that's why they call it fate. There was something very clean and simple about that. With the introduction of a fourth movie, however, that simplicity went out the window.

On the other hand, it did present an opportunity to break free of the structure which controlled the first three films—a good guy and a bad guy from the future, warring over the life of an innocent—and make the storytelling a little more surprising.

Can you talk about the challenge of picking up where the previous films left off, honoring those firmly established story points, and then trying to create something new that would propel the mythology forward?

The main challenge we faced was dealing with the fact that the first three Terminator films spend a great deal of time prepping you for what the world of the fourth one is going to look and feel like. We spent a fair amount of energy in early drafts, trying to craft environments that would be unexpected, something other than the usual bomb-blasted landscapes. One was a Skynet-built suburban environment in which humans were allowed to live "normal" lives, while of course being experimented upon from time to time by the machines. A particularly nice touch was a carpet of human bones beneath the artificial turf of the golf course. However, this notion did not survive very far into the development process.

In some ways, *Terminator 4* is a prequel that just happens to be set in the future. Can you talk about the difficulties of writing a story where the ending doesn't feel predetermined?

Well, the problem we faced with *Salvation* was that it all felt predetermined. The course of events had been pretty well laid out in the first three movies—Skynet tries to wipe out humanity, mankind finds back, under the leadership of John Connor, and ultimately triumphs. How do you get around doing something completely predictable?

The solution was, first of all, to give the movie a reason to exist. We faced this problem with *Terminator 3* as well. John and I floundered around for a while, trying to construct the third movie because our initial drafts felt like such a rehash of the second one. Only when we were given the go-ahead to let Skynet win this round, and nuke the planet, did we find we had a compelling ending to shoot for, after which the writing flowed quite readily. That ending seems obvious now, but it wasn't anything the producers had originally intended to do.

The answer for *Salvation*, we decided, was to kill John Connor—we figured nobody would see that coming. The reason Marcus Wright (Sam Worthington's character) is in the movie in the first place is that, upon Connor's death, he is destined to take over as the "new" John Connor. Very few in the Resistance even know what the man looks like, he's a disembodied voice on the radio to most of them. Being a cyborg himself, Marcus understands how the machines operate and is uniquely well-suited to go up against them.

If none of this sounds familiar, it's because this original ending got leaked on the internet, so director McG decided to change it, with the cooperation of the fourteen or so uncredited writers who were brought on board after us. As you may recall, it's Marcus Wright who now sacrifices his life, so that John Connor can receive an emergency field hospital heart transplant. I really hate that ending. *Terminator 2* **features much of the same cast as the first** *Terminator***. Apart from Arnold Schwarzenegger,** *Terminator 3* **has a largely different cast than** *Terminator 1* **and** *2***.** *Terminator 4* **has a different cast than the previous three films. So in some ways,** *Terminator Salvation* **is the third incarnation of the Terminator series. Can you talk a little bit about audience perception/confusion and managing a massive franchise like this?**
We concluded early on that there would never be any satisfying the serious fanboys. The chronologies of the first three films don't make sense, and never will. John Connor is the wrong age at the wrong time, etc. I only know this because I've been told, I'm not much for numbers myself. Likewise, there are folks out there for whom Eddie Furlong is the John Connor—sort of as Sean Connery is to Bond, I suppose. I'm an agnostic on the question of the "best" John Connor. I thought Furlong, Nick Stahl, and Christian Bale all brought something interesting to the role, though they don't exactly seem like the same person.

Terminator Salvation **is the first Terminator film without Schwarzenegger in a prominent role. Of course, thanks to CGI, a body double, and editing, he does have a brief and fun cameo. But aside from that, he's absent. Was there some concern that audiences wouldn't embrace a Terminator film without the series' most iconic figure.**
We were asked to come up with a cameo for Schwarzenegger early on. There was never serious talk of him having a major role since he was busy governing California at the time. As I recall, we had him playing a human being, one who would eventually become the model for the Terminator soldiers. We tried the same gag in *Terminator 3*, but it didn't make the final cut. However, you can find it in the DVD bonus footage.

Had *Terminator 5* **been a direct sequel to** *Terminator Salvation***, what would you have liked to have seen happen? How would you have liked to have seen the story continue?**
Full confession: I've never seen *Terminator 5*. So I'm probably ill-equipped to address its shortcomings if there were any. It had that *Game of Thrones* actress Emilia Clarke in it as Sarah Connor, right, so it can't have been all bad. To whatever extent we fantasized about a fifth installment in the Terminator series, it would have been a

The T-800
Illustration by Pat Carbajal

version with Marcus Wright as the lead. But directorial decisions during *Salvation* rendered that notion moot.

How would you like *Terminator Salvation* to be remembered?
To be honest, I'll always have warmer feelings toward *Rise of the Machines* than *Salvation*, largely because Jonathan Mostow, who directed *Terminator 3* and who is an old friend and former roommate, tends to be quite faithful to the script. Which is something screenwriters in particular appreciate. On the other hand, I will give McG props for creating what is undoubtedly the best-looking film in the series. I found that washed-out post-apocalyptic world fascinating. Moreover, though Mostow is no slouch as a director of action, McG crafted a sequence in the middle of the picture—the escape from the gas station through the capture on the bridge—that gives me goosebumps every time I watch it. I remember when John and I wrote that action, laughing and saying, "Nobody is ever going to be able to film this." I was happy to be proved wrong.

SECTION 5
Comedies

POLICE ACADEMY 4

Police Academy 4: Citizens on Patrol

Comedies, as a genre, don't lend themselves to sequels. Jokes work best when they are unexpected and contain elements of surprise. So when the jokes are told repeatedly, even with variations, the humor is blunted. Perhaps that's why even the most popular comedies of all time, have only spawned fewer than three sequels. *Airplane, Caddyshack, The Naked Gun, Wayne's World,* and *The Blues Brothers* have all created a sequel or two but didn't keep going. Yet, the *Police Academy* films have created six sequels.

The *Police Academy* franchise includes the seven-film series, which also spawned two television series, one animated *Police Academy* (1988–1989) and the other live-action *Police Academy: The Series* (1997–1998).

Despite its initial popularity, the *Police Academy* series is not necessarily well-remembered by cineastes. Viewers who have not watched the films since they were first released in the 80s might forget all but the broadest details. They might recall Steve Guttenberg as a smart-alecky police trainee with a disdain for authority, David Graff as Eugene Tackleberry, a Dirty-Harry-esque recruit, and Michael Leslie Winslow playing Larvell Jones, a man who uses his ability to create realistic sound effects to play tricks on anyone in his orbit.

In writing about the original *Police Academy* for *The New York Times*, Vincent Canby wrote, "*Police Academy* is a rude, crude, noisy, sometimes disarmingly funny, liberated-sexist low comedy. The movie, which opens today at the Warner and other theaters, is *Animal House* redecorated as a school for police officers."[77]

The New York Times was more complementary to the fourth entry: Janet Maslin wrote, The *Police Academy* series seems to shoot for an ever-younger crowd. The optimum viewer for *Police Academy 4: Citizens on Patrol*, which opened yesterday at the Criterion Center and other theaters, would be a 10-year-old boy. Even better, it would be a whole pack of them." The premise is that because the police can't patrol every area of the city at once, they start a program where citizens can help patrol their neighborhoods and "the *Police Academy* has offered train your citizens to better protect yourselves." The police and the community will "work and train" together. Of course, the citizens are only marginally competent and hilarity ensues. There are plenty of characters who get hit in the groin and plenty of ball puns including a moment where, in reference to golf balls, one character commands, "Don't ever touch my balls without permission." With a lot of balls-to-the-groin jokes, *Police Academy 4* is a surprisingly enjoyable film. With its fast pace and affable cast, it's everything Maslin's proverbial 10-year old boy could want. But *Citizens on Patrol* moves beyond balls to the groin humor to include golf balls to the groin, a dog licking a groin ("Are those wedding bells I hear, sir?") and fences to the groin.

Beyond the returning cast of characters, new recruits include future *Saturday Night Live* mainstay David Spade, as a skateboarding hipster and Sharon Stone, as a local reporter who is suspicious of the program. After someone seems to pass gas in court he's told, "Gee sir, I only thought you only got contempt of court if you opened your *mouth*." There's a gun-toting granny who shouts "freeze you scuzz-buckets" to perps, birds with diarrhea, and Bubba Smith, Michael Winslow—the "man of 10,000 sound effects" who uses his prodigious voice talents to distract, confuse, and confound criminals. Stay away if drawing-room farce is what you're after. On the other hand, pigeon jokes, torn pants, spilled food jokes, and cartoon pratfalls are all handled with dependable (and predictable) dispatch. One of the film's more ambitious moments concerns a Port-o-San that is moved, without the knowledge of its occupant, to the middle of a football field.[78]

Police Academy star Steve Guttenberg wrote about the film in his autobiography. He opined, "It had to happen. *Police Academy 4*. The vulgarity of it. We knew it was coming…We would joke about it, like an impending doom. We knew we would want to do it for the money but what artistic piggishness…Doing sequel after sequel sometimes has a slow and degenerative effect. It's like a drug that you build up a tolerance for, doesn't have the same hit to it."[79] Guttenberg also called it "greed" and "duping the audience."[80] He said that the director had to "save a flagging franchise after number three didn't perform as well as the studio would have liked." And "The fourth film had to perform."[81]

In the two interviews that follow, director Jim Drake and screenwriter Gene Quintano, discuss the fourth film in the series and the surprising staying power of the series.[82]

Jim Drake and Gene Quintano Interviews

Generally speaking, what makes a good fourth film?
Jim Drake: More of the same and some new elements. In this case, we had the gang training local citizens in crime prevention. Our group could be their old selves while the new individuals could find ways to bond with their teachers—taking on many of their distinctive characteristics.

Gene Quintano: A good fourth sequel—though that might be considered an oxymoron by some—requires balancing the familiar with the new. By then the central characters have a persona the audience expects and presumably likes or dislikes because seeing the ones you root against getting their comeuppance is part of the fun. You want to deliver the familiar without becoming tedious. Introducing new characters helps avoid the too familiar along with finding a story structure to accommodate conflict, failure, and redemption without being too heavy-handed. In the case of *Police Academy*, with an eye to the foreign market, the stakes and story structure had to be readily translatable. Since humor requires surprise the most difficult juggling act was between the comfort of the familiar and the fun of the new. Sometimes the challenge was to avoid going back to basically the same joke because it worked so well before.

What should be avoided?
Drake: Things to be avoided would be too many of the old jokes repeating themselves and not trying to find ways to expand the nature of the original characters. While

Steve Guttenberg as Carey Mahoney
Illustration by Pat Carbajal

horror, superhero, and sci-fiction movies routinely spawn sequels, there are few successful comedy franchises. Why don't comedies lend themselves to sequels?

While horror, superhero, and sci-fiction movies routinely spawn sequels, there are few successful comedy franchises. Why don't comedies lend themselves to sequels?

Drake: Unfortunately, whereas dramas and action films can always find new ways to tell their stories, comedies are limited by the characteristics of their principles. You can change the locale, but the audience will always demand that the principal performers try to stay the same. One way that the *Police Academy* films bucked the trend was to drop certain characters and introduce new ones. They also were able to find ways to make the principal characters take on more authority in each continuing film.

Quintano: Since comedy historically didn't travel well a large segment of the marketplace was soft. I have no data to support the following, but it seems comedy was readily available on television in the 80s whereas horror and sci-fi were few and far between so consequently film was where one had to turn. Many successful comedies have a central conceit that can be difficult to repeat (How many times can Kevin be left "home alone"?) whereas *Police Academy* could drop its characters into a myriad of situations that were organic to the setup. It was purely escapist entertainment with no pretensions to being anything else and while that may have rankled the critics it seemed to resonate with the audience. Warner Bros. was smart in that they let little time elapse between films: they were released annually, before the last one was forgotten or before much of the core audience had moved on. [Note: The first six films were released annually, usually in March. *Police Academy 1, 2, 3, 5*, and *6* were released in March. *Police Academy 4* was released in April. But there would be a 5-year gap before the seventh *Police Academy* film was released.]

How did you attempt to make *Police Academy 4* different than the previous films in the series?

Drake: I certainly was under the obligation to not broaden the characters too much, but I was able to find new ways to make the old seem new. By pairing the principals with the citizens on patrol, we could see the stars in a new light. They had a little more humanity and understanding than they had had in the previous films. Also, the love interest with Sharon Stone gave Steve Guttenberg a little more to do than he had done in the earlier films.

Quintano: An element of the later *Police Academy* movies was the introduction of new characters who played well against the regulars but also developed their own rapport, like Zed (Bobcat Goldthwait) and Sweetchuck (Tim Kazurinsky) who played so well off each other. *Police Academy 3* and *6* also had bigger set pieces, especially for the finale (jet ski and air balloon chases respectively). These opened up the pictures and created different perils that could be exploited comedically. The films had also become more PG in their humor which opened them up to a wider audience. So, know the characters, service them to the audience's expectations, introduce new characters, keep things surprising and create a bang-up finale that throws everyone into the mix allowing the characters we root for to shine.

What kind of feedback did you get from the studio? What was important to them?
Drake: We got very few notes from the studio. We were the only film they could comment on, however. The other films in production were directed by Clint Eastwood and Barbra Streisand and they would not allow the studio to give notes. One of the few notes we did get was that they felt the ninjas that Michael Winslow fought at the end of the film should somehow be introduced earlier. I came up with the idea that we had a jailbreak earlier on and we could discover the ninjas at that point. There was no explanation given as to what they were doing in jail, but it did seem to mollify the upper management.

Quintano: The Warner Brother executives were very involved in the *Police Academy* development process. Bob Daley, Terry Semel, Mark Canton, and Bruce Berman were all actively engaged in the development of the film's story structure and providing script notes, reflecting how important the franchise was to the studio. Notes centered on how to keep it fresh, the introduction of new characters, and big action sequences exploited for comedy. These elements had to remain accessible to the foreign market which tended to translate into more physical comedy. This was not a genre that received a lot of notes on character arc or motivation, no, the clarion call was always funnier, funnier, funnier!

In his autobiography, Steve Guttenberg indicated that you needed to "save a flagging franchise after number three didn't perform as well as the studio would have liked." He wrote that the "fourth film had to perform." What's it like to work on a franchise that has hit a rough spot and needs to be reinvigorated?
Drake: To be honest, I didn't know that the franchise was in trouble. We basically shot the script that we were given and then pared down the final film to fit a pre-existing time constraint that they had promised the theatre chains. The first rough cut was over two hours in length and after previewing it and considering what worked and what didn't, we cut it down to 78 minutes.

Quintano: The motivation is always in place to make a successful film—to do more—to do better and to feel it has to perform. The studio turned very quickly to developing *Police Academy 4* but there was no greater sense of urgency than for *Police Academy 3*. The fact is there were seven *Police Academy* movies so *3* was not much of a rough patch.

Personal note, out of more than twenty movies I have been involved with *Police Academy 3* is the only one still paying net profit after more than thirty years.

How did it help your job as a filmmaker that *Citizens on Patrol* was the fourth film?
Drake: One of the good things about shooting a sequel is that most of the cast and crew had worked together before. The only problem with this is that sometimes it felt like summer camp, and I was the new counselor. Also, by being the new guy on the block—the previous director (Jerry Parris, director of *Police Academy 2* and *3*) had passed away—the cast was more than willing to try some new directions that I gave

them. I think that I also brought a new perspective to the assignment which opened the cast up to playing along with me.

What appealed to you about directing *Police Academy 4*?
Drake: What appealed to me about directing *Police Academy 4* was the chance to work on a studio-financed picture with all the luxuries that entailed. This was my first big-screen comedy, and I learned a lot, at the studio's expense, as I went along. Also, it was being shot in Canada where I had worked before on *SCTV* (1976–84) and knew that the locations and crews would be first-rate.

Do you have a favorite line or gag?
Drake: My favorite line and gag in the picture came about in the looping session. When Bobcat Goldthwait and Tim Kazurinsky fall out of the airplane without parachutes when it is flying upside down, we cut to a shot of the crowd watching them. In the looping session, Bobcat ad-libbed, "Break your fall! Land on the kids!" The producer hated this, thinking it was cruel, but in a preview screening, it got one of the biggest laughs in the film.

It's been fun rethinking the making of the film with the attendant problems that went with it. But, overall, it was an enjoyable experience, and I was somewhat sorry when they asked me to do the next film and I was tied up on a television series.

Why were the *Police Academy* movies so successful?
Quintano: One of the key elements that enabled the *Police Academy* franchise to spawn so many sequels was its success in the foreign market. It was almost an axiom in the film business that comedy, for the most part, did not travel well: Comedies were more a reflection of culture (though some might argue lack of culture) than horror or sci-fi films. What scares one in New York will probably make one jump in Rome but what makes one laugh in Peoria may not play in Paris.

What both producer Paul Maslansky and Warner Brothers quickly understood was the universality of the police and the desire (with an ultimate appreciation for what they do) to make fun of them. The police force was a comedic environment that traveled and because it was primarily physical humor there wasn't a nuance of a language problem. A slip on a banana peel doesn't need explanation. With that in mind, keep the gags coming, humorously humanize the cops then let them save the day—evolved as the formula.

A few personal notes, I gained insight into the worldwide appeal of *Police Academy* on three different occasions. I encountered a *Police Academy 4* poster on the 14th-century wall circling the small village of Gubbio in Umbria, Italy.

Lance Kinsey, an actor in five *Police Academy* movies, gained insight into making a movie in Spain where he said, "I couldn't pay for my own drinks anywhere in Spain though back home in Brentwood I can't cash a check at the dry cleaners."

Directing a movie in France, I was approached by extras with *Police Academy* posters to autograph. I tried to explain that a writer's autograph on a poster tended to devalue it, but they were big fans and insisted.

Gene, while writing the film, did you think that the series could continue for a few more movies or did you think that *Police Academy 4* would be the last one?

Quintano: The studio turned quickly to the development of *Police Academy 5* so there was barely time to consider that they had made the last one. In fact, a story idea we had kicked around for *4* and one that Paul Maslansky had wanted to pursue for a while, became the plot for *Police Academy 5*.

Where does the film rank in the franchise?
Drake: Of course, the first film set the tone for the franchise, but in all modesty, I feel my film was second-best after that.

Quintano: Where does *Police Academy 4* stand in the 'pantheon' of Police Academy movies? Probably number four. The first film, which was a huge surprise success, obviously made possible all the others and the characters created by Pat Proft and Neal Israel became franchise stalwarts.

ERNEST 4
Ernest Goes to Jail

Ernest P. Worrell, the fast-talking, good-natured, naïve pitchman, was never intended to be the hero of ten movies, released in rapid succession over 13 years. Instead, Ernest was designed to hock products. Created by John Cherry, the co-head of advertising agency Carden & Cherry, Ernest first appeared in a commercial for an amusement park. The Park was so dilapidated that Cherry was reluctant to show it.[83] Instead, he hired Jim Varney to play Ernest, a fictional park-goer who could express his enthusiasm for the attractions. Ernest, as broadly and energetically portrayed by Varney, was so successful that he was repurposed and used in ads for numerous other companies. Over the course of his career, Varney appeared in spots for such diverse products as milk, natural gas, mattresses, ice-cream, pizza, soda (Coca-Cola and its competitor Mountain Dew), fruit drinks, car dealerships, and Cable Vision of Central Florida.

The format of the ads was consistent. Varney would speak directly to camera and address Vern, his unseen friend, and share his unbridled, but skewed passion for the product. In one ad, Worrell recites a poem about sour cream, "Roses are red. Violets are blue. Sour cream is white. And comes in a tube." The spots would end with Varney uttering his catchphrase, "Know-what-I-mean?" The spots were so popular, that Varney appeared in thousands of ads over the course of his career.

The unexpected success of the commercials led to a television series *Hey Vern, It's Ernest* (1988), a children's show that ran for one year and that won a day-time Emmy for Outstanding Performer in a Children's Series. In the show, in addition to playing his signature character, Varney played Ernest's family members, including Ernest's wife Edna, his sister, Bunny Jeannette Rogers, and his Auntie Nelda.

Ernest made his big-screen debut in *Dr. Otto and the Riddle of the Gloom Beam* (1985), a science-fiction comedy that was written and directed by Cherry. In it, Varney plays Dr. Otto von Schnick, a mad scientist, who throughout the film dons a series of disguises, including that of Ernest. Soon, Cherry and Varney realized that Ernest's character needed to be the star of the show, and not a supporting character. In *Ernest Goes to Camp* (1987), Ernest took center stage. A year later, *Ernest Saves Christmas* (1988) followed.

Ernest Goes to Jail, the fourth film to feature the Ernest character, was written by Charlie Cohen and directed by Cherry. In *Ernest Goes to Jail*, Varney plays a bank janitor who, while serving jury duty, is recognized as a dead-ringer for a death-row convict. The convict, also played by Varney, tricks Ernest into taking his place in jail. Through a series of mishaps, Ernest becomes magnetic, escapes jail by shooting electricity out of his hands, defies gravity, and stops the escaped convict from robbing the bank.

Perhaps not surprisingly, *Ernest Goes to Jail* was not embraced by critics. However, Caryn James of *The New York Times* offered faint praise in her review, "*Ernest Goes to Jail* so resembles a high-spirited cartoon that it is likely to be more amusing to children and less painfully obnoxious for parents than its predecessors…But the film is genial, smooth, and inoffensive. In the baffling world of Ernest, being able to give such backhanded praise is more than a grown-up could have hoped for."[84] Cherry, Ernest's co-creator, shrugged off the criticism. The director "gleefully" explained that the critics, "hate us." They're trying to find artistic value to something that's purely a commercial enterprise. It's like an art critic reviewing a baseball card."[85]

With box office receipts of an impressive $25 million, *Ernest Goes to Jail* was the second most successful Ernest film. *Ernest Saves Christmas* made $3 million more. *Ernest Goes to Jail* was also independently made and distributed through Disney's Touchstone label.

But after the sixth Ernest film *Ernest Rides Again* (1993) made only $1.4 million, the remaining four films went straight to DVD. By this time, the audience knew the formula—insert Ernest into an unexpected situation, and the fish-out-of-the-water comedy would follow. Later entries include *Ernest Goes to School* (1994), *Ernest Goes to Africa* (1997), and *Ernest in the Army (*1998), the last Ernest film. Varney, a gifted impressionist, and voice actor also appeared in Pixar's first two *Toy Story* films where he played Slinky Dog. Varney died from lung cancer in 2000. However, before Varney's death, Cherry and Varney were making plans for future installments, including one that would have sent Ernest to space.

About two-hour's worth of the Ernest commercials were collected and sold under the title *Ernest's Greatest Hits: Volume 1* (1986) and *Ernest's Greatest Hits: Volume 2* (1992). Ernest afficionados might have observed that there is a slight but important distinction between the depiction of the Cinematic Earnest and Ernest, the Pitchman. The Cinematic Earnest is gentle, sweet, childlike, and kind. Ernest, the Pitchman, sometimes has a bit of an edge to him. He can be a bit of a rascal. For instance, in one commercial, after Ernest quickly grows tired of listening to the jingle for a car dealership, he takes a hammer and smashes the radio and the nearby bowl of potato chips to bits. In another commercial, he throws a live grenade into a house. Granted, in the later example, Ernest is blissfully unaware of the damage that he's inflicted. Nevertheless, Ernest displays a mischievousness which, to me, is absent from his depiction of the character *Ernest Goes to Jail*.

I interviewed Charlie Cohen, the screenwriter of *Ernest Goes to Jail*, about his experience writing the film.

Charlie Cohen Interview

Can you talk about the development of the script for *Ernest Goes to Jail*?
I had never heard of Ernest when Disney came to me. They had read a broad comic script that I had co-written with a friend about a bunch of frozen Vikings who were dug up and came to life, ending up on a college football team. I don't know this for sure, but it seemed like they were having a hard time finding writers. Otherwise I'm not sure they'd have taken a chance on a young writer with no credits. In any case, once they got in touch, I started looking at all the Ernest stuff I could find. I wasn't wild about *Ernest Goes to Camp*, but there was a TV special *Ernest's Family Album*

(1983) that I thought was really funny and showed off all the many talents of Varney, so I signed on. I mean, I would have probably signed on anyway as it was my first job, but that made me sign on excitedly.

At the time I was very into *Pee Wee's Big Adventure* (1985), which is just terrific from start to finish, and proved that a broad comedy for kids could also be hip, smart, and edgy. I was also heavily influenced by an English TV show, *The Young Ones* (1982–1984), which did the same thing, though it was not for little kids. So the challenge I set myself was to, somehow, create an Ernest movie that would be a worthy successor to those.

What followed was an extensive period of me pitching story ideas both to John Cherry's manager and to Disney. I don't recall most of them but the one I really liked was called *Ernest Goes Bad* and had him being incorrectly sent to jail, winding up in the electric chair, and, ultimately, in hell. There, he helped the devil come to some better understanding of himself, although I can't remember how, and the devil sent him back to earth. Clearly, I was very naïve about the process and the, now obvious, fact that Disney had no interest in making a kids' film set in hell.

Anyway, John's manager responded with the idea of an "evil twin" film where Ernest is switched for his evil lookalike and the bulk of the action takes place in prison. I liked that and Disney was so worn down by this point they agreed as well, and I went off to write it.

Do you recall any of your other unused pitches?
I wish. Aside from the fact that in one he went to hell; I truly don't recall. They are all on a Kaypro CP/M computer somewhere in my garage; rather they are on the genuinely floppy floppy-discs that that computer used. Probably melted by now.

With *Ernest Goes to Jail* and the rest of the films in the series, I got the sense that they started with the comic premise and title and then found the plot.
I think that you may be right to the extent that they wanted to know the setting—camp, jail, etc. The good thing, as far as I was concerned, was that Disney seemed to look down on these films and so there wasn't all that much supervision about their storylines. They were more or less content to let me write it and then work on the script they got back.

I should say that I was not the only writer developing Ernest ideas. This is back in the day when studios would spend a lot of money developing lots of ideas and hire relatively cheap writers to write scripts for them. I had no idea at the time that other writers were writing Ernest scripts as well; that became clear later in the process.

What was important to the producers and studio about what they wanted to see in the script?
John "Buster" Cherry and his crowd, who had developed earlier Ernest movies, had written scripts for the next movies but, I believe, Disney nixed them. So what John wanted, really, was to do his own script with his own writers. Disney wanted something a little hipper, and also wanted more control over the project. They wanted to hire the writers—then fire them if necessary—so that they could be sure their concerns would be heard.

Jim Varney as Ernest P. Worrell
Illustration by Pat Carbajal

Let's discuss two notable moments in the movie. First, without any justification, the evil Ernest flies through the air.

I have always loved broad comedies and fantastical turns of events. The thing that, for me, makes that stuff work is to take all the progressions seriously and set them up. So if Ernest is going to become magnetic when he's electrocuted it was important to set it up at the start. Then, later, build and expand on that idea. Along those lines, I was never wild about the flying because, to me at the time, it didn't make sense.

What my original script had happen was that the final time he gets electrocuted a box of Miracle Grow gardening fertilizer fell on him and so, instead of becoming magnetic, he became huge. Ernest ended up bumping into an old black and white Godzilla monster who shoots fire at him, making him sneeze and his boogers landed on Mr. Nash, gluing him to the ground. Something like that. Looking back now, I'm not sure that makes any more sense than his flying, but for my young self, there needed to be an excuse, a la Miracle Grow, for things to happen.

Can you elaborate on your idea to have Ernest encounter the black and white Godzilla monster?

The basic gag was that he grew because of Miracle Grow, began to fight swat teams, who were trying to stop the enormous Ernest beast. In a couple of shots it grew to monster movie proportions. Then, as if called up by the genre it was playing off of, Godzilla and Mothra show up [and battle]. It was sort of a gag on the movie itself. It was my hat tip to the way I felt as a kid when *Blazing Saddles* suddenly busted loose of its chains and revealed itself to be all taking place in a movie studio [and not in the old West].

[Note: Cohen's script indicates his approach to depicting the battle between Ernest and Godzilla and Mothra. "Wherever possible, the following sequence should be made up of stock footage and shots from old monster movies, both black and white and in color. The Ernest footage that is intercut with these should be equally cheesy and fake. All effects must be cheap and bad."[86]]

The Miracle Grow idea sounds like a fun one. It has a kind of cartoon or child-like logic to it. I agree that you need some reason/to motivate the mayhem. I could not quite understand the reason why Ernest starts flying. Here's a theory, unsupported by the movie. Not only do magnets attract, but they also repel. Maybe the magnetic fields were reversed, and it gives the appearance of flight.

That would be a great reason if anyone had bothered to figure that out. But I'm sure they didn't worry about stuff like that; they just wanted the effect. I guess it's a writer's thing to want things to make sense. As a different director, the hilarious Belgian animator Niko Meulemans, once said to me in frustration: "Why, why, why, why, why?! Always with you it is the 'why!" Similarly, on another Disney project for Carol Burnett, I was working with the execs to figure out a funny and logical reason to get her character speeding down a ski slope when the exec burst out: "What is your problem? Just put Carol Burnett on skis and send her down the mountain. Woo-hoo. It's funny."

Let's discuss another moment. In another scene, Ernest shoots bolts of electricity

out of his body.

That only makes sense if you've started with a guy taking *in* all that electricity. You have to find some way for him to release it and that has the advantage of giving him momentary superpowers.

Ernest P. Worrell started as a character in commercials. Like the "Where's the Beef" woman, the Old Spice Man, and Flo from Progressive. Can you describe the character of Ernest? What did you keep in mind while writing him?

A lot of stuff for me starts with the voice. Jim Varney was such a great actor and Ernest was so sincere and well meaning. Kind of like a much, much dumber *Ted Lasso* [the Emmy nominated series starring Jason Sudeikis as an American coach who coaches a professional football in England]. Ernest is lovable because all he ever does is try to help. The whole premise of the commercials is he's always trying to give Vern good advice and to help him, even as he's destroying Vern's life. Like SpongeBob with Squidward, Ernest just wants to be friends.

The other fun thing about him for me is that he can barely conceive of others having evil intent. This allows him to be inadvertently brave, striding head-first into dangerous situations without considering what might happen.

All of this seems to me to be very much how a kid perceives the world. He or she is just trying to get along, to be nice to everyone and to be treated well, but the world is always much harder and more complex and judgmental than he or she imagines. It's really embarrassing to grow up. So, to watch a character who's even more awkward, well meaning, and wrong than you are, is a great thing. You can laugh at him which makes you feel more competent yourself while, at the same time, you root for him because you've been there too.

And, in a weird way, the Ernest character is very talented. He's able to perfectly impersonate other characters, like the crazy "aunt" type he pretends to be to get out of jail. And he's ambitious. He's always striving for more. He never expects others to take care of him. He's truly admirable. Finally, Varney had tons of charisma and you just have to watch him.

Ernest appears in 10 movies, a surprisingly large number. Who is the primary audience for the film?

As to the primary audience I never really thought about it. I know it's kids but, for me, the key was to make a movie that everyone would think was funny. More important, to make a movie I thought was funny.

I spent a lot of time as a teen watching old silent films by Charlie Chaplin and Buster Keaton and, at the time I was writing Ernest, I felt that modern slapstick had become lazy and clumsy. So it was important to me that all the gags be elegant and well-wrought.

While watching the film recently, I thought that Ernest reminded me of a mix of Pee-Wee Herman and Jim Carrey. Maybe with a little Jerry Lewis mixed in.

Yes. Exactly. And a touch of [silent-picture comics] Harold Lloyd, Charlie Chaplin, and Buster Keaton. That's the script. It's amazing and very cool to me that you got that from the movie.

Do you recall any strange or memorable notes that you were given about the script?
Oh boy. When I handed in the script, Disney liked it, but John Cherry hated it. John, understandably, wanted to do his own Ernest films and not have some kid hired by Disney come in and reconceive his series. The first thing I remember was he had me come in for a meeting. He sat me down so I could watch him going through the script page by page with a red marker, taking out pretty much all my jokes and replacing them with other stuff or saying his guys would "fix it." After four hours of this he had to go and scheduled another meeting with me; we were only halfway through the script. I called my agent and the Disney execs and told them that I didn't really think he was onboard with the script and that I couldn't bear to do that for another four hours.

Then the wonderful Frances Doel, a Disney exec, took me under her wing and, together, we planned out a revision of the script. I went off, wrote it, and handed it in. That's probably the best version of the script. Then nothing happened for about a year.

The story I've heard was that, for whatever reason, my script was shelved, and they kept developing the many other Ernest scripts they had in the pipeline. But none of them turned out well or maybe John was just not going to agree to anything that wasn't his; I don't know. A year later all the execs were being yelled at, the studio heads asking why there was no Ernest film being shot. They looked at what they had and deemed my script to be the closest to shootable.

The funny thing was, they only had my first draft. Frances Doel had moved on, so I now had different executives to work with. They gave me a lot of notes that were the same as the ones I'd gotten from Frances. I told them that they already owned a script with those changes and offered to send them the revised draft, but they insisted that they didn't want to "go back" and so they paid me to, essentially, hand in the same script they already had.

After that there was a long period of development with notes like "Make Better" and "Make funnier!" And each draft seemed to have a new executive with a new idea for a scene they wanted to add. The script got more and more bloated until they became worried that there was no way to cut it down. I said I knew a way to cut it and, for the third time, handed them a version quite like my first revised draft. That was approved to shoot.

John Cherry then took the script off to shoot and made pretty much all the changes he'd wanted to make in the first place and shot the film he wanted. When I saw it, I was horrified but, honestly, if I was him, I'd probably have done the same. This was his character and his baby, after all.

What else do you remember about writing the movie?
I remember using a lot of stuff from my life. Thinking about what he might do in the jury box, for instance, I was absently chewing on a Bic pen when it broke off and the ink got all over my mouth. So that's how that got into it. I remember taking a lot of walks around my neighborhood trying to come up with set pieces and stealing stuff from my surroundings.

How does *Ernest Goes to Jail* compare to the other Ernest movies?

Well, it's like them in a lot of ways. I like to think it has a slightly stronger plot and a bit more edge to it.

John Cherry directed eight of the nine Ernest films. Cherry said, "When we first started, they hated him, just hated him!"[87] There seems to be a love-hate relationship with the Ernest character.
John's not wrong. Disney looked down on slapstick, broad comedy, and John. I probably arrogantly looked down on him too. But to be fair, he wasn't very enamored of me either. I think to him I was just another kid Disney hired to keep him from having control.

Can you talk about your interactions with Jim Varney?
I wish I'd met him, but I never did. I did meet Gaylord Sartain, the fat pal of Ernest's and he was just a great, great guy. Very smart and a terrific actor.

You indicated that you didn't meet Varney. I would have thought that the studio or Cherry would have set up, at least, a quick meeting with him just so that you could hear what direction he wanted to take the character. Those meetings, even if they are intended to placate the talent, are fairly standard. Why do you think that meeting didn't take place?
Everyone involved seemed to be more aware than me that they were making a product. Cherry and company wanted a good product, one they understood. Disney just wanted something they could get away with that would make a predictable amount of money. But the idea of taking it seriously enough to have Varney meet me would not occur to the studio. And for Cherry, it would have weakened his control. What if I met Varney and he loved me? Then he would have wanted to make my draft. I was a writer for hire that was foisted upon Cherry. Why would he want to risk it?

If I sound bitter the reason is two-fold. One: I am a small man, who holds on to slights. Two: I really had a lot of respect for Varney and thought he was a great comic actor; it was truly disappointing I never got to meet him. They were pretty tight friends; had been through hard times together.

What was your reaction to the finished film?
Ok, I'm sorry but I absolutely hated it. I had been more or less told I was not invited to the set so the screening for cast and crew was the first time I had seen anything from it. I remember walking out after the film and someone in the crew saying I must be pretty excited. I just kept my mouth shut but I was almost in tears!

It was my first experience having my work manhandled by the process and I was totally unprepared for how different it was from my script. Not so much in what happened but in tone. It was like watching someone who had seen my version of the film tell his friend all about the movie and get all the details wrong. Almost every joke was replaced with, to my mind, a lesser version of the joke. Though I did like the line "Who would throw out a perfectly good dog?"

But again, looking back at it now, it really was John Cherry, the true author of Ernest, making the movie he wanted to make. I can't complain because my script was really well thought of by everyone who read it and it jump-started my writing career. Every development exec in town read it and seemed to love it. I benefited from low expectations: They all were amazed at how funny an Ernest movie could be.

It's nice to hear that the film jump-started your career. Can you elaborate on the impact that the film had on your career? It could have gone the other way.
It was the script, and the fact that I'd worked for a big studio, more than the movie itself that helped me. I would likely have never chosen to write such a broad, purely comic piece had I not been hired too. Sometimes, I've found, all those constraints and pressures of working for others forces you to get rid of all the stuff that you love but that no one really gets. So your "commercial" script is actually qualitatively better than your own "artistic" script. Sometimes. I also benefitted from the fact that no one expected a script for an Ernest movie to be good, much less innovative. So they were blown away by the script's gentle daring.

I love that you cared so much about the quality of the material you were writing. It sounds like Cherry and company were equally passionate about it, even if you both had different instincts. Your stories and observations underscore how challenging filmmaking can be, even if it is just perceived as another sequel in a long line of sequels. What some might dismiss as just another Ernest sequel is actually a passion project to some.
The one thing I found out working on this picture, is that as a rule, movies come out the way they do because the creators genuinely prefer them that way. I mean that, my whole life prior to this I assumed crappy comedy and crappy movies were crappy because they just didn't care. But working with John, I was shocked that it wasn't that he didn't care. He actually preferred his version. The final film was the film John Cherry wanted to make from the start. All that stuff I didn't like that I thought was too corny, too obvious, or just plain stupid was the stuff that he thought was hilarious, and just the right tone for their movie. And, conversely, all my "daring" crap that I thought gave it an edge and made it "hilarious" was either baffling or annoying to him.

This is kind of true for the Disney executives too. They had to appease their bosses, of course, so their comments were often vague and third hand. But they were all working really hard to make it as good as they could. Their problem was that, despite their best efforts, they were not really fans of slapstick and therefore just didn't get the project. One recurring note I got from studios, both during Ernest and over the years since, is that some of my stuff was "execution based." Finally, I asked what that meant, and it was explained to me that they needed scripts that, if they were done badly, they would still work. This explains all the emphasis on structure in Hollywood, and on the big plot arc. Those things make a story work even if they are told badly. If you have a strong plot, you can keep an audience tolerating your film even if your cast, director, etc., do everything wrong. Anyway, that's a theory of mine!

All of which is to say, I don't feel like any of them were as interested in making a great, groundbreaking comedy as I was. They were interested in not screwing up a lucrative franchise: in making an Ernest movie that would work and would serve its audience. I can't really blame them for that. But, of course, I do.

What did you learn from the experience?
I should probably say that, as a baby writer, I was not only naïve, but somewhat

arrogant as well. I felt it was my destiny to "reinvent and reinvigorate American slapstick comedy." The Disney execs were actually pretty good about gently bringing me to earth and reminding me that that was not the task. The task was to write an Ernest movie.

HOME ALONE 4

Home Alone 4: Taking Back the House

Home Alone (1990) was a monster hit. The family comedy, made on a budget of $18 million, amassed $476 million worldwide. *Home Alone* was the number one film for ten straight weeks, stayed in movie theaters for 200 days, and, at the time of its release, it became the third-highest domestic film of all time, behind *E.T.* and *Star Wars*.[88] By contrast, the fourth film in the series, *Home Alone 4: Taking Back the House* was a movie of the week.

In *Home Alone*, eight-year-old Kevin McCallister (Macaulay Culkin) is forced to defend his house when it's under attack by two inept burglars (Joe Pesci and Daniel Stern). *Home Alone* is written by John Hughes (*Ferris Bueller's Day Off*) and directed by Chris Columbus (*Harry Potter and the Sorcerer's Stone*), who both returned for the sequel. In *Home Alone 2: Lost in New York* (1992), Kevin is once again under attack by the two burglars, but this time he squares off against them in the Big Apple while he takes up residence in a ritzy hotel. *Home Alone 2* made over $350 million worldwide, $126 million less than the original. Still, a hefty haul for a comedy.

When Culkin effectively retired from acting in the mid-1990s, it seemed that the series had ended. But Hughes thought that he could continue the franchise without its adorable star. When Hughes decided to write *Home Alone 3* (1997), he set Culkin's character aside and instead created Alex Pruitt, a different eight-year-old boy whose parents also left him unattended at his house. This time, Alex's adversaries are not common burglars; instead, they are team of world-class thieves who have been hired by a North Korean terrorist organization to steal a microchip that has accidentally come into Alex's possession. If Alex fails to protect the chip, then the terrorists will be able to build a missile that air-defenses cannot detect or stop. The terrorist-themed premise, while decidedly adult for a family comedy, is not necessarily more intense than anything depicted in the first two films.

Home Alone 3, budgeted at $32 million, was directed by Raja Gosnell, the editor of the first two films. *Home Alone 3* brought in a respectable $79 million worldwide but it wasn't the box office hit that the studio was anticipating. *Home Alone 3* is not well-remembered but it does feature an early performance by Scarlett Johansson as Alex's older sister. Johansson, who was only 13 at the time of filming, demonstrates some pre-Black Widow toughness when she forces an FBI to give her classified information about the terrorists who are hunting her brother.

The series lay dormant until the early 2000s when the studio decided to produce a television movie for the ABC network. *Home Alone* 4 would feature the return of Kevin McCallister but this time he would be played by Mike Weinberg. *Home Alone* 4 is written by Debra Frank and Steve L. Hayes (*The Muppets' Wizard of Oz*, 2005), directed by Rod Daniel (*Teen Wolf*, 1985 and *Beethoven's 2nd*, 1993) and it was filmed in Cape Town, South Africa, an unlikely location to double for a quintessential American town. The filmmakers shot at Youngsfield Airbase in a hangar that housed the set of the McCallister's home.[89]

In *Home Alone 4*, Kevin is now 9-years old struggling to deal with his parents' impending divorce. All Kevin wants for Christmas is for his parents to get back together. But chances of their reunion seem unlikely; his parents live in separate homes and his father plans to marry his new girlfriend. Kevin is invited to spend Christmas in his father's mansion and reluctantly agrees. Once at the mansion, Kevin discovers that his dad's home is a fully automated "smart house" that responds to voice commands. Of course, Kevin's dad and his girlfriend Natalie have to leave Kevin so that they can prepare for the royal family's upcoming visit. But Kevin is not alone. Prescott and Molly, two members of the house staff, are there to keep him company and cater to his every whim. But the fun doesn't last. Marv Merchants, the burglar from the first two *Home Alone* movies, and his girlfriend Vera are scoping the house. Marv and Vera are working on a plan to kidnap the prince. Utilizing a series of elaborate traps and employing security measures that the smart house offers, Kevin keeps the royal family safe and staves off the bad guys. In the end, Marv and Vera are apprehended, Kevin's parents are reunited, and the royal family joins the McCallisters for the holiday.

Other straight-to-television sequels followed including *Home Alone: The Holiday Heist* (2012) and *Home Sweet Home Alone* (2021), which debuted on Disney+. In *Holiday Heist*, 10-year old Finn Baxter fends off Sinclair (Malcolm McDowell) and his gang of thieves who are trying to recover a lost Edward Munch painting that has been secretly stored in Baxter's house by a notorious bootlegger who previously owned the residence. It also features the return of Buzz McCallister (Devin Ratray), Kevin's older brother who is now a police officer. According to Buzz, Kevin calls the police every year on Christmas and makes a report about a child who has been left behind while their parents went away on vacation. Kevin is now the owner of a security company. Kevin's apparent desire to provide security to other families is no doubt shaped by his own terrifying experiences as a child.

Since *Home Alone 2*, Culkin has not appeared in any of the sequels. However, the actor reprised his role as McCallister in *Home Alone Again* with the *Google Assistant* (2018), a commercial for Google's artificial intelligence-powered virtual assistant. In *Home Alone Again*, the now-adult Kevin uses the product to enjoy his day home and alone and to defend his house.

The *Home Alone* series is hard to sequelize. Writers are forced to keep finding reasons why Kevin is "home alone" yet again (*Home Alone 2* and *4*). Kevin's repeated isolation and abandonment cast doubt on his parents' competence. Instead of putting Kevin through continual jeopardy, the filmmakers can create a new character and put them through the same paces (*Home Alone 3, Holiday Heist, Home Sweet Home Alone*). Either way, they are forced to repeat the same basic premise over and over. However, for a comedy to work, there has to be an element of surprise.

In the following interview, the screenwriters discuss the challenges of making a *Home Alone* sequel.

Interview with Debra Frank and Steve Hayes

How did you come to write *Home Alone 4: Taking Back the House*?

We had written a couple of projects for the producers, they liked our work, and we had a good working relationship with them. So, when Fox got the *Home Alone* sequel rights, they called us in to pitch.

The first two *Home Alone* films were big hits. They were blockbusters, which still rank as the top-grossing comedies of all time. How did the fourth film become a movie of the week?
Well, you'd have to ask the folks at Fox about that decision. Our best guess would be that *Home Alone 3* didn't do too well at the box office and its value as a feature franchise diminished. Moving to TV seemed like a good idea. We remember the Fox Family was excited to get the MOW [movie of the week] rights to the IP. And we were excited to get asked to pitch for the project because, TV or not, it was a classic franchise to be a part of.

***Home Alone 3* was a standalone film that did not include Kevin McCallister, the protagonist of the first two films, or his family. Can you talk about the decision to return to the original family?**
Not our decision, you'd have to ask Fox. But we'd guess that because the producers now had the right to use the original IP, they wanted to use the original family. And it was probably a big draw for getting TV ratings. When you think about a *Home Alone* movie, you think Kevin McCallister. I don't think most people could tell you the name of the kid's character in *Home Alone 3*. In retrospect, Steve thought that may not have been the best decision, as some literal-minded critics couldn't get over the fact that the same characters were being played by different actors.

Can you describe the writing process? How long were you given to write it?
The process was about the same as for all the MOWs we wrote. We took the basic concept and beat out the details of the story together, then we handed the story outline to the producers and they gave us notes, then we rewrote the outline. Then after revisions/approval from the network, we split up the scenes, wrote them separately, then traded and revised one another's scenes, then got back together to work out the kinks. That probably took a couple or three months.

Then the draft went to the producers, and they gave us notes. After incorporating their notes, the draft went to the network and they came back to us with notes, and we did another set of rewrites together. And that happened three or four times, with several weeks for each revision. Altogether the project took about six months or so.

There was a lot of last-minute tinkering once the production team got to South Africa, to accommodate the location. For instance, South Africa was not going to provide any Christmas-season snow, so we added references to the unseasonal weather and the final kind of meta-payoff where the smart house makes it snow at the end of the movie.

In the first two films, the McCallisters seem like a happily married couple. In *Home Alone 4*, they are separated. Can you talk about that decision?
That decision was made for us.

Can you talk about the idea of a "smart house" and having Kevin use the technology to thwart his adversaries? Kevin is, above all, clever. Was there any concern that his ingenuity would be lessened if he relied totally on technology to defeat the bad guys?

Again, the idea of the smart house came from the network and producers. It sort of became a character in the movie. The notion was to give Kevin bigger, broader resources—there was a sense that every trap you could set in a regular "dumb house" had already been done in the first three movies. Smart house technology was pretty recent, so it seemed like a good way to expand the slapstick possibilities. To expand his diabolical toolkit. We didn't think it lessened Kevin's ingenuity, just gave him a new, up-to-date array of weapons.

What are the most important things to keep in mind while writing a *Home Alone* film?

When writing a sequel for any film, you want to capture the essence of the characters. There's a sweet innocence to Kevin that is also mischievous and, at the same time, he has wisdom beyond his years. We watched the first two *Home Alone* movies to listen to their voices, (especially Kevin's) in order to duplicate their cadence and to get a sense of how they/he would react in a particular situation.

What did you want to avoid?

We wanted to avoid the out-there aspects of *Home Alone 3*, with its terrorist villains and missile-cloaking microchips and get back to the more intimate family focus that helped make the first two work so well. We wanted the *Home Alone* high jinks to have some emotional connection to Kevin and his family.

What was the hardest aspect of writing the fourth film in this series?

The challenge in writing the fourth film is keeping it the same, yet different. Kevin is home alone, encounters the antagonists, and uses his ingenuity to outsmart them. Originally, we pitched something completely different. It was an elaborately plotted story about a house exchange that took the family to Australia, where Kevin ran afoul of a rich hunter/collector and some poachers who were after a rare, endangered creature. Steve suggested calling the bad guy Rupert, which didn't go over well with our producers at Fox, who suggested it wouldn't be wise to use the name of the man who would be signing our checks.

When we heard back from the producers, they had decided not to go with that story. We don't remember why; maybe it was too expensive or too difficult using animals. So, they came back to us with the story about Kevin's mom and dad getting divorced, and Dad having a rich girlfriend who was planning a gala at her lavish smart house.

Of course, it was also a challenge to come up with new booby traps and slapstick gags, but that was a lot of fun, too. On the other hand, we wanted to make sure the slapstick didn't completely overshadow the emotional story of Kevin helping to get his parents back together. We wouldn't say it was the easiest, but perhaps, the most fun was writing the characters of Marv and Vera, the married couple bad guys; so in love but always arguing.

What's it like to be hired to write a movie like this? One might assume that the decision to make *Home Alone 4* as a movie of the week was made at the corporate level. It was a popular IP, that they felt they could exploit. I assume that you are a cog in a larger machine and not always the creative force behind every decision.
You assume correctly on both counts. Not sure as much thought was given to "protecting" the brand as to expanding it. Now there's a fifth installment, *The Holiday Heist*.

Did you have any ideas that you would have liked to have incorporated into the script but couldn't because they were not in keeping with the brand?
We wrote a gag involving Natalie [Kevin's father's girlfriend] having a life-size portrait of herself on the wall and ended up with her head stuck through it. But someone thought it made her look too narcissistic. That's the only one we seem to remember.

While the movie focuses on characters from the first two movies, their entire parts were recast. Was there any discussion of using any of the original actors?
No, first off, McCauley Culkin was 22-years-old, so by then, he should be able to stay "home alone." And the movie wouldn't work with just the parents (who would be too old to have a 10-year-old anyway); it would be quite odd to see the family and not the "real Kevin." Also, TV didn't have the cachet it has now, and you'd be hard-pressed to see a film actor doing a MOW, so we never considered it.

What are your thoughts on the finished film?
It's a cute family movie that was designed more for kids than adults. Debbie's daughters, who were the target age at the time, had friends over to watch it and they laughed and enjoyed it. When the plot-twist reveal of the identity of the burglars' "inside man," was revealed, one of the girls squealed "Ooh! That surprised me!"

And we thought the actors did a great job. French Stewart and Missi Pyle [who played the burglars] were very funny, Mike Weinberg [Kevin] had just been featured in the first *Project Greenlight* film and we thought he was adorable, and Barbara Babcock [the maid who is in cahoots with the burglars], who Steve had loved since she played Sergeant Esterhaus's sexy girlfriend Grace on *Hill Street Blues*.

Originally, I think we had the scene where the bathtub overflows and floods the house at the end of the movie. That was the final straw for Natalie's comeuppance. That and the young royal wanting to spend the holidays at Kevin's house. MOW writers are not involved once they hand in the script. So we're not quite sure what happened on the set during production but at one point we heard they were not going to do that scene, then we heard they filmed it on the last day of shooting because they had to take down the set anyway. Whatever the reason, the house flood is early on in the movie, and in the next scene, the house is fine. There is no cleanup, no mention of any water damage, nothing. That was kinda odd. But overall, we think they did a terrific job with all the elaborate physical bits, especially for a MOW which has a much smaller budget and so many more production constraints compared to a feature film.

SECTION 6
The Sex Comedy

EATING OUT 4

Eating Out: Drama Camp

The *Porky's* and *American Pie* movies are arguably the most famous sex comedy series. Both films titillated and shocked audiences with their crude humor, frank discussions about sex, and their cringe-worthy nude scenes, Even if the critics didn't respond, teenagers flocked to the films and multiple sequels followed. However, *Porky's* and *American Pie* are the exceptions.

When Cannon Films made *The Last American Virgin,* they hoped that they could produce a series of films. Cannon put the trio of male leads under contract for multiple pictures and they had good reason to believe that *Last American Virgin* could endure beyond one film. *Last American Virgin* was a remake of an Israeli film called *Lemon Popsicle* (1978), which was about the exploits of three teenagers in Tel Aviv, Israel in the 1950s. Cannon hired the director and co-writer of *Popsicle*, Boaz Davidson, to remake his own movie and to write and direct it. The *Lemon Popsicle* series lasted from 1978 to 2001 and consists of nine films and one spinoff movie. But *Last American Virgin* earned only $5.8 million, and it was nowhere near as successful as *Porky's*. However, with box-office receipts of less than six million dollars, the planned *Last American Virgin* series ended after just one film.

However, the fate of *Last American Virgin* was typical for sex comedies at the time. There were no sequels to *Fast Times at Ridgemont High* (1982), *Private School* (1983), *My Tutor* (1983), *Risky Business* (1983), *Hot Dog...The Movie* (1984) *Weird Science* (1985), *Secret Admirer* (1985), and *Hamburger: The Motion Picture* (1986).[90] There were a handful of sex comedies that eked out a sequel or two (*Zapped* and *Bachelor Party*), but most were just one-and-done.

Given the lack of sustainability of the storyline, it's particularly noteworthy when a sex-comedy series makes it to four. Such is the case with the *Eating Out* series which is five films strong. *Eating Out* is a sex comedy series aimed at the LGBTQ+ community. The five films were released in a brisk eight-year period, a breakneck pace to write, produce, edit, and distribute a collection of films.

The series consists of *Eating Out* (2004), *Eating Out 2: Sloppy Seconds* (2006), *Eating Out: All You Can Eat* (2009), *Eating Out: Drama Camp* (2011), and *Eating Out: The Open Weekend* (2011).

Filmmaker Q. Allan Brocka wrote and directed the first film and co-wrote the other four with Phillip J. Bartell. Brocka also directed the first, fourth, and fifth installments.

Allan Brocka Interview

For the uninitiated, how would you describe the *Eating Out* series?
The *Eating Out* series is a comedic celebration of what it's like to navigate the complications of LGBTQ sex, crushes, and self-love in your 20s.

***Eating Out* reminds me of the sex comedies of the 80s but aimed at an LGBTQ+**

audience. What were your inspirations?

Eating Out came from my love of what I call "college sex comedies" like *Revenge of the Nerds*, *American Pie*, *Meatballs*, and *Porky's*. I always laughed, and felt a little titillated and subversive watching them growing up, however, I longed to see LGBTQ characters who were celebrated and centered rather than ridiculed, punished, and desexualized.

I cannot imagine that when you made the first *Eating Out* film back in 2004 that you would have guessed that four sequels would have followed. How did a low-budget indie become a series?

I *never* thought there would be one sequel, let alone four. I wrote the script in film school as a joke. We had to write a script every semester. After I'd written all of my deep, meaningful dramas and high-concept big-budget films, I thought it would be fun to read really raunchy, sexy, and gay pages in class every week. The class loved it, it livened things up. When I finished the script, I put it at the bottom of my pile thinking nothing would ever come of it.

I met my *Eating Out* producer Michael J. Shoel on the film festival circuit as I toured with the comedic animated shorts, I made in film school. He asked if I had a script that could be made for $43,000 with two full frontal nudity shots. I said that's super specific, but yes, I do!

$43,000 was how much he had in the bank. He had been a distributor of LGBTQ titles and found that through his distribution network (mostly selling to video stores) he could make at least $60,000 with an LGBTQ title if it was decent and had brief nudity. He wanted to break into producing and was looking for a logistically easy-to-make script. I gave him *Eating Out*. He loved it and we were thrilled that we might make $17,000.

When we were shooting it, I did joke that if there was a sequel, we should call it *Sloppy Seconds*. The film was shot in 10 days in the middle of summer in Tucson, Arizona because that's where Michael lived. It was so hot our camera truck caught on fire canceling our first day of shooting. So, we lost our one day off and shot for 10 consecutive days.

The film was released to film festivals in 2004 and then theatrically in 2005. There was nothing like it at the time. Very few LGBTQ-centered films were comedic and sexy and spoke to LGBTQ youth. It took off in a way we never anticipated. It played nearly 100 film festivals and won a lot of prizes. Audiences laughed so much that they could not hear the dialogue. We decided to do a small theatrical release, and cities kept being added. We actually made our money back and then some with the theatrical release.

We realized the real impact when we released it on DVD. There were no streaming services at the time. For many LGBTQ people all over the world, DVDs were the only way to access LGBTQ stories. We grossed over $2 million in DVD sales.

About a year and a half after its release, my producer called me up and asked what I thought about a sequel. I said, "I have the perfect title!"

How did you come up with the concept of part four, *Eating Out: Drama Camp*?

Drama Camp is an homage to the summer camp theme that is often visited in the sex comedy genre, from *Meatballs* to *American Pie: Band Camp*, sexual awakenings at a camp seem to be an American tradition. It felt like something we just had to explore with *Eating Out* films as well. We started with the question: What would be some farcical sexual and romantic adventures of a camp comedy if the campers were largely LGBTQ? That's where the idea for Drama Camp came from.

How is *Drama Camp* typical of the series?
Drama Camp is typical of the series in a number of ways. Structurally, it begins with a sexy over-the-top scene that is not actually happening in real life and it ends with a post-credit tag scene that is purely there for eye candy. Like the other films, the central premise revolves around someone pretending to be something that they are not in order to get closer to someone that they like, which works somewhat then backfires, but ultimately, they discover that being themselves is what will make them truly happy.

In what way is *Drama Camp* different than the rest of the series?
Drama Camp is different in that it is the first of the films to introduce a major trans character with a romantic storyline. It is also the only film that ends with the central couple breaking up at the end of the film, rather than coming together. Many people were not thrilled with the "unhappy" ending but we ended it that way in order to set up part 5, *Eating Out: The Open Weekend*. *Eating Out: Drama Camp* was our *The Empire Strikes Back*.

What scene in *Drama Camp* is most emblematic of the series?
This would be the scene where Casey acts as the director during play rehearsal and directs his own boyfriend Zack to hook up with his scene partner Benji, knowing that both Benji and Zack have been wanting to hook up for a while now. The *Eating Out* films often contain a scene where two (or more) people hook up via the very active encouragement of a third party.

The trend in many sequels is to serve its core audience and not try to broaden the demographic or appeal to a general audience. Did you take that approach with your series?
We never aimed for a "general audience," but we absolutely made an effort to be more inclusive of people in our LGBTQ audience as the sequels came by bringing in lesbian, bisexual, and transgender characters, and storylines.

Can you talk about the decision to shoot parts four and five at the same time?
We filmed parts four and five simultaneously because we realized we could get more value for our money. When the budgets are so small and the shooting schedules are tight (10 days per film), a larger percentage of your money goes to basic things you need that don't really appear on screen like transportation, lodging, food, permits, etc. Combining the two films to a single 20-day shoot allowed us to save on many of those basic expenses and use the "extra" money for things like better locations, a nicer camera package, and a larger main cast.

Can you talk about the strategy of releasing both the fourth and fifth films in the

same year?

The films were released the same year because it was one of the conditions of one of the financers. In part four, *Drama Camp*, our central couple breaks up. In part five, *The Open Weekend*, they find their way back to each other. Also, in *Drama Camp*, our heroes win an all-inclusive vacation for putting on the best scene in the scene competition. *The Open Weekend* takes place during that all-inclusive vacation.

Most of the films I am writing about in the book are made through the studio system. How do you maintain a low-budget series?

I wish we had a studio backing stories like this. Longer shooting schedules and better resources for bringing up the overall quality would be wonderful. Those resources could also help to find and develop audiences. We exist only because our audience found us. The first two films were released before the social media explosion and we had zero advertising budget, so it was really word of mouth and playing at every LGBTQ film festival we could find that got us enough awareness to make an impact when they eventually released on DVD.

Another difficulty of a low-budget series is that each film gets harder to make. With micro-budget films, you need a lot of favors, freebies, and discounts to make ends meet. When you are making a fourth or fifth installment of something, it gets a lot harder to get those favors. People assume you must be making a ton of money and are just being cheap. While the first film did pretty well, the budgets since then have only increased and the avenues for recouping those budgets have only decreased.

***Eating Out* is a pretty outrageous title. Was there concern about selling it with that title?**

Eating Out was chosen for its outrageousness. There was never an alternate title. We wanted people to know exactly what the tone of the film would be with its title so there would be no surprises when the outrageous sex scenes, for the time, would pop up. There was some concern from some outlets with the second title *Eating Out 2: Sloppy Seconds*. Some places chose to list the title as only *Eating Out 2*.

Did you look at any other series as templates for yours?

We didn't really use any single series as a template for ours. With each of the first three installments, we assumed that would be the final film. When we got to parts 4 and 5, it gave us the opportunity to explore a storyline that could stretch across two films. We hoped there might be a part 6 and did set it up somewhat. But then, of course, part 6 never materialized, so to this day, it feels like something is missing.

The changing landscape of distribution pretty much killed the market for microbudget films like these. Before we could count on DVD sales along with licensing to make our money back. With the disappearance of DVD sales revenue, the only option is streaming licenses—well one license because they all want exclusivity—and that dollar amount simply does not pay enough to finance a small indie film if it isn't going to be an Oscar contender.

Like *Porky's* and *American Pie*, *Eating Out* has some fairly risqué scenes. Where is the line for you and did you ever worry about crossing it?

There are lines all over the place that we have no interest in crossing. Especially when sex and sexuality are involved. We are big on sex being celebrated and empowering. We try to avoid shaming and prefer celebrating the different paths people take. We also want to make sure that everyone involved is consenting, has agency, and is enjoying the sex that they participate in. Everyone who is objectified WANTS to be objectified. That sets us apart somewhat from the old heterosexual sex comedies.

The filmmakers of sex comedies often have to find the right balance between titillating nudity (sex) and raunchy humor (comedy). How did you balance that in *Drama Camp*?
Sexy and funny are a terrific combination. Often in real life we will use humor to broach sensitive or embarrassing topics. It's disarming and allows us to explore those topics further without fear and shame. It's similar in sex comedies, if the situations are funny, you can be a little more explicit without feeling like you're just watching a full-on porn film. Also, so many aspects of sex are just funny to me, for example the inconvenient mess of ejaculate. We don't talk about these things often, which to me, makes it even funnier when we do. Here's something so many of us experience and can relate to but never talk about…talking about it for the first time can be hilarious and cathartic.

What kind of cultural impact have you seen from the series?
The *Eating Out* series became somewhat of a rite of passage for LGBTQ youth of the Aughts and Teens. It shaped a generation of LGBTQ sexual awakenings and takes on our communities in ways I never would have imagined. And if I had, it might have been too overwhelming to process while making the films.

For many Millennials who came of age with the *Eating Out* series, the conversation around sex has only moved forward. Now with TV shows like Euphoria, Elite, Sex Education, and Generation exploring sex and relationships of LGBTQ youth so in-depth, the scenes in *Eating Out* seem almost quaint. It will be so interesting and beautiful to see where Gen Z takes our stories.

SECTION 7
Re-Edited Fourths

ROCKY 4

Rocky IV

Call it Rocky redux. Sylvester Stallone was not completely satisfied with the theatrical cut of *Rocky IV*, his hit 1985 sports drama. So 36 years later, Stallone re-edited the film, added new footage, and re-released the updated version as *Rocky IV: Rocky vs. Drago* (2021). Stallone has always been intimately involved in the series. In addition to starring as Rocky Balboa, the filmmaker wrote all six Rocky films and directed four of them. Stallone has also said that he wrote all of his dialogue for the spin-off movies *Creed*, for which he did not receive writing credit, and *Creed II*, in which he is credited as a co-writer.[91]

Stallone's decision to re-edit *Rocky IV* took some fans by surprise. The fourth film about the boxer was the most financially successful in the series. Still, Stallone felt that he could improve upon his original cut. *Rocky vs. Drago* features 40 minutes of new footage. However, the new iteration is only two minutes longer than the original cut. With few notable exceptions, Stallone did not simply reinstate entire previously deleted scenes. When he was recutting *Rocky IV*, Stallone used alternative angles and different takes from those he originally selected. For the new cut, the writer-director also added discarded lines, and he let the drama play out a little longer by having moments linger. Stallone described the process of identifying these moments as "panning for gold."[92] Stallone viewed re-editing *Rocky IV* as an opportunity to deepen the original movie and move away from the superficial crowd-pleasing aspects of his theatrical cut.

Stallone also admits that while making *Rocky IV*, he was overly influenced by the popularity of MTV, that he stylistically conceived the film as an "extended music video," and that he originally aimed for the "constant bombardment of the senses" and "synaptic overload."[93] In the feature-length documentary *The Making of Rocky vs. Drago*, Stallone acknowledges that *Rocky IV* is "too superficial" and that the film focused on the "physical battle" between the fighters and "ignored the mental one."[94] Stallone attributes his failure in letting the drama play out to his "lack of patience and confidence" as a filmmaker. Instead, he edited all the dramatic scenes to the quick in a misguided effort to get to the fight.

While retaining the music montages, the new cut also provides greater insight into the motivations of three main characters: Rocky Balboa, Ivan Drago, and Apollo Creed. In the original iteration, Apollo fights out of misplaced arrogance, Drago is an unquestioning machine serving the Soviet state, and Rocky's motivation for fighting Drago is simply revenge. In *Rocky vs. Drago*, we learn that Apollo wanted to fight Drago as an act of patriotism; Drago, who is now more physically and emotionally vulnerable, has mixed feelings about how his country is using him; and Rocky's relationship with Apollo is deeper than audiences were originally shown.

In *Rocky vs Drago*, Rocky's complicity in Apollo's return to the ring is underscored. In the new cut, Adrian (Talia Shire) pleads with Rocky, her husband, not to back Apollo in his effort to fight Drago. Adrian argues, "All this won't happen if you don't back it." By including this scene, Stallone holds Rocky partially responsible for his role in supporting Apollo's efforts to return to the ring, an act that will lead to his friend's death. However, Stallone balances this new moment by downplaying Rocky's accountability in a later scene. In *Rocky vs Drago*, it appears that Rocky is simply too late to "throw in the towel" and stop the fight. However, in the theatrical cut, Rocky has the necessary time to end the fight. Instead, he deliberately does not stop it. Of course, Rocky is simply following Apollo's express wishes. Still, Stallone apparently wanted to make the change and limit Rocky's culpability.

In *Rocky vs Drago*, Stallone lets the audience hear Rocky's inner-monologue, which we hear through a new voice over. In the first round, Drago knocks Rocky down. During this moment, the Italian-Stallion gives himself a pep talk, "Breathe. Don't be scared. You can do it. Get up. Get up. Get up." After the final fight, Stallone tones down Rocky's rousing speech where the pugilist talks about how the citizens of America and Russia are capable of change. The Mikhail Gorbachev character no longer gives Rocky a standing ovation; instead the President of the Soviet Union, walks out in disgust. The film also ends with a reprise of "Eye of the Tiger," a soaring song which works perfectly in *Rocky III* but is not thematically relevant to the fourth chapter. Stallone also re-edited the fight to remove instances of obvious "missed" punches, where the camera clearly picks up that the two actors did not make physical contact with each other.

In *Rocky IV*, Drago only spoke 9 lines of dialogue. Granted some of them were memorable—"I must break you" and "If he dies, he dies." In *Rocky vs Drago*, Stallone restores Lundgren's discarded dialogue. The additional moments humanize Drago, but they also make him less of an unstoppable force of nature.

Overall, this new cut allows *Rocky IV* to be more in keeping with the rest of the *Rocky* series, and less of a one-off jingoist action film. As Stallone puts it, "We just figured it out. Three and half decades later… This time it's going to be a drama, with all the superfluous goofy stuff out."[95]

Apparently, one of the "superfluous goofy stuff" was Sico, the robot-butler that Rocky gave to his brother-in-law Paulie (Burt Young). At first, Paulie is perplexed by Sico, this talking robot with a male voice box. But eventually, Paulie changes the robot's voice so that it sounds like a sultry female, implying Paulie develops romantic feelings for Sico.

Sico was operated and voiced by Robert Doornick, the CEO of International Robotics. For Doornick, Sico is not just a character in a Rocky movie. Instead, the robot was designed with an entirely different purpose. In the following interview, Doornick explains Sico's true function, his experience filming *Rocky IV*, and his thoughts about Sico's deletion from *Rocky vs Drago*.

Robert Doornick Interview

Before Sico appeared in *Rocky IV*, you received a call from Stallone's family for a different reason.
Sylvester Stallone's mother called my office. They had seen an interview where I was talking about using the robot with autistic children. As it happens, Stallone has an

autistic boy. They became very interested in having the robot meet his son. Eventually, Stallone said, "I'm going to put the robot in the next movie."

What was your reaction?
I thought that it was a cool idea. The robot had been in many sitcoms and other TV shows already. And I thought it was a cool idea for the robot to be in a *Rocky* movie. Business-wise, it was good for both of us. Because after the movie was produced, the robot continues to travel for many years, even to this day. The robot was a promotional tool for Stallone. By the same token, it was great publicity for our company.

What was Sylvester Stallone like?
Stallone was so nice. At the end of each workday, he wanted to go home, paint, and work out. He was such a pleasant man to work with. Always patient, kind, and compassionate. Sometimes he would bring in t-shirts and hand them out to everyone. Everybody wanted to please him. When someone is in a position of power and they're kind and compassionate, you want to please them. It's like with a teacher in a classroom, when they are nice you want to do well for them.

At the time, Stallone was married to Brigitte Nielsen [who plays Ivan Drago's wife Ludmilla]. Brigitte Nielsen came to the house while we were shooting the scenes. She did not know how the robot worked at the time. Stallone decided to convince her that the robot was artificially intelligent [and not controlled by a human operator]. Someone grabbed a balloon that was filled with helium, inhaled the helium, and started to talk like a chipmunk. Sico immediately said, "I could do that." Brigitte turned to Sico and said, "Impossible you're a robot. Robots cannot do things like that." Sico turned to a prop person and said, bring me a balloon, please. Everyone started to work on my side, including Stallone. Someone put a helium balloon on Sico's face and someone else put a balloon on my face. We both inhaled at the same time and the robot started speaking in a high voice. Brigitte said, "Oh, my god. That's amazing." Everybody else started laughing because she bought it. A few moments later, Stallone told her what happened and pointed to me. She was very angry that she was fooled.

We were having constant fun like that. But the beauty of Sico being operated by an actor with invisible wearable technology is that the robot can come to life at any moment and participate in any activity. Because of that, Stallone thought that the robot was so much for that he decided to write a couple more scenes for Sico. If you remember, Paulie was the recipient of a robot during the birthday scene.

I was going to ask you about that. Rocky's brother-in-law, Paulie, develops a romantic relationship with the robot.
There was a scene that was shot but taken out of the movie that explains that. In that scene, Sico and Paulie walk into Paulie's bedroom. Sico follows Paulie around saying, "You're not going to smoke a cigar in bed, are you? Because that really hurts my sensors. When are you going to take a shower? Change that T-shirt, too dirty." That makes Paulie angry. So Paulie opens up the back of Sico and reprograms the robot. That's why in a subsequent scene when the robot brings Paulie a beer, the robot speaks in a woman's voice. She says, "You're the greatest." Then Paulie says, "She loves me." But without that other scene, nobody in the audience knew why her voice

Sylvester Stallone as Rocky Balboa
Illustration by Pat Carbajal

changed. But the scene was too funny, and it took away from the dramatic feeling of the movie. So they took it out.

What else do you remember about the shoot?
A friendship developed very quickly, as soon as the robot arrived on the set. Stallone was immediately enamored with the robot. The robot became friends with all the actors, and it was a wonderful atmosphere. While we were standing by and not doing anything, we would put the robot in the back of a station wagon, and we would run to a school or hospital. It was a goodwill activity. This was all made possible because of Stallone.

After the movie was shot, we met a couple of times, including once in New York City. I was invited to this private affair and the robot was there too. Stallone made a grand entrance by stepping on Sico's platform. Stallone is not very tall, but he has a giant personality. But being on the platform, he was very tall. Stallone would say, [imitating Stallone] "Hey, you. Let's go over there." The robot would do some stand-up *shtick*. The robot would talk about his love life. They had a repartee. Whatever you said, he would always have the last word.

The Eighties are considered to be a time of excess. In *Rocky IV*, Rocky is extremely wealthy and is living an extravagant life in a mansion. Beyond comic-relief, Sico's purpose in the film is to represent Rocky's excess. Given your original intention behind the creation of Sico, what is your reaction to that perception?
That didn't bother me. We didn't shoot any scenes that showed the robot's true life purpose. Our job was to come, do the work, and go back home. What was important to me is that our company was making enough money so that we could reinvest that money to donate our services so that we can continue with our true mission.

What is that mission?
I think it's important to donate the services of the robot to inspire children to become more interested in the near future and to become architects of a better future. We want to motivate these kids because this world is extremely chaotic. It has been that way for several decades. We use the non-threatening robot, who is bigger than life, to address children. Children will listen to him much more than they would listen to me. But I speak to them through Sico. It's magical. We have these wonderful testimonial letters from educators, medical staff, nurses, therapists, who witness the magic of Sico.

What are the events like?
Sico walks into a room full of children, sometimes autistic children. We gather informally. I prefer to be on a gym floor rather than on a stage. I want the children to be on the same level as the robot. The robot will begin by asking, "Do you ever dream of creating something so far out and so extraordinary that it sounds and seems impossible to do? Do people tell you to stop dreaming about impossible stuff like that and that you're wasting your time?" Of course, most kids raise their hands. Because that's the age when we are extremely creative and have wonderful visions of our future.

The robot says, "I'm glad you raised your hand because I'm here to tell you that nothing is impossible. Let me explain to you why. Many years ago, I was a child, sitting in school, dreaming of building me, and people would tell him to stop wasting his time because robots would only exist in science fiction books. Computers did not exist at the time. So why dream about something that's impossible to create? But that same child decided to keep his dream alive. Do you know what happened? Technology caught up to his dream. Here I am. So tell me about your dreams." The kids will say, "I'm going to invent the teleportation machine." The robot says, "That's very interesting because there's a scientist in Austria right now who is experimenting with faxing small particles of matter from one location to another. This is the beginning of teleportation, why don't you pursue that further? Maybe you'll be the person to finish the job."

Most of the time, we would hear from school principals, and teachers after the robot had left saying how they were amazed how the children will start to talk to each other and form teams. They would say, "Let's try to create something unique inventing something extraordinary to save our planet." When you witness that, you can't help but think that you're on the right track. It's a non-profit gesture. We don't charge money for the robot to visit schools, hospitals, or clinics.

How did you sustain your business?
In those days, robots were very popular. Sico was the first robot of its kind. So we would get a tremendous amount of media attention. They would love to talk about "this crazy inventor." Every time we were on television, a school would call us and ask if we could come. We would say absolutely. Of course, we went broke doing that. We needed a funding mechanism so that we could continue to do this goodwill work for free.

Suddenly, we received a call from Lee Iacocca's office, who had recently joined Chrysler as the head of their corporation. His office said, "We saw how your robot was designed to bond very rapidly with any age, social, ethnic, or cultural group. We would like to use your robot in South America and throughout the United States to target our audience and to make them fall in love with our car." I said, "Absolutely, we know exactly how to do that." But when I got off the phone, I thought, "I don't know exactly how to do that."

But it was very easy. It turned out to be the same approach we used when we visited children at schools. The robot did extremely well for them. It was the beginning of our funding. We hosted all the major auto shows around the country and overseas as well. We ended up working for Ford, GM, Chrysler, Renault, Peugeot, and Mercedes. All the major car companies throughout the world rallied behind us. The press would say, "Can we have the robot visit us tomorrow at 6 am for the morning news show? We would get to the studio at 6 am. They, "Okay, we'll give you 30 seconds. And then you're on your way." But Sico would walk up and down the hallways and say, "Where is my dressing room?" The robot would say, "Make sure you favor my right side because I look better that way." The producers would laugh and without fail, they would say, "This is so entertaining. Can he stay and do the weather report? Can we have an interview with the key anchor people? Can the robot

Sico as Paulie's Robot
Illustration by Pat Carbajal

dance with them? Instead of getting 30 seconds of coverage, our clients are getting 30 minutes of coverage. So our clients loved us. Then we would go back to the shows. The audience, who just saw the robot on television, would flock to him and take photos. Sometimes people would say to him, "My grandmother is very ill. Do you think she'll be ok?" They thought the robot had the answers to everything.

I read that there was some talk of a Paulie-Sico spin-off television series.
That was for Burt Young and me. We became friendly. I said to him, "This relationship between you and the robot is so profound and so funny that we should consider turning it into a sitcom." He invited me over to his house in Hollywood, we sat down, and talked about writing it. I wrote the story myself. It would be the same character, Paulie. He's a down-and-out person who has a small daughter. The government has taken his daughter away because he's broke, and they say he's not capable of taking proper care of his child. He's destroyed by that because he and his daughter love each other.

Paulie's living in Los Angeles, on top of a garage. People don't think he's smart but he's quite clever with mechanical things. Periodically, he goes to Las Vegas to do a little work as a weekend security guard. One day, he's driving back from one of his Las Vegas jobs and sees this ball of fire coming down the road. He gets off the road and sees that the ball of fire is actually a spacecraft. He finds Sico who is having a problem with his spaceship. Sico comes from a different civilization. He thinks earth people are stupid. Especially Paulie. One thing leads to another, and it becomes an *Odd Couple* kind of situation [about mismatched roommates]. While Sico works on repairing his craft to return to his galaxy, he also tries to help Paulie get his act together and get his daughter back.

Of course, there are comical and also warm and fuzzy situations. Everybody tries to hide the fact that Sico is an alien. Paulie and Sico agree that if anyone asks, Paulie will say that Sico is a [store-bought] kit from Radio Shack. So that everybody buys it, Sico sometimes has to act as stupid as possible. Burt Young and I both wanted to do it. Unfortunately, he got called to work on another gig. Then we went away our separate ways and the concept faded. But it was very strong and very real.

As you know, Stallone re-edited *Rocky IV*. In his new version, Sico has been eliminated. How did you hear about it?
Everybody talks to me about anything related to Rocky. They were going to have to pay him royalties for life if they kept him in the movie. I understood the business aspect of it. Stallone and I are on friendly terms with each other. I knew why he was doing it. It didn't bother me.

There might be another reason. The Sico scenes are comical, and, in this new version, Stallone wanted to tone down the comedy and up the ante on the drama. Do you think that's a possibility why he cut Sico?
Yes, you're right. The storyline Stallone wrote for *Rocky IV* was very dramatic. Even when we were shooting, there was a lot of talk between the producers. They were saying that Sico should not have been in this movie because it takes away from the dramatic tone of the story. I understood that while shooting but I was not about to say,

"Let's tear this up the contract" and I'll go home. I understood their logic. I was quite happy to be in *Rocky IV*. I don't mind at all that they removed Sico. Mark, I'm totally satisfied. Sico was in the original movie, and he will be forever.

Sico is in SAG, the actor's union. Is that under your name or his?
His name.

How does that work?
I'll tell you what happened. SAG-AFTRA was headquartered in Manhattan. They were having a rally complaining about some issue. People were picketing in front of the headquarters with banners and signs. I said to them, "Why don't you have Sico? You want to draw publicity around this. Why don't you have Sico as an actor come?" They said, "That's a good idea." I said, "In exchange for that, make Sico a member of SAG." They said, "Sure, no problem at all."

To your knowledge, how many other robots are part of SAG?
None. Only Sico.

Can you talk about Sico's other public appearances?
When Disney opened the [*Star Wars* attraction] Star Tours pavilion in Disneyland, they invited the press to meet the actors and robots from the *Star Wars* movie. The problem was that C3PO, who is played by a British guy [Anthony Daniels] who I know, didn't look great in the costume when you saw it up close. In fact, it looked extremely bad. In the movie, it's perfect. But in real life, it's not. R2D2 is someone inside a garbage can. So the Disney people said to me, "We can't let the media meet these robots face to face." Disney built this platform so that the two robots would be elevated. But they wanted something else to represent the robotics technology in *Star Wars*. So Sico was invited. Of course, Sico has nothing to do with *Star Wars*, but he was there being interviewed about *Star Wars*. Sico is nowhere as popular as R2D2 and C3PO, but he has done much more [appearances] than them.

When Disney opened Epcot, Sico was invited because they wanted someone there with a robotic personality. They knew how to build animatronics but not mobile robots. Sico wound up working at nearly every Disney Park and some of their competitors too. Not too long ago, Sico was called to emcee the Spanish Music Awards, which is an annual show which takes place in Florida. It's a three-hour-long, live show. Sico was the first robot in the history of robotics to emcee a major televised show live. That show was televised live in front of 12 million people worldwide.

It sounds like you had some memorable experiences.
I remember we went to a promotional visit with a dinner at the private house of some millionaire. Stallone was there. So was Andy Warhol. Andy Warhol loved Sico. Andy Warhol walked around with this cheap camera. He was constantly taking pictures of everything around him. Andy Warhol was friendly with Keith Haring [the pop art artist]. Keith Haring's studio was right next door to my office in Manhattan, in SoHo. Keith Haring and Andy Warhol would periodically knock at my office door. They always wanted to see videos and pictures of what they were doing. He didn't have a tape machine or television in his studio. So, they would sit in my conference room

Carl Weathers as Apollo Creed
Illustration by Pat Carbajal

watching videos for hours. How cool is that?

Dolph Lundgren and I met in New York City at a nightclub to make a press appearance. We became friends. Sico has done it all. He has met royalty, kings and queens, and important people. He has even been asked to deliver command performance of the White House during the Reagan administration.

Where is Sico now?
He's at the office. We have a wonderful place that we call the robot garage.

Is he in good shape?
Sico is in very good shape. We have five different versions because the demand for the robot is extremely high at certain times of the year. Sico has evolved quite enormously since you've seen him in *Rocky IV*. From a technological standpoint, he's much more innovative. We give each generation of robots a different name. The eighth generation is called Millenia. Millenia comes on stage and delivers an entire performance completely on its own or remotely with an operator.

When Sico appeared in *Rocky IV*, what generation was he?
Sico Four.

Sico Four, *Rocky IV*?
Yes, Mark, I must tell you that I never made that connection. Sico Four and *Rocky IV*, that's true.

How has Sico's appearance in *Rocky IV* changed your life?
Not much really. I'm not the kind of person that thinks, "Oh my god, I'm in Hollywood." These jobs were only a means to an end. The jobs were a means to make money and reinvest that money so that we could donate our services to our true mission in life. When we finished work on *Rocky IV*, that was the end of our relationship. But that is typical of the way it works in Hollywood, even with actors. When the job ends, the relationship ends. That's the way it is. People say to me, "Why don't you call Stallone? Stay in touch with him?" I always say, "It's not my business to do that. I don't want to bother him with anything. I'm only the guy who supplies the prop."

Of course, I think of Sico as much more than a prop. But I don't think Stallone realizes how his name has helped me be a goodwill donor and allowed Sico to visit all these schools and hospitals. When I go, people look at Sico and say, "That's the *Rocky IV* robot." We always say that we're there thanks to Mr. Sylvester Stallone who made Sico famous as the *Rocky IV* robot. We have never stopped thanking Stallone for him hiring us. He's the man who made these visits to hospitals and schools possible.

SECTION 8
Lost Fourths

PORKY'S 4

Pimpin' Pee Wee

Porky's, as outlined in the previous chapter, was an influential film which defined sex comedies of the 80s. With its raunchy humor, emphasis on teenagers' efforts to lose their virginity, and the notorious scene where Pee-Wee, a sex-starved high school student, peeps on his showering classmates, the outrageous comedy was an outsized hit. Made on a shoe-string budget of $5 million dollars, the film grossed $160 million dollars worldwide. However, despite its popularity, the franchise initially ended after three films. The first three films in the series, *Porky's, Porky's II: The Next Day*, and *Porky's Revenge!* were released from 1982–1985, a four-year period. It would take another 27 years before the fourth Porky's film, *Pimpin' Pee Wee* was released in 2009.

There are times when a production company has a limited amount of time to make a sequel to a film before the rights revert back to the license holder. When a film is made to retain the rights, it is called an Ashcan Copy. Ashcan Copies are usually made inexpensively and quickly. The fourth Porky's film, *Pimpin' Pee Wee* is considered an Ashcan Copy.

After several failed attempts to make a sequel to the Porky's trilogy, including one by radio personality Howard Stern, the producers only had a limited amount of time to make the film before their time ran out. So they quickly cobbled together a limited budget and hired a neophyte screenwriter, Stephen Niver, to hammer out a script. In *Pimpin' Pee Wee*, a trio of college students open a brothel to raise money to repair an uncle's house that they had inadvertently trashed.

Even by modern standards, the film is raunchier than the previous installments. Whereas earlier *Porky's* explored such serious topics as anti-Semitism, *Pimpin Pee Wee*'s gross-out moments include having one of the boys getting thrown up on by a prostitute.

Another change made was the period. *Porky's* was set in the 1950s but *Pimpin' Pee Wee* features the same characters as the original, set in the present day. The decision to set it in modern times was likely a budgetary one. A period piece is simply more expensive. Even the running time of 78 minutes suggests that all expenses were spared.

Pimpin' Pee Wee wastes no time referencing Porky's shower scene or establishing its lewd tone. In the opening moments, Edward "Pee Wee" Morris (Adam Wylie) spies on co-eds engaged in a naked towel fight in a shower. The co-eds spot Pee Wee and instead of being outraged, they beckon him to join the festivities. However, Pee Wee's fantasies are shattered when his mother suddenly appears in the shower. Pee Wee wakes up; it was all a dream. The fantasy is shattered. Pee Wee's mom castigates him for wasting the summer and instructs Pee Wee to do something productive during his college break.

At the beach, Pee Wee meets his friends Tommy (John Patrick Jordan) and Anthony "Meat" Tuperello (Russ Hunt). The trio lament that they are not capable of attracting women. Later, Pee Wee goes to his Uncle Howard's lavish house. There, Uncle Howard tells Pee Wee that he's going on a three-week vacation. Uncle Howard offers Pee Wee a thousand dollars to look after his home while he's gone. Pee Wee agrees.

Pee Wee meets up with his friend and complains that he hasn't had sex in two years. His friends are equally randy and desperate for female companionship. So the trio agree to go to Porky's brothel to spend Uncle Howard's cash and have fun. There, Porky's daughter, Shelly (Whitney Anderson) tells her father her proposal to provide more equitable compensation and better working conditions for the women. But Porky dismisses Shelly's suggestions.

Pee Wee and Meat go to the backrooms to become intimate with the prostitutes. Tommy declines and instead goes to the bar where he meets Shelly. Tommy and Shelly strike up a conversation and exchange numbers. Before Pee Wee and Meat can consummate their relationship with the prostitutes, the boys cause a ruckus and are ousted from Porky's.

Determined to have a good time, Pee Wee, Meat, and Tommy decide to throw a wild party at Uncle Howard's beachside property. Tommy invites Shelly to the party. Scores of people fill Uncle Howard's house. The party is a raging success. However, Pee Wee inadvertently destroys Uncle Howard's antique vases, which are valued at $25 thousand dollars. Despondent, Pee Wee realizes that he doesn't have enough money to replace them in three weeks before Uncle Howard returns. Shelly comes up with an outrageous plan. Shelly decides to turn Uncle Howard's beach house into a brothel. Desperate to replace the broken items, Pee Wee agrees to the scheme and, in doing so, becomes the titular "pimp."

Shelly and the boys enact the plan and meet early success. However, Pee Wee's brothel encroaches on Porky's business. So Porky grabs a gun and marches off to Pee Wee's ad-hoc cathouse in hopes of ending either their lives or their business. At the house, Shelly intervenes and convinces her father to leave the boys alone. In the end, the boys raise the scratch to replace the broken items.

Originally titled *Porky's: The College Years*, the film was ultimately titled *Pimpin' Pee Wee*. Strangely, the *Porky's* name was dropped from the title. I suspect that the decision was not the producer's call. After all, what's the point in making a *Porky's* sequel if audiences don't know that the film is part of the series. Since the film's initial release, the *Porky's* branding has been restored and it has subsequently been marketed as *Porky's Pimpin' Pee Wee*.

Stephen Niver Interview

What makes a good Porky's sequel and what should be avoided?
Any *Porky's* should include the core gang, and a conflict with Porky [the owner of the local brothel], or another authority figure. Of course, there should be plenty of nudity and toilet/sex humor.

What were your marching orders?
Basically, I had to introduce the *Porky's* brand to the *American Pie* generation.

What was the hardest aspect of writing the fourth film in this series? The easiest?
I suppose the hardest part was coming up with jokes that work, since comedy can be so personal. The easiest part was crafting the characters. I've been a *Porky's* fan since grade school, so the characters were very familiar to me.

Unlike other franchises, such *Terminator* or *Highlander*, you didn't have to deal with an intricate mythology. Aside from the original's infamous shower scene, you had a fairly clean slate. How did this film continue the story of the original films?
The boys are still at odds with Porky, but the setting is modern-day.

Can you talk about how the story developed and how you decided which characters and what elements from the original you and the producers wanted to incorporate?
Ted Jarvis, [a character from *Porky's*] was in the first draft. Jarvis and Meat were like "dumb and dumber," playing off each other. However, it was decided to combine them, and involve Porky's daughter, Shelly Wallace, similar to 1985's *Porky's Revenge*. This time, the boys get back at Porky by opening a brothel on Angel Beach, which puts a serious dent in Porky's business.

Even by post-*American Pie* standards, the film is fairly risqué; it contains more nudity than the average teen comedy of today or of the 80s. Also, in terms of the Gross Out Comedy genre, it's fairly "gross." All sorts of fluids wind up on the main characters' bodies, including bird droppings, vomit, and seminal fluid.
The original script was actually a lot grosser! Apparently, it went through many changes on set. But I had no problem with that; Brian Trenchard-Smith is a legend and an absolute pro, so I knew that it was in good hands.

How quickly did you write the movie?
It came together fairly quickly. Maybe six weeks from outline to draft.

While the original is remembered for its outrageous humor and sexual situations, *Porky's* tackled some sensitive topics, including anti-Semitism. Was there any discussion about incorporating a more serious subplot to counterbalance the outrageous humor?
Alas, no. This was to be a sex comedy, through and through.

In some ways, the film is more of a continuation of the '80s Sex Comedy, told with modern sensibilities than it is a continuation of the story of the original movies.
I wanted it to be as packed with 80s sex comedy tropes as possible. I also wanted to keep the cell phone use to a minimum, and not rely too much on its convenience.

Do you have a favorite moment?
My favorite scene is probably the opening shower scene-dream sequence [that replicates the notorious scene from *Porky's* where Pee Wee peeps in the girl's shower] and the subsequent scene between Pee Wee and his mother [in which she chastises her son for pleasuring himself too frequently].

Did you hope to bring back any of the original cast in cameos where they would play new characters? If so, why didn't it happen?
It might've been interesting if the kids were the sons of the original Angel Beach boys, maybe with cameos from the original cast, but that wasn't discussed.

***Porky's* is an 80's iconic movie. However, until researching this book about fourth movies, I confess that I wasn't previously aware of *Pimpin' Pee Wee*. It seems like the film was made, like Roger Corman's Fantastic Four film, to protect a copyright.**
I wasn't involved beyond the script, as I was on another picture at the time. I can't believe that it's been nearly ten years now! I have no idea who even owns the rights, so your guess is as good as mine. I'm surprised that there hasn't been a proper video release, though, as I'm sure it would do all right.

SECTION 9
Unintended Fourths

MEATBALLS 4

Meatballs 4: To The Rescue

Each chapter of this book is meant to represent a different but representative aspect of how filmmakers approach the fourth chapter in a series. For instance, the Thunderball chapter represents the soaring heights of the Bond franchise and how the producers' confident attitude permeated every aspect of production. The *Psycho IV* interview represents how a classic horror franchise continued by making a prequel-sequel film. However, I am not including *Meatballs 4* in this volume to represent the fourth film in a comedy series. Instead, *Meatballs 4* is an outlier; the film was never intended to be the fourth Meatballs film.

Meatballs 4 started as a script entitled *Happy Campers*. The film went into production as *Happy Campers*, starring Lost Boy's actor Corey Feldman. But partway through the shoot Feldman and writer-director Bob Logan were informed that plans had changed. They were no longer making *Happy Campers*. Instead, they were told that they were making *Meatballs 4*. Needless to say, the news was a shock.

If you are unfamiliar with Meatballs 4, a brief synopsis might be useful. In it, Jack Nance (David Lynch's *Eraserhead*) plays Neil Peterson, the owner of Lake Side Camp. Lake Side is facing low attendance and financial ruin. So the camp's owner hires Ricky Wade (Corey Feldman), a popular counselor and water skiing instructor. Peterson tasks Ricky with boosting enrollment.

Monica Shavetts (Sarah Douglas), the owner of Twin Oaks, a rival camp, offers to buy Lake Side from Peterson so that she can take the property and build a vacation resort over it. Peterson refuses. But his financial hardships persist, and Peterson eventually decides to close the camp. Wade suggests a wager in which Lake Side and Twin Oaks face off at a water-skiing and jet-skiing competition. If Lake Side loses, Twin Oaks will buy them but if Lake Side wins, then Shavetts will pay off all of Lake Side's debts.

During the competition, Ricky is injured while water skiing because of poor sportsmanship by the rival camp. Neil Peterson, the elderly owner of the camp, then joins the competition, bringing the contest to a virtual tie. Ricky bravely ignores his painful injury, successfully performs the impossible triple-hinge (a mid-air triple flip), and wins the competition. The camp is saved.

In the following interview, writer-director Bob Logan explains how he unwittingly wound-up making *Meatballs 4*. Logan was playful during our conversation. When he started to explain a certain aspect of filmmaking, I told him that I was familiar with the concept. He gently chided, "I am not trying to speak down to you. I'm not condescending. By the way, condescending means…"

Bob Logan Interview

You did not intend to direct the fourth *Meatballs* film. What happened?
You should have been on a set when I found out.

Let us start at the beginning when you were making a movie called *Happy Campers.*

[*Children of the Corn* (1990) producer] Don Borchers bought a company called Moviestore Entertainment. It was an independent film company. Don was selling foreign rights to get money to make little independent movies. I had recently done a film called *Repossessed* (1990), a spoof of *The Exorcist*, with Leslie Nielsen and Linda Blair. Out of the blue, Don called me and asked, "What are you doing?" I said, "I'm playing with my daughter." He said, "Do you want to make a movie?" I said, "What movie?" Don said, "It's about the lake and craziness with the kids." Don did not mention anything about *Meatballs,* but he did not know about it at the time, either. I said, "Send the script over." Don said, "There is no script." I said, "What's the story?" He goes, "We don't have a story." I asked, "When do we start production? Two or three months from now?" He goes, "We are starting pre-production in six weeks. So it would be nice to have a script." It is like if you are planning to paint a house, it is nice to have a house first. Otherwise, you are painting the air.

Don said, "If we can negotiate something right now on the phone forget your agent for a minute. Just me and you, buddies." I said, "Okay, how much?" He offered me an amount. The amount of time I needed to work on it was ridiculously short because he needed the movie to be made and completed in three months. He called me in September, and they wanted to go to the Los Angeles Film Market in January and sell the film. So they wanted it complete.

I said, "You've got no script, you got no story, and you want to complete a movie and three months." Anyway, he offered me a certain amount of money. But for three months of my time, it was worth it. He said, "Give me a script next week."

I went to the Beverly Garland Hotel and locked myself in for a week and did my typical routine. This will sound perverted but trust me, it is not. It just saves time. I stripped all my clothes off and I started writing. Then, I would just write and write. When I got a little block, I would take a hot shower. For me, when the hot water hits the back of my neck, the ideas start flowing. I go back and forth from the shower to my computer, dripping wet. To this day, it still works.

Finally, at the end of seven days and nights, I finished the script. I sent it to Don, and he read it. He called me and said, "Let's start pre-production." I went into his offices, and they gave me a little office. I had three weeks to put the film together. We didn't have any locations. The only thing on board that we had was Corey Feldman. Don was able to get Corey. At the time, Corey was just trying to get any work that he could because he had some drug problems. Corey wanted to prove himself. He also knew me through *Repossessed.* He loved the movie and said he wanted to work with me.

We went to Bass Lake, which is north of Fresno, near Yosemite. We scouted it for two days and got what we needed. In the three weeks of production, we put together everything—locations, casting, and the stunt team. It was a hellacious three weeks. Then, we went up to Bass Lake to shoot the movie.

The schedule seems tight.

We only had three weeks—18 days—to shoot the entire film, including the ski sequences. It was a six-day work week. We'd have one day off. 18 days; that is it. That is fast, especially when you consider that we had stunts, and we were shooting on the water. We had a camera on one boat and the actor on another. But everything moves and you have to do it again.

Talk a little bit about the premise of the story.
It was almost a typical story. There is an old man played by Jack Nance who owns this little company, a camp. Across the lake is a competing camp and it's owned by a corporate woman. She has millions of dollars, the two camps are in competition with each other, and she is trying to drive them out of business. He is trying to stay in business. It is David and Goliath. Then it was a matter of figuring out the hero and his love interest and adding to the conflict. You must have a lot of stupid gags. Anyway, it was called *Happy Campers,* which I thought was a good title at the time.

How did *Happy Campers* become *Meatballs 4*?
That is about halfway into shooting the film. One night, after we broke, we had dinner. A guy by the name of Ken Badish, who was from the movie store, came up to the location with his wife. Ken tells me, "We're doing a little change in the film." I said, "How are you going to change it. We were still shooting the damn thing. What are you talking about?" He said, "We have to guarantee that we're going to make money. People know what [the phrase] Happy Camper means. But audiences want a title from an established movie. So, we paid to get the rights to the title *Meatballs*." I said, "What are you going to call it, *Meatballs 4*?" He said, "Yeah!"

If I get serious and if something really bothers me, then I get incredibly quiet. I just had to shut up and [Bobby gets close to the camera and stares]. I gave him one of those looks and he realized I was not too pleased. But he said, "That's what we're going to do. We've already made the decision." I said that I did not sign up for *Meatballs 4*. At the time I had already done two movies. One was *Up Your Alley* (1989), a little hundred-thousand-dollar film with Linda Blair. That is where I met Linda, I had the idea to do *Repossessed*. *Repossessed* costs millions. I was building my career up, so I did not want to be associated with a film that had a "four" at the end of the title.

I was quite upset, and I threatened to walk. We were halfway through the film and, of course, Ken did not want that. He said, "Let me have Don talk to you." I think he drove up to the set the next day.

Don and I had a long talk and it was just basically, "What are we going to do? We are being paid. Put it out, Bobby. Who cares? Don't worry it is not going to hurt your career. The movie is going to do either really well with the title or no one will remember it."

I tried to rationalize it because I did not want to leave my crew. My crew is my family. I did not want to leave the family high and dry. So I stuck with it. I was not pleased, but I stuck with it. I swallowed my feelings because you do not want the attitude to be negative. A positive attitude is especially important if you are making a comedy because negativity can ruin a film. Negativity just transcends into the movie, magically. That is how I found out.

Did you have to make any adjustments to the script to accommodate the *Meatballs* framework?

No, it was close enough to the first movie. Although, I understand that one of the *Meatballs* films had a space alien in it. [It is true. *Meatballs II* features a space alien]. So after I heard that, I thought, "Fuck it. If they have an alien, then let us have a giant rectum that skis." I did not care anymore. But no, it did not affect the script in any way, shape, or form.

It started as a fun project for me. But now that changed. Don was my employer and I thought that we should go finish the film and get it done. I felt used. I was backed into a corner. I could not leave. That would not help my career at all.

What was the cast's reaction? From what I have read, Corey Feldman did not seem pleased. [Looking back at his experience, Feldman said, "I never signed up to do *Meatballs 4*, nor would I have signed up to do *Meatballs* 4. I was completely swindled on that one."[96]]

No, Corey was not pleased. Corey was not pleased at all. This was a comeback for him. He wanted to be in something unique to him. But now that we were part four, we were not the starting line-up for the baseball team. Now, they are bringing in the Triple-A guys to finish off the game.

Did Corey, understandably, want to leave the film too?

As I recall, that was his reaction. He thought about it the same way I did. I do not blame Corey. We had long talks about it. We were very tight during the shoot.

I know that there are a lot of stories about Corey and him wanting to be Michael Jackson [who was Corey's friend]. But that is not my experience with him. Corey was a professional. He was never late on the set. He did not want to leave the cast and crew. And he also realized that it would not look good if he walked out of a film. It would make him look doubly bad and nobody would hire him. So he felt locked into the movie too. We all felt that way.

Everybody in the cast and crew had the same basic initial reaction, which was "What the fuck?" But then it became, "We've got a job to do. So let's finish it." Everybody was pretty much professional about it that way.

I'm not going to make it sound like people thought, "Oh my god! This movie has been retitled!" and that people were going crazy that the movie was retitled. No, it was not like that. But it was disappointing. A couple of people looked at it positively and that we would be associated with a hit. Yes, but it would be a hit three times removed. For the most part, it was not a big deal.

***Happy Campers* is a good title for a camp comedy. But I can also see the argument that there is an upside in being associated with *Meatballs*, a beloved comedy.**

Yeah, well they needed a good argument. But that bit of information is better to know beforehand. But we had a job to do, and I had already received half of my salary.

While we are talking about titles, the subtitle to *Meatballs 4* is *To the Rescue*.

I had nothing to do with that. When the movie went to VHS, they decided to give it a subtitle. I do not know why they chose that one. But I did not have anything to do with it.

I do not understand what it means.
I don't either. I don't either.

I can make the argument that the story for *Happy Campers* is cut from the same cloth as the original *Meatballs*. In both, a charismatic, sarcastic, wise-cracking leader, unites a group of underdogs who are battling a more popular and more powerful adversary.
I like your pitch. I'll buy it. That's what it was. They were going up against big corporate American. You see the story in a lot of movies from *Slap Shot* to *Major League*.

To help generate sales, is there a certain amount of nudity required for these types of films?
I am not sure that I would say that nudity was required but it was part of the deal. I was told that if there was nudity it would help the sale of the movie to HBO. I am not a prude, but I did not want to have nudity for nudity's sake. I tried to make those scenes a little funny. In the shower scene, the boys put the blue dye in the water and the women look like Smurfs. But I did not want it to seem cheap. They strongly hinted that they needed scenes like that and that they needed it to be rated R. But I did not want it to be a "hard R." I wanted it to be a "soft R." If you watch the movie, you will see that there are not a lot of bad words.

Can you talk about casting?
The casting director was Linda Francis, who has since passed away. Corey Feldman was the only one who was locked in. Originally, I had another actor to play the grandfather, the part that Jack eventually played. But we could not work out a scheduling issue. Linda called me and we were shooting those scenes in a day. I said, "I need someone up here." She suggested Jack because she had just worked with Jack on *Motorama* (1991) with Don. We cast him without even being able to talk to him. I knew Jack's work from *Eraserhead* and countless other films. So I committed to him over the phone with Linda. Then, Jack showed up the next day.

Who was originally cast as the grandfather, the part that Jack Nance played?
It was Brion James [who played a replicant in *Blade Runner*]. When he came to audition, he said, "I know I'm not going to get the role. I don't look like a traditional grandfather." I said that I did not give a shit about that. But there was a scheduling issue, and he could not do it. I cast Cristy Thom in a part that Asian-Americans do not always get to play. She was in Playboy and was dating Sylvester Stallone at the time. But normally you cast the blond with big boobs. I said that we should cast the Asian-Americans with black hair. I forgot her name for a moment. I tried to look at the poster, but her name was not on it.

I love that you have the poster on your wall. It suggests that you are proud of the film.
You got to be. When you think about how many people are on the planet and then you think of how many people get to be a director of the movie, aside from YouTube. I keep posters around just to remind me.

I get the impression that the movie was more or less what you intended it to be. You were still a hired gun and had to work within a framework, but within that framework, it was the story that you wrote and directed. You did not have to change to make it "more *Meatballs*." Title aside, *Meatballs 4* was more or less how you intended.

The movie is pretty much as I intended. To be honest, I was allowed to cast it the way I wanted. They trusted me and knew that I had written comedy for them before. They left me a good amount of [independence during the shoot] and in editing too.

What question do you wish more people would ask you about *Meatballs 4* but do not?

I wish people would ask, why is it called *Meatballs 4* and why did you do *Meatballs 4*? Well, you have my answer. I had no choice. That is one of the reasons I was interested in doing this interview with you. I wanted to clear the air a little bit and explain a little bit about the hell that happened.

What is your favorite story about working on *Meatballs 4*?

Sundays were our day off. On those days, I would hop on one of the many jet skis and go around the lake, as if I owned it. It is a massive lake. We built a ski ramp on it because it ties into the story. I went off of it a couple of times. The shoot was a real pressure cooker because of what happened with the script and what happened to the script as a result of what happened with Jack. But it is a long story.

I am ready. What happened?

Jack comes up to the movie and we got along. I would play pranks on him, and he would play pranks on me. I like playing pranks. I play pranks on set to keep it light. We were about a week into production, and it starts raining. It was a terrible storm, hellacious. We had to shut down production for the day. All the crew went back to their little cabins around the lake. I was in my cabin working on the script. Trying to figure out how to make it funnier. There is a knock on my door, and it was Jack. He was standing there, drenched. I said, "Jack, why are you here?" Jack said, "I think my wife just killed herself." Remember, we were playing pranks. So I thought he was joking, and I go for the humor, "Well, being married to you Jack, who can blame her?" A tear comes down his eye. I say, "Come on in."

A little back story on his wife. His wife was Kelly Jean Van Dyke, Jerry Van Dyke's daughter. She had drug problems and started doing adult movies to buy the drugs. Jack said, "I was just talking to her on the phone. I told her that I had had enough and that I wanted a divorce. But she said, 'If you divorce me, I'll kill myself.' Jack said, 'Don't be dramatic. I am going to let you go [and end this call]. I do not want to talk to you now. When I get back from the shoot, we can talk." She told him, "Jack if you hang up on me, I'm going to kill myself. I'm not kidding." Suddenly, the phone went dead.

Jack came to me saying, "Can I use your phone? She thinks I hung up on her and she's going to kill herself." I said, "Jesus, yes." I went to pick up my phone and there was no tone.

This was before cell phones. So I grab Jack and go to my rental car, and we drive to town. About an eighth of a mile away is this small town. We got into the bar, but the phone is dead. I said, "We need a phone badly and it's an emergency." Somebody yells "Go to the fire department about two miles down the line." So we hop into the car, and we were driving through the pouring rain. We get to the fire department, and no one is there. So we keep driving. Finally, we find a small police station and we pull in. There was only one person on duty. I explain the situation and Jack gives the cop her phone number. I take Jack to the side. I'm holding him and saying, "Don't worry. She going to be OK." The cop calls down to the LA police department and tells them the situation. I'm not sure how long we are sitting there. I assume that it's 20 or 30 minutes, but it seemed like an eternity. Jack's sobbing.

The phone rings and the cop picks it up. He talks for a second and then puts the phone down. The cop walks over to us and he looks at me before Jack looks up and shakes his head. The cop said, "We sent a unit down there and she's dead. She didn't make it. She hung herself.

I am not a religious guy, but I could see the soul leave Jack's body. At that point, it was just a body. The cops let us use their phones, and I called the base camp and I talked to Kris Krengel, yes, that is her name, Kris Krengel. Nice and talented woman. I told her to tell production what was happening, and I told her not to shut down the film. We get the team together and say we have got to take Jack home. We had a production assistant take him on the four or five-hour drive back to his house. One of the people on the crew reminded me that Jack had two handguns. He brought them up to go shooting in the mountains. I went to Jack before the production assistant drove him home and said, "Jack, trust me as a friend. There are no ulterior motives here. But hey friend, give me the guns." Jack gave me the guns and they take him home. So Jack won't be able to shoot any other scenes for the movie.

Now, remember when you shoot a movie you never film in order. But there are all these scenes that he was supposed to be in but will no longer be. But we already shot so much stuff with him. So we could not afford to shut down production and get another actor. We could not afford to reshoot everything. Our entire budget was about a million and a half and we already shot a lot of it. It was going to come down to this. I had to go through the script and find out what we already shot and what was left. Then, say, "From here forward, this is what we're going to shoot." I had to write him out of the script. We had to start shooting the next day.

I was up all night trying to figure it out. It was a 1000-piece puzzle and I had to move everything all around to make the story work. I was up all night. I don't know how I shot the next day, but I did. Now we're back to shooting out-of-sequence the rest of the script but without Jack's character now.

About six days later, Linda Francis, my casting agent calls. She said, "Jack just buried his wife, and he wants to come back and finish the movie." I tell her, "I rewrote the whole movie in a night. I shot other stuff without him. How do I do this again?" But what are we going to do? I cannot say no to him. I cannot say, "You can't come back to the production." I said, "Give me a night." So I go back to rewriting and I do that another night. It was just a killer. Suddenly, this deal I made for this little three-month job that was good money is not any longer. But Jack shows up the next day. And here is where it gets strange.

When I was writing the script, Jack's character has a granddaughter named Kelly. I named her after my daughter Kelly who was just three years old at the time. Jack's wife, who just killed herself, was named Kelly. The way the scheduling worked, that first scene he shot was not a comedy scene. Instead, it was one of the more serious scenes in the movie. It's a scene where he apologizes to his granddaughter Kelly for fucking up everything and ruining her life. The character was going to lose the camp and sell it. So he said that he is sorry for everything. But Jack's wife, who just killed herself was named Kelly.

We shot this scene in the cabin. Everyone was crying when she did it. It was a tough day for him, but he handled it so well. We were on location and could not see the dailies at all. But the shot was a dolly shot that starts in the distance and the camera slowly pushes in to a close-up. On the close-up, he apologizes, and the tears come down his face. It is a beautiful shot. After the shot, I asked my focus puller if it was okay, and he said it was. You have to go by their word. But we also shot a master shot. But later in editing, I see the footage. As soon as the shot started to move into him, the film goes completely out of focus. It stays out of focus until he said the last word of the last line. Then it goes out of focus. But I could not use the shot. It would have been beautiful. Instead, I went with the master shot, and I cut to the reaction shots. Then we finished the movie.

A couple of years later, Jack was killed. He went to a donut shop and some guy hit him. He went home. He had a contusion, and he did not know it. He was found dead the next day. [Nance was 53-years old when he died.]

Jack's performance is memorable. It is a broad comedy, but it is a lovely performance within it.
Jack was a good actor. The problem is that because of *Eraserhead*, Jack was stereotyped into playing these weird characters. But he also got the majority of his work from David Lynch. In addition to *Eraserhead*, Lynch put him in *Twin Peaks* and a bunch of other movies [*Dune, Blue Velvet*].

Any other memories?
One young lady on the crew started sleeping with another person who had a prominent position on the film. Her husband found out about it, came up to the location, and beat the shit out of the guy. So, I made the camera guy the director of photography for the day.

It was a young cast. They were between 19 and 23 years old. The film was a party film, so they are going to party off camera. I understand partying. Sam Kinison was my roommate. I wrote for Sam. But I told them, "I can't be your parents. But when you are on set, you have to be clean and sober. You have to remember your lines. If you do that, I do not care what you did the night before. But if you fuck up once, there ain't no twice."

It is easy to write out characters. I learned my lesson on that film when I had to write out a character, shoot some more, and then write him back in.

A friend of mine had a great line when it happened. He said, "You built a sculpture, then you had to knock it in half with a sledgehammer, rebuild that part, and then knock out the bottom part and reassemble that part." That is what I had to do with this film.

What is the legacy of *Meatballs 4*?
Residual checks. I know that sounds funny, but it is the residual checks that remind me of the movie. It's been about 30 years since it came out. At this point, the checks are usually twenty-seven dollars for a foreign TV deal. I recently got one for about $1,200. It is a nice little surprise when you get the green envelope from the Writer's Guild with a check inside. Residual is the sweetest eight-letter word in the world. It's a surprise. It's better than those Publisher Clearing House letters that say, "You might already be a winner." Generally, there is only enough to buy you lunch for that day. But that recent one was nice.

SECTION 10
Unmade Fourths

THE GODFATHER 4
The Godfather Part IV

The *Godfather* films are among the most celebrated films of all time. All three films were nominated for the Academy Awards for Best Picture and the trilogy earned 29 nominations in total. *The Godfather* and *The Godfather Part II* earned 11 nominations each and *The Godfather Part III* received seven.

Since the film series concluded in 1990, fans have been clamoring for a fourth part. But *Godfather* director Francis Ford Coppola insists that it is not always a good idea to continue a popular series, even if there is a demand. "I doubt a fourth film could happen. When you do every project, you demonstrate what you've got and what will be good that no one has ever seen before. When you make the second one, you've got to show it again...I have a theory that the fourth in the series in a tetralogy is always the weakest. The second one is usually the best. The third is sometimes good, sometimes not."[97]

Despite Coppola's misgivings, there were discussions about a fourth film. *Godfather Part IV* would follow the same structure as *Godfather Part II,* and it would be set in two time frames. The first period would be set in the past, telling the story of Sonny Corleone's pre-*Godfather* years and the second would be situated after *Godfather Part III,* exploring Vincent Corleone's (Andy Garcia) tenure as head of the family.

It is possible that Coppola's flirting with the idea was less about his own desire to continue the story than about his agreeing to make the film as a generous gesture to Mario Puzo, the author of the book and his co-screenwriter on all three films. The aging Puzo wanted to make sure that his children would be financially secure when he died. Coppola told the author he would arrange for Paramount to pay Puzo a million dollars to write the screenplay that Coppola would co-write without receiving compensation. A grateful Puzo agreed. However, Paramount Pictures rejected their proposal. According to Coppola, Puzo's million-dollar writing fee was too high.[98]

Without a film, *Godfather* fans could try to satiate their desire for a fourth film by experiencing the world of the Corleones in other media, including video games *The Godfather* (2006) and *The Godfather II* (2009) and three continuations novels *The Godfather Returns* (2004), *The Godfather's Revenge* (2006), and *The Family Corleone* (2012).

The Godfather and *The Godfather II* video games are loosely tied to the classic movies. The games recreate major scenes from the original films and introduce new characters whose missions are not always tied to the movie plots. James Caan reprises his role as Sonny Corleone in the first game and Robert Duvall returns as Tom Hagen in both adventures. Incredibly, Marlon Brando agreed to return to his Academy Award-winning role as Don Corleone. However, because Brando was too sick to perform, a sound-alike artist was hired to voice all of the actor's lines. Nevertheless, there is one scene in a hospital where Brando's performance can briefly be heard. *The Godfather* games became the subject of litigation. Mario Puzo's estate claimed that

Paramount owed them at least $1 million for their share of game profits. Eventually, the two parties settled out of court.[99]

Ultimately, some of Puzo's ideas for *Godfather IV* were incorporated into Ed Falco's continuation novel *The Family Corleone*. The cover of *Family Corleone* states that the novel is "based on a screenplay by Mario Puzo." However, *The Family Corleone* departs from the plans for *Godfather Part IV*. As noted, *Part IV* was going to be split into two time periods. But *Family Corleone* is set exclusively in the 1930s and it does not follow the events of *Godfather III*.

The release of *Family Corleone* was fraught. Paramount Pictures, which was not involved in the creation of the book, tried to block its release. According to a lawsuit that Paramount filed against the Estate of Mario Puzo, the film company allowed the estate to publish "one and only one" sequel novel—*The Godfather Returns*.[100] Paramount claimed that the Puzo estate published the second sequel novel *The Godfather's Revenge* without their "knowledge or authorization."[101] Paramount sued the Puzo estate and tried unsuccessfully to stop the release of the book. They claimed that the continuation novels "tarnish the legacy" of the films, mislead and confuse consumers into believing that the novels are part of the Paramount-owned and controlled Godfather franchise, which constitutes the three films and Puzo's original novel.[102] For its part, the estate claimed that Puzo always reserved book publishing rights and that they gave the studio repeated notification of their intention to publish additional novels.[103][104] Eventually, Puzo's estate and Paramount worked out an agreement. The terms were not made public. Lawsuit aside, *The Family Corleone* remains a fascinating, but incomplete, glimpse of the fourth *Godfather* film.

To learn more about *The Family Corleone*'s relationship to the unmade *Godfather Part IV*, I conducted the following interview with the book's author Ed Falco.

Ed Falco Interview

How did you come to write *The Family Corleone*?
My agent at the time was Neil Olson, of Donadio & Olson [the literary agency]. Neil also represented the estate of Mario Puzo. After Mario died, there was an open competition to write a sequel to *The Godfather*. Neil asked me at the time, 2001 I think, if I was interested in competing with other writers for the opportunity, and I declined. Mark Winegardner wound up winning that competition, and he wrote two sequels [*The Godfather Returns,* and *The Godfather's Revenge*]. In 2010, Neil offered me a chance to write a prequel to *The Godfather* based on unproduced pages from the screenplays for *The Godfather III* and *The Godfather IV*, which never got made. Altogether there were about 60 pages of script that made a rough arc for a film. I took those 60 pages and wrote a 400-page novel based around them and a larger group of characters of my own invention.

Can you describe the materials that you were given to work with?
Some of the 60 pages were from unproduced scenes in *The Godfather III*, and the others from *The Godfather IV*.

Do you know when they were written?
I don't know the exact dates. [Note, Falco later told me that the document he was working from was undated, but it was titled "Godfather III/IV Extracts."]

What story elements from the *Godfather IV* script excerpt did you use? What did you not use?
I used everything I could from both scripts. I can't remember specifically what I used and didn't use, but I do remember that I used everything I could from both scripts.

The plot for *Godfather IV* is said to be a prequel to *Godfather* and a sequel to the events of *Godfather III*. Did the pages that you saw confirm that?
I only saw select pages from *The Godfather IV*. All the pages were of scenes that were flashbacks to the period before any of the Godfather films or the novel.

Why were you given only a small amount of the screenplay and not the entire script? How did they determine what portion to give you?
I was only given those pages that were set in flashbacks to the 1930s, pages which I might be able to use in writing a prequel. I assume I was given the pages that might be useful for writing a prequel. Beyond that, I can't tell you anything about the whole script for The *Godfather IV*, or even if it exists. I never saw the whole *Godfather IV* script, only the pages from the script that were set prior to the beginning of the original Godfather story, the first *Godfather* movie, and the novel.

One way that your book differs from the unproduced script for *Godfather IV*, is that your story is a prequel to Puzo's Godfather and not a prequel and a sequel.
Have you seen the script for *Godfather IV*? I didn't know anyone had seen that script. I had no interest in writing a sequel. Once all those great characters are dead, well, what's left? Another Mafia movie I guess, but not a *Godfather* story, not a story of the original Corleone family.

Before you started writing your novel, you needed to get the blessing of the Puzo Estate. What was important to the Puzo family about how the characters would be depicted and how the series would continue?
Tony Puzo [Mario Puzo's son], representing the Puzo Estate, made no demands on how the characters should be treated or how the book should be written. I was free to do what I wanted with the larger story.

What kind of research and preparation did you do?
I read all of Puzo's writing, which included rereading *The Godfather* multiple times. I also read other novels written in the 1930s to get a sense of the vernacular. Beyond that, I read everything I could find on gangsters from that period, and the Mafia in particular. Of course, I watched all three *Godfather* movies many times, along with other gangster movies from the Depression era or about that period.

How did you navigate the two Corleone's worlds—the one from the movies and the one from the novels?
I wrote a prequel to Puzo's novel, but I also had the movies firmly in mind. Some of the flashbacks from the second movie make their way into *The Family Corleone*. For

instance, the scene of Vito returning to Italy to murder the Don who killed his mother. That scene in my novel is a literal translation of the movie scene, down to the clothes the characters wear.

What aspects of the franchise did you want to incorporate into your work?
The Godfather books and movies are all the corruption that results from misplaced or misunderstood ideals. Vito Corleone believes in the ideal of the family and in service to that ideal he becomes a murderer and irredeemably corrupts his family. By accepting violence as a means to an end, he destroys the family he meant to usher into a position of power, wealth, and safety. That theme is of great interest to me, and I embraced it. I was also especially interested in the character of Luca Brasi [The Godfather's enforcer, played by Lenny Montana]. He only gets a few minutes of screen time in the movie and yet is one of the most memorable characters. In the book, too, he doesn't get developed. He is the most feared and dangerous of Vito's henchmen, but Puzo only gives us a paragraph or so to explain why, and that doesn't come till near the end of the novel. I built much of my novel around Brasi, and I leave no doubt as to why he is so terrifying.

Once you decided to set the novel in 1933, some narrative decisions were made for you. For instance, Michael is in eighth grade and therefore cannot be a major part of this story. Can you talk about how you wanted to weave the characters throughout the narrative.
The plot revolves around Sonny's initiation into the family business. Vito didn't want any of his children in the business. Sonny was supposed to be a businessman. Sonny, however, wants to follow in his father's footsteps. The story follows his progress from a kid having a good time to becoming a true member of the family who must "make his bones" in a manner that turns him into the savage killer Puzo describes in the novel. In this sense, Sonny's arc in my novel is the same as Michael's arc in the movies. They are both illustrations of the corrupting power of the Corleone crime family. The difference is that Michael wanted no part of the business, while Sonny always wanted in.

Vito plays the same role in my novel that he played in Puzo's novel and in the movies. He's a man who follows his own code of honor, believing he's only doing what he must do to leave his children a life of wealth, power, and safety. He accepts the violence and danger of a life of crime—but he does so for his family. In the end, the violence and crime corrupt and destroy the family he meant to save from the violence and crime that he sees as having been thrust upon him.

Luca is the most purely evil of all the characters. One of the great differences between my novel and the rest of the *Godfather* franchise is that I'm harder on Vito. I mean to suggest that Vito and Luca are flip sides of the same coin. Vito needs Luca and Luca needs Vito. Together they're responsible for the violence and corruption that destroy their families and threaten the whole country.

According to Coppola, Mario Puzo referred to the time frame of the pre-*Godfather* years, as, "the 'happy years'—when we killed them, and they didn't kill us." Your book is set in this period. In the end, the family has won, and Sonny

seems to have the world on a string. They have not yet paid the price that is yet to come and will be depicted in Puzo's novel and the three films. For them, it's a "happy ending."

Sonny has killed his best friend to gain entrance into the family. He's been wholly corrupted. In the final page, when Sonny gets up on that platform, he's joining a contingent of men who are bound to die violent deaths, just as he will. Vito and Luca are both eating oranges. You'll recall how Coppola uses oranges symbolically throughout the movies. Vito is taking a polite bite out of his orange, while Luca is biting into his like an animal. But they're both eating an orange. Coppola avoided the obviousness of the apple. By the end of *The Family Corleone*, Vito has consolidated his power and is on his way to forming one of the most powerful crime syndicates in the nation. I don't see that as a happy moment, though I guess I can see your point since they think they're on top of the world. But they're only, really, at the beginning of an enterprise that will eventually destroy them.

The word "Godfather" does not appear in the title of your book. Was there any discussion of calling it "Godfather Something"? Having asked the question, I should add that the title *The Family Corleone* is a fitting one. It also helps distinguish your novel from the other continuation novels *Godfather Returns* and *Godfather's Revenge* and it suggests that your book would not focus solely on Vito.

I got to choose the title. I decided on *The Family Corleone,* and no one objected. I think I probably had *The Brothers Karamazov* stuck in my head as a pretty good title I could do a little riff on.

***Godfather IV* has not been made. Your book is not a novelization of a fourth *Godfather* film. However, there is a connection between the two. How would you characterize that connection?**

I don't really know how to answer that since I haven't read the screenplay for a fourth film, and I don't even know if one exists. There must have been pages written, since I got a handful of them, but no one, as far as I know, has seen a completed screenplay. But I can honestly say this: *The Family Corleone* could be a brilliant fourth film in the series. I wrote it so that a reader could go seamlessly from my novel to *The Godfather* novel, and then on to the movies. And honestly, I think the films wrapped up brilliantly with the second *Godfather* movie. Once Vito is dead and Michael's corruption is completed with the murder of his own brother, the story has been told and *The* Godfather saga is over. *The Family Corleone,* followed by the *Godfather I* and *II*—now that would be a brilliant film experience.

I understand that you wrote the book with the thought that it could be turned into a fourth film. How did that impact your approach to the book?
I wrote with an emphasis on scenes that could be easily translated to film, and on a plot that powered forward. I avoided material that could not be easily filmed. The meaning of the book resides in the action.

I was listening to Bobby Cannavale's excellent work as the narrator of the audiobook. Because he is an actor, he performs the dialogue and plays all the

parts. Cannavale even does a quasi-Brando interpretation. When viewed in this context, the novel becomes an audio drama that is closely linked to the film series.
Yes, exactly. Well put. Cannavale's reading is brilliant. *The Washington Post* listed *The Family Corleone* as one of the five best audiobooks of 2012. Cannavale does such a great job that after listening to the whole thing you feel you've seen the movie.

How would you characterize your experience writing the book?
I enjoyed the experience of writing *The Family Corleone* because I loved the movies, and because—I'm sure this will be surprising to many—I felt a lot less pressure than I typically feel when embarking on a novel. I mean, the characters were already there, and the overall arc was already there. I just had to come up with a few hundred more pages of plot and characters. Though my other novels and short stories have never found a popular audience, Neil picked me for the prequel because he knew my work. He knew I wrote literary fiction with a heavy noir influence. And he knew I was interested, always, in the conflict between the violence men carry in their very being, and their simultaneous desire to be decent.

SPIDER-MAN 4

Spider-Man 4

Spider-Man 4, intended to be the final chapter in Sam Raimi's hugely popular series about the wall-crawler, was never made. Fans of Raimi and Spider-Man can only speculate about what might have been.

Raimi's *Spider-Man* (2002) helped launch the current superhero boon that turned geek culture into a national obsession. Tobey Maguire's Peter Parker is a flawed and harried, yet sympathetic hero, and Raimi's *Spider-Man 2* (2004) is the rare sequel that was superior to a highly regarded original: it built on and deepened the audience's understanding of the characters.

However, *Spider-Man 3* (2007) was a major disappointment to fans and critics alike. The overstuffed film was bogged down with too many supervillains, Sandman (Thomas Hayden Church), New Goblin (James Franco), and Venom (Topher Grace). The inclusion of Venom, in particular, derailed and diluted the powerful dramatic conflict between Parker, his girlfriend Mary Jane Watson, and his best friend Harry Osborn (Harry's father, the original Green Goblin, was killed battling Spider-Man). Initially, Raimi resisted including Venom, an alien lifeform, in *Spider-Man 3* due to the character's "lack of humanity."[105] Raimi's vision for *Spider-Man 3* was "really about Peter, Mary Jane, Harry, and [Sandman]. But when we were done, Avi Arad, my partner, and the former president of Marvel at the time, said to me, 'Sam, you're not paying enough attention to the fans…you've made two movies with your favorite villains, and now you're about to make another one with your favorite villains. The fans love Venom, he is the fan-favorite.'"[106]

Despite reservations, Raimi relented. However, he couldn't conceal his feelings about Venom, and *Spider-Man 3* suffered for it. Raimi explained, "If the director doesn't love something, it's wrong of them to make it when so many other people love it. I think [raising the stakes after *Spider-Man 2*] was the thinking going into it and I think that's what doomed us. I should've just stuck with the characters and the relationships and progressed them to the next step and not tried to top the bar."[107] Despite its flaws, the movie was a blockbuster, grossing nearly $900 million. Still, it seemed series' fans were eagerly anticipating *Spider-Man 4*.

Various screenwriters, including James Vanderbilt (*Zodiac*, 2007), David Lindsay-Abaire (Pulitzer Prize-winning playwright), and Gary Ross (*Seabiscuit*, 2003), were hired to help craft the story for *Spider-Man 4*.[108] While Rami was said to be unhappy with their efforts, Sony Pictures was eager to keep the film's fast approaching 2011 release date. Instead of making a film that he didn't have complete faith in, and despite being deep into pre-production, Raimi walked away from the project. Sony scrapped the film entirely and unnecessarily rebooted the series with *The Amazing Spider-Man* (2012) and, its follow-up, *The Amazing Spider-Man 2* (2014), both directed by Marc Webb. Despite winning performances by Andrew Garfield (Peter Parker) and Emma Stone (Gwen Stacy), neither film matched the box office success of *Spider-Man 3*.

Sony seemed unsure of how to properly manage their franchise. There was talk of a third and fourth film in the reboot series, and spin-off movies featuring Spidey's foes the Sinister Six, and a rumored film implausibly focusing on Parker's beloved Aunt May. These ideas were abandoned. Baffled over the direction sequels should take, Sony wisely ceded creative control of the project to Marvel Studios rather than risk running the once-beloved franchise into the ground. Tom Holland was cast as the web-slinger in *Spider-Man: Homecoming* (2017), a superhero film disguised as a teen-comedy. Notwithstanding mostly favorable reviews, and the surcharge benefit for 3D tickets, *Homecoming* failed to surpass Raimi's *Spider-Man 3* at the box office.

Holland fared better with his next two Spidey films. *Spider-Man: Far From Home* (2019) made over one billion dollars at the box office and *Spider-Man: No Way Home* (2021) grossed nearly two billion, becoming the fifth most successful film of all time. The outsized theatrical success of *No Way Home* was due, in part, to the appearance of all three cinematic Spider-Men in the film. In *No Way Home*, sorcerer supreme Dr. Strange casts a spell that allows Garfield's and Maguire's Peter Parker to appear in the "universe" in which Holland is also Parker. All three Parkers join forces to bring down a cadre of villains. *No Way Home* resolves key plot points from both Holland and Garfield's respective film series. Yet, Maguire's life as Parker is decidedly more ambiguous. As a result, fans are left wondering, what happened to Peter Parker as played by Maguire and directed by Raimi? What would their *Spider-Man 4* have looked like?

Given Raimi's storytelling abilities—his visual inventiveness, his relatable and vulnerable characters, and his irreverent humor—along with the prevailing sense of diminishing returns in some of the post-Raimi Spider-Man movies, the assertion that Sony should have given Raimi creative control to make *Spider-Man 4* seems self-evident.

It is natural to wonder what form Raimi's fourth Spider-Man movie might have taken. To find out, I spoke with Jeffrey Henderson, the talented and lively storyboard artist, who worked intimately with Raimi during the pre-production phase of *Spider-Man 4*.

Jeffrey Henderson Interview

Tell me about your experience working on *Spider-Man 4*.
It was a crazy great experience. I am a huge fan of Sam Raimi's. His work was seminal while I was growing up. I loved *Army of Darkness* (1992) and *Darkman* (1990). There was also a mythology about his career. Sam wasn't from Hollywood; he was an outsider from Detroit. He put his first film on his dad's credit cards. He borrowed a lot of money and found a way to make the film himself. That's something I've always respected, it's inspiring. He also has a unique, off-kilter, singular sensibility.

I came in at the end of *Spider-Man 3*. I've been drawing for a long time, and I jump back and forth between a lot of different things. [Henderson also works as an actor, director, voice-over artist, and musician]. My first big job was *30 Days of Nights* (2007), which Sam produced. So I moved to New Zealand for a while to work on it. I met Sam briefly, but it was a perfunctory meeting where he said, "I'm Sam. Nice to meet you." That was really it. But Sam loves storyboard artists. When I came home, they hit me up about doing *Spider-Man 4*. I was thrilled because I'm a big Spider-Man fan and I'm a lifelong comic book geek. My style is steeped in old comics. It was also a big opportunity.

Sam and I worked together on the Sony lot. I don't get star-struck easily, but I have such an affection for him and his work. When Sam works, he gets excited and demonstrative. He's telling me the story of the movie, acting out the script. He's got a box of action figures and he's blocking out the action. Suddenly, I started laughing. I wasn't trying to be disrespectful, I just started laughing. He stopped, puts the action figures down, and asked, "What's so funny?" It all sort of hit me at that moment. I'm in Sam Raimi's office and he's acting out *Spider-Man 4* with Spider-Man toys. We're like a couple of five-year-olds sitting on the floor of our living room. I said, "Sam, no disrespect. But what sort of an alternate reality are we in where I'm having this conversation with you? What the hell is going on?"

We got along very well pretty quickly. Creatively, we were into the same stuff, and we have similar sensibilities. He's super collaborative. He's super open. He uses a lot of the same people for extended periods of time. He enjoys the process. He knows what he wants to do but he likes it if you've got a good idea. No matter where it comes from, he's open to it. Even before there was a script, he gave us all a lot of latitude to come up with ideas. We came up with ideas for set pieces and action pieces. For everything really, he wanted it all.

Later, I learned that *Spiderman 3* was a bad experience for him. He loves Spider-Man, but he also loves a very specific period of the character, which is the late 1960s to early 1970s. It's the John Romita-era and it's very much tied to Sam's childhood. [John Romita is widely considered to be one of the definitive Spider-Man artists.] That's what Sam wanted *Spider-Man 3* to be. But once they got into the production of *Spider-Man 3*, Sony kind of bullied him into putting Venom in that movie. Sam didn't want to do it. Not only did they push this late in the process, but Sam also didn't have any real affection or feel a connection with the character. He said, "Why don't you just let me make the movie that I want to make. Save Venom for a time when you inevitably reboot the series. Then, give it to someone who really loves Venom and will do it well."

Spider-Man 3 was kind of a mess. But he agreed to come back and make *Spider-Man 4* with the understanding that he could make the movie he wanted to make. He wanted some sort of promise or guarantee the same thing wouldn't happen again. We all thought that his first two Spider-Man movies were great and, even though *Spider-Man 3* sucked, it did make over three-quarters of a billion dollars. Rami was already an icon with a hugely popular body of work. You would think that after one or two of his Spider-Man movies alone they would have enough deference for his work to leave him alone. You could argue he had earned that right. Why didn't they say, "You just do what you want, and we are just going to cash the check." But he had the opposite experience on *Spider-Man 3*. It was really weird how they just turned on him. *Spider-Man 4* was predicated on that never happening again. He was already reluctant going in.

Spider-Man
Illustration by Pat Carbajal

Sam is a genuinely nice guy. I don't mean that as a euphemism. He's actually a nice man. If he has one flaw, it's that he can never be the bad cop. He needs someone else to do that. He's just not that guy who is going to be an ass. But sometimes in this business being an ass is what gets things done. Sam just doesn't have that thing in him. It's a great quality. But professionally, it hinders him because he doesn't like to fight it out.

But everyone was excited to work on *Spider-Man 4*. Dennis Gassner was the production designer, and he's worked on all these really great movies [*Miller's Crossing* (1990), *Bugsy* (1991), *Road to Perdition* (2002), *Spectre* (2015), *Blade Runner 2049* (2017).] He's like this mad genius. He's a really sweet older English gentleman. We were all coming up with some great stuff and Sam was excited. They were bouncing around with a bunch of different versions of the script. Then we started to see some red flags. The same shit was happening again. They were not letting him do what he wanted to do. You could see it going down the rabbit hole again. Gassner left the project and J. Michael Riva, who is also great, came on. [Riva worked on *Spider-Man 3* and *The Amazing Spider-Man*.] After *Spider-Man 4* folded, Riva did a couple of other films, including *Django Unchained* (2012), and then he passed away.

Storyboard artists are in a strange spot. In the entire production, we are the only people with the word "story" in our job title. Storyboarding has less to do with drawing than it has to do with the discipline of story. Drawing is just a means to that end. As storyboard artists, we're equal parts director and writer. A lot of what you do is subjective, and different directors employ storyboard artists in different ways. For Sam, it's an important part of his process. So when they started bouncing the script around, we'd all go off and work with different animatic teams. They would take our storyboards and animate them. The idea was to get a crude sense of what worked and what didn't. It would help Sam pitch his ideas to the studio. So even if they had conflicts about the story or the script Sam could say, "Look, I'm working on this. This is what it'll look like." We did quite a bit of that.

Casting and auditions were going on at the same time. It was an exciting time. But you could see dark things were coming and you'd say, "Oh man, it's happening to him again." I'm not sure about the time frame but it started about halfway through the process. I was with him when it happened. Sony came in and mandated the film would be in 3D. Sam said, "I know that 3D is big and trendy now with *Avatar* (2009), but I've never shot a frame of 3D before in my life. 3D is its own thing and I needed to know this even before we started pre-production." It's my understanding they were not willing to change the release date and, while we weren't behind, it was a massive movie and there was a lot to do. As hard as we were all working it was still going to be pretty tight. Plus, what Sam wanted to do with the story was going to be time- and labor-intensive. Throwing 3D on top of that…! It also felt arbitrary. Like someone said, '3D is hot right now and all the kids love it, so you've got to do it.' We were walking down the hall and Sam said, "They want me to meet James Cameron to consult about 3D." But I don't know if the meeting ever took place.

I was tasked with a completely different big thing. Every movie that Sam does that doesn't star Bruce Campbell has a great cameo for him. He has cameos [as different characters] in all three of Sam's Spider-Man movies. My job was to come up with cameo ideas. The one thing that bums me out about not making the movie is that the cameos would have been great. The opening of the movie was going to be this montage where Peter is no longer so angst-ridden about being Spider-Man. He's surrendered to the idea. He's full-on learning to love it and embrace it. So the whole beginning was going to be a montage of him taking down all these C and D-list villains, with a newspaper spinning at the camera. Because it was his last movie, he was going to show all of the villains. You'd see the Shocker, the Prowler, the Stilt-Man, and the Rhino. But it wouldn't have been the robot Rhino that you see in *The Amazing Spider-Man*. It would be a corny Rhino-bodysuit, with a little face sticking out and footie pajamas. Then Spider-Man would take them to the police station and the cops would clap for him. In one of the cameos, Spider-Man brings in Mysterio, with that ridiculous fishbowl helmet. Spider-Man throws Mysterio up against the counter, takes off the helmet and there's Bruce Campbell! He screams, "I'll get you Spider-Man!"

There was another cameo, which even today makes me laugh. Mary Jane is gone. That's one of the reasons Peter's completely into being Spider-Man. His personal life is in the shitter. It gets to the point where even Aunt May is dating and getting on with her life before Peter is. Peter goes to see her for their weekly standing dinner. He knocks on the door. She opens it and says, "Oh, Peter. I completely forgot about tonight." He says, "It's okay Aunt May," as he pushes himself through the door and there's Bruce Campbell as her inappropriately younger boyfriend. He's coming out of the back. He's got a towel on and he's all wet. He says, "I've got this May," and he sits Peter down on the couch. Aunt May goes to the other room. Campbell still has his towel on and he's still wet. He says, "Me and you have to talk Pete. I know this is awkward and I know it makes you uncomfortable. Your aunt is a woman, and she has needs." Peter goes, "Please stop talking, please stop talking."

How would you sum up the plot of *Spider-Man 4*?
That's a tough one because you're working on so many different drafts. I don't know what the definitive logline would be. The Vulture is thrown in jail by the evil forces who once employed him, and Peter Parker is free to be Spider-Man. *The Daily Bugle* is taken over and run by the Vulture's daughter. That gets messy because Peter and the daughter become affectionate. Then the Vulture escapes jail. The Vulture is a terrifying menace. Peter Parker is rediscovering his life while he is in full-on Spider-Man mode. In the takeover, *The Daily Bugle* has been turned into something that it never was. And all that is happening because the Vulture's daughter wants to know if her dad is really a monster or if she can save him. The whole third act is when she sees her dad dead. She finds all of his stuff and she decides she's going to take matters into her own hands.

What was Vulture's daughter's name?
I'm not sure they ever fixed on a name.

What can you tell me about the Vulture?
John Malkovich was cast as the Vulture, and they had a sick take on him. There was

a lot of stuff from *Spider-Man: Homecoming* that was based on *Spider-Man 4* or, at least, the draft that I saw. I thought *Homecoming* had a great take on it. Some of the concept stuff with Malkovich as Vulture was cool and some of the sequences, we came up with were badass. The way they were going to shoot the Vulture was cool. However, people's association with Vulture from the comics is that he's fundamentally stupid. He's an old guy, in a stupid green bodysuit with a fuzzy neckline with wings. That's lame. That's people's image of the Vulture. He's a reject from a David Bowie cover band. Our thing was you have to go the opposite way and make the Vulture the scariest, most hardcore, most intense badass that has ever been in a Spider-Man movie. He's going to be Joker-terrifying.

We worked on that a lot and had a lot of good ideas. That's why John Malkovich was great casting. Because he's got that intensity. He's scary intense. The take that they had on the suit was cool. It was almost like an H. R. Giger creation. It was sort of biomechanical. The wings folded out and had surgical steel blades on them, instead of feathers. I saw the tests where they put Malkovich in the suit. It was big. They were going to build practical wings.

Beyond the Vulture's look, how would you describe his character?
They came up with an interesting idea on why he's called the Vulture. He's the Black Ops guy they would throw under the bus. The movie opens with the Vulture on trial for all the stuff he's been thrown under the bus for. He gets indicted and jailed. The reason they call him the Vulture is because when he commits one of his horrible acts, there's nothing left but bones. Like a vulture. I thought that was badass.

I imagine their fight scenes would have been intense.
Most of the work I did while I was there working on a big set-piece. The big climactic event was at the end of the second act, and it was going to take place on the Citicorp building in New York, the one with the 45-degree angle roof. The Vulture's got Spider-Man and he's flying him over the city super high super-fast. Vulture builds up enough speed to literally launch Spider-Man. Spider-Man is falling. He can't web to anything. Like a missile, he crashes right into the top of the Citicorp Tower. He's so messed up and he's bleeding. The point of the scene was to establish that in order to launch the third act and raise the stakes, but the other thing we were trying to establish was that Vulture was the exact opposite of expectations. He was terrifying, brilliant, and badass. He crashes Peter into the roof of the Tower, and every time Peter tries to get up Vulture uses the arc of his velocity to swing around to swipe Peter with the blade edges of his wings. Vulture keeps on doing these passes and every time Peters puts his hands up, he cuts them again. Peter's all torn up. His costume is torn up and he can barely stand. When Peter finally manages to stand up, Vulture does a really big arc and uses all his velocity to crash right into him.

Vulture grabs Peter by the throat and smashes him up the length of that 45-degree rooftop. So he's got a big gash up his back. Peter is in bad, bad shape. It's the worst ass-kicking that Spider-Man has ever gotten on film. The Vulture is so intense, so angry, and so hardcore. Peter's trying to fight him off, but he's dazed and blacking out. Finally, the Vulture holds up an arm and the wing folds up until it's one big blade. He impales Peter through to the cement behind him. Vulture pins him, and he rips off

Peter's mask. We wanted to play with that trope that in every movie somebody knows who Peter Parker is. It happens in every single movie. I watched every Malkovich movie, and he always does this thing with his head. It's a head turn, kind of like a puppy. But instead of being cute, it's horrifying. At first, you think Vulture is going to show Peter mercy. Instead, Vulture starts screaming at Peter, "This is your fault. You know what you've done." Peter is blacking out and trying to fight him off. There's a POV shot in which what do you see is all blurry and out-of-focus. Peter's afraid he's going to die, and, in a last desperate effort, Peter pushes Vulture off as hard as he can. That breaks the blade. Vulture falls but lands on the ledge of the bottom of that 45-degree rooftop. That causes some of the blades to fold in on themselves, cutting him badly through his side. Vulture's wing is broken, so he can't fly. Now, Vulture and Peter are both jacked up. Vulture manages to get away by gliding through New York, crashing into the banks [of the Hudson River] outside of the city. We found this great old tugboat graveyard in Jersey City that we used as a reference. There are hundreds of shells of tugboats that are all rusted through. It looked crazy. It looks like something that came through Chernobyl. Vulture gets to the shore and dies right there.

But the big reveal is that once you see him roll off the ledge of the building and the camera pulls back, you see Vulture's daughter pounding on the glass of the tower next door. She's trying to get to him. But then she sees that Peter is Spider-Man. She sees that Peter has ostensibly just killed her dad. She kind of goes off the reservation and she and Peter have this terrible fight at the end. Sam wanted to imply Spider-Man died at the end. They were going to have this big parade, with an honor guard, in New York, and everyone would show up. Sam was going to populate the crowd with little kids wearing Spider-Man outfits. The last shot was going to be Peter in the crowd, hat pulled down, collar up. He's struck by the outpouring and amazing amount of love and support for him. Then he hands a kid a Spider-Man doll or something like that. I'm not saying that's the definitive or finished version of the story but that's the stuff I was working on with Sam.

In this version of the story, does Peter Parker definitively retire?
Sam's idea was that in his version of Spider-Man, Peter Parker is done. His rationale was that Peter had already given up his adolescence, his youth, his family, his security. He sacrificed himself physically and romantically. He's given up normalcy and security. Sam also thought that Peter was never aware of the impact he had on the people of New York, and he wanted to show that with the parade. Peter is just a neighborhood guy; he works in New York. He doesn't go all over the world; he's not a globetrotter like James Bond. He's just a kid. Sam thought it would be a very nice thing for Peter to see how much he meant to everyone while he's still alive and young enough and healthy enough to take it all in. Showing that and having him walk away leaves the possibility open that maybe he'll have a normal life. Maybe he'll be Spider-Man again someday but, at least at this point here and now, he's done. He needs to find his own life.

Spider-Man 4 **would have been released a year before** ***The Dark Knight Rises*,** **where Bruce Wayne retires. But in** ***The Dark Knight Rises*,** **Wayne passes the mantle to Dick Grayson. Typically, these films end with the notion that the**

superhero is out there, saving the day. Parker's retirement would have been a bold departure from that formula.
Exactly. Part of our mandate was to take all those tropes and turn them on their head. We wanted to take creative chances and take the film to places you don't expect. I love superhero movies, but they're often so bogged down with clichés and archetypes that they don't feel fresh. We were very conscious that we wanted to do something bold and weird. We wanted to play to Sam's sensibilities. He's kind of a quirky dude; he's an eccentric. We thought it would be beneficial to the series to follow Sam's sensibilities and not make it homogeneous. The idea that something must be a four-quarter tentpole that appeals to everyone never works. Big films never benefit from committees. Look at James Cameron, Christopher Nolan, and Alfred Hitchcock; they all have a singular vision and process. You should let them do their thing. But on the corporate or studio side, someone thought it was too eccentric for Spider-Man. But Spider-Man was invented by Stan Lee and Steve Ditko. Steve Ditko is the most eccentric artist who ever drew comics. Sam Raimi and Spider-Man are a perfect fit.

A big part of Rami's trilogy was the Peter Parker-Mary Jane relationship. You were saying that at the start of the film they were not together. Does Mary Jane (Kirsten Dunst) come back later in the film?
No, my understanding was that Mary Jane was just out of it. I don't know if that was a Sam call, a studio call, or an issue with Kirsten Dunst. I don't know what drove that decision creatively, but she was never part of it. There might have been one scene at the beginning where she finally left him for good. But in terms of the narrative and the character, if you're going to do a fourth movie, then you've got to take Peter someplace new. You have to. Otherwise, it's just lateral. And if the point was for Sam to go out on a high note, then he wanted to swing for the fences, take great chances, and not do the same shit all over again. In that regard, it was a great way to launch into that. Right off the bat, you defy the expectations. You break the trope and him from Mary Jane and all associated baggage. But the relationship with Mary Jane, Gwen Stacy in *Spider-Man 3,* was so stupid and ham-handed that Sam just wanted to wash his hands of the whole thing, to break free from *Spider-Man 3*. Clean the slate opens up a lot of narrative possibilities. Peter can date again. He can enjoy being Spider-Man. It goes to his head, and he stops thinking about other parts of his life. It's like rock stars who start to believe in their own bullshit.

They were going to have a major conglomerate come in and buy *The Daily Bugle* and make it totally trashy, the TMZ and *Daily Mail* route, the lowest common denominator. The daily paper tradition in New York is inherently filled with a lot of conflict. There was conflict with J. Jonah Jameson (J. K. Simmons) who puts Peter in this shitty little office. There's this woman who takes over and she's a corporate mouthpiece. But she also has a legit love of journalism. She's torn between her love of journalism and her love of money which comes from serving her corporate masters. It was interesting. The corporation is coming in and they are going to reassess everyone. Then her true identity is revealed. She's manipulated all this to find out if her father, the Vulture, was set up. She wants to clear his name and get him out of jail. But then she finds out that he is every bit as much of a bastard as she heard he is.

There were rumors that Anne Hathaway was cast as Black Cat.
I've seen that written [online] many times, but I never saw any mention of the Black Cat in any script that I saw, and I worked with Sam the entire time. As far as I know, Black Cat was not part of it.

Who would have played the Vulture's daughter?
They attached the part to a number of actresses. Kate Beckinsale was up for it. Anne Hathaway was up for it as well. Sam really wanted Angelina Jolie. I know Sam auditioned pretty much everyone but those were the main three. I saw Kate Beckinsale do a read with Tobey Maguire and she was great. I don't know what happened with Anne Hathaway or Angelina Jolie or how far they got. But as a reference point, they did ask me to use Angelina Jolie's likeness for a lot of the boards.

Was John Malkovich always the Vulture?
Early in the production, Sam spoke to Ben Kingsley about playing the Vulture. I did a couple of rounds of boards and concept designs with his likeness. But pretty early on it went to Malkovich. Malkovich would have been so badass.

Bryce Dallas Howard played Gwen Stacy in *Spider-Man 3*. Based on what you were saying, it doesn't seem like they were going to tell the iconic store where, while trying to save Gwen, Spider-Man inadvertently kills her.
No, and that's the whole thing. I think Sam wanted to wash his hands of the whole thing because *Spider-Man 3* was such a mess. He didn't want to explore storylines that were established in that movie. *Spider-Man 3* wasn't good, and I worked on it. Objectively, it wasn't. But "good" depends on your standpoint. Are you saying good creatively or good as the studio defines it, which is profitability. Those are two different languages.

If you say *Spider-Man 3* sucked to someone at the studio, they'll say, what do you mean it sucked? It made [nearly] $900 million. That's a conversation that gets you down a rabbit hole quickly. Look at the *Transformers* movies. I don't think you could make a reasonable argument that they're good movies, but they make billions of dollars. I don't begrudge anyone their fandom. But the argument is, because they make so much money, they're good by definition. Let's put it this way, I'll eat at McDonald's once in a while, but I don't have any delusions that it's good food. I don't confuse McDonald's with a good rib eye. I understand the studio's side. When they're playing with that kind of money, of course, they're going to be paranoid and do everything they can to protect their investments. They'd be foolish if they didn't. But there's a lot of politics between navigating creative and financial interests. A lot of times, they seem mutually exclusive.

Dylan Baker played Curt Connors, who becomes the Lizard, in two of Raimi's Spider-Man movies. Would Baker be the Lizard?
Not on the version that we were ultimately working on. There were a couple of drafts with the Lizard, but we didn't do any work on them. They wanted to go with the Vulture. I think they wanted to concentrate on the Vulture and one of the lessons they learned about *Spider-Man 3* is that sometimes too much is just too much. There were just entirely too many bad guys.

John Malkovich as the Vulture
Illustration by Pat Carbajal

But Sam had kicked around that idea a little bit. I think he might have wanted *Spider-Man 3* to be the Sandman and the Vulture [and not Venom] because that was the 1970s All-Star villain mashup. He also talked about using Lizard for *Spider-Man 4*. The first group that they had for *Spider-Man 4* was with the Lizard. And that's why the Lizard was the primary antagonist in the first reboot [Rhys Ifans played the part in *The Amazing Spider-Man*]. Sony just repurposed a lot of the script they already had. They didn't use Dylan Baker in the reboot as a little Lizard and I would have liked to have seen him. They spent three movies setting the guy up and it didn't pay off.

What happens with Vulture's daughter?
They had a thing with his daughter where the daughter picks up the mantle. At the beginning of the third act, she realizes that her dad really is this guy, then he gives her just enough information before he dies that she figures out where his lair is. It's a huge hidden complex. There's a great scene where she walks into it. The lights flicker, she's looking around and she's stunned that her dad has lived this whole secret life. She knew nothing about it. Then a center light comes on and she sees the big, winged apparatus in the middle. So she takes over and starts wearing his suit. At first, Peter is confused and freaked out. He thought he killed the Vulture and he felt terrible about it. So who the hell is this?

Then they fight?
Yes.

And Spider-Man wins the fight because he's Spiderman?
Well, no.

That's when she appears to kill him?
Right. She seems to kill him. Then she leaves him. Now she's heartbroken. Not only has she lost her dad, but she's also lost the man that she really cares about and feels deeply for. They were setting it up where the daughter and Peter end up becoming close. It was interesting and there's a lot of heart in it. Peter is not a little kid anymore. He's been through so much. He's a lot more street-smart now. He's a savvy grown-up. You can't keep him young forever. Tobey Maguire was around 35-years old at the time. He wasn't an 18-year-old anymore. But there were parallels to that era of comics. If you look at the early 1970s, the John Romita ones where Peter goes back between Gwen Stacy and Mary Jane Watson, it's sophisticated. It wasn't the lowest common denominator high school stuff. He was a young man, going to college.

In *Spider-Man 4*, Peter was trying to figure out what he wants to do with his life and the girl was very much in the same boat. She is an accomplished young woman who has been tasked with a huge takeover. She knows that everyone at *The Bugle* is hostile to her being there. They are hostile to the corporation, to their intentions, and to the change of format. Part of her agrees with them. She thinks it sucks too but she's the point person and she can't quit because it's a multibillion-dollar deal. In their own ways, they are both trying to figure out what to do and keep their conscience clean. Peter realizes how much of a burden it is to be Spider-Man. He comes home, he's alone. He gets beat up, he's alone. Even old-ass Aunt May is getting laid and he's not.

It's demoralizing. The daughter is also bound up in the pressure and the expectations of what she's doing. There's a lot of pressure, but at the end of the day, she just wants to know about her dad. She just wants to know who her father is and what he's done. And that's under the surface of everything. She's conflicted because she thinks a lot of people at *The Bugle* have valid points and she doesn't want to ruin the newspaper. She has a tremendous amount of respect for journalism. There were a lot of indictments about the TMZ culture, news that's not news, and reducing everything to sound bites. J. Jonah Jameson is too popular at the paper to be fired, so they demote him instead. He gets the shitty office and she takes his old office and you can imagine how happy he is about that.

After Spider-Man is presumed dead, after the parade, do they wind up together?
I don't think they did. They were looking for a context for that, where to go with it. They didn't want to just kill her off and they didn't want to make it a murder-suicide in the end. They didn't know where to go with it. But she and Peter were reflections of each other. She loses it. He kills the Vulture, and it affects him so badly that after the whole thing with her, it makes Peter give it up and walk away. He doesn't want to have to do that ever again. I think there's a little bit of that with her as well. She was put in this impossible situation, and she gets swallowed up as well. She became the very thing that her dad was. She wants to walk away from it too.

We also had a scene that would take place after credits. Peter would leave the parade, people celebrating him, and then it would go to credits. At the end of *Darkman,* we think Liam Neeson (Darkman) is dead. But in the last shot, there's a big crowd and people milling around the street. Bruce Campbell stops and turns around and it's obvious that it's Darkman but it's Campbell's face because that's the one he's adopted now? We were going to recreate that exactly with the actress who played the Vulture's daughter. The idea was that she didn't die. She's not gone either.

The last shot of *Darkman* suggests that Darkman, the hero, is still out there. Instead of saying the hero is out there, they were saying villain is still out there. How does a storyboard artist fit into a large-budget movie like this?
A storyboard artist is not part of any department. You work with the director singularly. We are in the Art Directors Guild but it's a weird fit because we don't have anything to do with the art department. The drawing part is ancillary to the story part. For a long time, Pixar didn't have scripts. Instead, they conceived whole movies and whole sequences visually because film, of course, is a visual medium. Sam is a visual director and he's very good at communicating visual ideas. It makes it very easy to work with him. He always respects the effort of others. It really matters to him. He loves the process, he loves actors, he loves storyboard artists, and he's very demonstrative. He's a blue-collar kid from Detroit and I was a blue color kid from Baltimore, so we had that in common. Even now, after all his success, he is still a little bit of an outsider.

There's a storyboard on your website with Peter Parker kissing someone. When I first saw it, I wondered if they wound up together.
No, that's kind of in the middle. It's after they started dating but before she finds out

that he's Spider-Man. They're both burdened with living these crazy, secret lives. It's about what they're giving up by living those secret lives. The more we talked about it, the more it made sense that these two people were defined by the pressure of navigating their secret lives. I thought that was interesting. They both have the same burden but neither one knows about the other. But they sense it. They touch on that a little bit in *Batman Returns* (1992) with Catwoman and Batman. I think if you live through something extraordinary, it leaves something in you that people who have had the same experience recognize. It's almost like a sixth sense. It's an indicator. I've heard that said about everything from serial killers to people who have suffered tremendous losses and tragedies. Those events imprint on you. Other people who have had that experience, even if they don't articulate it, can recognize it in somebody else. So that was part of it. I don't know how it would have ultimately played out in the script given all the politics but conceptually that was one of those things we talked about all the time. It was bold, narratively adventurous, and creatively cool. Sam didn't want to do the same old thing again. He wanted to go out on a high note, not just financially but creatively. He wanted to do something that he was proud of. He wanted to do something that was uniquely and distinctly his, as opposed to something that was half his and half the accounting department's.

You clearly have a great deal of admiration for Sam.
I wasn't in the Art Directors Guild yet. But Sam went to bat to get me into the union so I could be eligible to work on *Spider-Man 4*. Here's another story that illustrates my affection for him. Not too long before I started working for him, I had a number of family losses. I lost a lot of people at once and it was terrible. The first anniversary of my brother's death happened about halfway through my tenure on *Spider-Man 4*. They were doing a big charity concert in my brother's name in Baltimore. I went to Sam and told him about it in very broad strokes. He said, "Of course go. Don't even worry about it. You're doing great work. Don't even give me a second thought." Then he said, "What do you need?" I said, "I just need the time off." And he said, "No, what do you need from me? What can I contribute?" I'm going to get choked up even talking about this. He said, "It's a charity. I have a warehouse full of things. Put me down for whatever you think is appropriate and when you come back tell me what it is, and I'll sign and personalize everything. I'll take care of it. Go home and be with your family. Do the right thing." So I went home, and the event was a big success. The dad who won the auction had a kid who was an aspiring filmmaker. I came back, and Sam asked how it went. I told him. He said, "That's great." I come back at the end of the day, and I see Sam on his hands and knees on the floor of his office signing all these cool international Spider-man posters and a Blu-ray box set of his Spider-Man movies. But he didn't just sign them; he personalized them to the kid. He wrote, if you want to make movies, do good in school, be good to your parents and blah blah blah. Then he wrote, Hit me up when you're ready. Here's how to get a hold of me. I mean who does that? I had to go to the bathroom because I thought I was going to break down crying right in front of him. I'm like 6'3"; he's like 5' 3". He came up to me and said, "Hey buddy, how you doing? You're looking a little upset." Then he gave me this big hug. He said, "I wish I could do more," and I said, "Sam, you have no idea what this means

to me." He said, "Well, try not to do such shitty work. Try not to do such terrible work and we'll be even." When I say he's such a sweet guy I don't mean for a director, he's just a sweet guy. To this day, I still get choked up. It meant the world to me.

We also worked together on other projects. For years I worked on *Oz* [*Oz the Great and Powerful*, 2013], *Warcraft* [Raimi was initially attached to direct the 2016 film], and some other projects and development stuff. I know he's gotten calls about making other superhero movies, but I think he's reluctant to do them given his experience on Spider-Man.

Getting back to Spider-Man, it must have been challenging to work without a more polished script, or even an approach, that everyone could agree upon.
It was weird because the process was detached from the script. The script seemed almost amorphous. We never got the whole script. We would only get little pieces of it, only little chunks of it. That was an indicator that Sam was going to have to fall on his sword again and have all these story elements imposed on him. It was a great experience, but it was also a very strange experience. Sam and his producer, Grant Curtis, who became a wonderful friend, were wonderful. I was working with a lot of creative people, and we all felt like we were on fire. But there was a disconnect between all the things the studio said had to be in the script and the things that we were riffing on. There was a huge disparity between all the things that Sam wanted to do and his vision and what was being put on him by the studio. Then this malaise crept it and it was clear that they were doing it to him again. Morale started to go down. Then we started to hear whispers that the movie was going to be shut down, that Sam was going to leave.

We were in a weird vacuum because our job was to riff, riff, riff and, then Sam would say, "There's this thing I want to previs. [Previs, or previsualization, is a process where filmmakers use computers to create a rough layout of a scene.] I need you guys to help me pitch it." Suddenly, there'd be a real urgency to our work. We would do all these specific storyboards and animatic runs just to counter some specific dumbass' notes from the studio. Like I said, Sam is a sweet guy, and I would feel protective of him. I would be in these meetings with him, and you could see it physically wear on him. Sam was not good at hiding it; you could see it wear him down. They took something that could have been fun and wonderful, and it just wasn't anymore.

How did *Spider-Man 4* get canceled?
It finally got shut down right before Christmas. Grant called me. He said, "I'm sorry." I said, "You don't know me any apology I'm grateful to be there." He said, "I know, but I have to call 200 people today and tell them that they're out of work at Christmas time." That was a bummer. I had this conversation with Grant that I'll never forget. Before we hung up, I said, "I don't understand." We were so close to filming. There were probably already tens of millions of dollars pumped into it. We were already on staff, we were in previs, sets were already being built, and it had already been cast. That's a huge investment to suddenly cut and run from. I said, "How does that work?" He said, "Okay we're friends, but I'm going to lay this all out for you like a producer. Because if you want to produce, you're going to need to understand this." He said, "To the studio it doesn't look like they're going to lose $20 or $30 million, or whatever

it is. They look at it like we're gaining $100 million." I said, "That's the part that doesn't make any sense to me." He said, "Break it down like this. If you reboot you don't have to pay Toby, you don't have to pay Sam because they had guarantees and they had back end. All of that is off the table. Then they hire an up-and-coming director and an up-and-coming cast, and, because it's a career-making opportunity, you sign them for close-to scale and lock them in for three movies. The actors will make their money once they become stars from doing the reboot." So the studio saves tens of millions of dollars there.

Then he said, "The real thing, especially with something like Spider-Man, is that the movie is like a loss leader." He equated it to the food in a casino in Vegas. He said the movie represents a relatively small part of all the income generated from Spider-Man movies. The majority of the money comes from merchandising and licensing. Whenever they do a new Superman movie or reboot, they tweak the design just enough, so they have to renegotiate every deal with every vendor for every product worldwide. He said, "Think about the magnitude of that. We're talking about every action figure, every video game, every sippy cup, every fast-food premium, every sleeping bag, everything. If you reboot, you get to renegotiate all those deals from scratch, on your terms, all over the world. That is billions with a B. So while it is an astonishing amount of money to us, it pales in comparison to how much is generated by the merchandise." Remember Avi Arad, one of the *Spider-Man* producers, came from the toy business. Arad bought Toy Biz in the early '90s. That's what saved Marvel in the first place. [Arad and Isaac Perlmutter bought Toy Biz and, later, took control over Marvel Comics.] That's how he got to be a producer on *Spider-Man* in the first place. I'm not passing judgment; it's not an indictment. In terms of big-budget tentpole movies, that's how it works. That's why Disney and Pixar keep making *Cars* movies. I know the kids love them, but they generate ten times as much on merchandising as everything else, so they'll never stop making them. [More than $8 billion of *Cars* merchandise was sold in the first five years of its 2006 release.[109]]

Other than characters like Spider-Man, which is owned by Sony, Marvel Studios is in charge of many of their characters. Although now Marvel is making Spider-Man movies too. However, because Warner Bros. owns DC Comics, DC Comics films have to go through that extra level of bureaucracy. Marvel has a certain kind of autonomy that DC doesn't. There are some R-rated superhero films, but the rating does limit their ability to make kid's toys. Merchandising and licensing are a huge part of what drives that stuff.

I felt like even though it didn't come out I was a part of a weird little corner of the superhero universe. It's a shame. I really would have loved to have seen Sam go out on a high note. And that's why we were all inspired to do the level of work we did. There is a loyalty that comes with him being such a great guy. That loyalty goes above and beyond the paycheck. We were invested because we believed that Sam deserved an opportunity to go out the way he wanted to. We thought, "Let's make this kick-ass and leave nothing on the table. Let's go crazy."

It's too bad they didn't allow him to make his version of *Spider-Man 4*.
Spider-Man 4 would have taken the franchise and Peter Parker to a place they hadn't

been in any of the other movies. Vulture would have been a terrific, iconic, and terrifying villain. If we had been able to do what we were tasked with, it would have ended Sam's run on the series on a high note, creatively speaking. If they just let him do what he wanted to do, it would have been spectacular.

Appendix A

And So Fourth

Note: I tried to keep the introduction relatively short. I figured that most readers would likely want to get to the interviews right away. As a result, I eliminated large swaths from the introduction. For the few readers who want to further explore the minutia of fourth films, I offer the following.

How Sequels Change Characters

Sometimes sequels seem to inadvertently change the essential nature of a character. For instance, when we first meet them, John McClane and Ellen Ripley, in *Die Hard* (1988) and *Alien*, respectively, are not superheroes. McClane is a detective lieutenant with the New York City Police Department, and he is outclassed by his adversary Han Gruber, who seems to be a terrorist leader. Ripley is a warrant officer on a commercial freight spaceship; she is essentially a space trucker. In both films, the central characters are ordinary people who are placed in extraordinary circumstances. The more fraught their circumstances become, the more powerful their characters are called on to become. In the first *Die Hard*, McClane is nearly put out of commission when he is forced to walk across broken glass in his bare feet. By the fourth film, he is jumping from a semi-truck to an airplane and then, midair, from an airplane to the unforgiving pavement of a highway. Ripley spends much of *Alien* running scared. By the fourth film, she has super strength. She also loses much of her humanity. Literally. Weaver's character is no longer human, at least not strictly speaking. Instead, thanks to advanced technology, Ripley has been cloned.

Their return becomes unintentionally comical. Weaver expressed concerns about repeatedly returning to the franchise, saying that she did not want Ripley to become "a figure of fun" who would incessantly "wake up with monsters running around." As McClane says in a scene shot specifically for the teaser trailer for *Die Hard II*, "Why does the same thing keep happening to the same guy?" McClane has adopted the saying "Yippie kai yay" as his catchphrase. In the context of the original film, the Western quote made sense. It is part of a larger and ongoing conversation that McClane was having with Gruber. However, in later films, it almost becomes a weird fetish, which he utters before he kills each film's main bad guy. Timothy Olyphant, who played the villain Thomas Gabriel in the fourth *Die Hard* film, *Live Free or Die Hard*, remembers how Bruce Willis and the film's director Len Weisman agonized over when McClane should drop his bon mot. When Olyphant suggested that it did not have to be said at the climax of the film, that maybe it could be a throwaway line. They looked at him like he was crazy.

Similarly, the character of Paul Kersey, the architect-turned-vigilante in the *Death Wish* series was compromised over time. The power of the first film was that Kersey was an architect, with no law enforcement background and no lethal skills, who sought revenge on the men who killed his wife. However, to justify Kersey seeking revenge in ensuing *Death Wish* movies, other people who are important to him would have to die. In subsequent films, his daughter is violently attacked, and his housekeeper is killed, his friend is assaulted, his girlfriend's daughter overdoses from illegal drugs, his girlfriend Karen is killed, and his fiancée is threatened by her ex-husband, a mobster. It seems clear that Kersey is a crime magnet of sorts, and if he were serious about keeping people safe, he would stop forming meaningful relationships.

Screenwriter Gail Morgan Hickman resisted the direction taken by the *Death Wish* series. In Paul Talbot's book *Bronson's Loose: The Making of the Death Wish Film!*, Hickman explained, "It seemed to me that there's really only two ways to tell a vigilante story. One is to tell it really seriously [and to consider] the moral implications of living in a world where you can take the law in your own hands, [and] what that does to society, and what does that to you. If you're not doing to do that, if you're going to make it into an entertainment, then it has to be a cartoon." With Kersey single-handedly eliminating mobsters and taking on the war on drugs, *Death Wish IV* certainly became more cartoonish.

Much to the dismay of Victor Miller, who wrote the original *Friday the 13th*, the sequels changed Jason's nature. In the first film, he is a victim, but in later films, he became a villain, a killing machine. Miller said, "To be honest, I have not seen any of the sequels, but I have a major problem with all of them because they made Jason the villain. I still believe that the best part of my screenplay was the fact that a mother figure was the serial killer—working from a horribly twisted desire to avenge the senseless death of her son, Jason. Jason was dead from the very beginning. He was a victim, not a villain. But I took motherhood and turned it on its head, and I think that was great fun. Mrs. Voorhees was the mother I'd always wanted—a mother who would have killed for her kids."[110]

Genre-Busting
One way long-running franchises can stay fresh is to draw from different genres for different entries. For instance, the first *Child's Play* movie is a slasher-horror film, and the fourth entry is a horror-comedy. Similarly, the first Indiana Jones film, *Raiders of the Lost Ark*, was inspired by the movie serials of the nineteen-thirties and forties, and the fourth film *Indiana Jones and the Kingdom of the Crystal Skull* took inspiration from science-fiction movies of the nineteen fifties. But this is not a new strategy; this kind of genre-busting dates back to some of the earliest movie franchises.

From 1936 to 1946, Basil Rathbone and Nigel Bruce played Sherlock Holmes and Doctor John Watson in fourteen films. However, despite surface similarities in that Rathbone and Bruce played the crime-solving duo in all films, there are actually great differences between them. The first two films *The Hound of the Baskervilles* (1939) and *The Adventures of Sherlock Holmes* (1939) were set in Victorian times. But starting with the third film *Sherlock Holmes and the Voice of Terror* (1942), the setting was brought up to the nineteen-forties, the then-present day. Further changes were afoot.

Sherlock Holmes and the Secret Weapon (1943), the fourth film, takes the form of an espionage thriller. In *Secret Weapon*, Holmes has, in effect, joined England's war effort. The great detective faces off with Professor Moriarty who has joined forces with the Nazis in order to steal a scientific invention for a better bombsight, a device that enables atomic bombs to fall with accuracy. Other films would draw on other genres, including the supernatural (*The Scarlet Claw*, 1944), film noir (*The Spider Woman*, also 1944), and serial killer (*The Woman in Green*, 1945). As Amanda J. Field observed in *England's Secret Weapon*, "By the time the series ended in 1946, the films had retreated somewhat ambiguously from modernity straying first into ghosts-and-ghouls chiller territory and finally into horror."[111]

Prequels

Instead of making a sequel to the fourth film, filmmakers can create a prequel that depicts the events that happened before the fourth film. *The Phantom Menace* is a *Star Wars* prequel that tells the story of how Ben Kenobi found Anakin Skywalker, the young boy who would grow up to become Darth Vader. *Terminator Salvation* (2009) tried a similar approach. It told the story of how soldier Kyle Reese met John Connor, the leader of the robot resistance who in the first *Terminator* movie is sent back in time to protect John's mother Sarah Connor.

Hannibal Rising (2007) is a prequel to *Silence of the Lambs* (1991) and *Sum of All Fears* (2002) is a prequel to *The Hunt for Red October* (1990). Both films star different actors as younger versions of the main character, with Gaspard Ulliel and Ben Affleck taking over for Anthony Hopkins and Harrison Ford who replaced Alec Baldwin, respectively. Similarly, the fourth X-Men movie, *X-Men First Class* (2011), which is set in the sixties tells the origin story of the group of mutant superheroes. *Wrong Turn 4* (2011), subtitled *Bloody Beginnings*, tells the origins of a trio of deformed, inbred cannibals with colorful names, Three Fingers, One Eye, and Saw Tooth. The off-putting horror movie fits the definition of "torture porn" in which the cannibals eat someone alive, fondue style. *The Purge* (2013) is a violent thriller set in a suburban community in the United States that is celebrating the annual purge, the one day of the year when all crime is legal. In *The Purge*, a group of masked teenagers terrorize a family and eventually kill the father (Ethan Hawke). Because Hawke, the protagonist, is killed at the end of the movie. Later films did not have the option to focus their stories on his character, instead, they are set on subsequent Purge days. *The First Purge* (2018), as the name suggests, is a prequel that depicts the first time the twisted holiday was enacted. Similarly, the subtitle to the fourth Exorcist movie clearly announces that it is a prequel—*Exorcist: The Beginning*.

After playing Frank Martin, a mercenary who moves special goods, in three Transporter films, Jason Statham was ready to get out of the driver's seat. Ed Skrein replaced him for the reboot *The Transporter Refueled* (2015), which is about the early days of the former mercenary.

Bandit Goes Country (1994) is a prequel to *Smokey and the Bandit* (1977) and the fourth film in the series. Brian Bloom, who takes over for Burt Reynolds, would play the part in four 1994 TV movies *Bandit Goes Country*, *Bandit, Beauty and the Bandit*, and *Bandit's Silver Angel*, which were all released the same year.

Tremors 4: The Legend Begins, also a prequel, tells how the town of Rejection (later called Perfection and the location for the Tremors films) becomes inhabited by slug-like monsters called graboids. In this Western, Michael Gross plays the grandfather of Burt Gummer, the character he plays in the other Tremors films.

Prequel-Sequel

If a filmmaker can't decide whether to make a sequel or a prequel, why not do both? There are a modest number of sequel-prequel hybrids in the horror film genre. *Psycho IV, Saw IV,* and *Blood Raiser IV* all tell stories that happen before the events in the first film and also pick up sometime after that film concluded. In *Psycho IV*, Anthony Perkins reprises his role as the mother-loving/killing Norman Bates. But, employing flashbacks, the film depicts moments in Norman's life as a teenager, that were alluded to in Hitchcock's *Psycho,* and it picks up years later. *Saws IV* picks up after *Saw III*, and, like *Psycho IV*, it uses flashbacks to tell the story of how Johnathan Kramer became Jigsaw, a serial killer with a perverse code of ethics. In the case of *Saw IV*, it was necessary to depict Kramer's earlier exploits because he died in *Saw III*.

Hellraiser: Bloodline, the fourth *Hellraiser* film, is another notable sequel-prequel. The film is told in three time frames and tells the story of how three different generations of a family are connected to the Lament Configuration, a puzzle back that "opens up the doors to hell." The film opens in a space station in the 22nd Century and includes segments set in the 20th and 18th Centuries. There are some wickedly funny lines in *Bloodline*. When a security guard threatens Pinhead, the demon scolds, "What you think of as pain is a shadow. Pain has a face. Allow me to show it to you. Gentlemen, I...am.... pain." When another character sees Pinhead's face, which has had nails violently hammered into it, he cries, "For God's sake!" The demon responds, "Do I look like someone who cares what God thinks?" Despite flashes of wit, I tend to agree with the clerk at Blockbuster Video who, not wanting to waste her time, refused to allow my wife to rent the movie.

The fourth live-action Scooby-Doo film, *Scooby-Doo! Curse of the Lake Monster* (2010), is a TV movie *and* it's a prequel. However, it is not the first prequel in the series. The third *Scooby-Doo! The Mystery Begins* (2009) is also a TV movie and a prequel. As was *Bandit Goes Country* (1994), which is also directed by Hal Needham, the director of the first two Smokey and the Bandit movies.

Normally, a prequel takes place before the events of the first movie. However, *Terminator Salvation* is an exception in that it takes place after some of the key events of *Terminator* but before others. *Salvation* is a sequel to events that take place in modern times in *Terminator* but a prequel to the events that were depicted in the dystopian future, where androids hunt humans. However, given the time-traveling concept of the franchise, it is logical to leap back and forth in time.

Some part fours, deliberately eschew the first film's name, as is the case with the *Child's Play* series, which is about a children's doll named Chucky that is haunted and controlled by the spirit of a serial killer. The first two sequels were predictably called *Child's Play* 2 (1990) and *Child's Play 3* (1991). However, the fourth film *Bride of Chucky* (1998) dropped "Child's Play" and instead used the toy's name. The subsequent sequels retained the killer doll's name *Seed of Chucky* (2004), *Curse of Chucky* (2013), and *Cult of Chucky* (2017). Similarly, the first three *Hatchet* films were called *Hatchet* (2006), *Hatchet II* (2010), *and Hatchet III* (2013) but the fourth slasher film *Victor Crowley* (2017), is named after the titular killer.

Standalone

An alternative to going forward or backward is a standalone film, one that is largely separate from the continuity of the previous films. *Species: The Awakening* (2007) and *Howling IV: The Original Nightmare* (1988), the fourth *Species* and *Howling* movies are two such examples. The fourth Species film is the lone one that doesn't feature Natasha Henstridge's space-vampire, and the fourth *Howling* film is an attempt to faithfully adapt Gary Brandner's *The Howling*, the 1977 novel that inspired the series.

Unmade Fourth Films

The list of unmade fourth films is tantalizing. Everything from *Spider-Man 4* to *Godfather Part IV* has been rumored. Marvel's fourth *Avengers* film *Avengers: Endgame* was a runaway hit but the fourth film in Zack Snyder's DC superhero universe was never made. After Christopher Nolan concluded his Dark Knight trilogy, Warner Bros. executives gave Snyder the keys to their DC superhero kingdom. Snyder directed *Man of Steel* (2013), *Batman v Superman: Dawn of Justice* (2016), and *Justice League* (2017). However, the theatrical version of *Justice League* is not the director's cut, nor did it reflect Snyder's vision for the film.

Trouble started long before the film was released. Warner Bros. executives were keenly aware that Snyder's muscular and operatic style was in stark contrast to Marvel's family-friendly tone. So during the filming of *Justice League*, the studio asked Joss Whedon, the writer-director of the first two *Avenger* films, to work with Snyder and to write additional scenes for *Justice League*. But Whedon's initial contribution was not enough to satisfy them. When Warner executives screened Snyder's rough cut, they reacted negatively and demanded a major overhaul, a notion that Snyder vigorously resisted. But when Snyder needed to take some time off to deal with a family matter, he was forced off the film. The studio brought Whedon in to write and direct more scenes and to finish the movie.

Whedon's *Justice League* was a not entirely successful mix of two filmmakers, each with their own distinct style. Years later, when Warner Bros. launched HBO Max, their streaming service, the company needed high-profile projects for the service, and consequently, they hired Snyder to complete his films. Not only did Snyder continue to edit the rough cut of his film, but he also shot additional scenes for this revised version. Snyder's four-hour *Zack Snyder's Justice League* was released on HBO Max in 2021. But fans who were hoping that Snyder would neatly wrap up the storylines he set up in the previous films were disappointed.

Not only did Snyder not conclusively conclude his saga, but the director also teased plot points for the fourth film that he knew would never be realized. As a result, *Justice League* ends on a cliffhanger and unresolved storylines. But viewers will never see Superman and Lois Lane's baby, or see a romance between Lane and Bruce Wayne, or Lois die[112] because the additional movies will never come. Warner Bros. executives had hoped that the *Justice League* would end conclusively. Snyder said, "They didn't want me to suggest more films to come. They wanted me to cul-de-sac it as much as I could. I'm like, 'Look, that's just not the genre.' It's not the comic book genre to end the story, regardless of if we ever make [another] one or not."[113] In other words, Snyder deliberately set up a story for a fourth film that he knew he was unlikely to be given the opportunity to make.

Faux Fourths

On rare occasions, there is a question if the fourth film in a series actually exists. In 2018 a trailer debuted for *Dundee: The Son of a Legend Returns Home*, the third sequel to *Crocodile Dundee* (1986). The trailer shows Danny McBride as Brian Dundee, the long-lost son of Australian legend Crocodile Dundee who is going down under to search for his missing father. A second trailer includes scenes of Brian and Wally Jr., played by the Aussie Thor actor Chris Hemsworth. Both trailers and an elaborate website promised that the film would premiere in the summer. The website teased a little of the movie's plot and hints at Dundee's return. "Well, actually, he's missing in the Outback. And the only person who might be able to find him is the loudmouthed American son no one knew he had. Introducing Danny McBride as Brian Dundee. This son of a legend is forced to channel his Aussie roots as he embarks on the ultimate adventure in the land down under. It's time to live up to the family name. Unlike his father, Brian grew up as a city kid. But that won't stop him from picking up his dad's oversized knife and launching into the Australian outback, completely unprepared for what lies ahead." Other trailers feature parts for Margot Robbie as Lil' Donk, Hugh Jackman as the Prime Minister and Russell Crowe as newspaper magnate J. P. Steele, who is going to teach Dundee "who the most dangerous man in Australia is."

The accompanying poster for *Dundee: The Son of a Legend Returns Home* promised that the movie was "coming soon, mate."[114] It turned out, as many media critics suspected, that the trailer was not really for *Crocodile Dundee*, but instead, it was a teaser for an Australian tourism ad that would appear during the 52nd Super Bowl. Hogan also spoofed his association with his signature character in the meta-comedy *The Very Excellent Mr. Dundee* (2020). Playing himself, Hogan must navigate life as a fading star whose reputation is sullied and who is being courted to play Crocodile Dundee one more time.

In 2015, Liam Neeson appeared in a fake trailer for *Taken 4* that was aired on *Jimmy Kimmel Live!*. In the faux trailer, Neeson's retired CIA agent Bryan Mills is helping a friend recover a loved one who was taken. Whereas Mills' daughter and wife were taken hostage in earlier installments, in *Taken 4*, Mills' friend's dog is kidnapped. Eventually, Mills successfully retrieved the kidnapped canine. But success is short-lived. Mills soon discovers that one more thing has been taken—his friend's pants. Yes, somehow his friend's slacks were stolen—while he was wearing them. That is the tongue-in-cheek premise of the fake fourth Taken film.

A year later, Neeson would appear on *Late Night with Stephen Colbert* in yet another *Taken 4* parody trailer. This *Taken 4* seems to be more of a reboot than a sequel to the series. In the skit, Neeson is trying to land the part of an intimidating mall Santa Clause with an unusual set of skills. Neeson's Clause is intense and threatening as he warns children that he has a list and is going to check it twice to find out if they are naughty or nice.

The fourth movie in the *Sleepaway Camp* series is another fourth film which is not the fourth film. Following the success of 1983's *Sleepaway Camp*, two sequels were made, *Sleepaway Camp II: Unhappy Campers* (1988) and *Sleepaway Camp III: Teenage Wasteland* (1989). Promo footage for a fourth *Sleepaway Camp* was shot, but financing for the complete feature never materialized. Over 30 minutes of surviving footage of the promo shot, along with clips from the previous films, were edited together to make a quasi-fourth film, which was released in 2012 as *Sleepaway Camp IV: The Survivor*. The fourth complete film in the series was 2008's *Return to Sleepaway Camp*.

The fourth film in the *Barbershop* series is *Barbershop: The Next Cut* (2016). Yet, *The Next Cut*, the third part of a trilogy of films, is actually the *fourth* film made in the series. The third film produced is *Beauty Shop* (2005), a spin-off film.

Sometimes the fourth film will continue the story that was established in part 3, as is the case with *The Planet of the Apes* series and *Conquest for the Planet of the Apes*, which concluded the story that was established in the first three films. At other times, the series changes direction, as is the case with *Alien: Resurrection* (1997) after *Alien 3* (1992) definitively killed off Ripley, *Halloween IV*, which ignored the events of the Michael Myers-free *Halloween 3,* and which told the story about an evil corporation that was attempting to kill the people wearing their Halloween masks.

House Party 4: Down to the Last Minute (2001) is unrelated to the first three *House Party* films. But the fifth, *House Party: Tonight's the Night* (2013) is the fourth part of the story, as it is tied to the events of the first three films.

In the height of his fame, Arnold Schwarzenegger deliberately starred in a faux-four. A fictional fourth film plays a big part in the plot of the *Last Action Hero* (1993), a satire of action movies, in two ways. In the film, Austin O'Brian plays Danny Madigan, a young movie lover who goes to the movies to take solace from his everyday life and the loss of his father. Danny is a huge fan of the Jack Slater series. In the film within the film, the fictional series stars Schwarzenegger as Slater, a hard-boiled, wise-cracking police detective. Danny is particularly excited for the release of *Jack Slater IV*, the fourth film in the series. *Slater IV* stars Anthony Quinn, Charles Dance, and Art Carney, in his last film appearance. *Slater IV* gains even greater prominence when, after getting a hold of a magic ticket, Danny is transported into the fourth Slater movie. In fact, the bulk of *Last Action Hero* takes in this fictional fourth movie.

In 2020, Chris R. Notarile, a fan of the *Last Action Hero*, wrote *Jack Slaver V*, a radio play that is meant to serve as a sequel to *Slater IV*. It didn't make a big splash on the internet. However, a sequel to a faux-fourth film deserves honorable mention.[115]

Meta-Four

Scream 4 and *The Matrix Resurrections* have little in common—the former is a horror murder mystery former and the latter is an existential sci-fi action movie—but they are notable instances of part fours that are self-referential. Not only do the creators of *Scream 4* and *Matrix Resurrections* movies call attention to these movies *as* movies, but both frequently remind us that we are watching the fourth film in the series.

Both *Scream 4* and *Resurrections* contain scenes from past installments that are recreated in different forms—a film-within-a-film in *Scream 4*, and in *Matrix*

Resurrections by introducing a video game called *Matrix IV*. *Scream 2*, the filmmakers introduced *Stab*, a film-within-a-film that is based on the events in the original *Scream*. As the *Scream* franchise continued, so did the *Stab* movies, *Stab 2* echoes the events of *Scream 2*, and *Stab 3: Hollywood Horror* retells the events of *Scream 3*. So when a teenager in *Scream 4* inquires, "What is *Stab 4* about?" she is effectively asking, "What is *Scream 4* about?"

In *Resurrections*, Keanu Reeves returns as Neo, the leader of a resistance group that won the humans' battle against sentient machines. When *Resurrections* begins, Neo's memory has been wiped and he believes that he is a video game designer. He has also been tricked into believing that the events depicted in the first three *Matrix* films were games that he created. Neo is now tasked with creating a fourth *Matrix* game. In the same way that *Stab 4* echoes the events of *Scream 4*, the fourth *Matrix* game could mirror incidents from *Resurrections*.

The meta-commentary in *Resurrections* acknowledges the filmmakers' relationship to Warner Bros., the studio that owns the intellectual property rights to the *Matrix* series. Neo's business partner Smith (Jonathan Groff) explains, "Our beloved parent company, Warner Bros., has decided to make a sequel to the trilogy…They informed me they're gonna to do it with or without us… They made it clear they would kill our contract if we didn't cooperate." This line alludes to Warner Bros.' determination to make more *Matrix* films, with or without Lana and Lilly Wachowski, the creators of the series.

Other characters offer commentary about the inherent problem of making franchise movies. The Architect (Neil Patrick Harris), the creator of the computer simulation called the Matrix, grumbles, "Resurrecting you both was crazy expensive. Like renovating a house. Took twice as long, cost twice as much." The Architect could have been talking about the budget of *Matrix Resurrections*, which reportedly cost two-to-three times as much as the original film.

Scream 4 is similarly filled with meta-commentary. In fact, there is so much of it in *Scream 4* that the characters themselves acknowledge how meta the film is. One teenager complains to another about horror movies that the "whole self-aware post-modern meta-shit" has been "done to death." Much of the commentary is about the nature of horror film remakes. Various characters observe, "You do a remake to outdo the original;" that the only horror films currently being made are remakes; and that *Scream 4* is "less of a screquel [scream-sequel] and more of a screamake [scream-remake]." Even the killer known as Ghostface demands that her intended victim answer a trivia question about remakes. In response, the victim lists fifteen horror films that have been remade, including *A Nightmare on Elm Street* (1984) and *The Last House on the Left* (1972), both of which were directed by *Scream 4* director Wes Craven. Later in *Scream 4*, Gale Weathers (Courtney Cox), a writer whose book became the basis for the *Stab* series, observes that modern horror films are very "meta."

Both *Scream 4* and *Matrix Resurrections* allow the characters to anticipate the words of their online critics. Assessing a scary movie, a teenager in *Scream 4* snarks, "That was so fucking stupid. Pure horse shit. The death of horror right here in front of us!... These people don't know when to stop. They just keep recycling the same shit." In *Resurrections*, the villain castigates, "You've lost something, [Neo]. You're not what you used to be." Perhaps speaking for the filmmakers' worries about replicating past artistic and commercial success, Neo wonders, "What if I can't be what I once was?" Elsewhere, an executive at Neo's game company declares, "This [*Matrix 4* game] cannot be another reboot, retreat, regurgitated." Another employee counters, "Why not? Reboots sell."

Seeing Double: Two Part Fours
The Exorcist series is notable because the producers made two different films—*Exorcist: The Beginning* (2004) and *Dominion: Prequel to the Exorcist* (2005)—that were both intended to be part four. Let me explain. James G. Robinson, head of Morgan Creek, wanted to revive the dormant series. Caleb Carr, the author of *The Alienist* (1994), was brought in to write the screenplay and Paul Schrader, who wrote several movies for Martin Scorsese and who directed the eerie *Cat People* (1982), was hired to direct. Stellan Skarsgård was cast to play a young Father Merrick, the role played by Max Von Sydow in William Friedkin's 1973 film.

When Schrader turned in his cut to the studio, they were disappointed. Schrader had closely followed Carr's script, whittling down some long passages, and he delivered a thoughtful, contemplative film about the nature of good versus evil. However, Schrader's film was not the scary movie the studio wanted.

According to Schrader, the screening with Morgan Creek did not go well, "I showed it, and it was about two hours and ten minutes long. Jim [Robinson] was there. We talked a little bit about it. Not much. I said, 'It's a little long, let me pull out about ten minutes, and then I'll show it to you again.' I thought I'd get notes. I never got notes. Usually, at that point, you get notes, notes upon notes, notes about every single thing. When I showed a two-hour version the next week, Jim didn't show up for the screening. The editor was fired then, and I was told to go home. They wanted to re-edit the movie to make it scarier. I said, 'You can't re-edit it to make it scarier. You might be able to fix a few little things. The problem isn't the editing, the problem is the premise. You're not going to scare the Bejesus out of people when you have [Cheche] getting better [rather than degenerating]. It just doesn't work that way.' And I think they came to realize that because originally, they were just going to do some reshoots, and the reshoots kept getting bigger and bigger. Finally, they started to realize the only way to make a horror-driven film was to go in there and change the premise."[116]

Fearing that the movie-going public would dismiss a film that did not feature gore, the studio tried to re-edit the film. But the footage would not support their vision of the film. So, they hired Renny Harlin, who directed *Die Hard* 2 (1990) and *A Nightmare on Elm Street 3* (1987), to shoot additional scenes that would have more violence and gore. Harlin had other ideas. He did not want to just shoot a few scenes in another director's movie. He wanted to tell his version of *The Exorcist* and offered to shoot an entirely new movie. The studio agreed, re-hired Skarsgård to play the lead and off they went to reshoot the movie with a new script.

Skarsgård told the *New York Times*, "It wasn't really a script, but just a bunch of ideas about how to make the film scarier, basically by throwing in unmotivated scares in every second scene. I didn't like it and I didn't want to do it. But then Renny Harlin came on, who I've worked with before, on the [killer-shark film] *Deep Blue Sea* (1999) and who is a friend. In many ways, he's the opposite of Paul Schrader, so it was hard to imagine him working with Paul Schrader's material. But gradually Renny turned it into another movie and got Morgan Creek to reshoot the entire film or rather, make an entirely different film."[117]

Harlin's film was released as *Exorcist: The Beginning* and made just under $80 million, worldwide. It also became the most successful sequel in the *Exorcist* franchise.

At first glance, it seems that Morgan Creek's gamble to remake the film paid off at the box office. However, Harlin's film cost a reported $50 million to shoot, and it also had to bear the cost of Schrader's $30 million film. Additionally, there were marketing costs that can cost as much as half or more of the production budget, as well as the split in box office revenues that the studios must share with the theaters. In the end, Harlin's film lost the studio a lot of money.

Morgan Creek then realized that there was an opportunity to lessen their debt on the two films and to redress the little PR nightmare they created for themselves when they threw a nearly finished film by an esteemed filmmaker into a vault and seemingly threw away the key. Consequently, Morgan Creek asked Schrader to come back to finish editing, scoring, and sound mixing his film. But to keep costs down, they only gave him three weeks to handle all these post-production duties. Realizing that this was likely to be his sole opportunity to save his film, Schrader agreed.

Schrader's film was completed and released under the title *Dominion: Prequel to the Exorcist*. It received a modest theatrical release and garnered better reviews than Harlin's film.

In the end, *Exorcist* fans have two different part-four stories to choose from. Both films star the same actor and more or less follow the same plot. The films, however, are made by filmmakers who have polar opposite styles. *Dominion* is not Schrader's best film, but it is a worthy, if sometimes slow-moving, film about a man who is attempting to find his faith in God again, as it also explores the nature of evil. Harlin's film takes a radically different approach, which turns father Merin into an Indiana Jones action hero who can muscle his way through a fight with the devil.

In his review for the *Exorcist* fan site Captain Howdy, Erik Kristopher Myers writes: "The curious thing about the Exorcist franchise is that you have three films following the same narrative thread, but none of the chapters feel as though they belong to a greater whole. Each one plays too differently from the previous installment, destroying any sense of genuine continuity beyond names or locations. Schrader's film is the first to synthesize the elements of each one, whether intentionally or otherwise, and presents us with an *Exorcist* that owes as much to Friedkin as it does to Boorman and Blatty. At the same time, it also manages to achieve its own identity while still being directly linked to *The Exorcist*, *The Exorcist II: The Heretic* (1977), and *The Exorcist III* (1990). No other film in the series has a genuine marriage to each of its partners the way that Schrader's does."[118]

In an interview with the *New York Times*, producer Robinson describes the differences between the two different part fours: "The Renny Harlin version was a much more commercially shot horror film, and this one is much more cerebral. The masses that want to see these *Alien vs. Predator* movies want to see much more graphic violence. Paul's version is much more about the terror that resides in your own mind."

Blatty was blunter about the differences in the films, "After a slam-bang opening sequence, Harlin's prequel deteriorated into what was surely the most humiliating professional experience of my life, particularly the finale. I don't blame Renny Harlin, for he gave Morgan Creek, I promise you, precisely what Morgan Creek demanded: not shocking obscenity, but shocking vulgarity."[119]

Perhaps the only thing worse than making a box office failure is making an unreleasable film. Schrader noted that it "doesn't do anybody's reputation any good to be taken off a film, which is why I've worked so long to get this film to exist. Because no matter who you're talking to—your best friend, your wife—you tell them, you made a film that was really good, but they didn't release it," nobody believes you. They just look at you and think, 'Oh, poor Schrader. Look at the denial he's in. He really thinks he made a good film. Of course, he didn't. Nobody would pay for a $35 million film and then put it on a shelf.' You can't convince anyone it was any good because it's such financial folly. The greatest thing about having this film publicly seen is letting people decide for themselves, and I don't have to spend my life telling people, 'You know, that *Exorcist* film was actually pretty good.'"[120]

For many fans, it seemed that the *Exorcist* cinematic franchise was toast and that the money Morgan Creek spent on both films was folly. For 18 years, the rights to the *Exorcist* films lay fallow and, despite receiving some praise in fan circles, 2016's *The Exorcist* television series lasted only two seasons. However, in 2021, Universal paid a staggering $400 million to Morgan Creek and their partner Blumhouse Productions to create a sequel trilogy of *Exorcist* films.[121]

And So Fourth

As explored throughout this volume, there are myriad artistic and commercial reasons for creating fourth installments in popular series. Moviegoers get to see their favorite characters in new adventures; movie studios can hedge their financial bets by delivering the familiar yet simultaneously exploiting existing intellectual property; and filmmakers have more opportunities to ply their trade and express their creativity. In short, our seemingly unquenchable demand for sequels means movies will continue to go fourth.

APPENDIX B
List of Fourth Films

The following is a list of notable fourth films in popular series. It is not intended to be a complete accounting. Many, but not all of the films, are referenced throughout this book.

For ease of reading, I have omitted articles such as "The" or "A" before titles. Thus, *The Hunger Games* becomes *Hunger Games*. When the name of the franchise is not included in the title, I also include an identifier in parenthesis. For instance, *Sudden Impact*, 1983 (Dirty Harry) and *Sum of All Fears*, 2002 (Jack Ryan).

Determining a film's genre is not always straightforward. For instance, *Matrix Resurrections* could be considered either action or sci-fi; *Underworld: Awakening* could be characterized as either fantasy, action, or horror; *Rocky IV* could rank as either a drama or sports film, and *Lake Placid: The Final Chapter*, about a killer crocodile, could be filed under horror or, perhaps, even more broadly an animal movie, like Lassie or Rin Tin Tin.

Action
Death Wish 4: The Crackdown, 1987
Fast and the Furious: Tokyo Drift, 2006
Indiana Jones and the Kingdom of the Crystal Skull, 2008
John Wick: Chapter 4, 2023
Lethal Weapon 4, 1998
Live Free or Die Hard, 2007
Mad Max: Fury Road, 2015
Pirates of the Caribbean: On Stranger Tides, 2011
Rambo, 2008
Shaft, 2000
Substitute: Failure Is Not an Option, 2001
Sudden Impact, 1983 (Dirty Harry)

Action-Comedy
Bandit Goes Country, 1994 (Smokey and the Bandit series)
Beverly Hills Cop: Axel Foley (2023)
Home Alone 4: Taking Back the House, 2002
It's a Mad, Mad, Mad World 4, 1992
Jumanji: The Next Level, 2019
Men in Black: International, 2019
Midnight Run for Your Life, 1994
Police Academy 4: Citizens on Patrol, 1987

Animal Movies (Live Action)
Air Bud: Seventh Inning Fetch, 2002
Alvin and the Chipmunks: The Road Chip, 2015
Beethoven's 4th, 2001

Benji the Hunted, 1987
Francis Covers the Big Town, 1953 (Francis the Talking Mule)
Hills of Home, 1948 (Lassie)
Lighthouse by the Sea, 1924 (Rin Tin Tin)
White Fang and the Hunter, 1975

Animation
American Tail: The Mystery of the Night Monster, 2000
Bon Voyage, Charlie Brown (and Don't Come Back!), 1980
Care Bears: Journey to Joke-a-lot, 2004
Frosty Returns, 1992
Hotel Transylvania: Transformania, 2022
Ice Age: Continental Drift, 2012
Inspector Gadget's Biggest Caper Ever: The Case Of The Giant Flying Lizard, 2005
Land Before Time IV: Journey Through the Mists, 1996
Rugrats Go Wild!, 2003
Shrek Forever After, 2010
Starship Troopers: Invasion, 2012
TMNT, 2007 (Teenage Mutant Ninja Turtles)
Toy Story 4, 2019

Animation (Fourth Film Remakes)
Aladdin, 2019
Lion King, 2019

Comedy
Abbott and Costello Meet the Mummy, 1955
Barbershop: The Next Cut, 2016
Ernest Goes to Jail, 1990
Gidget Grows Up, 1969
House Party 4: Down to the Last Minute, 2001
Love Finds Andy Hardy, 1938 (Andy Hardy)
Madea Goes to Jail, 2009
Monty Python Live at the Hollywood Bowl, 1982
Pajama Party, 1964 (Beach Party series)
Return of the Pink Panther, 1975
Road to Utopia,1946, (Road to series)
Vegas Vacation, 1997

Comedy (Sex-Comedy)
American Reunion, 2012 (American Pie series)
Carry On Constable, 1960 (Carry On series)
Meatballs 4, 1992
Pimpin' Pee Wee, 2009 (Porky's series)
Revenge of the Nerds IV: Nerds in Love, 1994

Disaster
Concorde ... Airport '79, 1979
Sharknado: The 4th Awakens, 2016

Documentaries
28 Up, 1984
Born in the USSR: 28 Up, 2012
Growth Records Every 7 Years I Turned 20, 2013
High School Graduate of '92, Twenty Years Later, 2012
Jackass Forever, 2022
Up South Africa, 2013

Family
Casper's Haunted Christmas, 2000 (Casper the Friendly Ghost)
Dennis the Menace Christmas, 2007
Diary of a Wimpy Kid: The Long Haul, 2017
Herbie Goes Bananas, 1980
Muppet Christmas Carol, 1992
Parent Trap: Hawaiian Honeymoon, 1989
Pippi in the South Seas, 1970 (Pippi Longstocking)
Spy Kids: All the Time in the World, 2011

Fantasy
Harry Potter and the Goblet of Fire, 2005
Hunger Games: Mockingjay Part 2, 2015
Scorpion King: The Lost Throne, 2015
Twilight Saga: Breaking Dawn Part 1, 2011
Underworld: Awakening, 2012

Horror (Sequels)
Amityville 4: The Evil Escapes, 1989
Anacondas: Trail of Blood, 2009
Annabelle: Creation, 2017
Bride of Chucky, 1998
Candyman, 2021
Children of the Corn IV: The Gathering, 1996
Critters 4, 1992
Final Destination, 2009
Friday the 13th: The Final Chapter, 1984
Ghoulies IV, 1994
Halloween 4: The Return of Michael Myers, 1988
Hellraiser: Bloodline, 1996
House IV, 1992
Howling IV: The Original Nightmare, 1988
Jaws: The Revenge, 1987
Jeepers Creepers: Reborn, 2022
Lake Placid: The Final Chapter, 2012

Land of the Dead, 2005
Leprechaun 4: In Space, 1997
Omen IV: The Awakening, 1991
Nightmare on Elm Street 4: The Dream Master, 1988
Paranormal Activity 4, 2012
Phantasm IV: Oblivion, 1998
Prom Night IV: Deliver Us from Evil, 1992
Prophecy: Uprising, 2005
Pumpkinhead: Blood Feud, 2007
Puppet Master 4, 1993
Return of the Living Dead: Necropolis, 2005
Saw IV, 2007
Scream 4, 2011
Silent Night, Deadly Night 4: Initiation, 1990
Species: The Awakening, 2007
Texas Chainsaw Massacre: The Next Generation, 1994
Victor Crowley, 2017
Worst of Faces of Death, 1987
Wishmaster: The Prophecy Fulfilled, 2002

Horror (Comedy)
Abbott and Costello Meet the Mummy, 1955
Killer Tomatoes Eat France, 1991
Return to Nuke 'Em High Volume 1, 2013
Scary Movie 4, 2006

Horror (Prequels)
Exorcist: The Beginning, 2004
First Purge, 2018
Grudge, 2020
Hannibal Rising, 2007
Insidious: The Last Key, 2018
Tremors 4: The Legend Begins, 2004
Wrong Turn 4: Bloody Beginnings, 2011

Horror (Prequel-Sequels)
Hellraiser: Bloodline, 1996
Psycho IV: The Beginning, 1990

Horror (Remakes)
Cabin Fever, 2016
Evil Dead, 2013
Stepfather, 2009

Martial Arts
American Ninja 4: The Annihilation, 1991
Fist of Fury III, 1980

Kickboxer 4, 1994

Monsters (Classic)
Dracula Has Risen from the Grave, 1968 (Hammer's Dracula series)
Frankenstein Created Woman, 1967 (Hammer's Frankenstein series)
Ghost of Frankenstein, 1942 (Universal's Frankenstein series)
Godzilla vs. Kong, 2021 (Legendary's MonsterVerse series)
Invisible Agent, 1942 (Universal's Invisible Man series)
Mothra vs. Godzilla, 1964 (Toho's Godzilla series)
Mummy's Ghost, 1944 (Universal Mummy's series)
Son of Dracula, 1943 (Universal's Dracula series)

Musicals
Broadway Melody of 1940, 1940 (Broadway Melody series)
Sharpay's Fabulous Adventure, 2011 (High School Musical series, albeit a spin-off)
Step Up Revolution, 2012

Mysteries/Crime
Black Camel, 1931 (Charlie Chan)
Blood of Fu Manchu, 1968 (Christopher Lee's Fu Manchu series)
Evil Under the Sun, 1982 (Hercule Poirot)
Falcon's Brother, 1942 (RKO's Falcon series)
Murder on a Bridle Path, 1936 (Hildegarde Withers)
Murder, She Wrote: The Last Free Man, 2001 (Jessica Fletcher)
Nancy Drew and the Hidden Staircase, 1939 (Nancy Drew)
Saint's Double Trouble, 1940 (RKO's Saint series)
Shadow of the Thin Man, 1941 (Thin Man)
Sherlock Holmes and the Secret Weapon, 1943 (Basil Rathbone as Holmes)
Triumph of Sherlock Holmes, 1935 (Arthur Wontner as Holmes)

Romance
Four Mothers, 1941 (Four Daughters series)

Science-Fiction
Alien Resurrection, 1997
Conquest of the Planet of the Apes, 1972
Highlander: Endgame, 2000
Jurassic World, 2015
Matrix Resurrections, 2021
Predator, 2018
Resident Evil: Afterlife, 2010
Star Trek IV: The Voyage Home, 1986
Star Wars: Episode I—The Phantom Menace, 1999
Terminator Salvation, 2009
Transformers: Age of Extinction, 2014
Universal Soldier: The Return, 1999

Serials
Dick Tracy vs. Crime, Inc., 1941
Son of Tarzan, 1920
Son of Zorro, 1947

Spin-Off
Ocean's 8, 2018
Penguins of Madagascar, 2014

Spy
Bourne Legacy, 2012
Bullet to Beijing, 1995, (Harry Palmer)
Thunderball, 1965 (James Bond)
Mission: Impossible—Ghost Protocol, 2011
One of Our Spies is Missing, 1966 (The Man from U.N.C.L.E.)
Sum of All Fears, 2002 (Jack Ryan)
Wrecking Crew, 1969 (Matt Helm)

Sports
Bloodsport 4: The Dark Kumite, 1999
Cutting Edge: Fire and Ice, 2010
Kickboxer 4, 1994
Next Karate Kid, 1994
Rocky IV, 1985

Superhero
Avengers: Endgame, 2019
Batman & Robin, 1997
Citizen Toxie: The Toxic Avenger IV, 2000
Crow: Wicked Prayer, 2005
Dick Tracy Meets Gruesome, 1947
Incredible Hulk Returns, 1988
Return of the Six Million Dollar Man and the Bionic Woman, 1987
Superman IV: The Quest for Peace, 1987
Tarzan Finds a Son!, 1939
Thor: Love and Thunder, 2022
X-Men: First Class, 2011

Thrillers/Drama
Billy Jack Goes to Washington, 1977
Peyton Place: The Next Generation, 1985

Thrillers (Erotic)
Angel 4: Undercover, 1993
Poison Ivy: The Secret Society, 2008
Wild Things: Foursome, 2010

War
Dirty Dozen: The Fatal Mission, 1987
Expendables 4, 2023
Iron Eagle on the Attack, 1995
Jarhead: Law of Return, 2019
SEAL Team 8: Behind Enemy Lines, 2014

Westerns
Gambler Returns: The Luck of the Draw, 1991
Gunsmoke: The Long Ride, 1993
Call of the Prairie, 1936 (Hopalong Cassidy)
Magnificent Seven Ride!, 1972

Honorable Mentions

Adult
Debbie Does Dallas 4, 1988
Deep Throat 4, 1990
Devil in Miss Jones 4: The Final Outrage, 1986

Fourth Barbie Film
Barbie as the Princess and the Pauper, 2004

Titles with Four in them (but are not the fourth film in a series)
4 Days in May, 2011
4 for Texas, 1963
Fantastic Four, 1994, 2005, 2015
Four, 2013
Four Brothers, 2005
Four Christmases, 2008
Four Daughters, 1938
Four Days in September, 1997
Four Feathers, 1939, 1978, 2002
Four Flies on Grey Velvet, 1972
Four for Venice, 1998
Four Good Days, 2021
Four Horsemen of the Apocalypse, 1921, 1962
Four Kids and It, 2020
Fourth Kind, 2009
Four Lions, 2010
Four Seasons Lodge, 2009
Four Rooms, 1995
Four Seasons, 1981
Four Weddings and a Funeral, 1994
Fourth Man, 1983
Four Musketeers, 1974
Fourth Protocol, 1987

ACKNOWLEDGMENTS

My deepest thanks to the many people who supported me during the process of writing *Movies Go Fourth*.

I want to express my appreciation to all the artists who agreed to be interviewed. They were generous with their time and I'm grateful that they shared their memories and experiences with me. I'm also thankful to the wonderful assistants who helped facilitate those interviews.

I am also very grateful to you, the reader.

I'd especially like to thank Adam Davis, Jerry Kolber, John Rawles, Johanna Gendelman, and Sara Blumenthal. Similar thanks go to Lee Pfeiffer, James Page, Dr. Llewella Chapman, James Chapman, Clinton Rawles, Gary J. Firuta, Alan J. Porter, Dr. Lisa Funnell, Sean Longmore, Joseph Darlington, Mark O'Connell, Bill Kanas, Brian McKaig, and David Zaritsky. I would also like to thank Mark Ashby for his comments on the book. Additional thanks to Dan Murrell for his many forms of support.

I am delighted that Rob Hall designed the cover for this book. I am honored to include artist Pat Carbajal's exquisite illustrations in this work.

I owe a debt of gratitude to Phil Noble Jr., a writer whose work I admire, and who suggested the title for the book.

Utmost thanks also go to Jack Lugo for his council, feedback, support, and for pushing me to go big on the *Rocky IV* material.

Additional thanks to the RKO team, who include Ted Hartley, Mary Beth O'Connor, Brian Anderson, Steven Tolman, Amy McMillan, and Celia Castevens.

Thank you to Elizabeth Belasco, a wonderful, thoughtful, eagle-eyed editor.

I also want to thank my family for all of their support. I relied on Elliot Ravetz, who is always so generous with his time, advice, and love.

For my mom, the Honorable Sandra Edlitz, sending love and hugs.

I'd also like to thank my wonderful big sis, Tracy.

Additional love and thanks go to Gail Ravetz, Mark Visceglia, George Berger, Doctor Joan Shapiro, and Doctor Irving Shapiro.

I also want to remember my late, great father, the indefatigable Robert I. Edlitz.

Above all, I must thank Doctor Susan Shapiro, my wise, accomplished, and beautiful wife, and Ben and Doug, my two kind, funny, unique, and eclectic kiddos who make me immeasurably proud to be their dad.

Footnotes

[1] "Sir Michael Caine admits he has never seen the much-derided Jaws 4," January 15, 2016, https://www.independent.ie/style/celebrity/celebrity-news/sir-michael-caine-admits-he-has-never-seen-the-much-derided-jaws-4-34366505.html
[2] Christopher Reeve, Still Me, Random House, 1998, p199
[3] Aaron Sorkin, "Film Story Arc," MasterClass, 2016, https://www.masterclass.com/classes/aaron-sorkin-teaches-screenwriting/chapters/film-story-arc#
[4] "Eddie Murphy: I Just Wanted to Kill," *Comedians in Car Getting Coffee*, Netflix.com 2019
[5] Scott Wampler, "It's Official: Xander Cage Will Return in XXX 4," BirthMoviesDeath.com, April 17, 2018, https://birthmoviesdeath.com/2018/04/17/xxx-4-xander-cage-vin-diesel-sequel
[6] Derek Lawrence, "Fast & Furious writer open to sending franchise to space," Entertainment Weekly, July 7, 2019, https://ew.com/movies/2019/07/29/fast-furious-writer-space/
[7] Tony Williams, editor, George A Romero Interview, University Press of Mississippi, 2011
[8] Emily VanDerWerff, "The never-ending suffering of the legacyquel," Vox, Jan 2022, https://www.vox.com/culture/22890147/scream-5-matrix-4-legacyquel
[9] Nick Romano, "Lana Wachowski says bringing back Neo and Trinity for The Matrix 4 helped her grieve," Entertainment Weekly, September 2021, https://ew.com/movies/lana-wachowski-neo-trinity-return-matrix-4-helped-her-grieve
[10] Geoff Boucher's Twitter account, https://twitter.com/geoffboucher/status/1015371669945270272
[11] James Hibberd, "Sylvester Stallone Gets Candid About Career, Regrets, Feuds: "I Thought I Knew Everything," *Hollywood Reporter*, November 7, 2022, https://www.hollywoodreporter.com/tv/tv-features/sylvester-stallone-interview-rocky-rambo-tulsa-king-1235254384/
[12] Director Steven Spielberg, *Jaws,* written by Peter Benchley, Carl Gottlieb, with uncredited writing by John Milius and Robert Shaw, based on the novel by Benchley.
[13] Chris Evangelista, "Universal Approached Steven Spielberg About A 'Jaws' Reboot, And He Rightfully Said No," SlashFilm.com, June 22, 2021, https://www.slashfilm.com/581871/jaws-reboot/?utm_campaign=clip https://www.slashfilm.com/jaws-reboot/
[14] Pamela McClintlock, "Box-Office Milestone: 'Jurassic World' Becomes No. 3 Movie of All Time Hollywood Reporter.com, July 22, 2015, https://www.hollywoodreporter.com/news/box-office-jurassic-world-becomes-810460
[15] Mark Daniel, "Christian Bale talks 'Ford v Ferrari', the films that got away, Batman and his real dream job," *Toronto Sun* November 15, 2019, https://torontosun.com/entertainment/movies/pure-bloody-excitement-christian-bale-puts-pedal-to-the-metal-in-ford-v-ferrari
[16] David Hochman, Does the Bat have 9 lives? "Looking to the future of Batman," *Entertainment Weekly*, June 20, 1997, http://ew.com/movies/1997/06/20/future-batman/
[17] Chris Nashawaty, "Every *Mission: Impossible* Movie Ranked, May 22, 2021, Esuquire.com, https://www.esquire.com/entertainment/movies/gmp36504562/best-mission-impossible-movies-tom-cruise-ranked/?__twitter_impression=true&s=03
[18] Christopher Reeve, *Still Me*, Ballantine Books, 1999
[19] Daniel Kremer, *Sidney J. Furie: Life and Films*, p.288, The University Press of Kentucky, 2015
[20] Mark Rosenthal and Lawrence Konner, *Superman IV* script, posted on Superman Homepage, https://www.supermanhomepage.com/movies/superman_IV.txt
[21] Mark Rosenthal and Lawrence Konner, *Superman IV* script, posted on Superman Homepage, https://www.supermanhomepage.com/movies/superman_IV.txt
[22] Mark Rosenthal and Lawrence Konner, *Superman IV* script, posted on Superman Homepage, https://www.supermanhomepage.com/movies/superman_IV.txt
[23] Nina Easton, 'Superman' Lawsuit Trail Date Set for April 16', Los Angeles Times, Feb 1, 1990, http://articles.latimes.com/1990-02-01/entertainment/ca-1469_1_superman-iv
[24] http://thecomicscode.weebly.com/superman-the-confrontation.html

[25] Mark Rosenthal and Lawrence Konner, *Superman IV* script, posted on Superman Homepage, https://www.supermanhomepage.com/movies/superman_IV.txt

[26] Jack Shepherd, *Independent*, "George Clooney apologies for 'destroying" Batman and Robin 18 years later," May 26, 2015

[27] *Shadows of the Bat: The Cinematic Saga of the Dark Knight*, 2005

[28] Owen Gleiberman, "Batman Forever," *Entertainment Weekly*, June 23, 1995

[29] http://horror.wikia.com/wiki/List_of_deaths_in_Jaws_series

[30] Michael de Guzman, *Jaws: The Revenge*, Shooting Script dated January 23, 1987, HorrorLair.com, http://www.horrorlair.com/scripts/jaws_the_revenge.txt

[31] Michael Caine, What's it All About, Century. p. 445, 1992

[32] Steve Biodrowski, *Cinefantastique, 1990*, as quoted on HitchcockMaster.wordpress.com

[33] *The Washington Post*, November 04, 1990, as quoted on HitchcockMaster.wordpress.com

[34] Kyle Anderson, "All the *Friday the 13th* Movies Ranked," Entertainment Weekly, April 25, 2014, https://ew.com/article/2014/04/25/friday-the-13th-tv-show-movie-rankings/

[35] Robert Englund and Alan Goldsher, *Hollywood Monster: A Walk Down Elm Street with the Man of Your Dreams*, Pocket Books; 2009

[36] Craig Marks and Rob Tannenbaum, "Freddy Lives: An Oral History of Nightmare on Elm Street," *Vulture*, October 20, 2014, https://www.vulture.com/2014/10/nightmare-on-elm-street-oral-history.html

[37] Robert Englund and Alan Goldsher, *Hollywood Monster: A Walk Down Elm Street with the Man of Your Dreams*, Pocket Books; 2009

[38] Bill Koenig, "007 movies listed by number of tickets sold, 1995-present," *The Spy Command* https://hmssweblog.wordpress.com/2015/11/25/007-movies-listed-by-number-of-tickets-sold-1995-present/?fbclid=IwAR0zgsZSwbMSifu0LwJHkhYkfjmKgdvLtrJAvYMuR20_YVoaujQu5uiAX6I. Also James Chapman.

[39] Robert Sellers, *The Battle for Bond*, Tomahawk Press, 2008, P.169

[40] Michael Coate, "Bond Goes Wide: Remembering "Thunderball" on its 50th Anniversary," Digital Bits, December 29, 2015

[41] Ibid.

[42] Unknown writer at British Board of Film Censors, http://www.bbfc.co.uk/case-studies/archive-thunderball

[43] Unidentified author at the British Board of Film Censors, Exception Form Memo dated November 29, 1965, page 2, http://www.bbfc.co.uk/sites/default/files/attachments/thunderball-final.pdf

[44] Ibid, page 7

[45] Ibid, page 2

[46] Ibid, pages 7

[47] Ibid. page 7

[48] Pauline Kael, "Dirty Harry: Saint Cop," *New Yorker*, January 15, 1972

[49] Pauline Kael, "Dirty Harry: Saint Cop," *New Yorker*, January 15, 1972

[50] Ibid.

[51] Roger Ebert, "Dirty Harry," July 1, 1971,https://www.rogerebert.com/reviews/dirty-harry-1971

[52] Roger Ebert "Dirty Harry is Not Fascist," April 4, 2008, https://www.rogerebert.com/letters/dirty-harry-is-not-fascist

[53] *AFI's 100 Years...100 Movie* Quotes, June 21, 2005 http://www.afi.com/100years/quotes.aspx

[54] Scott McGee, "The Outlaw Josey Wales," http://www.tcm.com/this-month/article/79824%7C0/The-Outlaw-Josey-Wales.html

[55] A.O. Scott, "Just When You Thought It Was Safe to Go Back Into The Jungle, *New York Times*, January 25, 2008, https://www.nytimes.com/2008/01/25/movies/25ramb.html

[56] TV Tango.com, "November 25, 1984, Sunday," http://www.tvtango.com/listings/1984/11/25/movie

[57] Mark Newbold, "Caravan of Courage: Celebrating 30 Years of an Ewok Adventure," StarWars.com, November 26, 2014, http://www.starwars.com/news/caravan-of-courage-celebrating-30-years-of-an-ewok-adventure

[58] Warren Bill, "George Lucas: Father of the Force," Starlog Yearbook, Volume 3, 1988
[59] Luke Farr, "Disney Axes Three Feature-Length Star Wars Films From Canon," Ace of Geeks.net, April 15, 2015, http://aceofgeeks.net/disney-axes-three-feature-length-star-wars-films-from-canon/
[60] Jonathan Rosenbaum, Discovering Orson Welles, p2, University of California Press, 2007
[61] Ibid, p246
[62] *Everything or Nothing: The Untold Story of 007*, 2012
[63] Eriq Gardener, *Hollywood* Reporter, "MGM Faces Class Action Over James Bond Box Set Mission Two Bond Films," April 7, 2017, https://www.hollywoodreporter.com/thr-esq/mgm-faces-class-action-james-bond-box-set-missing-two-bond-films-992172
[64] Pablo Hidalgo, *Star Wars: The Essential Reader's Companion*, p2, Del Rey, 2010
[65] Ibid.
[66] Ibid.
[67] Pablo Hidalgo, Twitter, Jan 30, 2017
[68] StarWars.com, April 25, 2014, http://www.starwars.com/news/the-legendary-star-wars-expanded-universe-turns-a-new-page
[69] Bristol Bad Film Club, "Exclusive Interview: Warwick Davis Discusses The Ewok Films, 40 Years of Star Wars and Willow 2, Bristol Bad Film Club, May 28, 2017, https://www.bristolbadfilmclub.co.uk/2017/05/28/exclusive-interview-warwick-davis-discusses-the-ewok-films-40-years-of-star-wars-and-willow-2/
[70] Leland Chee writing as Tasty Taste on StarWars.com, December 6, 2006, https://web.archive.org/web/20070227204935/http://forums.starwars.com:80/thread.jspa?threadID=152583&start=1050
[71] Graeme McMillan, "'Star Wars': Now the Spinoffs Will Matter (Some of Them, Anyway)," *Hollywood Reporter*, January 07, 2014
[72] Ibid.
[73] Charlton Heston, "In the Arena," Simon & Schuster, 1995
[74] Dale Winogura, "Charlton Heston Taylor Apes 1 and 2," *Cinefantastique*, p28, Summer 1972
[75] Chris Knight and Peter Nicholson, "Paul Dehn, Scriptwriter Apes 2,3 and 4," *Cinefantastique*, p28, Summer 1972
[76] Dale Winogura, "J. Lee Thompson, Director Apes 4," *Cinefantastique*, p23,.Summer 1972, http://pota.goatley.com/magazines/cinefantastique-summer-1972.pdf
[77] Janet Maslin, "Police Academy 4", *The New York Times*, April 4, 1987, https://www.nytimes.com/1987/04/04/movies/film-police-academy-4.html
[78] Janet Maslin, "Police Academy 4", *The New York Times*, April 4, 1987, https://www.nytimes.com/1987/04/04/movies/film-police-academy-4.html
[79] Steve Guttenberg, *The Guttenberg Bible: A Memoir*, Page 264, Thomas Dunne Books, May 8, 2012.
[80] Steve Guttenberg, *The Guttenberg Bible: A Memoir*, Page 266, Thomas Dunne Books, May 8, 2012.
[81] Steve Guttenberg, *The Guttenberg Bible: A Memoir*, Page 266, Thomas Dunne Books, May 8, 2012.
[82] The Jim Drake and Gene Quintano interviews were conducted separately but were combined together.
[83] Lisa Belkin, "Ernie: A Commercial Success Story," *The New York Times*, June 8, 1987, https://www.nytimes.com/1987/06/08/movies/ernie-a-commercial-success-story.html
[84] Cary James, "Ernest Again, Invulnerable To Life's Inanimate Objects," *The New York Times,* April 7, 1990, https://www.nytimes.com/1990/04/07/movies/review-film-ernest-again-invulnerable-to-life-s-inanimate-objects.html
[85] Lisa Belkin, "Ernie: A Commercial Success Story," *The New York Times*, June 8, 1987, https://www.nytimes.com/1987/06/08/movies/ernie-a-commercial-success-story.html
[86] Charlie Cohen, *Ernest Goes Bad*, page 105, undated draft of the script.
[87] Kathy Kalafut, "Ernest's Transition from TV to Film," *Entertainment* Weekly, April 13, 1990, https://ew.com/article/1990/04/13/ernests-transition-tv-film/

[88] Scott Mendelson, "'Home Alone' Is The Next Fox Franchise To Get Assimilated Into The Disney Collective," Forbes, August 12, 2021, https://www.forbes.com/sites/scottmendelson/2021/08/12/home-alone-next-fox-franchise-to-now-part-of-disney-collective/?sh=204e21784c16

[89] Jill Stanford, "Cape Town: South Africa's Tinseltown," *Engineering News*, May 5, 2003, https://web.archive.org/web/20190322020434/http://www.engineeringnews.co.za/article/cape-town-south-africas-tinseltown-2003-05-05

[90] *The Wild Life* (1984), the sex-comedy, is sometimes referred to as a sequel to *Fast Times at Ridgemont High*. After all, both films are coming-of-age stories that were written by Cameron Crowe. However, *Wild Life* is not a sequel to *Fast Times*. Instead, they are thematically linked.

[91] Jason Ingolfsland, "How Sylvester Stallone Changed Creed I And II To Make It More Comfortable," Cinemablend, May 2020, https://www.cinemablend.com/news/2495651/how-sylvester-stallone-changed-creed-i-and-ii-to-make-it-more-comfortable

[92] *The Making of Rocky vs Drago*, Director John Herzfeld, Balboa Productions, 2021

[93] *The Making of Rocky vs Drago*, Director John Herzfeld, Balboa Productions, 2021

[94][94] *The Making of Rocky vs Drago*, Director John Herzfeld, Balboa Productions, 2021

[95] *The Making of Rocky vs Drago*, Director John Herzfeld, Balboa Productions, 2021

[96] Will Harris, "Corey Feldman on child actors, his favorite roles, and the Goonies sequel," *The AV Club*, December 12, 2012, https://www.avclub.com/corey-feldman-on-child-actors-his-favorite-roles-and-1798235206

[97] Andy Morris, "The Godfather Part IV," September 24, 2012, GQ http://www.gq-magazine.co.uk/article/gq-film-godfather-part-four

[98] Andy Morris, "The Godfather Part IV," September 24, 2012, GQ http://www.gq-magazine.co.uk/article/gq-film-godfather-part-four

[99] Leslie Simmons, "Puzo estate sues over 'Godfather' games," Hollywood Reporter, June 2008, https://www.hollywoodreporter.com/news/general-news/puzo-estate-sues-godfather-games-114138/

[100] "Paramount Pictures Corporation vs Anthony Puzo, as Executor of the Estate of Mario Puzo," Feb 17, 2012, https://www.scribd.com/doc/82339753/Godfather-Complaint-1

[101] "Paramount Pictures Corporation vs Anthony Puzo, as Executor of the Estate of Mario Puzo," Feb 17, 2012, https://www.scribd.com/doc/82339753/Godfather-Complaint-1

[102] "Paramount Pictures Corporation vs Anthony Puzo, as Executor of the Estate of Mario Puzo," Feb 17, 2012, https://www.scribd.com/doc/82339753/Godfather-Complaint-1

[103] Eriq Gardner, "Paramount, Mario Puzo Estate Settle 'Godfather' Lawsuit," Hollywood Reporter, December 21, 2012, https://www.hollywoodreporter.com/business/business-news/paramount-mario-puzo-estate-settle-406160/

[104] "Answer and Counterclaim," March 12, 2012, https://www.scribd.com/doc/85258769/Puzo-Paramount-Answer-amp-Counterclaim

[105] Frank Palmer, "Spider-Man 3: the Film That Destroyed The Tobey Maguire Franchise," Screengeek.com, July 8, 2017, https://www.screengeek.net/2017/07/08/spider-man-3-the-film-that-destroyed-tobey-maguire-franchise/

[106] Ibid.

[107] Ibid.

[108] Nikki Finkie and Mike Fleming, "Exclusive: 'Spider-Man 4' Scrapped: Sam Raimi & Toby Maguire & Cast Out; Franchise Reboot for 2012, Deadline, January 11, 2010; http://deadline.com/2010/01/urgent-spider-man-4-scrapped-as-is-raimi-and-cast-out-franchise-reboot-planned-21993/

[109] George Szalai, *Hollywood Reporter*.com, February 14, 2011, https://www.hollywoodreporter.com/news/disney-cars-has-crossed-8-99438

[110] Victor Miller personal website, http://victormiller.com/faq.php

[111] Amanda J. Field, *England's Secret Weapon: The Wartime Films of Sherlock Holmes*, Chaplin Books, 2019

[112] Austen Goslin, "Everything Zack Snyder has said about the story for his Justice League 2 and 3," Polygon.com, March 23, 2021, https://www.polygon.com/movies/22347059/justice-league-2-plot-zack-snyder

[113] Anthony Breznican, "Zack Snyder Explains That Enigmatic Justice League Ending," VanityFair.com, March 18, 2021, https://www.vanityfair.com/hollywood/2021/03/zack-snynder-justice-league-ending-explained

[114] DundeeMovie.com

[115] JACK SLATER V (a radio play by Chris R. Notarile), https://www.youtube.com/watch?v=0czbqmguoqoz

[116] Jason Stringer, "Exclusive Interview with Paul Schrader," Captain Howdy.com, May 24, 2005, http://captainhowdy.com/2005/03/exclusive-interview-with-paul-schrader

[117] David Kehr, "Double Your Pleasure? Early 'Exorcist,' Take 2," *New York Times*, May 2, 2005, https://www.nytimes.com/2005/05/02/movies/double-your-pleasure-early-exorcist-take-2.html

[118] Jason Stringer, "Dominion: The First Review," Captain Howdy.com, May 20, 2005, http://captainhowdy.com/2005/05/dominion-the-first-review

[119] David Kehr, "Double Your Pleasure? Early 'Exorcist,' Take 2," *New York Times*, May 2, 2005, https://www.nytimes.com/2005/05/02/movies/double-your-pleasure-early-exorcist-take-2.html

[120] Jason Stringer, "Exclusive Interview with Paul Schrader," Captain Howdy.com, May 24, 2005, http://captainhowdy.com/2005/03/exclusive-interview-with-paul-schrader/

[121] Rebecca Rubin, Brent Lang, "Universal Spends $400 Million on New 'Exorcist' Trilogy Starring Ellen Burstyn, Leslie Odom Jr.," Variety.com, July 26, 2021, https://variety.com/2021/film/news/universal-exorcist-trilogy-1235027500/

ABOUT THE AUTHOR

Mark Edlitz has worked as a writer and producer for ABC News, NBC-Uni, CNBC, Discovery ID, and National Geographic Channel's *Brain Games*.

Edlitz's writings about pop culture have appeared in *The Huffington Post*, *Los Angeles Times Hero Complex*, *Moviefone*, and *Empire* magazine online.

He wrote and directed the award-winning independent film *The Eden Myth* and directed *Jedi Junkies*, a documentary about extreme *Star Wars* fans.

Edlitz's book *How to Be a Superhero* includes interviews with actors who have played superheroes over the past seven decades.

His book *The Many Lives of James Bond* consists of original interviews with artists who have created James Bond movies, novels, television, radio dramas, comic books, and video games. It also includes a large collection of interviews with actors who have played 007 in different media.

His third book *The Lost Adventures of James Bond* reveals previously undisclosed scenarios for Timothy Dalton's abandoned third and fourth Bond movies, questions Toby Stephens about playing 007 on the radio, delves into the unproduced Casino Royale play, and exposes the secret history of James Bond Jr., the animated series about 007's nephew.

Edlitz lives in New York with his wife and two children.

ABOUT THE ILLUSTRATOR

Artist Pat Carbajal started as a political cartoonist for various national newspapers in Argentina. He then moved on to portrait art, illustrations, children's books, comic books, and storyboards for commercials.

Pat started producing art for the American market in 2007 when he illustrated covers for *Timeline of The Planet of the Apes* by Rich Handley for Hasslein Books. In 2009, he painted covers for the Bluewater Productions biography series, which were based on the lives of influential American women. Rock stars were the next subject for Pat. Bob Dylan, Jim Morrison, and Jimi Hendrix were the legends who were featured in *Rock and Roll Comics: The Sixties*, followed by Ozzy Osborne, AC/DC, and Guns N' Roses in *Rock and Roll Comics: Rock Heroes.*

The first graphic novel that Pat completely illustrated was *Allan Quartermain,* which was written by Clay and Susan Griffith and published by Bluewater. Together with Clay and Susan, he created the character of The Raven for Bluewater's *Vincent Price Presents*, a classic horror comic book that starred Hollywood screen legend Vincent Price. Pat made his debut as a writer in the following issue of the comic.

For Hasslein Books, Pat illustrated the covers and interior art for Lexicon of *The Planet of the Apes*, *Back in Time: The Back to the Future Lexicon*, *A Matter of Time: Back to the Future Chronology*, and *Total Immersion, The Red Dwarf Encyclopaedia.*

Pat has also supplied illustrations for *The Many Lives of James Bond* and *The Lost Adventures of James Bond.*

Pat creates exclusive designs for t-shirts with Rotten Cotton and produces comic book and cover artwork for Eibon Press, with a series of horror graphic novels based on cult movies, including *Maniac*, Lucio Fulci's *Zombie*, and *The Beyond.*

Pat lives in Argentina.

www.ingramcontent.com/pod-product-compliance
Lightning Source LLC
Chambersburg PA
CBHW081353070526
44583CB00020B/2543